# Neighborhood Justice

# Neighborhood Justice

## Assessment of an
## Emerging Idea

## Roman Tomasic
## Malcolm M. Feeley

Longman
New York & London

**NEIGHBORHOOD JUSTICE**
**Assessment of an Emerging Idea**

Longman Inc., 19 West 44th Street, New York, N.Y. 10036
Associated companies, branches, and representatives
throughout the world.

Developmental Editor: Irving E. Rockwood
Editorial and Design Supervisor: Frances Althaus
Cover Design: Dan Serrano
Manufacturing and Production Supervisor: Robin B. Besofsky
Printing and Binding: BookCrafters, Inc.

**Library of Congress Cataloging in Publication Data**

Main entry under title:

Neighborhood justice.

  Bibliography: P.
  Includes index.
  Contents: Towards the creation of a complementary
decentralized system of criminal justice/Richard Danzig—Varieties of dispute
processing/Frank E. A. Sander—Influences of social organization on
dispute processing/William L. F. Felstiner—[etc.]
    1. Compromise (Law)—United States—Addresses,
essays, lectures. 2. Criminal justice, Administration of—United States—Addresses, essays, lectures.
3. Neighborhood justice centers—United States—
Addresses, essays, lectures. I. Tomasic, Roman.
II. Feeley, Malcolm.
KF9084.A75N45                    345.73'05                    81-8249
ISBN 0-582-28253-5               347.3055                     AACR2

Manufactured in the United States of America
9 8 7 6 5 4 3 2 1

# Contents

# Tables

# Introduction

Roman Tomasic
Malcolm M. Feeley

The last two decades have witnessed a significant social movement aimed at reforming the legal system. Massive amounts of governmental and foundation aid have been made available to institutions, such as the police, prisons, legal services, and therapeutic and educational agencies, to expand their capacities, broaden services, and develop new alternatives for coping with disputes. Whether all these actions actually lead to improvements remains problematic, as more often than not the problems tackled are rooted in the structure of society while the solutions build upon existing pillars of these structures. Still, the problems are serious and the efforts significant. The purpose of this volume is to bring together new or heretofore difficult to obtain materials that assess an important component of this important movement.

A major concern among proponents of this reform has been the development of new and more effective ways to handle so-called small claims and petty criminal offenses. Responding to long-standing complaints that the courts are overloaded, too costly, and too time consuming to afford ordinary citizens access to justice, and that the formality of the courts precludes them from identifying root causes of interpersonal disputes and, hence, affecting lasting settlements, a number of reforms have been put forward to simplify and supplement existing legal processes. While some of their assumptions about the capacity of existing court alternatives and resources are questionable, reformers nevertheless have insisted upon pushing ahead with attempts to promote their new ideas. They have been encouraged by the perception of a crisis in law, calls for delegalization, plans for simplification of legal processes, and attacks on professionalism in general (see, e.g., Unger, 1976).

The belief that the legal system has become too complex and unresponsive to meet community needs for justice has led to two types of efforts. One of these has been to simplify and streamline court structures and procedures. The other has involved attempts to remove disputes from the court entirely by taking them to less formal, more responsive forums. Both of these strategies for reform are however part of the recent overall attack upon formalism that has become so fashionable of late, although there is evidence to suggest that it is part of an episodic concern within the legal system, and indeed that we may already be witnessing the early stages of a countershift (Abel, 1981). This fluctuation is of course by no means a new phenomenon; historically we have seen the pendulum of legal change swing from poles such as formality and informality, complexity and simplicity, professionalism and lay decision making, adversary and inquisitorial approaches, and the poles of greater and lesser concern for individualization. Indeed these fluctuations reflect tensions inherent in the law itself, expressing as it does a multiplicity of conflicting and competing goals (see, e.g., Nonet and Selznick, 1978; Packer, 1968).

This current movement for delegalization, simplification, and informality has been directed at a wide variety of activities—ranging from rethinking antitrust laws and deregulation of major industry to the development of alternatives to handle petty criminal and civil disputes— and itself is part of a still broader concern with increasing access to justice (Cappelletti, 1978–79). A survey of the entire range of concerns in this movement is well beyond the scope of a single volume, and here we propose to examine only one aspect of this important movement, the emergence and operations of informal alternatives to courts for handling minor criminal and civil grievances. Known generically as *neighborhood justice centers*, these institutions, which now number well over one hundred in the United States, vary widely in structure and mission. Despite this, they share a number of essential features: they are designed as alternatives to courts; handle both criminal and civil grievances; rely on voluntary participation by the disputants; and employ techniques of mediation and compromise rather than compulsory formality and the winner-take-all approach of courts. Proponents of neighborhood justice centers argue that these features of these new institutions, along with their community base, enhance the likelihood that root causes of grievances can be explored and effective settlements reached. Some proponents go on to argue that by removing minor issues from the courts, those issues remaining before the courts will have the opportunity to be more effectively handled, even as those being removed will also be handled more effectively.

Even as we have argued that this current embrace of informality is part of a historical ebb and flow, we also recognize its distinctiveness. What does seem to be unique about the current interest in informal alternatives to courts is the extent to which it is being supported by established political, legal, and judicial organizations. This channeling of legal reforms by elites raises questions concerning the extent to which fundamental changes are likely to emerge from efforts at court reform in improving effective access to justice. There is something ironic about *state* control and bar association support of *informal* justice experimentation. For a movement that ostensibly has a local basis and is promoted as an alternative, it is curious that calls for greater use of informal justice techniques are mainly coming from, or else are mainly supported by, the national government, and are fostered by legal and judicial elites. This suggests that informal justice will be promoted only as long as it advances the formal justice system and the national legal organizations. If this is so, it could then be argued that informal justice may be subject to the interests of the formal justice system. Moreover, informal procedures may oddly enough be seen simply as a reflection or aspect of the formal legal structure. While it remains to be seen if the above argument can be applied to legal institutional change generally, this is one of the major themes as it applies to the neighborhood justice movement considered in the concluding section of this volume.

More generally we think that it is vital to examine rigorously the nature of alternative programs as early as possible. All too frequently in the past, new social programs have failed to be subjected to close scrutiny early in their lives. In the criminal justice system, the pretrial diversion movement is a good illustration of this. First formally proposed in the mid-1960s, and heavily funded and frequently hailed as a bold new experiment by government for years, the first full-scale evaluation of a diversion program was not reported until 1980 (Baker and Saad, 1979). It tended to confirm what by then a growing number of skeptics were coming to believe: that formal pretrial diversion programs had been oversold, and that they accomplished few if any of their original goals. Arguably, disenchantment with pretrial diversion programs might have been forestalled had they been adequately evaluated early enough to allow for their refinement. Alternatively, had the limits of diversion been known earlier, programs of this nature might more readily be replaced by more appropriate ones. The legacy of the diversion experience weighs heavily upon subsequent reform efforts in the lower courts, such as the current neighborhood justice initiative, despite the desire of proponents of the latter movement to distance themselves from the former.

We see important similarities in the appeal with which both of these ideas have been generated, and the speed with which efforts to develop them has been mounted. Like pretrial diversion programs a decade ago, neighborhood justice centers have been rapidly adopted and widely embraced in a relatively short order. Now widespread in the United States, support for the concept has also been picked up by reformers in Canada, Australia, and elsewhere. The rapid proliferation of neighborhood justice centers underscores the urgency for accurate and independent assessment of their effectiveness. The need for such evaluations is probably most vital for reformers themselves. The failure to examine reform initiatives critically could well lead to needless disenchantment. We recognize, of course, that the reformer must be something of a salesperson, and as such vigorously promote what he or she regards as the virtues of the product. Still, the honest reformer, like the honest politician, should reflect on the possibility of a subsequent disenchantment with oversold ideas, especially if it is felt that evolutionary reform is the only realistic strategy with which to deal with the current problems of the legal system.

Although neighborhood or community justice centers are relatively new in formal structure and terminology, the techniques and concepts upon which they are based have been with us for a much longer period of time. Some of these, like mediation, are in fact quite ancient, having long been used in one form or another in many non-Western societies and in important segments of commercial enterprises within the West (see Nader and Todd, 1978). The modernization of traditional soceiities has further altered the nature of mediation techniques and procedures. China, India, Burma, and Tanzania are good illustrations of this. Unfortunately, when the traditional model of mediation was imported into Western countries, it was further transformed. This can also be seen in the models of lay justice that we find in socialist societies, such as China, Cuba, Poland and the Soviet Union. The transplantation of dispute-processing institutions has inevitably involved their transformation and grafting upon existing social mechanisms.

The enthusiasm and haste with which some traditional models have been revived or applied to Western societies has led many reformers to ignore the problematic features of this transformation process. First, some have assumed that the nature and consequences of mediation and informal justice in traditional cultures are clear-cut, and that the technology of simpler societies could readily be applied in communities in the industrialized West. Ironically, traditional societies have themselves been moving away from informal justice techniques like mediation, as have some socialist societies, and the significance of so-called lay courts in other countries is on the decline. Second, those who enthusiastically embrace traditional models of dispute settlement have tended to assume either that informal forums do not already exist in Western societies, or else that they are ineffective. Although such assertions should have been subject to investigation before or early on in the process of establishing informal dispute settlement centers, these concerns are only now beginning to receive significant attention. By ignoring the existing institutions for obtaining informal justice through existing lower courts, functionally (as distinguished from geographically) organized communities, and private government, proponents of justice centers have been faced with lack of interest and clients, unanticipated opposition, and open resistance, all of which might have been reduced or avoided had existing patterns of informal disputing forums been mapped beforehand. Third, trying to emulate the benefits of the seemingly voluntariness in dispute resolution in many traditional settings, reformers have failed to appreciate the coerciveness of public opinion in cohesive traditional cultures. As such, reformers can be faulted for underestimating the importance of coercion, tradition, and other forms of legitimate authority.

But then, reformers, policymakers, and politicians are impatient people, often preferring, and perhaps requiring as a condition of initiation, attractions of bold and decisive new programs, to the less immediately rewarding commitment to background research and quiet incremental adjustments of existing institutions. The political attractiveness of the justice center model in seeming to be an appropriate response to problems being experienced by the courts has provided a major incentive for "experimentation" with this model. This once again raises a critical problem of reform: while it is understandable and perhaps desirable and inevitable that reformers and their supporters will be enthusiastic about their reform proposals, once these proposals begin to take on institutional or bureaucratic form, it becomes increasingly difficult to subject the basic assumptions of the reform agenda to critical scrutiny and independent evaluation. Reformers are naturally unwilling to see their institutional innovations jeopardized by too close a scrutiny from independent evaluators who do not necessarily share their enthusiasm for the reform. John Dewey's hope for the liberal society as the experimenting society and New Federalism's vision of "states as laboratories for experimentation" notwithstanding, government funding agencies—and we might add, foundations as well—often cannot afford to see their programs fail. As such, they too often resist careful assessment. Consequently, all too often adequate evaluation is not forthcoming or, when it is, the findings come too late to have significant impact upon the improvement of the programs being evaluated. While it is hoped that this does not occur within the neighborhood justice center experience, we see signs that it is occurring due to the failure to examine first *existing* informal institutions of disputing in Western societies. Indeed one of our hopes is that this volume will encourage more sophisticated examination of this popular new idea.

None of the above should however be taken as a rejection of the importance of informal justice or of the desirability of finding ways to handle disputes by simpler means so as to ensure improved access to justice. The problems addressed are serious, and efforts to deal with them are desirable and should be encouraged.

However we should ask to what extent these goals are already being served, as well as what functions are currently being carried out by existing structures. Indeed, it is ironic to note that just as it is completing its more-or-less successful campaign against justice of the peace and other forms of lay-administered justice, the organized legal profession in America is coming to embrace another type of informal justice in the neighborhood justice centers. Additionally, research on the structure and functioning of established courts increasingly reveals that these courts are not the remote and rigidly formal institutions that black-letter law would have them be. They often operate with flexibility and a concern for compromise and substantive justice that would surprise proponents of neighborhood justice centers (see, e.g., Carter, 1977; Utz, 1978; Feeley, 1979; and Nonet and Selznick, 1978). Additionally many trial courts also encourage reliance on self-help to emerge as potential litigants bargain under their shadow, (Mnookin and Kornhauser, 1979). Indeed it may even be that the problems of court congestion and delay serve important sociolegal functions for both the court bureaucracy and the litigant, and that elimination of these "problems" may foster still other problems elsewhere in the justice system (Levin, 1977). It has, for example, been argued that justice centers may actually limit access to justice by keeping cases out of court. Finally, there is some evidence to suggest that access to the formal legality and authority structure of the lower courts is an important symbolic mechanism vital to effective justice and to effective settlement, even if direct advantage of it is not taken. (Lezerson, 1981). If this is so, it suggests that it may be at least as important, if not more important, for reformers to improve procedures within the courts and to examine the informal activities conducted as auxiliaries and in their shadows that do promote alternatives separate from and outside the court structure. With adequate research and proper concern, the neighborhood justice center experience should provide us with answers to such questions.

In examining the impact and effectiveness of the neighborhood justice center approach to reform, it is important to appreciate that court reform has been on the agenda of reformers for quite some time, and that many of the same problems continue to frustrate reformers. We need only turn to the work of Roscoe Pound, Arthur T. Vanderbilt, and the legal realists such as Jerome Frank. More recently, this fact has been emphasized in Raymond T. Nimmer's important study, *The Nature of System Change* (1978), and Joel Handler's book, *Social Movements and the Legal System* (1978). Nimmer (1978:2) points out that despite the injection of considerable funds into the court reform effort over the years "... the problems of yesterday remain the problems of tomorrow." One reason for this, he points out, is that change agents have paid but scant attention to the social environment of their reforms and failed to anticipate the likely adaptive responses to efforts from within the judicial process itself. Taking this further, it could be argued that one major reason for the failure of pretrial diversion programs and the possible failure of the justice center movement may be their capture by officials of the judicial process who in turn use them for their own rather than the clients' needs.

The progress or perhaps lack of real progress in court reform, as

Raymond T. Nimmer has so effectively illustrated, must force reformers to reexamine some of the grosser claims that they make when seeking to promote their ideas. The extent to which the alternatives movement has been characterized by polemic and a preeminent concern with appeal and appearance rather than with purpose and reality needs to be assessed. Of course, this is not a problem unique to the area of court reform for it arises in all areas of public policy. Indeed the dilemma may be inherent in contemporary liberalism (Feeley and Sarat, 1980). Still, with the expansion of the role of the national government in recent years, the gulf separating policy initiation from policy implementation has widened and created a paradox: the very means required to mobilize innovative policies are the same forces that subsequently serve to frustrate implementation, bold promises, overexpectation, oversimplification—all of which yield to disillusionment and disappointment. This same point is made in different fashion by Murray Edelman (1964, 1978) in his continuing work on the symbolic nature of reforms or, as he recently put it, "words that succeed and policies that fail." Clearly, legal reform is as political as the implementation of policy initiatives generally. However, while this has tended to be well recognized for nonlegal issues (e.g., housing, welfare, environmental policy), it has been much more rare for court reformers to confront seriously problems of symbolic politics raised by their initiatives perhaps because, as Stuart Scheingold (1973) has so brilliantly shown, lawyer-reformers typically view the legal process as an alternative to, rather than a part of, the political process.

The costs of reforms need also to be more carefully assessed, although this is frequently notoriously difficult to do with any accuracy. Costs must to be assessed in terms of such things as the impact of court reform proposals upon the remainder of the court system, the duplication of existing informal mechanisms that serve similar functions perhaps more effectively, as well as the usual economic costs of establishing new structures and processes. For many reformers this kind of cost assessment, if honestly and rigorously done, is simply unacceptable and perhaps itself politically too costly. Yet if past experience is to be of any guide, an inventory of these costs and the social impact of court reforms is vital if there is to be any chance of a departure from the pattern of underachievement of reformist goals that has been noted.

The above discussion raises important questions that need to be asked of the neighborhood justice center movement. The essays and research reports collected in this volume seek to provide some answers as well as to raise further questions in this vein. Taken together, these contributions provide a valuable glimpse into this fascinating but problematic new reform. If we achieve our aim as editors, these materials will also provide a guide for resolving some of the uncertainties within this growing and important movement. Still there is considerable and perhaps unfounded optimism reflected in the very asking of these questions, in that they assume that acceptable answers *can be* found within the existing social structure.

Despite this, it is encouraging to note that in recent years there has been a growing awareness in government circles that legal change cannot be bought cheaply, and that one of the prerequisites of effective policymaking in the legal area is a greater commitment to research and greater appreciation of the relation of legal institutions to social structure. For many years it was thought that while massive funds should be made available, for example for basic medical research, legal change could be allowed to go on with minimal attention to basic issues. The history of court reform, especially in respect to alternatives, shows how wrong this judgment has been. While it is true that government cannot wait until all the results of exhaustive research are at hand, the history of repeated failure clearly requires that more attention be given to the broader issues that individual reform proposals raise. While it is still too early definitively to judge the neighborhood justice movement as yet another instance of a reform failure, there is now sufficient information available to enable some hard questions to be asked by appraising the judgments of reformers who provided the early rationales for this movement and by assessing the early experiences of some of the more carefully watched programs. We hope that this volume brings important policy issues to a broader audience and contributes to the more sophisticated analysis of this intriguing but elusive movement.

The four chapters in Part I are all authored by recognized experts on alternative to courts. Richard Danzig, Frank Sander, William Felstiner, and Daniel McGillis have all written or spoken widely on the theory and practice of neighborhood justice centers, and their work has played a significant role in giving life to and shaping thinking within this movement. Three of the four pieces in this section—all but the one by McGillis—have been published previously and have been influential among the small group of people reflecting upon this movement. Our purpose in bringing them together and reprinting them here is to make them more accessible to a much larger audience, as well as to use them to impart a much needed broader perspective on the matterials contained in Part II. The contribution by McGillis reviews a vast amount of his prior work, reports on developments in a wide variety of neighborhood justice centers, and updates as well some of his previously reported work. Here for the first time he has drawn his most important observations and presented them in a form readily accessible to a broad audience.

While there are of course a great many themes and variations in the very complex alternatives movement, the views reported by these four distinguished and insightful observers of this new movement are representative of the key rationales and concerns of the neighborhood justice movement. Taken together these four selections provide an excellent summary of major rationales lying behind this movement and provide an excellent introduction to, and perspectives on, the case studies in Part II and assessments in Part III of this volume.

Part II contains a number of case studies of recent examples of the neighborhood justice experience. The chapter by Leonard Buckle and Suzann Thomas-Buckle, a first report on their important and continuing research, does what we argued above needs to be done: it carefully and painstakingly maps out informal dispute-processing alternatives already in place in communities. Janice Roehl and Royer Cook report on an evaluation of three Justice Department-sponsored neighborhood justice centers in Atlanta, Kansas City, and Los Angeles. William Felstiner and Lynne Williams describe in careful detail one of the earliest community mediation programs, located in Dorchester, Massachusetts. The study by Robert Davis, reported here for the first time in published form, is the most sophisticated and important evaluation of a mediation center to date. This evaluation of the Brooklyn mediation program employs and faithfully executes a sophisticated experimental design. As such it stands as a model for further research in this area and as dramatic refutation of the oft-heard charges that programs are "too new" to be subjected to systematic quantitative evaluation and that program officials will not tolerate random assignment required for experimental research.

Part III contains four broad ranging assessments of neighborhood justice centers. Sally Merry's contribution examines the elusive notion of "success" in the neighborhood justice movement, although her observations have obvious implications for policy initiatives in general. Richard Hofrichter offers a sharp and penetrating criticism of neighborhood justice centers which views them in broad social and political context. William Clifford's chapter raises important questions about the adaptability of mediation across cultural settings. Finally Roman Tomasic's chapter provides a comprehensive review of the major assumptions and problems of this movement. In many respects his chapter serves as a check-list of things to be considered by those interested in promoting neighborhood justice centers.

Finally, we call attention to the extensive bibliography at the conclusion of this volume. The alternatives movement has received impetus from a wide range of sources and people. Its proponents run the gamut from professional anthropologists to Supreme Court justices. Advocates for community courts are found among radicals and conservatives. Similarly, critics come from diverse and surprising places. In turn, proponents and critics alike have drawn on a diverse literature—law, anthropology, political theory, psychology, philosophy, history, sociology, and an array of cultural experiences—to develop their theses. While we have made an effort to give an array of views and assessments of the neighborhood justice movement as it is developing in the United States, its intellectual and experiential roots are much too wide ranging for us to have provided representative views of each of its major components. Instead, we have sought to provide an extensive, if not exhaustive, bibliography in order to facilitate continued inquiry by our readers. In doing this we have also taken care to list a number of important unpublished reports and studies that are part of the vast fugitive literature in this field.

Finally, a note of clarification. Several chapters in this volume contain a large number of references. Because of extensive overlap, we have provided a common source for full citation. All references found in the editors' introduction and the chapters by Danzig, Felstiner, McGillis, Buckle and Thomas-Buckle, Roehl and Cook, Felstiner and Williams, Davis, Merry, Clifford and Tomasic are listed in full in the bibliography at the end of this volume.

# PART I

## Rationales

# 1

# Towards the Creation of a Complementary, Decentralized System of Criminal Justice[*]

**Richard Danzig**[†]

Perhaps no institutions in urban America offer so much evidence of their shortcomings and so little of their successes as those bureaucracies which compose our municipal criminal justice systems. City police doubtless retard urban crime; city courts commendably adjudicate some important cases; city jails manage to hold most of their prisoners for the duration of their terms. But what is salient to the informed citizen and the academic alike are the facts that city police cannot keep city streets free from crime; that major metropolitan courts abrogate their principal function by not adjudicating the guilt or innocence of a majority who come through their doors; and that city and country prison systems probably inspire recidivism as frequently as they reduce it. In sum, a strong case can be made that America's criminal justice systems neither control, nor consider, nor correct criminality. One thinks of them as Dr. Johnson thought of the performing dog: the wonder is that they perform at all.

[*] Copyright 1974 by the Board of Trustees of the Leyland Stanford Junior University. This is an edited version of an article first published by Richard Danzig in (1974) Stanford Law Review 26: 1–54, and reprinted by kind permission of *Stanford Law Review* and Richard Danzig. Footnotes renumbered.

[†] Work on an earlier draft of this paper was supported by the Association of the Bar of the City of New York. A precis of the earlier draft appears in W. Farr, L. Liebman, and J. Wood, Decentralizing City Government: A Practical Study of a Radical Proposal for New York City 106–19 (1972). I am indebted to the Bar Association for its financial support, to Professor Liebman for his close involvement with the work, and to Professor Farr and Mr. Wood for their general supervision of the project. I am also grateful to numerous colleagues and friends of the Stanford and Yale Law School faculties for their helpful comments. Of course, neither the Bar Association nor these individuals bear any responsibility for the contents of this Article.

2

This Article focuses on one among the myriad of ideas that have been put forward as cures or at least crutches for the American municipal justice system: the idea that increased effectiveness can be achieved by decentralization of some or all of the operations of existing systems. My aim in the pages that follow is neither to bury this idea nor to praise it. Either exercise would be facile. The idea of decentralization in relation to criminal justice systems has been much discussed, but too little developed to warrant judgment. Nothing now exists to praise but a shadowy, unreal idea, or to bury but a pitiable, incomplete straw man. Instead of "evaluating" the notion of decentralization, the aim of this Article is to make it real and thereby to make it something that the interested reader can understand and preliminarily assess for himself. My proposition is that only when this job has been done—and this Article does no more—can the idea be tested in practice, and that only after being tested can it finally be evaluated. . . .

At the outset it is necessary to concede that however ambitious the effort which follows, by phrasing the issue in this manner certain key questions have been circumvented. First, there is no discussion here of how districts ought to be demarcated; I take that as given. Second, there is no discussion of how cabinets ought to be elected, whom they ought to represent, etc. Third, I take the liberty of using the terms "district", "neighborhood", and "community" almost interchangeably without reference to the fact that, obviously, they are not synonymous. Fourth, I make no attempts to assess whether the costs of decentralization *in general* exceed the benefits. These questions are not avoided because they are unimportant, but rather, simply because there are other important questions—those about the operational possibilities for a decentralized system—which are less discussed, but which when answered may give us a clearer fix on the questions put aside.

## Working Principles

In designing a neighborhood criminal justice system intended to operate concurrently with a municipal system, I have been guided by seven working principles. The reader will better understand and be better able to evaluate the institutional choices made if he is familiar with and makes his own judgments about those principles. I therefore begin by isolating and describing them.

### The Choice of a Neighborhood-Based System

Experimentation with a neighborhood-based system of criminal justice appears to be attractive for at least three reasons. First, decentralization may be expected to improve the operation of the police, the courts, and the prisons by bringing home the responsibilities of these institutions to the community and—what is equally important, but more often over-looked—the responsibility of the community for these institutions. Whether it be instanced by the views of some citizens that the police are pigs, or of some police that some citizens are animals, or by the im-periousness of many judges who view their courts as their kingdoms, or by the physical and social isolation of the prisoner and his keepers, we are repeatedly confronted by the gap between society at large, its cri-minal caste, and those assigned to deal with that caste. If the plan here proposed brings police, courts and corrections to the city's communities, and forces these communities to come to terms with their own criminals, then it will more than justify the financial costs, psychological frictions, and administrative inconveniences that it will foreseeably entail.

Second, there are substantial advantages to physical decentralization besides overcoming the "out of sight, out of mind" syndrome that has long been society's main theme in relation to the inner workings of police stations, the "downtown" courts, and the upstate (or island iso-lated) jails. The very functioning of a system is inhibited by its physical isolation. The length of the trip to family court discourages the use of its facilities. The distance from community to jail retards work-release programs and the continued social intercourse of the community resi-dent and the prisoner. Even if no benefits were realized from having the criminal justice system under community control, putting parts of that system *in* communities would have significant advantages.

Third, decentralization is conceptually and emotionally closely tied to a particular type of innovation which in my view offers much promise in the context of criminal justice systems: the use of paraprofessionals. It would be naive to divorce the pursuit of community control from the community's desire for jobs; this is, in part, what makes hospitals and schools particularly intensive battlegrounds. The search for patronage on the part of a community's would-be governors, and for employment on the part of the governed, can be usefully directed in a system whose two preeminent present characteristics are a shortage of manpower, and the educational, social, and psychological gap between those who run the system and those who are run through it.

## The Emphasis on System

By scaling down the institutions dealt with in this Article, decentraliza-tion emphasizes the fact that each bureaucracy is only one component in the complex process by which society handles crimes and criminals. The outputs of one agency are the inputs of another: legislatures define crimes and thus criminals whom the police are charged with apprehending; police arrests make court prosecutions; court convictions become penal cases; often ex-convicts become criminals once again and the system recycles. The systemic perspective views a change in one component subsystem as forcing changes in the others. Widening or narrowing the definition of crimes increases or decreases police, court, and correction business; changes in police techniques may overburden or free the time of judges and prison staffs; judicial rules may force new police techniques or leave some laws unenforceable; the sentencing patterns of judges may be affected by perceptions about the prison environment and by the knowledge that for each convict put into prison another must be let out or given less attention and space.

The systemic perspective, which has become increasingly popular in professional thought about criminal justice over the last decade, is basic to an understanding of why we should decentralize and of how the alternatives formulated in this Article should be tested. Thus, to the question of "why decentralize?" the systemic perspective adds a fourth answer to those given in the previous section: decentralization may facilitate integration of the criminal justice system.

Instruments of coordination designed to make the present centralized criminal justice process function as a coherent system often do not exist in our cities. Where they do exist, as in New York, they are commonly too sporadically convened (e.g., New York's Urban Action Task Forces) or too unwieldy (e.g., Mayor Lindsay's Criminal Justice Coordinating Council) to induce a coherent systems approach. There is a good reason to believe that a decentralization which narrows the size of the jurisdiction and thus puts the different institutions in the same building, or which at least puts their heads periodically in the same room, will improve the effectiveness of the process. Certainly it will increase the possibilities of constructive multiorganizational innovation.

The systemic perspective also leads to certain observations about our methods of procedure when we do decide to decentralize. We ought not to decentralize one component in the system while leaving others untouched. Such an effort would be likely to increase friction between the municipal and the neighborhood organizations and to frustrate both parties. The ineffectiveness of occasional attempts to decentralize only one component of a law enforcement system has demonstrated the dangers only of a system fragmentation, not of decentralization. A new system must avoid this trap by stepping further ahead to a wider—and thus probably more successful—program.

## The Emphasis on Creation of a Complementary System

Whatever the faults of the present system, it does some things well. City prisons are notably effective in preventing escapes; the courts have developed an impressive mechanism for protecting the constitutional rights of defendants; though sometimes abused, the police power to use firearms is generally exercised with restraint and sobriety. In these and other respects the centralization of a municipal system affords advances.

These and related advantages should not be ignored in revising existing systems. There is no virtue and much danger in decentralizing what is done well centrally. Does our commitment to reintegrating persons into society extend so far that we would want prisons located in our housing projects? Would we really want a man to be compelled to stand trial before his neighbors? Would citizens be safer if the authorized use of violence were delegated to community patrols of local residents?

Answering these and related questions in the negative, and feeling that even if some felt differently they would have to recognize that the majority of voters would not share their feelings, I start from the premise that if decentralization is to be successful it will involve the construction of a complementary system, supplementing and in some areas substituting for, but nowhere destroying or totally displacing, the existing apparatus.

Cast in this mold there is even the possibility that those entrenched in the existing bureaucratic system may find the phenomenon of decentralization complementary to their work rather than hostile to it. A coexisting system will threaten them less if it has modest goals, and if it undertakes only those activities which the bureaucracy dislikes—those it does badly and for which it is criticized.

Defining a supplementary system by what the existing system does badly has advantages of a more positive sort than simply reducing damage or hostility. So long as the new system is presented as supplementary, it avoids situations where the costs exceed the benefits of decentralization simply by assigning these situations to the municipal rather than the neighborhood system. Particularly at its outset, when the decentralized system is likely to be flooded with managerial and political problems, the presence of an established system as a depository of activities temporarily or permanently better left centralized is a valuable outlet.

Operationally, the continued existence of the established system opens the attractive option of checkerboard decentralization. The schemes here outlined permit communities to choose to assume functions as alternatives to the municipal system, but, because the municipal system remains intact, they do not compel such assumption. Thus, for example, a middle class neighborhood need not assume a law enforcement role simply because a poorer neighborhood wants an alternative to the way that role is now performed.

Conversely, so long as they are presented within the context of an alternative system at the neighborhood's option, offering communities criminal justice options does not permit the municipality to "cop out" of areas and problems it would rather not handle. Decentralization will thus be a means of increasing the range and impact of city services, not a ploy for abandoning them.

Structuring the neighborhood system as an alternative also permits us to build a fail-safe mechanism into the system's design. In many of the arrangements outlined below individuals may opt out of the neighborhood system, or the established municipal system may reassert its control, if the neighborhood alternative is operating inappropriately or ineffectively (e.g., by oppressing or ignoring minorities). Doubtless some will object that this is "mock decentralization"—that it leaves power in the same hands which have always held it. But in an area as sensitive as criminal justice it seems at this time neither politically feasible nor socially wise to advance a plan which delegates control to neighborhoods without contingent recourse to a central authority. As will be evident below, the fail-safe mechanisms often make change possible without legislation; they make it possible for the central institution to intervene in cases of great concern without dismantling the whole apparatus of decentralization, and, therefore, they open the way for more daring innovation than could be attempted on an all or nothing basis.

Proceeding on the basis of creating a neighborhood system which is to be complementary to and coexistent with the existing system requires a presumption which should be made explicit here. I do not envision a supplementary system which draws heavily on the existing system for its financial support. Such dependence would rouse hostilities from entrenched civil servants certain to doom even the most worthy of plans. This plan therefore does not take money out of the present budget of the city's police department, courts, or prisons. Rather, it assumes that stepped up funding which would otherwise flow to these agencies can be diverted to community activities, partly because the community activities are worthy in themselves, and partly because they do improve existing agencies' ratios of resources to tasks by assuming some tasks they now perform. The expectation of increased funding is probably more reasonable in relation to the criminal justice system than to other city services; federal support and municipal allocations both seemed committed in this direction.

## The Assuagement of Professional Concerns

Decentralization is an apparent threat to the professionalization of the criminal justice system. But decentralization and professionalization are conceptual half-brothers. A consideration of their common elements suggests a way of bringing them to coexist, to mutual benefit.

Viewed from the inside, by the policeman, judge, or jailor, professionalization is a means by which a law enforcement job is more sharply defined, raised in prestige, and insulated from external control; it is a route by which law enforcement personnel can lay claim to being self-regulated, self-taught through training by those already in the profession, and self-perpetuating through control of recruitment. In contrast, decentralization suggests less job specialization, external (i.e., community) imposition of discipline and direction, external control of job entry and training, and—it is believed—a consequent loss of prestige. Despite these real differences, the two concepts share certain important characteristics.

*Control of legal institutions.* The first common characteristic of professionalization and decentralization is that both are substitutes for an otherwise intolerable lack of control by the legal system over individuals empowered to act on behalf of that system. The actors in the present criminal justice system are effectively released from control by the physical isolation noted above and by the extraordinarily unrestrained character of their working environment. The patrolman enjoys exceptional freedom from on-the-job supervision by his station-house-bound superiors; the judge performs his tasks certain in the knowledge that no agency other than his own can reverse his case decisions, and that in most criminal cases appeal will be prohibitively expensive and time consuming; and the jailor operates in a milieu characterized by an extreme paucity of statutory guidelines, by the general incapacity of his wards to mobilize the political system in their own behalf, and by an insufficiency of manpower which leaves administrators hardly capable of operating, much less of closely supervising or reviewing, the operation of the city's prisons.

The lack of statutory control is not an accident, consequent on mistakes made in the administration of the present system. The enduring essential character of this problem is suggested by the famous query: "Who shall guard the guardians?" Professional mores (through professionalization) or close community observation and control (through decentralization) seem more trustworthy mechanisms for preventing police corruption, judicial insubordination, prison brutality, or gross inefficiency and laziness throughout the system than more laws, more police, more judges, and more jailors would be. Viewed in this context, decentralization and professionalization are both attempts at coping with the same fundamental difficulty in the criminal justice system: a lack of close control by society at large.

*Danger of isolation.* The two phenomena are similar in their negative as well as positive aspects. Both risk suffering from insularity and inbreeding because both assert control by isolating the subject agency: in one case from professionals in other fields, paraprofessionals, politicians, and just plain people; in the other case from professionals, "experts" of all sorts, and, in general, anyone without credentials originating in the defined jurisdiction.

This mutual rejection of "outsiders" makes it difficult to delegate real control of a professionalized bureaucracy to a community or, conversely, to professionalize a bureaucracy which is truly community-controlled. But the similarities in the control function of decentralization and professionalization suggest that *when isolated in separate bureaucratic spheres* professionalized and decentralized institutions may both reduce objectionable aspects of the present system. This observation reinforces the arguments for a scheme of coexisting, complementary systems. In my opinion, a key to successful municipal operation of police, courts, and prisons lies in determining which functions already have been professionalized, which may be feasibly and appropriately professionalized in the near future, and which are not easily or should not be professionalized. The latter are ripe for decentralization. Thus formulated, decentralization becomes not a force in opposition to professionalization, but rather a force well coordinated with it, a force which in fact speeds professionalization by sharpening the role definition the professional is seeking to assume.

## Attention to Externalities as a Yardstick to Decentralization

Decentralization will be unsuccessful if one district's exercise of control has significant adverse consequences for other districts. Economists have labeled such extramural consequences of intramural transactions "externalities," and it seems obvious that governmental power over conduct with minimal or no extradistrict effects is more appropriately decentralized than power over conduct which has more numerous and significant externalities. Hence, the decision whether to delegate responsibilities to an alternative system is like a decision whether to leave transactions in private hands, or to subject them to government regulation. A contract to produce power is no longer left to a consumer and producer to negotiate; it is regulated by government as a representative of all those third parties who, though outside the transaction, will be affected by it—in the power-production case by the population and diminution in resources it may cause.

In cases which generate significant externalities limited to a small geographic area, decentralization permits delegation of authority to a surrogate more likely to represent those affected by the transaction than a centralized government. The principle of externalities thus suggests a further advantage to the construction of a complementary, neighborhood-based system of criminal justice: such a system enhances the probability that those who will create and operate their criminal justice system will be those, and only those, affected by it. Loitering or raucous noisemaking may, for example, generate externalities for disapproving East Harlem residents if such activities are permitted there, but there is no self-evident reason why residents of Queens should partake in the governmental decision which might regulate or restrict these phenomena. Significant externalities do not reach that far.

This general principle leaves two critical problems unresolved. First, what utilitarian calculus indicates when those outside a district are affected significantly enough to gain entry to the decisionmaking process? Second, how are psychological externalities to be weighted? I have found no logically compelling answers to these questions. Moreover, if the problem is considered abstractly, I see no hope of evolving an answer or answers which could be generally acceptable. Each man's resolution of these problems depends, *inter alia*, on his sense of vulnerability, of anguish over the conduct of his fellow man, and on how he values his own and others' right to live without intrusion and restraint. Despite these difficulties, the rule of thumb provided by a judgment of the impact of externalities is basic to the fabrication of a scheme of decentralization. In concrete instances, particularly when a comparison must be made between alternatives, a commonsense application of the rule often seems to yield a generally accepted conclusion.

## Commitment to Experimentation

Nothing said in this Article should be taken to mean that the time for looking has passed and that we are ready to leap. Though advanced with enthusiasm, recommendations based on so rudimentary a collection of observations as those presented here should be tested in practice (and doubtless modified) before it can be decided whether and how they should be put into effect on a large scale. This Article should be read only as a blueprint for experimentation.

The checkerboard pattern associated with casting our model as a complementary system should permit experimentation at modest cost in selected districts. Moreover, even this expenditure is predicated on more than theory. The majority of institutional arrangements here proposed have been selected because they would draw on the experience of existing projects: ventures run by foundation and municipal agencies, or operating programs in other cities and countries. (These pilot programs were designed with an aim other than decentralization in mind but all seem adaptable, and indeed seem to be strengthened by adaptation, to a neighborhood system).

Thus the system presented here is designed to move from existing knowledge, empirically derived, to a scheme of larger, more coordinated experiments, and then ultimately, to a higher level of implementation.

## A Reality Constraint

In the pages that follow I have limited myself to proposals that I believe have a reasonable chance of implementation over the next five years, given the constraints imposed by bureaucratic inertia, the political and economic self-interest of those involved in the criminal justice system, public indifference or fear, and scarcity of resources. I have permitted myself to be "optimistic" only in presuming that public fear of crime will work against inertia and indifference and produce funding in this area even while other city responsibilities may be given fewer and fewer resources relative to demand.

## Institutional Arrangements

### Legislation

*Advantages of local legislation.* Society creates its criminals by using its laws to define crimes. One of the most salient issues in current jurisprudential discussion is whether we create too many criminals by labeling too many forms of conduct "crimes." This is an issue particularly relevant to decentralization. If street loitering is a way of socializing in a community whose streets are more hospitable than its tenement living rooms, or if playing the numbers in a slum is no different from playing poker in the suburbs, why should the suburban concept of crime be imposed on inner city society. So long as externalities are minimal, shouldn't each community be free to define its own crimes?

There can be no doubt that within New York and other cities, neighborhood styles already affect the regulation of neighborhood crime, but the process proceeds sub rosa at the discretion of individual civil servants. When police overlook assaults in black areas which would produce arrests in silkstocking districts, or when judges vary sentencing patterns to conform to their vision of the mores of the complainant and offender, the resulting pattern of law enforcement is subject to neither community nor legislative control. This conduct is a particularly undesirable manifestation of rule by civil servants. In the all too frequent worst cases, the criminal justice system is molded to conform to an outsider's stereotype of community conduct. In the rare cases where the civil servant goes beyond stereotypes and does correctly perceive patterns of community conduct, the operation of the system will probably conform to the lowest common denominator of present affairs, rather than to the ideals of the community. Delegating the legislative power of criminal code definition to a neighborhood government would beneficially reassert the community's control of the conduct of its own system. In the face of community legislation, neither policy nor judges would be so likely to assume that "this law doesn't really apply to these people."

Community control over a portion of the penal law also implies neighborhood decisionmaking in a critical area previously left almost entirely to the discretion of civil servants: resource allocation. With resources far too scarce to perform all law enforcement jobs, the overbreadth of state and city codes leaves the criminal justice bureaucracies to make choices between enforcement alternatives which the larger polity has shirked. Permitting communities to narrow the code is thus almost synonymous with asking them to make their own program choice in regard to some aspects of law enforcement. They may, of course, opt out of this choice by keeping their codes as overbroad as the state's now is. But at least the delegation of legislative power opens an opportunity which state legislators, because of the pressures of some areas and interests which do want the widest possible code, are not likely to seize.

Other decentralization plans attempt to strengthen community control of enforcement patterns by suggesting that police precinct commanders and neighborhood leaders meet regularly to discuss enforcement priorities. But this method of decentralization spawns at least four unnecessary tensions. First, by leaving state and city legislative directives unmodified, while at the same time introducing another stream of directives to the police captain, a plan which recommends police-community collaboration sets up an undesirable conflict between legislative authority and popular control. Second, because the appearance of deference to legislative direction must be maintained by both police and neighborhood leaders, district modifications of central decisions tend to be negotiated out of sight and implemented through tacit pressures. This is hardly a desirable way to increase community control of police activity. Third, while community direction on a legislative plane has a chance of being acceptable to the police, lay pressures toward particular allocative decisions within a given legislative framework seem much more intrusive on the would-be professional's performance of his professional role. Standard police doctrine teaches that the community should be kept out of operational decisions. Though the mystique of these decisions is exaggerated, this doctrine is bureaucratically understandable, and deeply rooted. Fourth, any procedure by which the community informally negotiates its enforcement priorities with local police obfuscates responsibility for the consequences of these decisions. When the costs of nonenforcement are incurred, both parties react by berating each other. This Article therefore suggests that communities be empowered to proceed legislatively in choosing whether they will label prostitution, gambling, homosexuality, drunkenness, marijuana use, vagrancy, and disorderly conduct as "crimes," and, if so, how, up to certain levels, they would punish perpetrators of these activities.

*Proposed method of implementation.*   A good way for the state to delegate this power might be for it to adopt a variant of the procedure used in the enactment of the "model acts" or "uniform codes" now popular in American law. Under this variant it is suggested that the state legislature (in regard to the first five of the named categories of "crimes") and the city council (in regard to the latter two categories) might pass legislation similar to that now enacted, but make the application of the legislation contingent on local areas adopting the bill. The legislature could authorize local areas (in New York, neighborhood districts) to adopt the bill with lesser, but not greater, penalties than those specified in the enabling legislation. In this way a neighborhood council would be spared the cost and furor of hammering out legislation, and would instead be asked to make a relatively simple choice, comprehensible to all neighborhood residents. State restraints on the upper limits of penalties and the definition of offenses would protect those who might be accused of crimes, and the uniform nature of the act would facilitate the comprehension of a district's laws by police (who might be transferred from district to district), judges (who might handle cases from several districts), travellers, and new residents. The system of enactment by local authorities based on authorization contained within the enabling act also leaves a fail-safe mechanism in the hands of the state or city. If, for example, the externalities of certain conduct are greater than was at first recognized, or if a district becomes a bulwark of organized crime, the state or city can simply repeal its enabling ordinance.

Those who regard the overexpansiveness of codes as a crime against society may not be entirely happy with a scheme of local option which permits continued "overbreadth" in some areas. If drunkenness is a disease, and such 'crimes without victims" as prostitution, gambling, homosexuality, and drug use have no physical consequences for the nonparticipant, what right does any government, even a decentralized one, have to harass this activity and imprison its perpetrators? The short answer to this point is that the proposed scheme does not inhibit efforts at reform of the criminal code at the state level. By giving states the power to set a maximum, but not a minimum, on punishment of conduct regarded as criminal, it becomes easier to restrict the overbreadth of a code and no harder to diminish it.

A longer reply is worth considering because it illustrates some of the values of decentralization to the conservative as well as to the radical. Though an argument that "crimes without victims" should be exclusively the concern of those voluntarily engaged in such transactions is powerful, our political and moral tradition recognizes the significance of psychic externalities. The psychic distress of being exposed to offers of prostitution, displays of homosexuality, the sight of drunks, and the thought of all three has historically been minimized through efforts at the control of deviance. Though there would seem to be no acceptable ground for allowing distress generated merely by the thought of these (and similar) activities to retard their operation, there is force to the contention that when these activities are publicly conducted they generate suffering for those who would, but cannot, avoid contact with them. Shouldn't a group of citizens have the option of insulating their residential neighborhood from public forms of conduct (a category which does not include speech, or private conduct) they find psychologically undesirable, even if physically inconsequential? Viewed from this perspective, decentralization gives groups of citizens the capacities to construct their own public life styles in areas sheltered in part by criminal codes of their own choosing (up to limits designed to protect the due process rights of those who might deviate). The checkerboard pattern of different codes in different areas should give each individual an opportunity to select a community which fits his life style, while at the same time it leaves sheltered those communities whose life styles demand shelter.

This legislative plan, built around the device of neighborhood discretion in opting in or out of uniform acts, flows nicely from our principles. It is neighborhood based and brings the community and its criminal justice system closer together, to the benefit of both; it operates in a manner which maximizes the prospects of peaceful coexistence with the state's legislative power; it comports well with the professionalization of the agencies which must administer it; and its area of operation is defined so as to minimize externalities.

## A Community Moot

Periodically there appears in the literature of criminal law—either in commentary on foreign legal systems or in a revisionist approach to our own—a glimmering of recognition that a court could do very different things from those we are accustomed to its doing. This perspective is of pressing relevance to decentralization.

*Need for a new court model.* So long as we think of courts as adjudicators of guilt, they are extremely unlikely candidates for decentralization. At the outset of this Article it was acknowledged that there are some things the existing system does well and that these should be preserved. A prime example was the trial mechanism which affords due process to the accused. The courts, it may be conceded, do not give as many defendants the benefits of a due process trial as they should, but this only points to a need for more courts or for improving the workings of courts. If distance, professional objectivity, a "blind" treatment of all individuals as though they were alike, and a highly controlled, even rigidified, procedural system are the underpinnings of due process (it would seem that they are), then certainly reformers attempting to expand the opportunity for a due process trial should not call for decentralization of the court system. By these lights the last things we want are paraprofessionals as judges, community mores as standards, and a neighborhood as a forum.

At their best, then, courts should be responsive to higher principles than the sentiments of those who are judged or, more especially, those who do the judging. Where is there a role for community control in such a pure—and surely correct—vision of the process? Moreover, as commonly conceived, courts also seem irrelevant to decentralization because each case involves so little policy input once a legislative code has been framed, and each case (except for the most spectacular) yields so little of consequence to the political arena when it is resolved. What can the average citizen contribute and what does he care?

These perspectives change radically, however, if we stop thinking of courts as adjudicators, and view them instead as parts of a therapeutic process aimed at conciliation of disputants or reintegration of deviants into society.[1] One author has labelled these contrasting conceptualizations as the battle model and the family model.[2] Another, writing as an anthopologist, compares the function and style of parallel court systems in Liberia in similar terms.[3] A court system, established by the British, was primarily adjudicative, while a tribal "moot" performed an integrative, conciliatory function. Whereas the court was characterized by social distance between judge and litigants, rules of procedure which narrowed the issues under discussion, and a resolution which ascribed guilt or innocence to a defendant, the moot emphasized the bonds between the convenor and the disputants, it encouraged the widening of discussion so that all tensions and viewpoints psychologically—if not legally—relevant to the issue were expressed,[4] and it resolved disputes by consensus about future conduct, rather than by assessing blame retrospectively.[5] The consensual development of solutions was aided by the fact that while the "court" emphasized the trappings of authority and coervice power, the moot "takes place in the familiar surroundings of a home. The robes, writs, messengers, and other symbols of power which subtly intimidate and inhibit the parties in the courtroom, by reminding them of the physical force which underlies the procedures, are absent."[6] While courts often proceed in a mysterious, almost Delphic fashion, obscure and therefore unpersuasive to the people caught up in the system, a moot has a better chance of molding consensus because it operates in an everyday manner as well as milieu.[7]

Despite the differences between a tribal culture and our own, isn't there a place for a community moot in our judicial system.[8] Such a moot might handle family disputes, some marital issues (e.g. paternity, support, separation), juvenile delinquency, landlord-tenant relations, small torts and breaches of contract involving only community members, and misdemeanors affecting only community members. The present system does not, after all, perform the job of adjudication in most of these cases. Civil proceedings are generally avoided because the parties are too ignorant, fearful, or impoverished to turn to small claims courts, legal aid or similar institutions.[9] Many matters which may technically be criminal violations will not be prosecuted because they are viewed by the prosecuting authorities as private and trivial matters. The criminal adjudicative model seems particularly insufficient and a system of conciliation correspondingly well advised when we know that due to institutional overcrowding and established patterns of sentencing the vast majority of misdemeanants and some felons are not likely to be imprisoned. For these defendants, the judicial process is not a screen filtering those who are innocent from those who will be directed to the corrrective parts of the process. Rather, it is the corrective process; as such it fails to be more than a "Bleak House,"[10] profoundly alienating, rather than integrating.

The arguments for abandoning the adjudicative model have received some recognition in two of the function areas of court work which a moot might assume: those related to juveniles[11] and to family disputes.[12] But New York's Family Court,[13] reorganized in 1962[14] and again nominated for reorganization in 1969,[15] retains the trappings of the adjudicative model.[16] Judges, 30 to 40 years older and of an entirely different social stratum from those who typically are summoned to appear before them,[18] preside in downtown courts from raised benches, deciding cases involving charges of juvenile delinquency,[19] assaults between family members, divorce and nonsupport. The physical, social and psychological distance between a judge and the citizens before him cannot be overcome, nor can the circumstances of a situation be penetrated in the limited time available for each case; decisions by fiat rather than conciliation are therefore necessary.[20]

*Workings of the proposed moot.* A neighborhood moot, however, might handle segments of this case load[21] in a different manner. Again, we are dealing with activities (assaults between family members, juvenile delinquency which does not reach the level of felony, marital relationships other than divorce) which do not have significant externalities. Again, the bankruptcy of the professional in handling these problems has many times been noted, especially by the professionals themselves.[22] Here also the existing system is overburdened and undermanned.[23] If a less elaborate community-based system assumed a defined portion of the case load, it would leave the regular court time to function in cases where its professional skills were relevant.

The usefulness of nonprofessionals assembled through the forum of a moot is suggested by therapeutic practices which secure progress with personal and family problems by building a pattern of supportive conduct among friends and neighbors.[24] The family court only treats parties in the courtroom environment; a moot would begin with the recognition that people's problems may be resolved or intensified—if not caused— by the milieu in which they dwell. Operating in that milieu the moot is designed to stimulate emotional and tangible support from those on the block and in the tenement, the people among whom the disputants live and on whom they depend.

The method of operation of such a moot could vary experimentally with each community. Typically, however, it might draw its "business" from referrals by social agencies, the community police,[25] the neighborhood attorney, the municipal police, the existing court system, and from voluntary submissions by individuals who wished the services of the body. A salaried counselor accepting such requests for a moot might then arrange sessions at a time and place suitable to the participants: the complainant, the persons about whom he has complained, and those invited by these parties or the counselor. If a necessary party refused to attend, a counselor would simply refer the other parties to the municipal justice system. This possibility should often secure the cooperation of those who in the court system would be defendants.[26] A significant attraction to complainants is that the moot holds promise of being more conveniently located, more considerate, and much faster in processing cases that the municipal system.[27] Moreover, there is evidence that a number of would-be complainants do not proceed through the regular police and court system because they do not want the offender to be "harmed" or because they think that the incident is a private, not a criminal, matter.[28] For such people, the informal, private, noncoercive style of the moot may be very appealing. Because the moot has no power of compulsion and does not preempt regular court action, a complainant has nothing to lose by turning first to it. Refusal to give the counselor power to compel attendance is not likely, therefore, to leave a moot without cases.

A moot might be public or private, held in the home of a party, in a community meeting hall, or in the counselor's chambers, with a presumption in favor of private meetings in the counselor's chambers, unless all parties agreed otherwise. Typically, moots might function by the counselor asking the complainant to state his grievances and his requested remedies, by having the person complained about respond, and then by allowing general discussion and questioning between all those present.[30] It would be hoped that through such open discussion a range of grievances running in both directions would be aired and better understood,[30] that the counselor might be able to suggest future conduct by both parties to reduce tensions; and that both friends and relatives invited by the participants might serve as "witnesses" and participants in the consensual solutions evolved, thus joining community officials in keeping the peace.[31]

It will be seen from this brief description that in some cases it is hoped that the moot will have effects beyond the judicial and even the correctional function. The moot as recommended would be unique in prompting *community discussion* about situations in which community relations are on the verge of breaking down. When the juvenile who loiters around a shop now receives a police record and warning,[32] antagonisms between him and his peers and shopkeeper and police are increased rather than relieved. If the complaint were replaced by a moot discussion, to which the teenager brought his friends, the shopkeeper his associates (including his family, other shopkeepers, his employees), and the police their officers charged with working with juveniles, there would be a fair chance for the kind of interchange which has proved valuable when staged as a one-event "retreat" in other communities.[33] Depending, no doubt, on the passions and personalities involved, the skill of the counselor, and the root causes of tension, there is reason to hope that such sessions would be useful.

No legislation would be necessary to initiate the moot; the cooperation of individuals associated with the existing court system would be the only prerequisite. Insofar as the moot might prove ineffective in some cases or areas, complainants could be expected to reinitiate their cases in the municipal courts. The alternative system is thus backed up by the established system.

## Conclusion

In this Article overcriminalization and overcentralization are linked. Externalities, due process considerations, danger, the need for professional training and dispassionate commitment all make community handling of "true crime"—crime with victims, crime which provokes a passion for retribution and a need for extended incarceration of the "criminal"—a poor subject for community controlled decentralization. Conversely, however, "crime without victims," "crime" which the complainant wants restrained but without elaborate procedure or punishment of the offenders, "crime" born to negligence or bureaucratic error, "crime" which does not call for isolation of the offender but rather his better integration into society—this is a problem best defined and dealt with by the community in which it arises. Centralized organizations either ignore these problems or mishandle them by squeezing some unlucky and haphazardly chosen few into a system which adjudicates, condemns, isolates, and punishes. In contrast the community institutions recommended here are designed to conciliate, comprehend, reintegrate, and help community disputants, deviants, delinquents, and just those with problems.

Those who support this plan should do so not because they want community control of the operations of the current system, but rather because they want a new system; one which fills a need overlooked in urban America to date.

## Notes

1. "For the most part, litigation is a way of viewing the past through the eyes of the present. But perhaps justice is best done by starting with the present —with present needs and present demands—and using the past only where it reveals equitable considerations which will provide guidance in shaping a remedy. . . .

"We are still—in contract law, in domestic law, in landlord-tenant law, in tort law—engaged in a quest for fault, for "who did what when" as a way of deciding how the risk should be borne and who should pay, perform or provide remedy. Yet, in domestic relations, industrial injuries, automobile accidents, we are finding that the quest for fault is time consuming, elusive and not particularly productive in terms of enabling human beings to get back on their feet and to cope with the present or chart a rational course for the future." Cahn and Cahn, *What Price Justice: The Civilian Perspective Revisited*, 41 Notre Dame Lawyer 932 (1966). The Cahns propose the creation of a "Neighborhood Arbitration Commission" and other institutions less relevant to this discussion.

2. Griffiths, *Ideology in Criminal Procedure, or a Third "Model" of the Criminal Process*, 79 Yale L.J. 359. Though Griffiths does not discuss the point, he could fairly argue that, insofar as it has developed the tool of arbitration, modern labor law provides us with an extended and successful experience in the operation of the family model. *See generally* A. Cox and D. Bok, Cases and Materials on Labor Law 518–23 (6th. ed. 1969).

3. Gibbs, *The Kpelle Moot*, 33 Africa 1 (1963), *abridged and reprinted in* Law and Warfare 277 (P. Bohannan ed. 1967); Gibbs, *Poro Values and Courtroom Procedures in a Kpelle Chiefdom*, 18 Sw. J. Anthropology 341 (1962). Though Gibbs' insights have been taken as the starting point for this discussion, the anthropological literature is not without other examples of the same system in other cultures. *See e.g.*, in Mexico, Nader, *Styles of Court Procedure: To Make the Balance*, in Law in Culture and Society 69 (L. Nader ed. 1969); in Africa, Harries-Jones, *Marital Disputes and the Process of Conciliation in a Copperbelt Town*, 34 Human Problems in British Central Africa 29 (1964); and in India, Cohn, *Some Notes on Law and Change in North India*, 8 Economic Development & Cultural Change 79 (1959), in P. Bohannan ed., Law and Warfare 139 (1967), and L. Rudolph and S. Rudolph, the Modernity of Tradition 254 (1967).

Comrades' Courts in the Soviet Union bear some resemblance to the moots here proposed, particularly in their encouragement of neighborhood participation and their emphasis on total examination of the situation of the offender. But they differ markedly from the moots chronicled above and here recommended because of their coercive power (either through punishment or record-keeping), their adjudicative emphasis (guilt or innocence determined by a tribunal of judges), and their link with the centralized state machinery. *See generally* Lipson, *Law: The Function of Extra-Judicial Mechanisms*, in Soviet and Chinese Communism: Similarities and Differences 144 (P. Threadgold ed. 1967); Berman and Spindler, *Soviet Comrades' Courts*, 38 Wash. L. Rev. 842 (1963). Note also Stanley Lubman's contrast between the emphasis on "right and wrong" in present Chinese communist mediation proceedings and the lack of such emphasis in traditional Confucian efforts at mediation. Lubman, *Mao and Mediation: Politics and Dispute Resolution in Communist China*, 55 Calif. L. Rev. 1284 (1967).

Cuba's "popular tribunals," though performing conciliatory functions and "organized . . . in the neighborhood, so that neighbors and acquaintances of those being judged can attend the trials . . . and . . . judges sitting in these trials come from the same community in which they live and work," Manual De Los Tribunales Populares De Base VI (1966) quoted in Berman, *The Cuban Popular Tribunals*, 69 Colum. L. Rev. 1317, 1318 (1969), are also constructed on the coercive adjudicative model, *see e.g.*, Berman's description: "[T]he 'A pie!' cry when the judges enter and exist . . . coupled with the armed and uniformed crier, gives the Popular Tribunals an aura of formality and authority which is not insignificant'. *Id.* at 1342.

The community institution recommended in this Article has been called a "moot" to emphasize that it is more like the Kpelle than the communist system.

4. M. Gluckman, *The Judicial Process Among the Barotse of Northern Rhodesia* 51 (1955), notes the advantages of the same all-encompassing technique in Barotse courts.

5. Griffiths calls this a "distinction between a punitive and a best-interests proceeding." Griffiths, *supra* note 2, at 411. The Rudolphs write: "The village tribunal, because its members reside among the disputing parties and find their own lives touched by their discontents, is less anxious to find 'truth' and give 'justice' than to abate conflict and promote harmony." L. Rudolph and S. Rudolph, *supra* note 3, at 258. Nader quotes Professor Hahm's observation that "analogous Korean proceedings prefer peace to justice, harmony to truth, and mediation to adjudication." Nader, *supra* note 3, at 84.

6. Gibbs, *The Kpelle Moot*, 33 Africa 1 (1963), *abridged and reprinted in* Law and Warfare 277, 282 (P. Bohannan ed. 1967).

7. Curiously, Gibbs does not emphasize this point. *But see* Srivinas, *The Social System of a Mysore Village*, in Village India 18 (M. Marriot ed. 1955): "I do not hold that justice administered by the elders of the dominant caste is always or even usually more just than the justice administered by the judges in urban law courts, but only that it is much better understood by the litigants." Jessee Berman's comment on the Cuban Popular Tribunals is similar, "Perhaps it is not unfair to say that it is deemed more important that the people know the judges, than that the judges know the law." Berman, *supra* note 3, at 1335.

8. It should be noted that other writers have called for the creation of neighborhood courts, and that some institutions of this sort are actually operating in the United States, but the emphasis in these programs has been on an adjudicative rather than a conciliatory forum. *See e.g.*, Elson and Rosenheim, *Justice for the Child at the Grassroots*, 51 A.B.A.J. 341 (1965): "In essence, our proposal is to transplant a certain group of cases from the juvenile court itself to a community panel created by the court specifically to hear and dispose of those cases." *Id.* Note especially *id.*, at *344–45*, discussing operating prototypes of such panels.

See also the description of the East Palo Alto, California, Community Youth Responsibility Program in Hager, *Neighborhood Court Judges Its Own Juvenile Offenders*, L.A. Times, Dec. 25, 1972, at 1, col. 5, and (in more detail) Urban and Rural Systems Associates, Evaluation of the Community Youth Responsibility Program, undated.

9. *See generally* Eovaldo and Gestrin, *Justice for Consumers: The Mechanisms of Redress*, 66 NW. U.L. Rev. 281 (1971). After surveying the present range of options for consumer litigation, the authors conclude that "new approaches are needed which can transcend the limits of our traditional legal framework," *id.*, at 302, and urge experimentation with arbitration techniques which would circumvent traditional court procedures.

10. I have borrowed Dickens' phrase from Schrag, *Bleak House 1968: A Report on Consumer Test Litigation*, 44 N.Y.U.L. Rev. 115 (1969), who uses it to describe the delays encountered in litigating consumer protection cases in New York City's courts.

11. V. Stapleton & L. Teitlebaum, in Defense of Youth: a Study of the Role of Counsel in American Juvenile Courts 103 (1972), quote Jane Addams:

"There was almost a change in *mores* when the Juvenile Court was established. The child was brought before the judge with no one to prosecute him and none to defend him—the judge and all concerned were merely trying to find out what could be done on his behalf. The element of conflict was absolutely eliminated and with it, all notion of punishment as such. . . ." The Stapleton and Teitlebaum discussion underscores ways in which a thrust toward legalization has undermined this orientation.

12. *See generally* Foster, *Conciliation and Counseling in the Courts in Family Law Cases*, 41 N.Y.U.L. Rev. 353 (1966).

13. A civil court, but one included in this Article because of the obvious relevance of its work to the criminal justice system.

14. *See* Family Court Act, N.Y. Judiciary-court Acts 111–1019 (McKinney 1963 & McKinney Supp. 1973). Association of the Bar of the City of New York, Children and Families in the Courts of New York City (1954) describes the operation of the New York system prior to 1962. The report prompted the 1962 Family Court Act.

15. *See* Directors of Administration of the Courts, first and second Judicial Departments, a Study of the Family Court of the State of New York within the City of New York and related agencies and recommendations concerning their Administration (1969).

16. In part this is a result of a constitutional mandate called into play wherever coercive detention of significant duration is a likely outcome of a procedure. *See In re* Gault, 387 U.S. 1 (1967); Hogan v. Rosenberg, 24 N.Y. 2d 207, 247 N.E. 2d. 260, 299 N.Y.S. 2d 424 (1969). In part it is due to the administrative ambiance which envelops a high volume bureaucratic operation. "Impersonal attendants perform their duties with clipped routine, underscoring alienation. In the waiting rooms of the larger New York boroughs it is not unusual for fifty or sixty persons to be gathered. As each case is called the name of the respondent is shouted out in full voice by a court employee dressed like a police officer. The name of the youngster is likely to be called a second time if he does not leap forward immediately, lest a moment be wasted. Observers find it ironic to recall the words of the Illinois Family Court Act, which expressed the intended spirit of the New York Law as well: 'The children . . . as far as practicable . . . shall be treated not as criminals but as children in need of aid, encouragement and guidance'." Paulson, *Juvenile Courts, Family Courts, and the Poor Man*, in the Law of the Poor 370 (J. tenBroek ed. 1966).

17. Only one of the 30 Family Court judges who listed a birth date in the 1970 *Martindale-Hubbel* was born after 1924. The average age of judges listed there is 59.

18. *See generally* Paulson, *supra* note 16, at 371.

19. The unfortunate individual and institutional impacts of this labeling are discussed in Langley, *The Juvenile Court: The Making of a Delinquent*, 7 L. & Soc'y Rev. 273 (1972).

20. The New York Family Court's failure as an instrument of conciliation is suggested by the fact that of the 44,675 new cases it received in 1968–69, exactly 10 were for conciliation in an effort to avoid divorce or separation. Report of the Judicial Conference, State of New York for the Judicial Year July 1, 1968, through June 30, 1969, at 288, 319. Statewide, the number of conciliation proceedings in family courts declined from 520 in 1963–64 to 163 in 1968–69—the

only decline in cases received by Family Courts except for a marginal decrease in neglect cases. *Id.* at 288. This lack of activity is not a problem in itself because conciliation bureaus established in 1967 have actively offered conciliation services in divorce and separation cases. *See id.* at 50, 106. But the Family Court's incapacity to play this role in divorce cases suggests its inability to abandon the adjudicative model in dealing with juvenile delinquents or family offenses.

21. It is not proposed that the moot entertain either adoption or divorce proceedings. Other cases could be handled either by the moot or family court, according to the preference of the litigants. *See* text accompanying notes 140–43 *infra*. The moot's resolution of support or similar cases could be given force simply by framing agreed results in the form of a contract between the parties.

The distribution of the case load in New York City's Family Court is as follows:

Types of cases in New York City Family Court 1968–69

| *Proceeding* | *Percent* |
| --- | --- |
| Juvenile delinquency | 20 |
| Person in need of supervision | 11 |
| Neglect and permanent neglect | 9 |
| Adoption | 2 |
| Support | 29 |
| Family Offense | 11 |
| Paternity | 17 |
| Other | 1 |

Source: Report of the Judicial Conference *supra* note 20.

22. *See* J. Polier, *A View from the Bench* (1964); Paulson, *supra* note 131; Tolchin, *Experts Wonder If Family Court Is Doing Its Job*, N.Y. Times, Jan. 18, 1964, at 24, col. 3. All the foregoing specifically refer to the Family Court in New York City. Griffiths remarks generally that "[t]here is common agreement that the juvenile court movement—measured against its initial ideals and expectations—is more or less of a failure." Griffiths, *supra* note 2, at 399.

23. The Family Court, "still suffers from acute shortages of necessary personnel and auxiliary services. . . . [The shortage] not only adversely affects the quality of the Court's work, but is creating a backlog of cases awaiting hearing or disposition of near critical proportions."[11] Report of the Judicial Conference *supra* note 20, at 287. During 1968–69 the city's Family Court disposed of 34,935 petitions, about the same number as in the previous year, but 44,675 petitions were received. *Id.*, at 288.

24. *See* Davidson, *To Treat a Disturbed Person, Treat His Family*, N.Y. Times, Aug. 16, 1970, 6 (Magazine), at 10; text accompanying note 28 *infra*.

25. The Family Crisis Intervention Unit referred 34.8 percent of the families it dealt with to the Family Court, U.S. Dept. of Justice, N.I.L.E.C.J. Report—Training Police as Specialists in Family Crisis Intervention (1970), at 30.

26. Excellent cooperation from juveniles has been obtained in East Palo Alto, *see* note 28 *supra*, when the experimental system is described as an alternative to police and court processing.

27. "An enormous amount of time is wasted by the parents of children pulled into court. Little or no attempt is made to space appointments for court hearings. Everyone is told to come at 9:30 in the morning, and the reception

rooms fill with employed mothers and fathers who lose more wages with each passing hour.

"Waiting to appear in the court is not only expensive for those the court must serve, but the waiting often proves to be futile. A case scheduled to be heard may not be ready and an adjournment will have to be ordered, with the consequent loss of another day's pay for parents." Paulson, *supra*, note 16 at 373.

The community moot might hold most of its hearings on evenings or Sundays. Without lawyers or forms, continuances would be much less likely than in Family Court. The speed with which hearings could be initiated by the moot would add to its therapeutic advantages. "[T]he hearing takes place soon after a breach has occurred, before the grievances have hardened." Gibbs, *supra*, note 6, at 282.

28. A National Opinion Research Center Survey of 10,000 households in 1965 revealed that only about 50 percent of all crimes were reported to law enforcement authorities. Thirty-four percent of those who did not report an incident explained that they did not want the matter treated as a criminal affair or the offender harmed. Ennis, *Crime, Victims and the Police*, in Modern Criminals 87, 94 (J. Short ed. 1970).

29. In the moot, the parties are encouraged in the expression of their complaints and feelings because they sense group support. "The very presence of one's kinsmen and neighbors demonstrates their concern." Gibbs, *supra* note 6, at 284.

Not every type of community will have a cultural milieu conducive to the expression of such grievances, nor could we expect every potential participant in any given community moot to be open to this approach. See the comments on cultural barriers to the expression of feelings, in J. Spiegel, *Some Cultural Aspects of Transference and Countertransference*, in Individual and Familiar Dynamics 160, 161–75 (J. Masserman ed. 1959).

30. "In the moot the parties . . . are allowed to hurl recriminations that, in the courtroom might bring a few hours in jail as punishment for the equivalent of contempt of court." Gibbs, *supra* note 6, at 286.

31. Of course the impact of social pressure will vary greatly with the "culture" and structure of the community in which the moot is held. Schwartz, *Social Factors in the Development of Legal Control: A Case Study of Two Israeli Settlements*, 63 Yale L.J. 471 (1954), notes several factors relevant to the greater influence of informally expressed opinion in one kibbutz than in another. The kibbutz with less primary group interaction, agreed norm-definition, peer-group identification, and self-selection by emigration or immigration is more likely to rely on more formal legal mechanisms. This suggests some reasons why a moot might be less effective in a New York slum than in a more primitive, rural community. But whether subgroups within an urban slum share enough of these characteristics to a great enough degree to make a moot worthwhile or whether they are so lacking in them as to make it impractical, must, in the absence of experiment, be a matter of conjecture. *See also* Kawashima, *Dispute Resolution in Contemporary Japan*, in Law in Japan 41 (A. von Mehren ed. 1963), for a discussion of "social-cultural" factors prompting the Japanese to resolve disputes through reconciliation or conciliation rather than litigation.

32. In New York a YD-1 form records a complaint made to the police, but

not processed by the courts (and therefore not confirmed by judicially examined and approved evidence). Taken collectively the forms create a dossier, later used by schools, welfare agencies, and courts (in sentencing) as though it implied guilt. At present the system faces legal challenge as an invasion of privacy and a violation of the constitutionally mandated presumption of innocence. I am here proposing that the community moot, which would compile no records suggesting guilt, replace the YD-1 in New York and like systems in other cities.

33. In the moot, "rewards are positive, in contrast to the negative sanctions of the courtroom. Besides the institutional apology, praise and acts of concern and affection replace fines and jail sentences." Gibbs, *supra* note 6, at 288.

# 2

# Varieties of Dispute Processing[*]

## Frank E. A. Sander[†]

In 1975, in an article entitled "Behind the Legal Explosion", published in the *Stanford Law Review*,[1] Professor John Barton pointed out that if federal appellate cases continued to grow for the next 40 years at the same rate at which they have grown during the last decade, then by the year 2010 we can expect to have well over one million federal appellate cases each year, requiring five thousand federal appellate judges to decide them and one thousand new volumes of the Federal Reporter each year to report the decisions. Since the number of cases initiated in the federal system each year is approximately ten times the number of decided appeals, one can readily extrapolate Professor Barton's projections to the trial level. And if one keeps in mind that in the State of California alone about four times as many actions are commenced each year as are commenced in the entire federal system, one begins to get some sense of the magnitude of the total problem.[2]

But I believe that one should view these dire predictions with a healthy skepticism. Litigation rates, like population rates, cannot be assumed to grow ineluctably, unaffected by a variety of social factors.[3] Nor should it be assumed that there will be no human intervention that could dramatically affect the accuracy of Professor Barton's projections.

Thus one concern to which we ought to address ourselves here is how we might escape from the specter projected by Professor Barton. This might be accomplished in various ways. First, we can try to prevent disputes[4] from arising in the first place through appropriate changes in the substantive law, such as the adoption of a no-fault principle for automobile injuries or the removal of a criminal sanction for certain

* Reprinted with the permission of West Publishing Co. and Frank E. A. Sander from 70 F.R.D. 111–134. Copyright © 1976 by West Publishing Co. Condensed; footnotes renumbered.

† I am indebted to a number of colleagues and friends for helpful comments on earlier versions of this paper.

conduct.[5] A less obvious substantive law issue that may have a bearing on the extent of litigation that arises is whether we opt for a discretionary rule or for one that aims to fix more or less firmly the consequences that will follow upon certain facts. For example, if a statute says that marital property on divorce will be divided in the court's discretion there is likely to be far more litigation than if the rule is, as in the community property states, that such property will normally be divided 50-50. I wonder whether legislatures and law revision commissions are sufficiently aware of this aspect of their work.

Another method of minimizing disputes is through greater emphasis on preventive law.[6] Of course lawyers have traditionally devoted a large part of their time to anticipating various eventualities and seeking, through skillful drafting and planning, to provide for them in advance. But so far this approach has been resorted to primarily by the well-to-do. I suspect that with the advent of prepaid legal services this type of practice will be utilized more widely, resulting in a probable diminution of litigation.

A second way of reducing the judicial caseload is to explore alternative ways of resolving disputes outside the courts, and it is to this topic that I wish to devote my primary attention. By and large we lawyers and law teachers have been far too single-minded when it comes to dispute resolution. Of course, as pointed out earlier, good lawyers have always tried to prevent disputes from coming about, but when that was not possible, we have tended to assume that the courts are the natural and obvious dispute resolvers. In point of fact there is a rich variety of different processes, which, I would submit, singly or in combination, may provide far more "effective" conflict resolution.[7]

Let me turn now to the two questions with which I wish to concern myself:

1. What are the significant characteristics of various alternative dispute resolution mechanisms (such as adjudication by courts, arbitration, mediation, negotiation, and various blends of these and other devices)?
2. How can these characteristics be utilized so that, given the variety of disputes that presently arise, we can begin to develop some rational criteria for allocating various types of disputes to different dispute resolution processes?

One consequence of an answer to these questions is that we will have a better sense of what cases ought to be left in the courts for resolution, and which should be "processed"[8] in some other way. But since this inquiry essentially addresses itself to developing the most effective method of handling disputes it should be noted in passing that one by-product may be not only to divert some matters now handled by the courts into other processes but also that it will make available those processes for grievances that are presently not being aired at all. We know very little about why some individuals complain and others do not, or about the social and psychological costs of remaining silent.[9] It is important to realize, however, that by establishing new dispute resolution mechanisms, or improving existing ones, we may be encouraging the ventilation of grievances that are now being suppressed. Whether that will be good (in terms of supplying a constructive outlet for suppressed anger and frustration) or whether it will simply waste scarce societal resources (by validating grievances that might otherwise have remained dormant) we do not know. The important thing to note is that there is a clear trade-off: the price of an improved scheme of dispute processing may well be a vast increase in the number of disputes being processed.

## The Range of Available Alternatives

There seems to be little doubt that we are increasingly making greater and greater demands on the courts to resolve disputes that used to be handled by other institutions of society.[10] Much as the police have been looked to to "solve" racial, school and neighborhood disputes, so, too, the courts have been expected to fill the void created by the decline of church and family. Not only has there been a waning of traditional dispute resolution mechanisms, but with the complexity of modern society, many new potential sources of controversy have emerged as a result of the immense growth of government at all levels,[11] and the rising expectations that have been created.

Quite obviously, the courts cannot continue to respond effectively to these accelerating demands. It becomes essential therefore to examine other alternatives.

The chart reproduced below attempts to depict a spectrum of some of the available processes arranged on a scale of decreasing external involvement.[12]

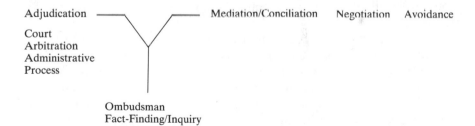

At the extreme left is adjudication, the one process that so instinctively comes to the legal mind that I suspect if we asked a random group of law students how a particular dispute might be resolved, they would invariably say "file a complaint in the appropriate court". Professor Lon Fuller, one of the few scholars who has devoted attention to an analysis of the adjudicatory process, has defined adjudication as "a social process of decision which assures to the affected party a particular form of participation, that of presenting proofs and arguments for a decision in his favor."[13] Although he places primary emphasis on process, I would like for present purposes to stress a number of other aspects—the use of a third party with coercive power, the usually "win or lose" nature of the decision, and the tendency of the decision to focus narrowly on the immediate matter in issue as distinguished from a concern with the underlying relationship between the parties. Although mediation or conciliation[14] also involves the use of a third party facilitator (and is distinguished in that regard from pure negotiation), a mediator or conciliator usually has no coercive power and the process in which he engages also differs from adjudication in the other two respects just mentioned. Professor Fuller puts this point well when he refers to "the central quality of mediation, namely, its capacity to reorient the parties toward each other, not by imposing rules on them, but by helping them to achieve a new and shared perception of their relationship, a perception that will redirect their attitudes and dispositions toward one another."[15]

Of course quite a variety of procedures fit under the label of adjudication. Aside from the familiar judicial model, there is arbitration, and the administrative process. Even within any one of these, there are significant variations. Obviously there are substantial differences between the Small Claims Court and the Supreme Court. Within arbitration, too, although the version used in labor relations is generally very similar to a judicial proceeding in that there is a written opinion and an attempt to rationalize the result by reference to general principles, in some forms of commercial arbitration the judgment resembles a Solomonic pronouncement and written opinions are often not utilized. Another significant variant is whether the parties have any choice in selecting the adjudicator, as they typically do in arbitration. Usually a decision rendered by a person in whose selection the parties have played some part will, all things being equal, be less subject to later criticism by the parties.

There are important distinctions, too, concerning the way in which the case came to arbitration. There may be a statute (as in New York and Pennsylvania) requiring certain types of cases to be initially submitted to arbitration (so-called compulsory arbitration). More commonly arbitration is stipulated as the exclusive dispute resolution mechanism in a contract entered into by the parties (as is true of the typical collective bargaining agreement and some modern medical care agreements). In this situation the substantive legal rules are usually also set forth in the parties' agreement, thus giving the parties control not only over the process and the adjudicator but also over the governing principles.

As is noted on the chart, if we focus on the indicated distinctions between adjudication and mediation, there are a number of familiar hybrid processes. An inquiry, for example, in many respects resembles the typical adjudication, but the inquiring officer (or fact finder as he is sometimes called) normally has no coercive power; indeed, according to Professor Fuller's definition, many inquiries would not be adjudication at all since the parties have no right to any agreed-upon form of presentation and participation.

But a fact finding proceeding may be a potent tool for inducing settlement. Particularly if the fact finder commands the respect of the parties, his independent appraisal of their respective positions will often be difficult to reject. This is especially true of the Ombudsman who normally derives his power solely from the force of his position.[16] These considerations have particular applicability where there is a disparity of bargaining power between the disputants (e.g., citizen and government, consumer and manufacturer, student and university). Although there may often be a reluctance in these situations to give a third person power to render a binding decision, the weaker party may often accomplish the same result through the use of a skilled fact finder.

There are of course a number of other dispute resolution mechanisms which one might consider. Most of these (e.g., voting, coin tossing, self-help) are not of central concern here because of their limited utility or acceptability. But one other mechanism deserves brief mention. Professor William Felstiner recently pointed out that in a "technologically complex rich society" avoidance becomes an increasingly common form of handling controversy. He describes avoidance as "withdrawal from or contraction of the dispute-producing relationship" (e.g., a child leaving home, a tenant moving to another apartment, or a businessman terminating a commercial relationship). He contends that such conduct is far more tolerable in modern society than in a "technologically simple poor society" because in the former setting the disputing individuals are far less interdependent.[17] But, as was pointed out in a cogent response by Professors Danzig and Lowy, there are heavy personal and societal costs for such a method of handling conflicts,[18] and this strongly argues for the development of some effective alternative mechanism. Moreover, even if we disregarded altogether the disputes that are presently being handled by avoidance—clearly an undesirable approach for the reasons indicated—we must still come to grips with the rising number of cases that do presently come to court and see whether more effective ways of resolving some of these disputes can be developed.

The preceding brief appraisal of the various primary processes is misleading in its simplicity, for of course rarely do the processes occur in isolation. Often adjudication involves an element of conciliation. Professor Stewart Macaulay describes an interesting example of such a situation in his analysis of the Wisconsin Department of Motor Vehicles' activities in monitoring the relationship between automobile franchisors and franchisees. Although the Department's only formal responsibility was whether to hold hearings with a view to possible revocation of the franchise, in fact the intervention of the Department served a mediative role by compelling each party to consider seriously the contentions of the other party, and hence led to settlement in a great number of cases.[19] Similarly, as already pointed out, fact finding may very closely resemble adjudication. Moreover when we look at the way the various processes occur in particular institutions, there is often an elaborate interplay of the individual mechanisms. For example, a grievance under a collective bargaining agreement is usually first sought to be negotiated. If the parties cannot settle the case they go to arbitration, but the arbitrator may first seek to mediate the case. Finally there may be an attempt to review the arbitrator's decision in the courts.

## Criteria

Let us now look at some criteria that may help us to determine how particular types of disputes might best be resolved.

### Nature of Dispute

Lon Fuller has written at some length about "polycentric" problems that are not well suited to an adjudicatory approach since they are not amenable to an all-or-nothing solution. He cites the example of a testator who leaves a collection of paintings in equal parts to two museums.[20] Obviously here a negotiated or mediated solution that seeks to accommodate the desires of the two museums is far better than any externally imposed solution. Similar considerations may apply to other allocational tasks where no clear guidelines are provided.

At the other extreme is a highly repetitive and routinized task involving application of established principles to a large number of individual cases. Here adjudication may be appropriate, but in a form more efficient than litigation (e.g., an administrative agency). Particularly once the courts have established the basic principles in such areas, a speedier and less cumbersome procedure than litigation should be utilized. . . .

With respect to many problems, there is a need for developing a flexible mechanism that serves to sort out the large general question from the repetitive application of settled principle. I do not believe that a court is the most effective way to perform this kind of sifting task. In Sweden, in the consumer field, there is a Public Complaints Board which receives individual consumer grievances. Initially the Board performs simply a mediative function, utilizing standards set up by the relevant trade organizations. If initial settlement is impossible, the Board issues a nonbinding recommendation to both parties, which often leads to subsequent settlement. Failing that, the grievant can sue in the newly established Small Claims Court. But another aspect of its activities is to seek to discern certain recurring issues and problems that should be dealt with by legislation or regulation.[21]...

## Relationship Between Disputants

A different situation is presented when disputes arise between individuals who are in a long-term relationship than is the case with respect to an isolated dispute. In the former situation, there is more potential for having the parties, at least initially, seek to work out their own solution, for such a solution is likely to be far more acceptable (and hence durable). Thus negotiation, or if necessary, mediation, appears to be a preferable approach in the first instance. Another advantage of such an approach is that it facilitates a probing of conflicts in the underlying relationship, rather than simply dealing with each surface symptom as an isolated event.

Consider, for example, a case such as might be heard in the recently established mediation session of the Dorchester (Massachusetts) District Court. A white woman (Mrs. W.) has filed a criminal complaint for assault against her black neighbor (Mrs. B.). The facts, as they emerge at the mediation session, are that Mrs. W. has for some time gratuitously taken care of Mrs. B.'s two young children so that Mrs. B. can go to work. On the day in question one of the B. children for the second time in a row broke the expensive eyeglasses of one of the W. children, and had been generally out of control. Mrs. W., having reached the end of her rope, struck the child. When Mrs. B. heard about this, she marched over to Mrs. W. and hit her. Mrs. W. thereupon filed a criminal complaint.

Fortunately the Dorchester District Court, like a number of other courts around the country,[22] has a program under which, if the clerk or judge deems the case appropriate, and the two parties are willing, the case can be referred to a panel of three trained mediators drawn from the local community. The panel will attempt to let each of the disputants fully state her side of the story, and then, through skillful probing, will seek to elicit points of tension in the underlying relationship (here, the increasing sense of exploitation felt by Mrs. W. as an arrangement deemed temporary became long-term). Finally, the mediators will attempt to work out an agreement which seeks to alleviate the long-run tensions as well as resolve the immediate controversy (here, for example, that Mrs. B. might agree to work with the social service component of the mediation project to try to find some alternative child care arrangement, and that she would pay five dollars per month to reimburse Mrs. W. for the broken glasses). Such a solution (unlike the aborted criminal adjudication) would most likely be acceptable to both parties; more significantly, it would have a therapeutic effect on the long-term relationship between these two individuals because it would permit them to ventilate their feelings, and then help them to restructure their future relationship in a way that met the expectations of both parties. In addition it would teach them how they might themselves resolve future conflicts. Thus there is a strong likelihood that future disputes would be avoided, or at least minimized.

Of course, it might be suggested that a court could also induce such a settlement. But quite aside from the unlikelihood of a busy court being able to create a climate that encourages the disputants to ventilate their underlying grievances, there is a world of difference between a coerced or semi-coerced settlement of the kind that so often results in court and a voluntary agreement arrived at by the parties. . . .

To be sure we have had a traditional aversion to judicial involvement in the going family, except where it is compelled by considerations of health or safety.[23] But I wonder whether that policy is not traceable to the coercive quality of the typical adjudicative intervention, rather than to a notion that the family must inevitably be left to struggle with its own internal conflicts. Of course in a sense we have developed a mediative solution for most family conflict—social work and family therapy. Still where there is a breakdown of the family as a result of death or divorce, the courts have customarily become involved and it is here that alternative dispute resolution devices—particularly mediation—need to be further explored.[24]

In the field of corrections, an interesting new program was recently begun at the Karl Holton facility in Stockton, California, by the California Youth Authority working in collaboration with the Center for Correctional Justice and the Institute of Mediation and Conflict Resolution. Instead of utilizing the usual authority-dominated grievance procedure, the drafters opted for what they called "the mediation approach".[25] It consists at the first level of a five person committee, one of whom (a middle management official) acts as Chairman, the other four being voting members—two inmates and two staff members. Review of the decision—or of the opposing views in case there is a tie—by the director of the facility or his delegate is then provided for, and finally recourse can be had to an outside independent three-person review board set up under the auspices of the American Arbitration Association. The decision of this board is only advisory, but the director of the facility must promptly indicate whether he will comply with it, and if not, to state his reasons for not doing so. Thus while the ultimate power of decision remains in the person in charge, aggrieved individuals are given maximum opportunity first to air their views freely in a mediational context and then, if that fails, to have their views presented for evaluation by a disinterested outsider.

Initial experience under this process is revealing. In contradistinction to the polarization that might have been expected at the initial level where two inmates are pitted against two officials, in only 10 out of the first 212 cases did the first step grievance committee result in a 2-2 tie. In all other cases a majority decision resulted. Moreover recent research suggests that the presence of a viable grievance mechanism is a significant factor in preventing prison riots.[26]

Such an internalized grievance procedure, with limited last resort recourse to outside agencies, would appear to hold great promise for many disputes within an ongoing institution, such as a school, a welfare department, or a housing development. In view of the multifaceted nature of this type of grievance process, one might hope that if a case following such a procedure subsequently came to court, the court would give great, if not conclusive, weight to the prior determinations.[27]

## Amount in Dispute

Although, generally speaking, we have acted to date in a fairly hit-or-miss fashion in determining what problems should be resolved by a particular dispute resolution mechanism, amount in controversy has been an item consistently looked to to determine the amount of process that is "due." The Small Claims Court movement has taken as its premise that small cases are simple cases and that therefore a pared-down judicial procedure is what is called for. Next to the juvenile court, there has probably been no legal institution that was more ballyhooed as a great legal innovation. Yet the evidence now seems overwhelming that the Small Claims Court has failed its original purpose; that the individuals for whom it was designed have turned out to be its victims.[28] Small wonder when one considers the lack of rational connection between amount in controversy and appropriate process. Quite obviously a small case may be complex, just as a large case may be simple. The need, according to a persuasive recent study, is for a preliminary investigative-conciliational stage (which could well be administered by a lay individual or paraprofessional) with ultimate recourse to the court. This individual could readily screen out those cases which need not take a court's time (e.g., where there is no dispute about liability but the defendant has no funds), and preserve the adjudicatory process for those cases where the issues have been properly joined and there is a genuine dispute of fact or law. Obviously such a screening mechanism is not limited in its utility to the Small Claims Court.[29]

## Cost

There is a dearth of reliable data comparing the costs of different dispute resolution processes. Undoubtedly this is due in part to the difficulty of determining what are the appropriate ingredients of such a computation. It may be relatively easy to determine the costs of an ad hoc arbitration (though even there one must deal with such intangibles as the costs connected with the selection of the arbitrator(s)). But determining the comparable cost of a court proceeding would appear to pose very difficult issues of cost accounting.[30] Even more difficult to calculate are the intangible "costs" of inadequate (in the sense of incomplete and unsatisfactory) dispute resolution. Still, until better data become available one can probably proceed safely on the assumption that costs rise as procedural formalities increase.

The lack of adequate cost data is particularly unfortunate with respect to essentially comparable processes, such as litigation and arbitration. Assuming for the moment that arbitration would produce results as acceptable as litigation—a premise that is even more difficult to verify —would cost considerations[31] justify the transfer (at least in the first instance) of entire categories of civil litigation to arbitration, as has been done in some jurisdictions for cases involving less than a set amount of money? One difficulty in this connection is that we have always considered access to the courts as an essential right of citizenship for which no significant charge should be imposed, while the parties generally bear the cost of arbitration. Thus although I believe, on the basis of my own arbitration experience, that that process is, by and large, as effective as and cheaper than litigation, lawyers tend not to make extensive use of it (outside of special areas such as labor and commercial law), in part because it is always cheaper for the clients to have society rather than the litigants pay the judges.[32] Perhaps if arbitration is to be made compulsory in certain types of cases because we believe it to be more efficient, then it should follow that society should assume the costs, unless that would defeat the goal of using costs to discourage appeals.[33] I will have more to say about this subject later.

## Speed

The deficiency of sophisticated data concerning the costs of different dispute resolution processes also extends to the factor of speed. Although it is generally assumed[34]—rightly, I believe—that arbitration is speedier than litigation, I am not aware of any studies that have reached such a conclusion on the basis of a controlled experiment that seeks to take account of such factors as the possibly differing complexity of the two classes of cases, the greater diversity of "judges" in the arbitration group, and the possibly greater co-operation of the litigants in the arbitration setting.

## Implications

1. At one time perhaps the courts were the principal public dispute processors. But that time is long gone. With the development of administrative law, the delegation of certain problems to specialized bodies

for initial resolution has become a common-place. Within the judicial sphere, too, we have developed specialized courts to handle family problems and tax problems, among others.

These were essential *substantive* diversions, that is, resort to agencies having substantive expertise. Perhaps the time is now ripe for greater resort to an alternate primary *process*. As I have indicated earlier, such a step would be particularly appropriate in situations involving disputing individuals who are engaged in a long-term relationship. The process ought to consist initially of a mediational phase, and then, if necessary, of an adjudicative one.[35] Problems that would appear to be particularly amenable to such a two-stage process are disputes between neighbors, family members, supplier and distributor, landlord and tenant.[36] Where there is an authority relationship between the parties (such as exists between prisoner and warden or school and student) special problems may be presented, but, as indicated earlier, such relationships, too, are, with some adjustments, amenable to a sequential mediation-adjudication solution.[37]

Receptivity to such an alternative primary process imposes special obligations on the Bar. Although we know relatively little about the participation of lawyers in conciliation processes, it is possible that there will be a lesser role for lawyers in this new world. Perhaps this simply calls for more diverse training in the law schools, but in the first instance it also poses a test to the Bar of its capacity to support innovative experimentation despite a temporary adverse economic impact for the profession.[38]

As regards the nature of the adjudicative tribunal, we should give strong consideration to greater use of arbitration, particularly where we are dealing with specialized issues or issues whose confines have been fairly well chartered out by a contract between the parties, by governing legislation or by prior court decision.[39]

2. Although others more competent will be addressing themselves more directly to criminal adjudication, I am impressed by the experimental work that has been undertaken under the auspices of the Law Enforcement Assistance Administration (LEAA) to divert certain types of minor criminal offenses (e.g., ones like the case earlier described between Mrs. B. and Mrs. W.) to a mediational proceeding. Such a process readily fits under the general rubric described in the immediately preceding section; but it can also be seen in the larger context of a movement towards a community "moot," offering informal and supportive services to community members.[40] Such institutions of course have a rich anthropological heritage.[41] Whether, in our alienated and divisive society, these institutions are hopelessly out of place, or whether they represent the last hope of a regained sense of community, remains to be seen.[42]

3. While the mediation-arbitration model earlier referred to is one useful format for processing certain types of cases, another device that

bears further utilization is what might be called the screening-adjudication model. I have already made reference to this in connection with the discussion of Small Claims Courts, and in a sense it might be argued that what I am describing is but another name for pretrial. But, as indicated earlier, there is a considerable difference between a judicial suggestion that the case ought to be settled for $X, and a quick preliminary "costing out" or "screening out" by a separate body.[43] . . .

An interesting experiment along these lines is the so-called Michigan Mediation System.[44] Here a three-person panel made up of a member of the plantiff's bar (selected by the bar association), a member of the defendant's bar, and a trial judge sit together as a panel for a period of two weeks to hear primarily tort cases in which the liability is acknowledged but there is dispute about the damages. The panel first reads such documentary evidence as there is and then discusses each case with the lawyers for the parties for about half an hour; no oral evidence is allowed. The Board then indicates what it believes the case is worth. If the case is not settled for this sum, then the plaintiff must receive at least 110 percent of this sum in order to avoid being taxed for the costs of trial (at a stipulated sum set so as to include a figure for attorneys' fees); the defendant must pay a similar fee if he does not settle and the recovery is more than 90 percent of the amount set by the mediation panel.

This approach, though promising, was criticized by the Chairman of the recently established Litigation Management and Economics Committee of the A.B.A. Section on Litigation on the ground that it comes too late in the process, after "considerable pre-trial and discovery expense has already been incurred." He suggests instead a program of mandatory arbitration for certain classes of cases, such as those involving claims of $25,000 or less. To avoid an overly rigid application of arbitration to cases for which another dispute resolving mechanism might be more suitable, he proposes that the mandatory feature would be waived upon a showing that another process would offer a more "fair and efficient adjudication of the controversy." "Conversely, arbitration could be required in those cases exceeding the jurisdictional limit of mandatory arbitration upon a showing that arbitration would be a more fair and efficient method of resolving the controversy.[45] This is an innovative and promising suggestion that deserves careful study.

4. What I am thus advocating is a flexible and diverse panoply of dispute resolution processes, with particular types of cases being assigned to differing processes (or combinations of processes), according to some of the criteria previously mentioned. Conceivably such allocation might be accomplished for a particular class of cases at the outset by the legislature; that in effect is what was done by the Massachusetts legislature for malpractice cases. Alternatively one might envision by the year 2000 not simply a court house but a Dispute Resolution Center, where

the grievant would first be channelled through a screening clerk who would then direct him to the process (or sequence of processes) most appropriate to his type of case. The room directory in the lobby of such a Center might look as follows:

| | |
|---|---|
| Screening Clerk | Room 1 |
| Mediation | Room 2 |
| Arbitration | Room 3 |
| Fact Finding | Room 4 |
| Malpractice Screening Panel | Room 5 |
| Superior Court | Room 6 |
| Ombudsman | Room 7 |

Of one thing we can be certain: once such an eclectic method of dispute resolution is accepted there will be ample opportunity for everyone to play a part. Thus a court might decide on its own to refer a certain type of problem to a more suitable tribunal.[46] Or a legislature might, in framing certain substantive rights, build in an appropriate dispute resolution process.[47] Institutions such as prisons, schools, or mental hospitals also could get into the act by establishing indigenous dispute resolution processes. Here the grievance mechanism contained in the typical collective bargaining agreement stands as an enduring example of a successful model. Finally, once these patterns begin to take hold, the law schools, too, should shift from their preoccupation with the judicial process and begin to expose students to the broad range of dispute resolution processes.[48]

5. I would be less than candid if I were to leave this idyllic picture without at least brief reference to some of the substantial impediments to reform in this area. To begin with there is always the deadening drag of status quoism. But I have reference to more specific problems. First, particularly in the criminal field, cries of "denial of due process" will undoubtedly be heard if an informal mediational process is sought to be substituted for the strict protections of the adversary process.[49] In response to this objection it must be asserted candidly that many thoughtful commentators appear agreed that we may have over-judicialized the system, with concomitant adverse effects on its efficiency as well as its accessibility to powerless litigants.[50] This is not the place to explore that difficult issue, but we clearly need to address ourselves more fully to that question.

A related concern is the one concerning the need to retain the courts as the ultimate agency of effectively protecting the rights of the disadvantaged. This is a legitimate concern which I believe to be consistent with the goals I have advocated. I am not maintaining that cases asserting novel constitutional claims ought to be diverted to mediation or arbitration. On the contrary, the goal is to reserve the courts for those activities for which they are best suited and to avoid swamping and paralyzing them with cases that do not require their unique capabilities. . . .

## Conclusion

It seems appropriate to end this fragmentary appraisal on a modest note. There are no panaceas; only promising avenues to explore. And there is so much we do not know. Among other things, we need far better data than are presently available in many states on what is in fact going on in the courts so that we can develop some sophisticated notion of where the main trouble spots are and what types of cases are prime candidates for alternative resolution.[51] We need more evaluation of the comparative efficacy and cost of different dispute resolution mechanisms. And we need more data on the role played by some of the key individuals in the process (e.g., lawyers). Do they exacerbate the adversary aspects of the case and drag out the proceedings (as many family law clients believe), or do they serve to control otherwise overly litigious clients (as trial lawyers often assert)? What is the optimal state of a country's grievance machinery so that festering grievances can be readily ventilated without unduly flooding the system and creating unreasonable expectations of relief?

Above all, however, we need to accumulate and disseminate the presently available learning concerning promising alternative resolution mechanisms, and encourage continued experimentation and research. In this connection we must continue to forge links with those from other disciplines who share our concerns. Their differing orientation and background often give them a novel perspective on the legal system. . . .

## Notes

1. J. Barton, Behind the Legal Explosion. 24 Stan. L. Rev. 567 (1975).

2. For the federal data, see Annual Report, Administrative Office of the U.S. Courts; for California, see Annual Report of the Administrative Office, 1975, p. 82.

3. See, e.g., A. Sarat & J. Grossman, Litigation in the Federal Courts: A Comparative Perspective, 9 Law & Soc. Rev. 321 (1975); A. Sarat & J. Grossman, Courts and Conflict Resolution: Problems in the Mobilization of Adjudication. 69 Am. Pol. Sci. Rev. 1200 (1975).

4. For present purposes I use the word "dispute" to describe a matured controversy, as distinguished, for example, from a "grievance" which may be inchoate and unexpressed.

5. See generally Johnson, Kantor & Schwartz, Outside the Courts: A Survey of Diversion Alternatives in Civil Cases, 1977, Denver, National Center for State Courts; M. Rosenberg, Devising Procedures that Are Civil to Promote Justice that Is Civilized, 69 Mich. L. Rev. 797 (1971).

6. See L. Brown & E. Dauer, Preventive Law—A Synopsis of Practice and Theory, in The Lawyer's Handbook (rev. ed. 1975 Am. Bar Ass'n); see also the same authors' forthcoming casebook on preventive law to be published by Foundation Press.

7. I would suggest the following criteria for determining the effectiveness of a dispute resolution mechanism: cost, speed, accuracy, credibility (to the public and the parties), and workability. In some cases, but not in all, predictability may also be important.

8. The term "dispute processing" rather than "dispute settlement" is borrowed from W. Felstiner, Influences of Social Organization on Dispute Processing, 9 Law & Soc. Rev. 63 (1974).

9. The Berkeley Complaint Management Project, under the direction of Professor Laura Nader, is presently pursuing some of these questions; a book entitled "How Americans Complain" is contemplated. A similar inquiry is being undertaken by the Center for the Study of Responsive Law in Washington, D.C.

10. See, e.g., A. Stone, Mental Health and Law—A System in Transition (Dept. H.E.W. 1975).

11. In the federal system, the area of largest civil litigation growth has been that involving the newly expanded statutory causes of action (e.g., civil rights actions, social security claims, etc.). See, e.g., Annual Report, Administrative Office of the U.S. Courts, 1974, p. 390.

12. I have selected this factor as one that seems to me rather critical, but there are obviously other aspects in which the various processes differ and which must be considered (e.g., method and cost of selection of third party, qualifications and tenure of third party, formality of proceedings, role of advocates, number of disputants, etc.). Some of these are referred to interstitially in the ensuing discussion. Another factor that is often said to play a differing part in the various processes is the relevance of norms. But see M. Eisenberg, Private Ordering Through Negotiation: Dispute Settlement and Rulemaking. 89 Harv. L. Rev. 637 (1976), suggesting that dispute settlement negotiation closely resembles adjudication in its frequent recourse to norms. See also A. Sarat & J. Grossman, Courts and Conflict Resolution: Problems in the Mobilization of Adjudication, 69 Am. Pol. Sci. Rev. 1200 (1975).

13. L. Fuller, Collective Bargaining and the Arbitrator, 1963 Wis. L. Rev. 1, 19. See also L. Fuller, The Forms and Limits of Adjudication (unpub. mimeo).

14. For present purposes the terms "mediation" and "conciliation" will be used interchangeably, although in some settings conciliation refers to the more unstructured process of facilitating communication between the parties, while mediation is reserved for a more formal process of meeting first with both parties and then with each of them separately, etc.

15. L. Fuller, Mediation—Its Forms and Functions, 44 So. Cal. L. Rev. 305, 325 (1971).

16. See W. Gellhorn, When Americans Complain (1966); P. Verkuil, The Ombudsman and the Limits of the Adversary System, 75 Col. L. Rev. 845 (1975); B. Frank, Ombudsman Survey (A.B.A. Sec. Ad. Law). New Jersey has recently established a broad-scale Department of the Public Advocate, containing a Division of Rate Counsel, a Division of Mental Health Advocacy, a Divi-

sion of Public Interest Advocacy, and a Division of Citizen Complaint and Dispute Settlement. N. J. Sta. Ann § 52: 27E (Supp. 1975).

In addition to these public investigating officials, there are of course a host of private complaint processors employed by individual companies, by trade organizations, or by the media.

17. See W. Felstiner, note 8 *supra*. Of course, as Felstiner notes, there are exceptions to this generalization. For example there may be enclaves having the characteristics of the simple society within the complex society, and sometimes overriding personal factors determine whether or not avoidance will be utilized in specific situations.

18. See R. Danzig & M. Lowy, Everyday Disputes and Mediation in the United States: A Reply to Professor Felstiner, 9 Law & Soc. Rev. 675 (1975). See also L. Nader, Powerlessness in Zapotec and U.S. Societies (mimeo).

19. See S. Macaulay, Law and the Balance of Power (1966).

20. L. Fuller, Collective Bargaining and the Arbitrator, 1963 Wis. L. Rev. 32–33.

21. See D. King, Consumer Protection Experiments in Sweden (1974). Cf. E. Steele, The Dilemma of Consumer Fraud: Prosecute or Mediate, 61 A.B.A.J. 1230 (1975).

The Swedish Public Complaints Board is one of five innovative dispute resolution mechanisms that is currently being studied by the Access to Justice Project, based at The Center for the Study of Comparative Procedure at the University of Florence, Italy, under the co-direction of Professor Mauro Cappelletti of that university and Professor Earl Johnson of the USC Law Center in Los Angeles. The Access to Justice Project will soon be publishing a number of documents detailing dispute resolution mechanisms in a number of countries (including the United States), as well as various theoretical studies.

22. For a comprehensive survey of these efforts, see, D. Aaronson, B. Hoff, P. Jaszi, N. Kittrie & D. Saari, The New Justice—Alternatives to Conventional Criminal Adjudication (Instit. for Advanced Studies in Justice, American University, Dec. 1975). See also J. Stulberg, A Civil Alternative to Criminal Prosecution, 39 Albany L. Rev. 359, 367 (1975), and Exploring Alternatives to the Strike, Monthly Labor Rev., Sept. 1973, p. 33, for a description and evaluation of the American Arbitration Association's somewhat comparable 4-A ("Arbitration-as-an-Alternative") project, and R. Nimmer, Diversion: The Search for Alternative Forms of Prosecution (Am. Bar. Found. 1974).

23. See C. Foote, R. Levy & F. Sander, Cases and Materials on Family Law, Chapters 1A and 6B (2nd ed. 1976).

24. See, e.g., S. Roberts, A Family Matter, 38 Mod. L. Rev. 700 (1975), discussing an English case in which various sums were contributed by a man, his brother and his parents towards the purchase of a common household. After they had lived there for 13 years, the mother died, leaving her estate to her sons in equal shares. A dispute then arose between the two brothers as to their respective shares. The writer opines that formal adjudication does not appear to be the best way to settle this kind of dispute.

25. See J. M. Keating, Arbitration of Inmate Grievances, 30 Arb. J. 177 (1975). For a discussion of some other models in this setting, see Note, Bargaining in Correctional Institutions: Restructuring the Relation Between the Inmate and the Prison Authority, 81 Yale L. J. 726 (1972). See also J. M. Keating, V.

McArthur, M. Lewis, K. Sebelius & L. Singer, Toward a Greater Measure of Justice: Grievance Mechanisms in Correctional Institutions (Center for Correctional Justice, Washington, D.C., 1975); Seen But Not Heard: A Survey of Grievance Mechanisms in Juvenile Correctional Institutions (Center for Correctional Justice, Washington, D.C.).

26. See R. Wilsnack, Explaining Collective Violence in Prisons: Problems and Possibilities, to be published in A. Cohen, G. Cole & R. Bailey, Prison Violence.

27. See United Steel Workers v. American Mfg. Co., 363 U.S. 564, 80 S. Ct. 1343, 4 L. Ed. 2d 1403 (1960); United Steelworkers v. Warrior & Gulf Nav. Co., 363 U.S. 574, 80 S.Ct. 1347, 4 L Ed. 2d 1409 (1960); United Steelworkers v. Enterprise Wheel & Car Corp., 363 U.S. 593, 80 S.Ct. 1358, 4 L.Ed. 2d 1424 (1960).

28. B. Yngvesson & P. Hennessey, Small Claims, Complex Disputes: A Review of the Small Claims Literature, 9 Law & Soc. Rev. 219 (1975).

29. A somewhat similar function is performed by law students as part of the Night Prosecutor Program in Columbus, Ohio. See Citizen Dispute Settlement (LEAA 1975).

30. A rudimentary beginning towards cost comparisons was provided in the evaluation report of the Philadelphia 4-A ("Arbitration-As-An-Alternative") project. See note 22 *supra*. The evaluators found a "direct" cost of $83.60 per project case as compared with a "direct" cost of $141 for each court case. But, as the evaluators note, there are many questions about such a comparison. To begin with, the figures depend upon the volume of cases, and with respect to court cases assume an average rather than a marginal cost allocation. And there is no attempt to control for the possibly differing complexity of the two classes of cases. See B. Anno & B. Hoff, Refunding Evaluation Report on the Municipal Court of Philadelphia's 4-A Project, Blackstone Associates, Washington, D.C., Feb. 25, 1975.

31. Other conceivable objections to such a proposal (e.g., denial of the right to a jury trial) are considered below.

32. Several Boston lawyers have told me this when I asked them why they did not use arbitration to a greater extent in connection with separation agreements.

33. This appears to be the practice in Pennsylvania. See National Conference on the Causes of Popular Dissatisfaction with the Administration of Justice, Resource Materials, pp. 91–93.

34. See, e.g., the Blackstone Associates report, note 30 *supra*, indicating disposition of 88% of project cases in an average time of 49 days, whereas that was the shortest time in which the court disposed of any case. See also Resource Materials, note 33 *supra*.

35. In some past experiments, such as the 4-A project, the initial phase is denominated arbitration. But conciliation always represents an important initial step in that operation, see, e.g., Stulberg, *op. cit. supra* note 22, and the question then becomes whether the mediation and arbitration should be performed by the same person. I have earlier indicated my doubts about such a coalescence of functions. In addition, the use of separate personnel, though perhaps more expensive and time-consuming, makes possible the use of individuals with different backgrounds and orientations in the two processes.

36. For some other examples, see L. Nader & L. Singer, Law in the Future —What Are the Choices? Paper prepared for Conference Sponsored by California Bar, Sept. 12, 1975.

37. Conversely, where the relationship is one of pure bargaining but it is desired to have limited adjudicative intervention in case agreement cannot be reached, the final offer arbitration device sometimes utilized in public sector employment is available. See, e.g., Massachusetts Acts, 1973, ch. 1078. Under this process the arbitrator is limited in his decision to a choice between the last offer of the two parties. The obvious purpose is to engender good faith bargaining. See, e.g., Industrial Relations, Oct. 1975, for a number of articles seeking to evaluate the practice.

38. This assertion is based on the assumption that some of this new mediational work will displace work previously done by lawyers. But, as pointed out earlier, much of it may simply substitute for what is now being handled by avoidance.

39. Compare H. Edwards, Arbitration of Employment Discrimination Cases: An Empirical Study, to be published in the 28th Proceedings of the National Academy of Arbitrators by B.N.A., suggesting an uncertain command by labor arbitrators of the federal law of employment discrimination. See also D. Feller, The Impact of External Law Upon Labor Arbitration, paper delivered at National Conference on the Future of Labor Arbitration in America, to be published by the American Arbitration Association.

40. See R. Danzig, Towards the Creation of a Complementary, Decentralized System of Criminal Justice, 26 Stan. L. Rev. 1 (1973); Comment, Community Courts: An Alternative to Conventional Criminal Adjudication, 24 Am. L. Rev. 1253 (1975); J. Jaffe, So Sue Me! The Story of a Community Court (1972)

41. See, e.g., Law in Culture and Society (L. Nader ed. 1969); J. Gibbs, The Kpelle Moot: A Therapeutic Model for the Informal Settlement of Disputes, 33 Africa 1 (1963), reprinted in Rough Justice: Perspectives on Lower Criminal Courts (J. Robertson ed. 1974).

42. For an optimistic answer to this question, see D. Smith, Book Review, 87 Harv. L. Rev. 1874 (1974). It is interesting to note that with the notable exception of the Jewish Community Board, whose work is the subject of the cited review, and a few other institutions, most of the experiments to date have involved alternatives to the criminal courts. Is this the result of some conceptual notion, or, as I suspect, because, like the reputed response of Willie Sutton, the famed bank robber when asked why he robbed banks, "that's where the money is"?

43. See V. Aubert, Courts and Conflict Resolution, 11 J. Conflict Resolution 40, 44 (1967), suggesting that failure realistically to appraise a legal claim is one major reason for taking it to court rather than settling it. Other reasons given are irrational on the part of litigants (e.g. undue pride or stubborness) or the indivisibility of the claim in issue (e.g., child custody).

44. S. Miller, Mediation in Michigan, 56 Judicature 290 (1973).

45. See R. Olson, An Examination of the Judicial Process: A Discussion of Modifications and Alternatives to Our System of Dispute Resolution, to be published in the Summer 1976 issue of Litigation, the journal of the A.B.A., Section

on Litigation. The concept of "more fair and efficient adjudication of the controversy" is borrowed from Federal Rule 23(b).

Mr. Olson's Committee is presently undertaking a nationwide survey, through interviews with judges, court administrators and experienced practitioners, of innovative approaches to reducing the time and expense of litigation as well as of promising alternative dispute resolution mechanisms.

46. See, e.g., *Kamm v. California City Dev. Co.*, 509 F.2d 205 (9th Cir. 1975) (trial court in land fraud class action was justified in dismissing class action on basis of agreement that defendant would utilize arbitration to process potential multiple claims against it). But cf. *Rizzo v. Goode*, 96 S.Ct. 598, 46 L. Ed. 2d 561 (1976) (improper for district court to order creation of program by City of Philadelphia Police Dept. for processing recurring complaints of police misconduct.

47. Consider, for example, the provision of the Magnuson-Moss Warranty Act which requires the FTC to promulgate rules establishing procedures for informal dispute settlement mechanisms which must be exhausted before any lawsuit can be commenced under the Act. See Public Law 93–637, 88 Stat. 2183, and the implementing regulations adopted by the FTC, 40 Fed. Reg. 60190 (Dec. 31, 1975). Compare the suggestion that each statute creating substantive rights contain a judicial impact statement.

48. This presents an excellent opportunity for law students who seek to do creative field work, e.g., by helping a telephone company to set up a grievance mechanism or studying the operation of the local ombudsman.

49. Cf. L. Rubenstein, Procedural Due Process and the Limits of the Adversary System, 11 Civ. Rights-Civ. Lib. L. Rev. 48 (1976).

50. See Johnson, Kantor & Schwartz *op. cit. supra* note 5, Chapter VI. See also H. Friendly, "Some Kind of Hearing", 123 U. Pa. L. Rev. 1267 (1975).

51. Apart from deficiencies in particular states, comparisons are particularly hampered by the lack of comparability among the data.

# 3

# Influences of Social Organization on Dispute Processing[*]

### William L. F. Felstiner[†]

Man is an ingenious social animal. Institutionalized responses to inter-personal conflict, for instance, stretch from song duels and witchcraft to moots and mediation to self-conscious therapy and hierarchical, profes-sionalized courts. The dispute processing practices prevailing in any par-ticular society are a product of its values, its psychological imperatives, its history and its economic, political and social organization.[1] It is un-likely that any general theory encompassing all of these factors will be developed until there have been many piecemeal attempts to understand something of the influence of each.

This paper first outlines several types of social organization and analyzes certain forms of dispute processing. It then suggests that these forms of dispute processing either depend on an availability of resources (such as coercive power or pre-dispute information) which varies with social organization or have different negative consequences in different social contexts. Finally, the paper explores the implications of this link-age between social organization and dispute processing for certain re-forms currently advocated in the U.S. . .

[*] Reprinted with permission from *Law & Society Review* 9: 63–94, 1974. Condensed; most notes have been excluded. All references included in the text of this chapter are found in the bibliography at the conclusion of this volume.

[†] I received substantial encouragement in working through this analysis from Jane Collier, Richard Danzig, Robert Stevens and David Trubek and valuable direction from Richard Abel, Celestine Arndt, Richard Canter, Marc Galanter, Robert Kidder and Mark Peterson.

## Ideal Types of Social Organization

Social organization in these propositions means any regularities in geographic, economic, kin or other relationships among people within a single society. But in any particular society alternative and competing institutions may organize the same relationships. As a consequence, analysis of the effect of social organization on any social process is extremely complicated. In the same society, for example, families may either be nuclear or cohere on extended lines. Vocations may or may not persist across generations. Neighbors may be friends or strangers. We know very little about the regularity with which these variables associate. Since the effect of social organization on forms of dispute processing cannot be explored using a real empirical base because the data do not exist, insight must come, if at all, through the use of ideal types.

Two ideal types of social organization will be contrasted: a technologically complex rich society (TCRS) and a technologically simple poor society (TSPS). In a TCRS the family unit is nuclear (conjugal) and biological (*see* Nimkoff & Middleton, 1968: 35). Marriage and its functional equivalents are unstable, are not arranged, and constitute a liaison between individuals rather than between family groups. Relationships between extra-nuclear family members are either unimportant —in that they are not a source of companionship, therapy, economic or political support, education, ceremony or self-definition—or they tend to be grounded not upon kinship but upon the same factors which give rise to relationships outside the family. Adults infrequently live in the same neighborhood as their parents, siblings or adult children. Financial assistance in old age is the responsibility not of the family but of the state. Working members of a family do not share work sites or occupations.

In a TCRS friendships are unstable; long-term interpersonal relationships are difficult to maintain. Adults do not live where they have lived as children and are schooled in more than one locale. They do not live in one house or neighborhood for an adult life, and they are not employed in one place for a working life. Friendship is geared to rough equivalence in economic status, and individuals do not proceed up or down the economic scale at the same pace as any particular acquaintances. Because of access to convenient transport, social intercourse is little restricted by proximity: friends are not necessarily neighbors and neighbors are not necessarily friends. Especially in urban areas, friendships tend to be routine rather than intimate, reflections of Alexanders's autonomy-withdrawal syndrome (1966: 19–33).

Vocational mobility in a TCRS is high, although more from job to job than from occupation to occupation. If the requirement of specialized skills tends to reduce mobility between occupational strata, the labor market has few other structural impediments; group barriers are progressively ineffective and nepotism is unimportant. Only a small proportion of the labor force is self or family employed, working in agriculture or in jobs acutely restricted in locale. Disfavored occupations (manual, farm and domestic labor, food services, low-level factory employment) account for only a small proportion of total employment, and consequently relatively few workers with disfavored jobs are competing for jobs in favored occupations. The work force has received a substantial general education; many opportunities to develop the specialized skills required of a technologically advanced industrial apparatus are available.

Residential mobility also is high in a TCRS. Housing availability rarely inhibits moves. Although the trauma and burdens of moving are worse for women than men, a move is neither extremely uncomfortable nor administratively difficult. Jobs are not fungible because contacts, customers, seniority and local custom make each one somewhat singular, but a move generally does not require a change of occupation. Few moves are inhibited by the prospect of disturbing close family relationships because in most instances the family lives somewhere else to begin with. The process of making new familiars out of strangers is not encumbered by differences in language, eating habits, dress or notions of acceptable behavior. A move spells no greater cultural than social sacrifice. Climate is valued over history, and facilities (aesthetic, sport, spectator) over nostalgia. No space-confined relationship with the dead, immediate or long past, exists. Whatever artifacts, religious, educational and child-rearing practices, entertainment, dress or manners are left behind will be found virtually duplicated at the new doorstep. The anxiety of moves is reduced by the experience of earlier non-traumatic moves. Local moves do not mandate a change of job, of friends, of family relations or of cultural context.

A crucial dimension of the social organization of a TCRS is the range and importance of the interaction of individuals with large-scale bureaucratic organizations. Such enterprises dominate relationships which involve employment, credit, consumer purchasing, education, health and welfare services and government.

In a TSPS the family unit is generally extended and frequently includes significant fictive elements. Marriage is either a relationship of restricted contact reflecting purdah considerations or else tends to be unstable. In either case marriages are generally arranged by family elders and constitute relationships between family groups as well as between marriage partners. Family relations beyond husband and wife dominate social organization. Whether it be a matter of clan, lineage, sib, avunculate, *jati*, co-residence or some other extended family or functionally equivalent (e.g., compadre) arrangement, the enlarged family is the basis for economic, political, ceremonial and therapeutic sustenance, general education and companionship. Young people, married or not, tend to be subject to significant older generation control until the older generation dies. Since the old have no savings and no pension, and the state has no resources for them either, they are, by choice or default, dependent on their family. Vocational separation between generations is unusual; farmer begets farmer, weaver begets weaver. In a TSPS, in other words, people tend to be aggregated with their parents, children and other kin in residence, in work and in responsibility.

In a TSPS the geographical range of non-family liaisons is restricted. Friends tend to be neighbors, neighbors tend to rely on each other for economic cooperation and significant public works projects require community cooperation as much as government assistance. Local politics are governed by shifting alignments which reflect personal loyalties and economic opportunities more than ideological or programmatic differences. The full picture of interpersonal relations is a complicated, highly articulated cross-cutting network in which individuals are involved on their own account and as representatives of kin-based groups. It is conventionally contrasted to the nuclear family centered, unconnected, single-stranded organization of societies resembling a TCSR. (P. Cohen, 1968: 152–54; Nader and Yngvesson, 1973: 912).

The contrast in residential mobility between a TCRS and a TSPS is not as stark as the difference in type of family relationships. In a TSPS a move of any distance may be tantamount to exile, an anxious passage to a place where language, food and manners are foreign or distasteful and where cultural artifacts, especially those geared to religious activity (temples, shrines, holy places) may not be easily reproduced. More importantly, moves may eliminate family and extra-family (compadre, age set, faction, clique) support crucial to economic and emotional health. In a TSPS most long distance moves involve country people moving to cities and therefore generally require a change of occupation. On the other hand, a move in a TSPS may be no more than an easy transfer, often made in groups, from a village to an urban neighborhood peopled with acquaintances who have migrated to the city from the same village. Economic and cultural as well as social dislocation may then be tempered by the existence of an island of the familiar and supportive in a sea of the strange and indifferent. Nevertheless, moves in a TSPS are much more dependent upon tying into an existing social network at the destination and involve more economic hardship, social and cultural alienation and emotional trauma than do moves in a TCRS.

Vocational mobility is also lower in a TSPS. Higher unemployment means more competition for jobs when existing employment arrangement are severed. Ascriptive preferences and nepotism are commonplace. A significant proportion of the labor force is self or family employed and thus involved in work which is restricted in locale. Social contacts tend to precede rather than follow vocational opportunities.

The crucial role of large-scale organizations in a TCRS is not duplicated in a TSPS. Employment may be with major enterprises, but is generally not; credit is extended by individual money lenders and merchants rather than by commercial banks and large stores; consumer purchasing is carried on in small shops; primary education is provided in small local schools; and health services are indigenous and individualized rather than imported and bureaucratic. Only in the administration of welfare (i.e., public works projects, famine relief) and other government activities does the citizenry of a TSPS confront bureaucracies comparable to those which dominate social life in a TCRS.

## Components of Forms of Dispute Processing

The basic question underlying this paper is whether the consequences of, and the availability of resources required by, *any* form of dispute processing vary with social organization. This proposition will be explored through analysis of adjudication, mediation and avoidance as they are applicable to disputes in which individuals or small groups are involved.

Adjudication and mediation are distinguishable from negotiation and self-help by the necessary presence of a third party, someone who is neither asserting nor resisting the assertion of a claim in his own behalf nor is acting as the agent of such a party. Conventionally we label as adjudication that process in which the third party is acknowledged to have the power to stipulate an outcome of the dispute, although in many instances such power will be exercised only when the adjudicator is unable to persuade the disputants to agree to an outcome. In mediation, on the other hand, outcomes are produced by the third party only when he can secure disputant consent to proposals of accommodation (Collier, 1973: 26; Fuller, 1971: 308; Kawashima, 1963: 50). By avoidance I mean limiting the relationship with the other disputant sufficiently so that the dispute no longer remains salient. Avoidance resembles Hirschman's (1970) notion of exit. But avoidance, unlike exit behaviour, does not necessarily imply a *switch* of relations to a new object, but may simply involve *withdrawal* from or contraction of the dispute-producing relationship.

In adjudication, outcomes may be sensitive to a wide range of extrinsic factors including class membership, political alliances, economic consequences and corruption, but in the main the behavior of the disputants is evaluated by reference to generalized rules of conduct. Most such rules are not immutable, but they are stable. Adjudication as a consequence tends to focus on "what facts" and "which norms" rather than on any need for normative shifts. This concentration on the behavior of the disputants, rather than on the merits of abstract rules, creates a significant potential for psychological trauma. The effect of losing a dispute is to be told that what you consider as history was either an illusion or a lie, that what you considered normatively appropriate behavior is characterized as anti-social, and that what you consider your property or your prerogative will now, because of your failings, by fiat become your enemy's (Aubert, 1969: 286).

The psychological consequence is frequently to alienate the loser from the adjudicative process... One would, therefore, expect that loser compliance with adjudicative decisions is produced not by their merits, but by the coercive power which they command. Unconvinced of their original error, losers respond to an adverse decision only because the consequences of not responding would be worse.

The predicted association of adjudication and coercive power appears to be borne out empirically. Wimberley's Guttman scale for legal evolution lists twenty-seven societies which use courts (defined as institutions possessing socially recognized authority to make binding decisions). Eighteen of those societies maintained a court-directed police force and five of the remainder used automatic ordeals (Wimberley, 1973: 81, 82), that is compulsion by the will of the gods (Roberts, 1965: 209). And all nine of the court/no police societies had strong corporate kin groupings suggesting an internal coercive potential which does not depend upon specialized functionaries. (For a counter-instance *see* Schlegal, 1970: 171). The variety of coercive power employable by different adjudicative systems is extensive. Mild social ostracism or negative public opinion (Gough, 1955: 50; Mayer, 1960: 264–66; Bohannan, 1957: 68), closed access to marriage partners (Srinivas, 1954: 157), termination of all social intercourse (Hitchcock, 1960: 243; Llewellyn & Hoebel, 1941: 103), banishment (Canter, 1973: 9; Brandt, 1971: 209–10), protected self-help (Pospisil, 1964: 147–48) and police action (Collier, 1973: 103; Gluckman, 1955: 222) are common.

The relationship between social organization and adjudication appears to depend not only on the availability of coercive power, but also on the presence or absence of social groups... To the extent that adverse adjudicated decisions will be ignored unless compliance can be coerced, compliance will depend on the threat of some sanction acceptable to, and generally administered by, a group. To the extent that judicial specialization reflects general social role differentiation (Abel, 1974: 288), many societies are simply not sufficiently differentiated to produce wandering adjudicators...

Adjudication requires expertise in the social rules governing behavior and, frequently, in the secondary rules governing the conduct of disputes. This expertise is relatively easy to create on a mass basis. The expertise required of a mediator is different. Since successful mediation requires an outcome acceptable to the parties, the mediator cannot rely primarily on rules but must construct an outcome in the light of the social and cultural context of the dispute, the full scope of the relations between the disputants and the perspectives from which they view the dispute. Mediation, then, flourishes where mediators share the social and cultural experience of the disputants they serve, and where they bring to the processing of disputes an intimate and detailed knowledge of the perspectives of the disputants. In the absence of such shared experience and such pre-processing knowledge, the effort a mediator would have to make to fill the gaps would be disproportionate to the social stakes involved in the dispute. Because of these characteristics of mediation, deliberate mass production of mediators is generally infeasible. On the other hand, since the outcomes it produces are consensual and are generally compromises, mediation need not be backed by coercive power.

Why is it important for a mediator who does not know the disputants to acquire insight into their priorities and feelings as a part of the mediation process? Let us assume that mediated outcomes are of two kinds. They may be personality independent in the sense that the mediator is able to suggest a result which adequately meets the interests of each disputant as those interests would be identified by any persons in their positions. In such situations the mediator's ingenuity is affected only by his understanding of the disputants' manifest interests. It may well be feasible to acquire such information adequately during the mediation.

On the other hand, an outcome may be personality dependent in the sense that an acceptable scheme which sufficiently meets the demands of both disputants must reflect these demands as they idiosyncratically view them. In this case the feelings of the disputants are crucial and the possibility that a mediator will acquire sufficient insight during mediation is more doubtful. The difficulty may arise in part because the disputants are not particularly self-conscious about their own feelings and therefore fail to give the mediator adequate information so that he may understand them. Even when the disputants are conscious of their feelings, they may nevertheless restrict their communications to the mediator to matters they believe will promote their cause on an instrumental, rather than an effective, level or according to motives which they believe it is acceptable for them to maintain rather than expose their real, but embarrassing, needs. In either case the information presented to the mediator is probably not as rich as the more general information available to a mediator who has widely shared experience with the disputants. It would be imprudent to set theoretical limits to the successes of mediative geniuses, but for the run-of-the-mill mediators upon whom institutionalized mediation must be based long-term and relatively intimate prior association with the disputants may be highly functional in all settings and necessary for reaching personality dependent outcomes (*see* Gulliver, 1969: 40–48).

Adjudication and mediation are relatively visible processes. They tend to be public to the group in which they take place, notorious within the group and didactic for the group. Avoidance, on the other hand, is more difficult for an outsider to identify and is less frequently reported. . . .

The most important social characteristic of avoidance for dispute processing theory is its variable costs. To understand that variation one has only to focus on Gluckman's (1955: 19) classic distinction between single-interest linkages and multiplex relationships, those which serve many interests. The cost of avoidance is always a reduction in the content of the relationship which has been truncated or terminated. If the relationship was geared to a single interest, only that interest is affected. If the relationship was multiplex, all the interests are affected, even though the cause of the avoidance grew out of only one. The difference, for example, is between losing a sibling only and losing a sibling who is also a neighbor, a companion, a therapist, a political ally, an economic co-adventurer and a ceremonial confederate (*see* Nader and Metzger, 1963: 590–91).

## The Effect of Social Organization on Institutionalizing Different Forms of Dispute Processing

For our purposes, then the key to adjudication is groups and coercion, to mediation is shared experience, and to avoidance is its variable costs. Within any society on an institutional basis, we should expect to find less adjudication where groups are infrequent and the coercive power which can be marshalled is weak, less mediation where shared experience is rare and less avoidance where avoidance costs are high. What insights concerning the distribution of forms of dispute processing might these propositions produce in the ideal type societies described earlier? In a TSPS either adjudication or mediation will occur at the level of face-to-face groups such as kin units, factions and villages. The coercion necessary for adjudication rests ultimately on the group's power to expel contumacious disputants. Since the group's functions are central to the members' well-being, participation in group adjudication and adherence to adjudicated outcomes are self-generating. The size of such groups and the intensity of relations within them make mediation a realistic alternative to adjudication: the requisite knowledge of dispute context and participant perspective are available without inordinate mediator efforts. Whether groups in any particular society will use both institutionalized adjudication and mediation, or one more than the other, may then be a function of considerations other than social organization. Values and their psychological derivatives may in some contexts be crucial ingredients. The stress on mediation in eastern societies has often been attributed to the importance of Confucian distaste for conflict and self-assertion (J. Cohen, 1967: 60; Hahm, 1969: 20; Kawashima, 1963: 44) while antipathy to self-arrogation and authoritative control has had the same effect in hyper-egalitarian western societies (Evans-Pritchard, 1940: 180–84; Emmett, 1964: 47, 80–89; Miller, 1955: 271–72, 283–86; Yngvesson, 1970: 95–96, 258). On the other hand, despite the conventional notion that mediated compromises better preserve the continuing relationships characteristic of small communities or multiplex groups (Nader, 1969: 87–88; Nader and Yngvesson, 1973: 912), adjudication is quite common in such situations (see Hitchcock, 1960: 261–64; Srinivas, 1954: 155; Cohn, 1965: 83; Gluckman, 1955: 80–81; Moore, 1970: 331; Gibbs, 1962: 345; Collier, 1973: 36–39; Metzger, 1960: 36). Sometimes institutionalized mediation is available as a step preceding such adjudication (Hitchcock, 1960: 242; Cohn, 1967: 143; Moore, 1970: 327; Collier, 1973: 26–28), sometimes it is not (Srinivas, 1954: 159; Gibbs, 1967: 380–83; Nader and Metzger, 1963: 586–87), and sometimes one cannot tell (e.g., Gluckman, 1955: 26).

As the size of the groups on which one focuses in a TSPS grows, from village to tribe or from extended family to sub-caste, adjudication will become the dominant form of dispute processing. Mediation is no longer feasible because, whatever the shared general social and cultural experience, no specific mediators nor occupants of specific social positions will possess as a matter of existing experience sufficient information about the particular perspectives and histories of the particular disputants to be able efficiently to suggest acceptable outcomes. Adjudicative expertise in rules, on the other hand, is either widely possessed where the rules are not specialized (in the sense that they are readily available only to professionals) or can be generated on a mass basis where specialization is important.

The frequency of avoidance as a form of dispute processing in a TSPS should be affected by its high costs. These costs would be incurred whether avoidance takes place within the kin group, within a non-family multiplex relationship, or in economic activities. Within the family if disputants terminate or decrease their contacts, relations between groups, which may have political and economic as well as social connotations, are jeopardized as well. Where marriages are arranged, decisions about who marries whom are generally made on prudential grounds, in a corporate process and under the influence of past social relations. As a result, disputes which are processed by avoidance will cast a long shadow, interfering with the future marriage prospects of many group members (*see* Beals, 1961: 33). Use of avoidance as a technique where the disputants, such as parent and grown child or siblings or affines, live and work and conduct other important activities together, is logistically difficult and psychologically dangerous—the repressed hostility felt toward the other disputant is likely to be shifted to someone or something else. Even worse, the failure to express or act upon predictable hostility will in many societies lead to accusations of witchcraft against the person who hides his antagonisms (*see* Collier, 1973: 222). Yet physical separation, by moving residence or work, may be socially infeasible, economically disastrous and emotionally traumatic. Since many. relationships beyond the family are multiplex, avoidance as a reaction to a dispute impairs not only the interest out of which the dispute arose, but all other interests shared by the disputants (*see* Van Velsen, 1969: 138). As Moore (1973: 738) points out for the Chagga, "the continuing control exercised by the lineage neighborhood nexus over its members is illustrated by every dispute it settles. No man can hope to keep his head above water if he does not have the approval and support of his neighbors and kinsmen." This analysis should not be construed to imply that avoidance would never or rarely occur in small communities in technologically simple societies. In fact, in nomadic tribes, where avoidance by physical separation is easy, dispute processing by such tactics is commonplace (Furer-Haimendorf, 1967: 22–23). The point is rather that avoidance has high costs in a TSPS and one would as a result expect significant use of other forms of dispute processing which are more likely to aid the maintenance of threatened, but important, social relationships.

In both a TCRS and a TSPS adjudication is predictable at the level of the state which is a group with an important normative system and substantial coercive power. The degree of use of such adjudicative process will depend upon the extent to which it is viewed as expensive, degrading, alien, slow, time-consuming, ineffective and destructive, upon the available alternatives and their characteristics and upon litigant objectives.

In both types of societies adjudication may also be an important form of dispute processing within large-scale organizations. Such organizations must establish a normative system to govern their operations: coercive power is located both in their power to expel constituents and in their power to vary tasks and rewards. Rules and compulsive power may explain why adjuducation can work if it is established. But they do not entirely explain why it is established. Making decisions in particular cases is inevitable. Where there are rules and power, the people with the power will enforce some rules. Whether that process is controlled by people who are directly affected by their own decisions or by people who are importantly influenced by considerations of neutrality will depend upon locally prevalent values and on the countervailing power, individual or organized, of those subjected to the rules. If organized political opposition (labor vs. management, students vs. administration) exists within organizations, controversies about past behavior are more likely to be adjudicated by a third party than decided by a participant (*see* Weber, 1967: 335–56). And the more a society values procedural fairness over instrumental efficiency, the more likely it is that the same result will occur. Mediation within organizations may be equally feasible since in the operations of an organization extensive shared social, cultural and personal experience is generated. And adjudicative and mediative institutions may co-exist within an organization (at my university decanal adjudication is paralleled by ombudsman mediation).

Between outsiders who have some contact with a large organization and the organization, a significant amount of dispute processing may be a special form of avoidance termed "lumping it." In lumping it the salience of the dispute is reduced not so much by limiting the contacts between the disputants, but by ignoring the dispute, by declining to take any or much action in response to the controversy. The complaint against the retail merchant or the health insurance company is foregone although the complainant's grievance has not been satisfied, or even acknowledged, and although interaction between the individual and the organization is not altered. It would be uncommon for such grievances to be mediated since there is little incentive for the organization to change its posture. Because of the discrepancy in size and power even the threat of withdrawal by the individual is futile to coerce compromise by the organization. And no adjudication short of the government courts may be possible because no other power exists to coerce decisions against the organization (*see* McGonagle, 1972: 72–75).

The clearest difference between dispute processing in a TSPS and a TCRS should be located in disputes between individuals or family and social groups. The availability of adjudication and mediation and the high costs of avoidance in a TSPS have been examined. The opposite conditions are predictable for a TCRS: adjudication and mediation of such disputes will be hard to institutionalize and avoidance will carry significantly lower costs. The obstacle to adjudication of inter-personal disputes in a TCRS is the limited coercion available to agencies other than government courts. The forms of coercion available in non-government adjudication in a TSPS depend either on membership in groups, especially kin-related groups, or on participation in multiple interest relationships. In a TCRS such groups and associations are either non-existent or weak. One cannot be influenced by public opinion if there is no relevant public, nor exiled from a group to which one does not belong. What sanction in a neighborhood of single interest relationships might a neighborhood adjudicator employ? With what, after childhood, can most parents threaten a children or an uncle a niece? (Turner, 1970: 414).

At the same time structural factors exist in a TCRS which reduce the utility of adjudicating interpersonal disputes in government courts. To the extent that such courts are staffed by specialists, as one would expect them to be in such a society unless it is organized according to a revolutionary socialist ideology, the rules they apply will tend to become specialized, importantly procedural and alien from everyday norms

(Abel, 1974: 270–84). Specialized rules will require litigants to hire professional counsel. Professional counsel means added expense, inconvenience and mystification. Government courts frequently process a large volume of routine quasi-administrative matters (foreclosures and evictions, divorce, collections, repossessions and the filing and marshalling of liens). These routine matters, coupled to a high criminal caseload and a sensitivity to the demands of due process and to the autonomy of judges which impedes reforms aimed at efficiency, tax the government courts' capacity to process individual interpersonal cases quickly (Sykes, 1969: 330–37). If court litigation may be fairly characterized as costly, slow and alienating, we can expect relatively little use to be made of it in situations in which, as in most inter-personal disputing, the economic stakes are low (Danzig, 1973: 44), unless, as in divorce and custody cases, a government imprimatur is an absolute necessity.

This analysis is not entirely compatible with Black's (1973a: 53) belief that use of government courts is a stage in an evolutionary process reached when sub-government controls are weak or unavailable. First, considerable data point to high simultaneous use of government and sub-government dispute processing. The best documented instance may be colonial India (Rudolph & Rudolph, 1967: 260–62; Galanter, 1968: 69), but there is no evidence that nineteenth century America witnessed proportionately less interpersonal litigation than mid-twentieth century America despite more cohesive kin and residential systems (*see* Friedman, 1973: 338). And second, Black entirely ignores the role of avoidance: he does not consider the possibility that as "communities" and their informal controls disappear, the need for any external civil dispute processing between individuals may also substantially fade.

Institutionalized mediation of interpersonal disputes will also be infrequent in a TCRS. Because of the crucial importance of shared experience in mediation, the less role differentiated a social unit, the more mediators will be available for disputes of varying origin. . . .

The relatively weaker bonds of family, of friendship, of job and of place in a TCRS make institutionalizing adjudication and mediation difficult, but they also reduce the negative consequences of avoidance. Avoidance behavior between generations within a family, for instance, generally will not seriously threaten either disputant's economic security, political position or ceremonial or therapeutic opportunities. Reducing as well as eliminating contact within a continuing social framework is relatively easy where relations are more formal than functional. . . .

Where there are pockets within a TCRS where social organization is more like that postulated for a TSPS, then one would expect that avoidance, having higher costs, would be less important and that adjudication and mediation, being more feasible, would be more frequently institutionalized. Such pockets are likely to arise where there are unassimilated ethnic minorities with a strong tradition of internal government or where a pattern of social discrimination severely limits the economic, residential and social mobility of distinctive minority groups. This qualification is not meant to impy that every ethnic ghetto will be organized and use the dispute processing machinery of a Punjabi village but simply that dispute processing will in important respects be a function of social organization. And the social organization which exercises that influence will be the local version, however the dominant majority organizes its affairs.

To summarize this section, adjudication and mediation, on the one hand, and avoidance, on the other, are complementary. Where adjudication and mediation are feasible, avoidance is costly; where avoidance has tolerable costs, adjudication and mediation are difficult to institutionalize. This complementarity has a logical base. The same set of social circumstances which makes one set of processes available frustrates the other and vice versa. The predicament of unorganized individuals who have a dispute with large organizations of which they are not members may be an exception: adjudication and mediation are generally unavailable and avoidance costly to the individual. It is this social pathology which has probably led to recent calls for ombudsmen in government, in universities and for public utilities (*see* Gellhorn, 1966: 25, 28–29, 215–217).

## Implications of the Analysis for Dispute Processing Reforms in the United States

One of the frequently criticized aspects of life in America is the failure of the society's institutions to cope adequately with the people's grievances against each other. Ordinary courts cost money and time, are slow and mystifying, and tilted against the poor, the uninitiated and the occasional user (e.g., Galanter, 1974; Wald and Wald, 1968: 34–37; Carlin and Howard, 1965: 381–429). Small claims courts are alleged to have been transformed by sellers of consumer goods and services into taxpayer supported collection agencies (Small Claims Study Group, 1972: 128; *Calif. Law Rev.*, 1964: 884–90; Bruff, 1973: 12, 13). Although there is an occasional note to the effect that "private-informal dispute settlement . . . is significant in complex societies" (Grossman and Sarat, 1973: 14), the references to non-government institutionalized adjudication or mediation in the United States are very sparse except within organizations, within organized commercial activities and within some minority groups. This paper suggests that much of the slack may be absorbed by avoidance. The degree to which avoidance is as much an empirical reality as it is a sociological possibility will need to be determined through field studies. Whatever such studies may reveal, current dissatisfaction is so pervasive that advocacy of consciously engineered reform and creation of dispute processing institutions is hardly likely to abate. The sponsors of neighborhood ghetto courts (Statsky, 1974; Hager, 1972; Cahn and Cahn, 1970: 1019), community moots (Danzig, 1973: 41–48), reoriented small claims courts (Small Claims Study Group 1972: 197–213), clergy dominated dispute processing for religious minorities (Balderman, 1974: 41–42) and mediation systems for public housing, consumer-merchant and private criminal complaints (Abner, 1969: 12–18) will not be convinced by social scientists that avoidance is an adequate substitute for their proposed reforms. But their reforms may perhaps be more effective if they heed the influence of social organization on what they set out to do.

Let us use Danzig's proposed neighborhood moots as an example. He advocates a transplant of the Kpelle (Liberia) moot to American urban neighborhoods. Danzig (1973: 47–48) is alert to the effect of cultural differences and aware that moot success may depend on the level of "primary group interaction." But he does not suggest how frequently sufficient primary group interaction occurs in any American neighborhoods. Moreover, Danzig (1973: 46) seems insensitive to the role of the mediator, suggesting only that he be a "salaried counselor." Gibbs (1967: 288–9), on the other hand, pays considerable attention to the importance of the social position of the Kpelle mediator. Selected by the complainant, he is a kinsman and town chief or quarter elder. He can produce a therapeutic effect because he is "a member of two social systems," that of the disputants (kinsman) and of the wider community (elder). In my terms Danzig's mediator is unlikely to be functional unless he shares significant intimate experience with the disputants. If such a criterion is ignored or cannot be met in counselor selection, the Kpelle experience may be impossible to duplicate. The Kpelle moot, moreover, is not really mediation. It decides who is mainly at fault, it imposes sanctions and requires apologies (Gibbs, 1967: 280, 283). It can exercise such coercion because it is an institution of a group—a village quarter composed of several virilocal polygamous families (1967: 279). Gibbs (1967: 287) highlights the crucial role of group approval. In addition, in an earlier article (1962: 341–42) he reports that the Kpelle have internalized a particularly strong respect for authority. A successful transplant of the Kpelle version of a moot thus may require a psychological set and social organization which parallels the Kpelle's as well as counselors with high quotients of shared experience with their clientele.

Religious courts open to secular disputes are not unknown in the U.S. (*Columbia Journal of Law and Soc. Probs.*, 1970: 56–68; Balderman, 1974: 18–20). Their supposed advantages over civil courts are speed, less expense, less specialized procedures, privacy and adjudication by members of the same minority group as the disputants and according to its value system. (*Columbia Journal of Law and Soc. Probs.*, 1970: 68–70). Balderman's (1974: 30, 34) study of Jewish courts in Los Angeles, however, indicates that they are rarely used as alternatives to civil courts. The religious courts are employed rather to hear claims which the civil courts will not (Jewish divorces, conversions) and to define the nature of Jewish religious life.

Advocates of minority group institutions as an alternative to government courts, such as the Bet Tzedek proposal in Los Angeles (Balderman, 1974: 41), ought to face the question of why existing religious courts may have failed to fulfill this function. These institutions are adjudicative. They may compel compliance with their decisions either through resort to government courts based on party execution of irrevocable arbitration agreements or through the persuasive effect of community pressure. As one would predict, the existing Jewish courts in Los Angeles are able to mobilize community coercion when the disputants are members of a functioning, closely knit group and are unable to do so where they are not. Thus, disputes involving synagogues and synagogue personnel are effectively adjudicated while those between Jews who play no special religious role remain troublesome (Balderman, 1974: 20–30). One might expect that the necessity of hiring a lawyer and of invoking civil court process would make the arbitration agreement rather ineffective. Empirically this seems to have been the case in Los Angeles. Despite the fact that the losing party often fails to obey the Jewish court's decision, the rabbis of that court cannot recall a single instance in the past twenty-five years in which the prevailing party has sought government court coercion through enforcing the obligatory arbitration agreement (Balderman, 1974: 19).

New institutions, then, ought to be adjudicative only when they expect to serve a clientele which is socially organized to coerce its members into compliance with decisions without secondary recourse to government courts. Where dispute processing is to be provided for a different kind of social unit, it would be well to recognize at the outset that only mediation may be effective, and to maximize the use of third parties who are likely to share the social and cultural experience of the disputants and who have some pre-processing information about them as personalities—a neighborhood notable is preferable to a trained social worker or lawyer who is an "outsider" (*see* Yaffe, 1972: 58, 266–67).

Innovative neighborhood "courts" have recently begun to operate in New York City and East Palo Alto, California (Statsky, 1974; Hager, 1972). In New York, mediation is conducted by non-professional neighborhood residents who secure extensive information about the backgrounds and personalities of juveniles referred to the mediators and of the adults with whom they are quarreling. In East Palo Alto neighborhood judges adjudicate complaints against juveniles and penalize offenders with neighborhood work tasks. Although the behavioral theories implicit in these two approaches are obviously different, each of these institutions seems to be more sensitive to the different prerequisites of mediation and adjudication than are the advocates of neighborhood moots and religious arbitration boards.

In any event, the effect of such reforms, even if they were adopted by a single community, is limited. Juvenile problems and problems within families and within religious groups could be processed in a new forum. But neighborhood disputes, work disputes, consumer disputes and citizen-government disputes would be unaffected. For these disputes, either avoidance is adequate or major changes must be made in government courts, particularly in small claims courts. Since the need for such a court reform has been apparent for decades (Smith, 1924: 9; Nelson, 1949: 239; *Stanford Law Review*, 1952: 238), the utility of avoidance must be viewed as a blessing. In a world that is too infrequently symmetrical, our inability to process many disputes by adjudication or mediation may generally be balanced by a lesser need to do so.

## Notes

1. This paper reflects a preference for the term "dispute processing" instead of the more common "dispute settlement." My aversion to "dispute settlement" is based on the conviction that a significant amount of dispute processing is not intended to settle disputes, that a greater amount does not do so and that it is often difficult to know whether a dispute which has been processed has been settled, or even what the dispute was about in the first place (*see* Collier, 1973: 169; Gulliver, 1969: 14–15; Gibbs, 1969: 193). These questions persist even when issues in dispute are sharply defined, as by written pleadings. In many such formal cases one or all of the parties seek something other than a resolution, even an advantageous resolution of the matter in dispute. Such a phenomenon is recognized in the U.S. (Sykes, 1969: 330; Nader, 1965: 19) and is thought to be endemic in India. Litigation is used as a skirmish or an important maneuver in economic and political warfare: the expense, inconvenience and disgrace of court involvement imposed on one's opponent outweigh one's concern about the end result of the ostensible dispute, if ever an end result is intended (Kidder, 1973: 137; Cohn, 1967: 154; Rudolph and Rudolph, 1967: 262). It does not then seem to make sense to talk about a "settlement" process when frequently it is not demonstrable that settlement is the objective of the process, and when it is often impossible to determine what is to be settled or whether that result has been achieved. The term "dispute processing" avoids all these difficulties.

# 4

# Minor Dispute Processing: A Review of Recent Developments *

### Daniel McGillis

Interpersonal conflicts routinely arise in all societies, and every society develops institutions for coping with them. These mechanisms range from the informal community hearings common in some African societies in which relatives and neighbors discuss disputes before a local mediator (Gibbs, 1963; Danzig, 1973; Smith, 1972) to formal courts of the industrialized societies (Sarat and Grossman, 1975). Within any society disputants are likely to have a number of options for pursuing their complaints. They can "lump it" by seeking to avoid the dispute (e.g., by eliminating contacts with the other disputant), negotiate their differences directly, have the dispute mediated by a third party either formally or informally, bring the matter to the attention of a fact finder or ombudsman, or take the matter to a court.[1]

Societies vary greatly in their use of these various alternatives. Americans tend to rely heavily upon the formal court processing of disputes. Extrapolating from California data, Johnson et al. (1977: 1) estimate that approximately 10 million new civil cases are initiated each year in American courts, a figure that averages out to approximately 5,000 per 100,000 population. In comparison, Sarat and Grossman (1975: 1208) have reported very low civil litigation rates in many other countries (e.g., 307 per 100,000 population in Norway, 493 per 100,000 in Finland, etc). American criminal caseloads are also comparatively high.

---

* Eds. Note: Portions of this chapter are drawn from D. McGillis, *Neighborhood Justice Centers*, Washington, D.C.: U.S. Government Printing Office, 1981. All references in the text are found in the bibliography at the conclusion of this volume.

Countries which do not rely heavily upon the courts are not without conflicts; instead they tend to have well-developed alternatives for dispute processing. Some have strong traditions supporting the resolution of disputes within family or neighborhood groups. For example, Cohen (1967: 1201) has noted that in China "most civil disputes between the individuals are settled by extrajudicial mediation" involving the efforts of local individuals. The Soviet Union and a number of European countries have also developed formal nonjudicial mechanisms for the processing of disputes, although they differ significantly in form and structure from the Chinese models (Berman, 1972; Felstiner and Drew, 1979; Cappelletti and Garth, 1978; Lubman, 1967).

Patterns of use of dispute settlement mechanisms within· societies are not static, however. Every society has a range of dispute processing options, and emphases among these options change over time. For example, even though China has long stressed extrajudicial dispute settlement, the government is currently actively promoting increased availability and use of adjudicatory forums. In a series of highly publicized acts, China has recently adopted an extensive new code of criminal law and procedure, new constitutional safeguards, revitalized the legal profession after a period of virtual banishment, and reopened law schools closed for many years (Chen, 1980). In contrast, in the United States there is a pronounced trend towards "delegalization." Major examples include efforts to simplify legal procedures (e.g., no-fault divorce, no-fault automobile insurance laws; see Johnson et al., 1977); efforts to decriminalize certain offenses and deinstitutionalize convicted offenders (Abel, 1979), and the growth of alternatives to the courts (e.g., mediation centers; see Sander, 1977). In commenting upon such variations in an earlier time, Pound (1922: 54) noted that there is a "continual movement in legal history back and forth between justice without law, as it were, and justice according to law."

Recent American efforts to develop nonjudicial dispute processing forums for the handling of "minor" disputes are reviewed in this paper.[2] These forums vary enormously in their philosophies, goals, and structures. The individual programs often have relatively modest aims and aspirations, yet in the aggregate the projects raise many fundamental questions regarding the appropriate relationship of the state to its citizenry. Earl Johnson (1978) of the University of Southern California Law Center noted recently that "it is somewhat ironic that 'small" claims and what many deem 'simple' disputes—rather than large cases or complex controversies—have compelled a rethinking of the prevailing model of dispute resolution." This rethinking has helped to illuminate the widely varying assumptions held regarding the appropriate role of the justice system in American society. Debates have occurred regarding many facets of the justice system.

For example, views differ considerably regarding the definition of justice. Are specific processes required as a precondition for the rendering of "justice"? Some (e.g., Fuller, 1979) have argued that minimal procedural elements include the impartiality of third-party hearing officers, opportunities for parties to present their side of the controversy fully, and relatively equivalent capabilities of parties to pursue their claims (with professional assistance provided when the process is too complex for a layperson to negotiate unaided). Are specific "just" *outcomes* required, and how are these to be assessed by outside observers? What role should collective "social justice" play in the rendering of justice in individual cases? Disagreements have also occurred regarding the *proper level of access to justice system mechanisms*. Should such mechanisms be universally available for virtually all disputes, as some have proposed (see Cappelletti and Garth, 1978, for a discussion of this issue)? Or due to economic and other factors, is the value of courts intrinsically symbolic and much of their force indirectly conveyed by conferring "bargaining endowments" to disputants in the shadow of the justice system (Mnookin and Kornhauser, 1979; Galanter, 1979a)? The *types of appropriate justice system* mechanisms have been discussed extensively in recent research literature. Some (Fetter, 1978: 179–205) have noted the merits of the current adversarial system and have suggested ways in which it could be strengthened; others (Sander, 1976; Johnson et al., 1977; Garafalo and Connelly, 1980) have discussed potential advantages of alternative processes (mediation, arbitration, and the like) for use in certain types of cases; and still others (Buckle and Buckle, 1977; Feeley, 1979) have documented how the American civil and criminal justice systems are already predominantly purveyors of "negotiated" settlements.

The diversity of goals asserted for nonjudicial dispute processing mechanisms has been striking (McGillis and Mullen, 1977). Some believe that nonjudicial forums can increase *access to justice* because they facilitate prompt hearings, reduce or eliminate legal costs, schedule dispute settlement hearings at convenient hours and locations, and the like. Some stress *improved efficiency*, arguing that reliance on informal alternatives will free the courts to attend to more serious cases. Others argue that mediation provides an *improved process* for handling disputes because disputants are able to explore the underlying problems contributing to the dispute without the restrictions of rules of evidence, time limitations of typical lower court hearings, and the presence of attorneys as intermediaries in the discussion. Still others point to potential *community benefits* deriving from mediation, arguing that such community-based programs, if developed in neighborhoods and administered locally, can increase direct citizen participation in major life decisions, reduce community tensions through effective conflict resolution, teach citizens how to solve problems collectively, and more generally improve the quality of community life.[3] Many of the nonjudicial projects have sought to address varying combinations of the above goals.

The great variety of goals and philosophies has resulted in ideologically diverse individuals endorsing the development of nonjudicial forums often for very different and at times incompatible reasons. For example, the recently enacted federal Dispute Resolution Act of 1980, designed to support research and funding for nonjudicial dispute-processing mechanisms, received support from such diverse groups as the National Chamber of Commerce and Ralph Nader's consumer advocates; the Conference of Chief Justices and 1960s-style community activist groups; and the American Bar Association and vociferous critics of professionalism. Not surprisingly it was the multifaceted nature of the four basic goals noted above that facilitated agreement among such traditional adversaries.[4]

As might be expected, the wide diversity in project goals and proponents has resulted in virtually every approach and its opposite being advanced as a means of promoting dispute settlement. Major variations include differences in the amount of coercion employed on disputants (from quite substantial coercion to a virtual lack of coercion),[5] types of linkages to the justice system (outright sponsorship, informal appended relations, and independence), variations in the role of law and lawyers (from central importance to virtual rejection of their role), and enforceability of settlements (from civil court enforceability—e.g., arbitrator's awards, mediation settlements converted into judgments of the court—to reliance totally upon disputant maintenance of the agreement) (McGillis and Mullen, 1977: 47–54, 65–70, 71–76). This paper summarizes some of the major variations in the existing nonjudicial projects.

## Minor Dispute Processing Projects

Projects for the mediation and/or arbitration of minor civil and criminal disputes have been developed in approximately 30 states during the past five years. The total number of such projects is roughly 140, and some states have been particularly active in project development (e.g., Projects are operational or developing in 17 Florida cities, 14 New Jersey cities, 10 New York cities, 9 Massachusetts cities, and 9 California cities). Projects exist in every region of the continental United States and in Honolulu as well (American Bar Association, 1980).

The term *minor dispute center* will be used as a generic label for all of the nonjudicial projects discussed in this report. Projects included under this general label have a wide variety of local titles including "citizen dispute settlement center," "neighborhood justice center," "community mediation center," "night prosecutor program," "community board program," "urban court project," and others.

## Development of Initial Projects

A major stimulus for the development of the early nonjudicial projects appears to have been a growing concern in the late 1960s and early 1970s regarding the justice system's difficulties in handling minor civil and criminal disputes. Recurrent problems found in many courts included extensive delays, high costs, assembly-line procedures, and citizen dissatisfaction with the quality of justice rendered. James Kilpatrick, a syndicated columnist, summarized the situation by noting, "The major problem of American justice is not the gargantuan lawsuit. These take care of themselves. The major problem lies in the inability of our system to deal promptly and justly with the little cases that can create 'festering sores and undermine confidence in society.'" Such "little cases" are, of course, major events in the lives of the citizens involved in them and include such common matters as assaults and batteries among relatives and acquaintances, landlord-tenant battles, disputes about shoddy workmanship, and the like.

The earliest minor dispute center projects appear to have been developed by prosecutors in response to perceived needs for improved handling of minor criminal cases. The Philadelphia Municipal Court Arbitration tribunal has one of the longest lineages. The project was established in 1969 through the joint efforts of the American Arbitration Association, the Philadelphia District Attorney, and the Municipal Court, and provides disputants involved in minor criminal matters with the option of proceeding in court or selecting binding arbitration. The Columbus, Ohio, Night Prosecutor Program was begun about the same time and employs mediation rather than arbitration in an effort to reduce court caseloads and effect more satisfying outcomes. Initially two local law professors served as mediators; the project now handles over 10,000 cases per year.

Both the Philadelphia and Columbus projects received LEAA funding, and the Columbus project was designated an Exemplary Project by a board of LEAA officials in 1974. As a result, extensive documentation of the project was prepared, and the National Institute of LEAA sponsored nationwide seminars to advocate replication of the project. Programs modeled after the Columbus project were developed in many Ohio communities. In addition, the Miami, Florida, project, among others, credits the Columbus project as a major stimulus to its development, and the Miami project in turn stimulated the development of projects in at least nine other Florida cities. Other major projects which have inspired replication include the Institute for Mediation and Conflict Resolution's Dispute Center in Manhattan, the San Francisco Community Board Program, the Rochester Community Dispute Services project, and the Boston Urban Court Program. Recently developed projects often tend to be eclectic and borrow features from a number of the established programs (see, e.g., ABA, 1980).

## Project Characteristics

Projects vary widely in their approaches to nonjudicial dispute settlement. Major differences include types of: (1) disputes handled, (2) project sponsorship, (3) case referral sources, (4) dispute settlement techniques, and (5) hearing officer characteristics. The balance of this section briefly reviews variations among programs on each of these five characteristics and illustrates the wide variety of project forms, functions, and philosophies.

### Types of Disputes Processed

Projects vary considerably in the types of cases handled. Some projects process a broad variety of minor civil and criminal matters while others limit themselves to specific types of disputes such as small claims cases or criminal, domestic, consumer, or housing-related matters. Regardless of the types of disputes processed, virtually all projects tend to place their primary focus upon disputes occurring among individuals who have an ongoing relationship, whether as relatives, landlord-tenant, employer-employee, neighbors, and so on. These cases are viewed as amenable to mediation and arbitration due to the possibilities for compromise and the potential interest of the parties in arriving at a joint settlement. The following examples illustrate the variations in case criteria among dispute settlement projects.

### Programs Handling Both Civil and Criminal Matters

Many projects have very broad case criteria and handle a wide variety of both civil and criminal matters. Criminal matters include assault, assault and battery, criminal mischief, and larceny, while civil matters typically involve landlord-tenant, consumer-merchant, and employer-employee disputes. Strict categorization of many matters as either criminal or civil is, of course, not possible. For example, an assault may be treated as a crime or a tort, and handled in criminal or civil courts, or both. In attempting to categorize cases roughly as either criminal or civil, one recent evaluation of five dispute settlement projects in Florida defined a criminal matter as "any act by an adult where a possible violation of a state statute or municipal/county ordinance has occurred," and civil issues as all disputes where "no possible governmental sanction or penalty can be levied" (Dispute Resolution Alternatives Committee, 1979: 3). Following these definitions, the Florida evaluators report dramatic differences in the criminal/civil case mix of Florida projects: for example 84 percent of the Jacksonville Project's caseload was categorized as criminal in contrast to only 19 percent in St. Petersburg/Clearwater. Overall in the 2,500 cases studied by the evaluators in the five Florida dispute settlement projects, 41 percent were categorized as criminal and 59 percent civil (Dispute Resolution Alternatives Committee, 1979: 17). A similar classification approach resulted in approximately 40 percent of cases in Atlanta, 72 percent in Kansas City, and 42 percent in Los Angeles being considered criminal (Cook et al., 1980). The wide variations in the actual caseload mixes typically reflect differences in primary referral sources; some projects have strong ties to criminal courts, others to civil courts, and still others to neither or both.

In the civil area, most projects are hesitant to process disputes between disputants varying greatly in power because of concern that the more powerful party will have little incentive to compromise; thus, disputes betwen individuals and large organizations are often not processed. Some projects, however, have encouraged more powerful parties to participate. For example, in Fairfax County, Virginia, merchants are required to agree to process consumer complaints through mediation at the consumer's request as a precondition for membership in the local Chamber of Commerce.[6]

In the case of criminal matters, most projects handle only misdemeanors. But the New York Institute for Mediation and Conflict Resolution Dispute Center occasionally handles felonies (such as felonious assaults and even rape) when they involve acquaintances. And an experimental center in Brooklyn handles only felonies. This latter project was initiated in response to a recent study of the Vera Institute of Justice which found that in New York, felony cases among acquaintances were generally not successfully prosecuted (Vera, 1977: 81). Although such cases comprise a large proportion of the court's caseload (e.g., 56 percent of violent crime cases), the majority are dismissed due to lack of complainant cooperation.[7] In Washington, 75 percent of assault cases involve persons with prior relationships and nearly 90 percent of these cases are also dismissed. The Vera researchers called for alternatives to the present choice between full prosecution and outright dismissal and recommended mediation as a promising option.

The Florida project evaluation cited earlier has noted the value of mediation in criminal cases. The researchers concluded that the five Florida projects studied were effective for both civil and criminal cases, but reported that disputants referred to (mediation) programs by criminal justice personnel were more likely to appear for scheduled hearings, reach agreements, and be satisfied with the (mediation) process than were participants with civil law matters (Dispute Resolution Alternatives Committee, 1979: 59). Similarly evaluations of the three Department of Justice Neighborhood Justice Center projects also report that criminal justice system referrals are more likely to result in hearings than other types of referrals (Cook et al. 1980).

Some projects process a large volume of "bad-check" cases in addition to the rest of their caseload. For example, the Columbus Night Prosecutor Program handles over 10,000 "bad-check" cases a year (McGillis and Mullen, 1977: 108–211). Many critics have argued that this type of case is not suited for mediation and have suggested that processing such cases can harm a project's image by making it appear to be a collection agency. Supporters of "bad-check" case processing have responded that informal mediation in such cases is a more humane approach to settling bad-check cases than arrests or threats of arrest and have argued that such hearings are in fact successful.

## Programs that Focus on Small Claims Matters

In 1977 the district court in Portland, Maine, began a pilot project using mediation in small claims cases. The project provides disputants the option to mediate small claims cases prior to formal adjudication. Preliminary data from an extensive evaluation conducted by Professor Craig McEwen of Bowdoin College indicate that mediation clients are significantly more satisfied with their case's processing than court clients, and that mediated settlements are more likely to be carried out than are adjudicated judgments. The mediation project has been implemented in courts across the state and has begun to handle selected domestic matters such as alimony and custody disputes (Greason, 1980: 579).

In Massachusetts in 1978, court reform legislation provided that disputants involved in small claims cases must have the option of taking their case to mediation as well as the courts. Complainants will be informed of the availability of mediation at the time of initial filing and from the bench at the time of the court hearing. This is apparently the first instance of a statutorily mandated option of mediation in small claims, although a number of jurisdictions in New York, California, Pennsylvania, and Ohio have had compulsory arbitration of minor civil matters (within a given monetary range) for some time (Judicial Council of California). The compulsory arbitration hearings are typically conducted by a panel of attorneys, and disputants have the right to a trial *de novo*, for which the appellant must pay the arbitration costs. In New York City, parties involved in a small claims suit are given the option to have the dispute arbitrated by an attorney. The choice of arbitration waives the parties' rights to appeal. The Los Angeles federally sponsored NJC has been quite heavily involved in mediating small claims, and referral forms to the NJC are automatically appended to the filing forms in small claims courts. The project also has staff in the courts who can immediately mediate issues referred directly to them from the bench.

## Programs that Focus on Criminal Matters

As was noted earlier, some projects primarily handle criminal matters (e.g., criminal matters constitute 84 percent of the Jacksonville caseload and 72 percent of the Kansas City caseload). These projects accept both criminal and civil matters but have developed particularly successful linkages with criminal justice agencies.

Very few projects are explicitly designed to focus exclusively on criminal matters. One of these is the Brooklyn program, discussed earlier, which is designed to deal with felony charges involving acquaintances. Another is the Massachusetts Adult Mediation/Restitution Program developed in 1978 with support from LEAA. This latter project terminated after the federal funds were expended. It operated in three Massachusetts District Courts (Woburn, Lowell, and Cambridge) and dealt exclusively with misdemeanor cases, most of which involved controversies between strangers. Referrals were received from the bench at court hearings and defendants were required to admit to facts sufficient to establish guilt before the judge would continue the case and refer it to the project. The program primarily handled minor property offenses. Community people served as mediators and mediation hearings tended to focus upon the specific terms of monetary or service restitution. The conception of the project differs considerably from other mediation projects which typically initiate hearings with the assumption that either or both of the parties may have committed offenses against the other. While discussions in the Adult Mediation/Restitution Program could involve compromises between the two disputants, they did not begin with the initial neutral stance typically associated with mediation, and in many respects the project was a restitution project that only employed some of the trappings but not the substance of mediation.

## Programs that Focus on Domestic Matters

Mediation has become an adjunct to many family crisis intervention programs (McGillis, 1980). In some projects social workers meet with the husband and wife separately in an attempt to arrange suitable referrals and assistance, while in others the two parties are brought together for informal mediation. These sessions often focus on family violence, but as well mediate such divorce-related issues as child custody and visitation. Family crisis intervention projects are operated by a host of different agencies. In some communities, they are sponsored by the police (e.g., the Police Foundation supported an experimental police-based project in Norwalk, Connecticut), in others by probation departments (e.g., the Aid for Battered Women project in New Bedford, Massachusetts), conciliation courts, and private nonprofit agencies. Divorce mediation services staffed by lawyers and social workers are being developed in many cities, and clients are charged fees for the services.

## Programs that Focus on Consumer Matters

Numerous consumer dispute-processing projects have been developed in recent years (McGillis, 1981). The Better Business Bureau has established programs in many cities which provide for the sequential use of conciliation, mediation, and arbitration. Most cases are settled prior to the arbitration stage. The National Association of Home Builders has established the Homeowner's Warranty Corporation, which employs a similar three-step approach, with similar results when it is employed. The Magnuson-Moss Warranty Act has encouraged the development of this type of dispute-processing program to enforce product warranties generally and mandates the Federal Trade Commission (FTC) to facilitate ways to resolve warranty disputes. The Ford Motor Company and other automobile companies are experimenting with various approaches to the mediation of automobile warranty cases. Numerous trade associations have developed dispute resolution efforts, such as the Major Appliance Consumer Action Panels and the Furniture Industry Consumer Action Panels, which investigate complaints by consumers and make nonbinding recommendations for their resolution. In a number of states an executive office of consumer affairs and/or the state attorney general's office now provide consumer complaint departments which can provide conciliation services by telephone or through the mail.

## Programs that Focus on Housing Matters

During the past few years a number of project designed to mediate housing-related controversies have been created (McGillis, 1980). Housing mediation projects are particularly prevalent in California and some have very large caseloads. For example, the San Jose Housing Service Center reports that it handled over 34,000 referrals from August 1975 through April 1979. The California legislature in 1980 passed a resolution recommending development of housing mediation projects statewide. In Denver, ACTION has funded a housing mediation project which is sponsored by the Denver Commission on Community Relations and the Colorado Bar Association. The Department of Housing and Urban Development (HUD) has also funded an extensive research and technical assistance program to explore alternative housing dispute mechanisms.

## Program Sponsorship

Three major types of sponsors of nonjudicial dispute settlement projects are common: public sponsorship, private sponsorship with close ties to the justice system, and private sponsorship with a community orientation.

## Public Sponsorship

Project sponsors have included state-level agencies (e.g., Massachusetts Attorney General's Office consumer complaint project), local courts (e.g., the Miami Citizen Dispute Settlement Program), Prosecutor's offices (e.g., the Columbus Night Prosecutor Program), city manager's office (e.g., the Kansas City Neighborhood Justice Center), county governments (e.g., the Portland, Oregon, Neighborhood Mediation Project), and police departments (many police departments sponsor family crisis intervention units).

## Private Sponsorship with Close Ties to the Justice System

A number of projects have been sponsored by private organizations with close ties to the local justice system including the Orlando Citizen Dispute Settlement Project sponsored by the local bar association, the Rochester Community Dispute Service Project operated by the American Arbitration Association and the Institute for Mediation and Conflict Resolution Dispute Center in New York.

## Private Sponsorship with a Community Orientation

A number of projects developed under the sponsorship of local private organizations rely primarily upon community control of operations and obtained referrals of cases directly from the community rather than justice system agencies. The San Francisco Community Board Program and the Los Angeles Neighborhood Justice Center both have this orientation. Projects of this type tend to stress the value of decentralization, return of control regarding major decisions to the community, the need to develop leadership skills within the community, and related issues along with improved dispute processing.

## Case Referral Sources

Case referrals come from a variety of sources. Evaluators of the five Florida projects discussed above found that police and prosecutors' offices accounted for nearly two-thirds of all referrals, while the remaining referrals were distributed among many other sources, including walk-ins, court clerks, legal aid, city hall, news media, consumer protection agencies, private attorneys, judges, and several other governmental agencies (Dispute Resolution Alternatives Committee, 1979: 16). A similar pattern of referral sources holds for many other projects, although in some jurisdictions one source produces the majority of referrals, for example, the bench (Boston), court clerk (Rochester), prosecutor (Jacksonville), police (Orlando), and walk-ins (Los Angeles Neighborhood Justice Center).

## Dispute Settlement Techniques

Projects employ a variety of dispute-processing techniques including conciliation, mediation, and arbitration. Each approach will be discussed briefly in turn. It should be noted that most projects are eclectic in approach and employ a variety of techniques to settle disputes.

*Conciliation.* Many projects attempt to settle disputes through phoned or letter contact with the respondent (defendant) prior to the scheduling of a formal hearing. While some projects limit themselves to this approach (e.g., various state-level consumer complaint projects) and advise complainants to proceed on their own to other forums if conciliation fails, others view conciliation as only a first step and provide their own mediation and arbitration services if conciliation fails.

*Mediation.* Face-to-face mediation of conflicts between disputants is a common procedure used in many projects. Techniques of mediation vary considerably; some projects use panels of up to five mediators, while others rely on a single mediator. Some projects have relatively brief hearings (e.g., an average of 30–45 minutes in Miami), while others have quite lengthy hearings (e.g., over two hours on the average in Boston). The American Arbitration Association and the Institute for Mediation and Conflict Resolution both tend to stress the value of caucuses between individual disputants and hearing officers (with the other disputant leaving the room for a short while) as a technique for finding the "bottom line" of each disputant. This approach is used extensively by projects in Rochester and Cleveland. Some other projects tend to reject the caucus approach and stress the development of communication skills on the part of disputants. Such projects have disputants carefully explain their positions and then require the other party to repeat the essence of their opponent's position. Some projects employ written resolutions (e.g., Boston), and one project (Los Angeles) notes on its resolution agreement form that the mediated resolution reached by consent is enforceable in court.

*Arbitration.* Projects that employ a formalized arbitration procedure (e.g., New York City, Rochester, etc.) have the authority to make binding agreements enforceable in court. These projects typically attempt to mediate the dispute first and resort to imposed arbitration awards only after mediation has failed. The New York City project reports that only approximately 5 percent of its cases reach arbitration; the remaining 95 percent of the cases are mediated, and the mediated agreements are then written up as enforceable consent agreements. The Rochester project, which relies on similar procedures, reports that 40 percent of its cases proceed to imposed arbitration (McGillis and Mullen, 1977). Comparative data on the relative effectiveness of the two approaches are not as yet available. The difference between mediation and arbitration becomes blurred in some projects in which the prosecutor is the sponsor, and the threat of criminal charges for failure to maintain a mediated agreement is very real.

## Hearing Officer Characteristics

Hearing staff characteristics vary widely among projects and include lay citizens who have received training in mediation or arbitration techniques (e.g., Boston, Rochester, and New York), law students (e.g., Columbus), and lawyers (Orlando). Some telephone conciliation projects (e.g., the Massachusetts Attorney General's consumer project) employ undergraduates on internships. The Maine small claims court mediation effort has relied heavily upon retired persons, and this approach has interesting parallels to the role of elderly persons as dispute resolvers in many unindustrialized societies (Greason, 1980).

## State Initiatives

As interest in alternative dispute-processing mechanisms has grown, some state governments have developed legislation, technical assistance, and research-assessing dispute-processing needs. Recent major state actions are briefly described below.

California has enacted legislation to encourage the development of alternative dispute-processing institutions, and Florida (HB 707), and New York (A 6188) have also proposed similar legislation. The New York bill would provide $1 million for the support of nonjudicial dispute projects. The California bill had initially included $1 million for project support but the provision was dropped in light of Proposition 13. The Florida bill does not include any appropriations (see McGillis, 1980b).

All three of the bills provide for the confidentiality of case-related material. The California law provides that all memoranda, files, and written agreements are confidential and privileged and are not subject to disclosure in any judicial or administrative proceedings. Similarly, all communications are privileged. The Florida bill provides a similar broad protection. Confidentiality has been a concern among program advocates from the outset, and statutory provisions of confidentiality would be valuable. At present, projects must rely on attempts to negotiate agreements from local prosecutors' offices that confidential information gathered by mediators will not later be demanded in court.

In Florida the Supreme Court has directed the Office of the State Courts Administrator to provide local jurisdictions with technical assistance in establishing local mediation projects. As of 1981, this office had evaluated five Florida projects, developed a detailed manual for use by projects, conducted a statewide conference in informal dispute resolution, and initiated a major public information campaign. In New Jersey, the Department of the Public Advocate recently sponsored a national conference on dispute resolution mechanisms, and representatives from the various New Jersey dispute settlement projects participated in the meeting.

In many states, bar association committees, judicial special committees, and other groups are studying the need for nonjudicial dispute resolution mechanisms. The Alaska Judicial Council recently completed such a study, as did the Special Committee to Study Alternative Means of Dispute Resolution of the Massachusetts District Court. The latter study led to the creation of experimental projects in Salem, Framingham, and Taunton, Massachusetts. Recently promulgated Standards for the Prosecution and Defense in New York State cite the development of accessible nonjudicial dispute processing mechanisms as a top priority.

## National Initiatives

A variety of federal efforts have been developed to encourage minor dispute-processing innovations including the Department of Justice Neighborhood Justice Centers program and the federal Dispute Resolution Act. The Neighborhood Justice Center Program was established by the National Institute of Justice and projects were funded in Atlanta, Kansas City, and Los Angeles. [Editor's note: A report by evaluators of this effort is included in this volume (see pp. 91–110).] The Dispute Resolution Act was discussed earlier in this paper, and the program is designed to establish a national resource center to serve as a clearinghouse for information, provide technical assistance, and conduct research in the dispute settlement field, as well as to authorize funds for the establishment of experimental dispute-processing mechanisms. Prospects for funding of the Act appear very dim due to the current severe federal budgetary restrictions.

## Conclusions

This chapter has provided a brief summary of recent developments in minor dispute processing in the United States. The diverse origins and goals of current dispute-processing innovations were discussed, and major project characteristics were reviewed. Major state and national initiatives were also noted.

Befitting the diversity of project philosophies, goals, and procedures, a comparable diversity is emerging in the interpretation of project achievements. Some project evaluators and observers have viewed the mediation programs very favorably (Cook, Roehl, and Sheppard, 1980), while others have serious reservations (Tomasic, 1981). A number of factors have contributed to the difficulty in definitively evaluating the merits of the mediation efforts. The following are some of these problems.

1. *The lack of a consensus on project goals.* As was discussed earlier, there is substantial disagreement over program goals and criteria for judging program success. Major goals include relieving the overcrowded justice system, improved access to justice, enhancement of community power, and improved resolution of conflict. Some projects claim to pursue all these goals, while others focus on only some of them and may reject some others.

2. *Limitations in currently available evaluation data.* While there have been a number of evaluations of these new dispute-processing projects, most of them have examined programs with diverse civil and criminal caseloads, and there is little information regarding the specialized minor dispute-processing projects. Only one evaluation to date has employed an experimental design and randomly assigned disputants. [Editor's note: A report on this study is included in this volume; see Robert Davis, pp. 154–170.] The study assessed the Brooklyn program for felony dispute processing, and similar research on minor civil and criminal case processing is needed.

To date most evaluations have focused upon descriptions of project caseloads, referral sources, and other "process" data. As a consequence, little information is available regarding the long-term impact of mediation versus court case processing, comparative costs of judicial and nonjudicial resolution, and the like. Similarly, we know very little about the differential impact of varying approaches to dispute settlement (e.g., conciliation, mediation, arbitration, and adjudication) and of varying types of hearing officers (e.g., lawyers, laypersons, social service professionals). The scarcity of precise empirical data on program achievements and impacts encourages a diversity of views regarding the merits of programs, and suggestive evidence can be mustered to support an extremely wide range of positions regarding nonjudicial dispute-processing forums.

3. *Difficulties in generalizing from newly developed projects.* Many evaluations to date have focused on "experimental" projects funded by the federal government or private foundations. While valuable, such evaluations may be limited in their generalizability because they typically focus only on the first 12 to 18 months of a project's life, during its start-up period. The initial period of a project's life is far from typical of routine operations. Felstiner and Williams' (1980) study of the Boston Urban Court project is a notable exception to this practice. Evaluations of additional established projects are needed in order to assess their longer range operations and impact.

## Prospects for the Future

The growth in the number and variety of minor dispute-processing projects has been striking in recent years. Federal budgetary cutbacks coupled with the severe restrictions in state and local budgets may inhibit the rapid development of dispute-processing projects in the coming years, and "natural-selection" processes in city councils and county commissions may separate successful programs from those that were less successful. Some of the established projects may begin to face growing problems with bureaucratization, although it remains to be seen if large caseloads in some of the older projects will lead to delays in case processing, reduced time allotted to hearings, and growing unresponsiveness to clientele characteristic of mature bureaucracies. The specter of overburdened assembly-line mediation systems replacing overburdened assembly-line court rooms is not an attractive one, and it is hoped that reform of such systems will not be on the agenda of justice system reformers of the 1980s.

Regardless of the short-term prospects for individual dispute-processing projects, it appears that the widespread support for non-judicial forums for minor dispute processing may herald a major shift in American jurisprudence. Fuller (1971, 1979) has written prolifically and compellingly on the limits of adjudication for the handling of certain matters. His concerns appear to have been validated nationally with the development of mediation centers. Sander (1976) documented in his Pound Conference essay the "rich variety of different processes . . . which singly or in combination may provide far more 'effective' conflict resolution" for certain types of disputes.

The detailed jurisprudence is yet to be written. The continuing experimentation across the country may point the way to the development of a more highly differentiated and coordinated justice system, with different forums and procedures suited to different types of human conflict.

## Notes

1. See D. McGillis and T. Mullen (1977) for further discussion of options available to disputants.

2. The term *'minor' disputes* will be used in this paper to encompass a wide variety of civil and criminal matters. The civil matters will typically fall within small claims court monetary limits and the criminal matters include a diverse group of misdemeanors (e.g., assaults and threats typically among acquaintances). The term is not meant to imply that the disputes are unimportant; clearly many such "minor" disputes are major events in the lives of the disputants enmeshed in them.

3. See for example, R. Shonholtz, *Review of Alternative Dispute Mechanisms and a Government Proposal for Neighborhood Justice Centers* (San Francisco Community Board Program, unpublished manuscript, 1977) and the American Friends Service Committee Grassroots Citizen Dispute Resolution Clearing-

house newsletter, *The Mooter* (available from Paul Wahrhaftig, 4401 Fifth Avenue, Pittsburgh, Pennsylvania, 15213) for an explication of the community benefits potentially arising from the use of community-based conflict resolution mechanisms.

4. For background and history on this act, see *Dispute Resolution Act Hearings before the House Judiciary Committee*, July 27, August 2, 1978 (Serial Number 68) Washington, D.C.: U.S. Government Printing Office, 1978, and *Dispute Resolution Act Joint Hearings Before the House Judiciary and Commerce Committees*, June 6, 7, 14, and 18, 1979 (Serial Number 25) Washington, D.C.: U.S. Government Printing Office, 1979, for detailed discussions of the Dispute Resolution Act and reasons for its development.

5. For example, some projects affiliated with justice system agencies strongly urge respondents to attend mediation sessions (e.g., the Citizens Dispute Settlement Project of the City Attorney's Office in Minneapolis, Minnesota), while other projects conscientiously attempt to avoid the impression of pressuring disputants to participate in the projects (e.g., the San Francisco Community Board Program). Some differences in intake strategies are reviewed in McGillis and Mullen (1977).

6. A copy of the Fairfax County Business/Consumer Code of Ethics can be obtained from the Fairfax County Department of Consumer Affairs or the Fairfax County Chamber of Commerce.

7. [Editor's note: A report on the Brooklyn project by Robert Davis is found on pp. 154–170 of this volume.]

# PART II

## Case Studies

# 5

## Doing unto Others: Disputes and Dispute Processing in an Urban American Neighborhood [*]

Suzann R. Thomas-Buckle[**]
Leonard G. Buckle

### Introduction: Neighborhood Justice Centers and Self-Help Justice

Recent innovations, such as Neighborhood Justice Centers (NJCs), attempt to provide people with disputes a larger number of options for resolving their problems. Planners of such reforms often assume that disputants must choose between no assistance at all or whatever relief may be offered by the police and the civil and criminal courts. Their proposals focus on development of a middle range of alternatives. The NJC movement in particular is intent upon expanding choices for disputants who know each other well. These people, the reformers believe, are often ill-served by the courts, and as a consequence are likely not to pursue their grievances.

Unfortunately, planning for NJCs has taken place without much

[*] The support for this project comes from the German Marshall Fund through fellowships awarded to the authors. Much of the field research and many of the ideas presented in this paper can be attributed to Timothy Eckels, Allen Lee, and Nancy Reichman. Their contributions are considerable, but the many discussions we have had have blurred the authorship of specific insights and make it impossible for us to give individual credit where it is due.

Scott Cook, Dvora Yanow, and Elena Papa joined us at a late phase of the project and have provided assistance in the preparation of this paper.

[**] This chapter was prepared especially for this volume. All references in the text of this chapter are found in the Bibliography at the conclusion of this volume.

prior research on how people with disputes actually choose (and evalu-ate) various courses of action.[1] As a consequence, NJCs have been de-signed without adequate knowledge of whether the justice system is weak because it does not provide enough alternatives or because many people, including those with minor disputes, prefer other means to re-solve their problems. At present there is also only a vague understand-ing of how people in this country pursue grievances, including disputes among aquaintances. Do Americans in fact have large numbers of unre-solved minor disputes that grow out of long-standing, valued rela-tionships? To what extent do they already have resources available to understand the roots of their grievances and to gauge when action is advisable? Finally, what is the relationship between existing institutions and neighborhoods? Do neighborhoods, as the NJC movement suggests, provide crucial but deteriorating support for disputants? Clearly, there is a need for careful empirical research before any solution on a grand scale is proposed. Indeed, we must first determine if there is a problem, and if so, if it is amenable to public intervention.

At a minimum, we feel, judicial reformers should know what the market for an NJC is likely to be. Will people tend to avoid it because they prefer to help themselves? Are there other satisfactory means of resolving troubles already in place? Are they perhaps likely to find NJCs so attractive that they will come to depend on them for a wide range of services? Ideally, NJCs could emerge from and supplement existing in-formal systems already treating neighborhood troubles.[2] Whatever the case, it seems certain that considerable research on existing dispute re-solution institutions should *precede* large-scale social planning in this area.

In the following pages, we report some of our findings from an empirical study of dispute processing and neighborhood structure. Although not until later will we deal fully with NJCs and their prospects for success, our findings here address fundamental questions about the premises upon which NJCs are based. This chapter describes the social structure and interactions and the kinds of disputes and ways of resolv-ing them in one urban neighborhood.

In general, we did not find much evidence of a "market" for an NJC-like intervention. For instance, we found more collective disputes than individual disputes and many more disputes involving strangers rather than aquaintances. In addition, we found that residents use and strongly prefer an already existing, apparently effective, set of informal neighborhood-based options for resolving disputes. Furthermore, the ways that residents use these options suggests that the sort of help they feel they need from third parties is very different from that offered by NJCs.

In brief, what we found was reliance on self-help. Most respon-dents were reluctant to bring in outsiders, preferring to deal directly with adversaries. When third parties were invoked, it was as advocates and advisers, not as negotiators, and those called upon were most often people seen as part of the neighborhood. These patterns may reflect an unwillingness to negotiate, a deep distrust of formal institutions, strong penchant for self-reliance, and a growing sense of mutual interdependence among residents.

This indigenous, informal system of self-help justice, however, is hardly flawless. Access to the existing informal institutions is not uniform. Some people use them with ease, while other are badly disadvantaged by them. Since there is no consistent means of regulation, self-help justice can easily degenerate into violence. Finally, because the institutions of self-help justice have no formal structure, there is no accountability, either to the residents or to the society at large. It is clear, therefore, that there are some serious issues to be considered in deciding how to incorporate this information into planning for NJCs and other alternatives to formal adjudication.

In the following sections, we will discuss our findings in more detail. We first describe the intent of our study and its site, asking in what sense it serves as a "neighborhood" for its occupants. We then outline what our respondents reported to us as troubles,[3] the mechanisms they employed to resolve them, and the system of self-help which seemed to be at work in their neighborhood. We conclude with some efforts to link our findings about disputing in one urban community to some of the underlying premises of the NJC reform.

## Background: Studying Johnson Square

Our research focused on a place we call Johnson Square,[4] a three-block area in Waterford, a municipality of 100,000, located in a large, Eastern metropolitan area. Most of the residences in the Square are turn-of-the-century two- and three-family wood-frame houses set on lots little wider than the dwellings. Three brick apartment buildings—each with six or more units—complete the residential portion of the Square. At the boundaries of our study site are a variety of small businesses—warehouses and small factories built along a declining rail line to the south, and restaurants, specialty shops, and an amusement parlor lining an arterial street to the north.

The social and economic characteristics of Johnson Square are similar to those of Waterford and the metropolis of which it is a part. While most of the frame dwellings are owner occupied, the apartment buildings have absentee owners. Most of the businesses are owned by people who live in the suburbs and generally do not regard the residents of the Square as either customers or employees. Residents themselves are ethnically and racially diverse, although there is a large group of French people who came to Waterford from Canada. Most of the households are working—or lower-middle class, with some students and a few professionals comprising the main exceptions.

The Square has few institutions, such as governmental agencies, churches, or community groups within its boundaries. For example, the French-language Roman Catholic church is several miles away, and the nearest Roman Catholic church is regarded by many people in the Square as the "Irish parish" and is not generally used by residents. No other religious body seems influential in the Square. Waterford provides what residents see as important services in Johnson Square, yet no City Hall offices are housed there. The legal aid office, for example, is quite removed from the Square, the Waterford Municipal Court is at the other end of the city, and most government offices are located near City Hall, several miles away. Only the East Waterford Planning Team seems at all rooted in the Square, but it is not located there and its mandate includes the whole East End of Waterford.

Even though the area contains none of these institutions— sometimes seen as important dispute processors—its compactness, racial and ethnic diversity, and middle- to working-class structure made Johnson Square attractive as an initial site for our research. Since we wanted to understand the processes of disputing as a whole, we did not wish to go into the neighborhood with prespecified variables to test. We wanted instead to develop as rich as possible a fabric of information, by conducting what Weiss (1966) calls a holistic study.[5]

## Neighborhood Boundaries

When we asked residents what they saw as being "their neighborhood", they suggested geographical areas as large as Waterford and as small as a few adjacent houses. When they talked more generally, though, it became clear that geography is only one of several ways people in Johnson Square express the dimensions of their neighborhood. For many of them the concept carries with it a very strong sense of "entitlement" to make claims for city services. Likewise, residents tend to incorporate selectively into their notion of neighborhood a variety of events and institutions, important as part of the neighborhood but well beyond what they saw as its boundaries. For example, the East Waterford Planning Team is seen by some as part of the neighborhood, as are hearings, committee meetings, and social activities in other parts of the city. On the other hand, many respondents restricted their perception of neighborhood to subgroups within the Johnson Square community, for example, homeowners as opposed to renters, or long-term as opposed to short-term residents. As one homeowner said of the apartment tenants:

The live here, but they aren't *really* here—you know, they don't expect to raise their children here and send them to the neighborhood schools—they just don't plan to stay here *forever*.

Likewise, residents of the apartment buildings often describe the one building in which they live as their—somewhat isolated—neighborhood. Even within these subgroups, there are still further distinctions. As one long-term resident put it:

> I have a lot of family here and I guess you could call them my neighborhood. The others in the neighborhood I just say 'Hi' to when I see them in the street.

Owners, employees, and customers of the local businesses have only the most limited identity as part of the neighborhood. Few participate in it, and they are not perceived by local residents as "part of the neighborhood."

## Social Interaction

Day-to-day relations among the neighbors of Johnson Square are polite but distant. Even among the long-term residents, the notion of what neighbor-to-neighbor contact ought to be does not suggest the highly valued, ongoing warm relationship that "neighbor" is sometimes seen as connoting. As one resident put it:

> A good neighbor is someone who keeps to himself but is there if needed. You borrow a cup of sugar [for a party] but you don't invite them to the party.

Another long-term resident commented even more forcefully:

> Yeah, I know just about everybody in the neighborhood, but they're not my friends; I guess I like to know who they are, but that's all there is to it.

## Mutual Assistance

Though residents generally do not see the Square as a place where neighbors are close friends, they do talk about interactions with their neighbors in the process of dealing with trouble. Groups of residents do emerge in response to a neighbor's request for help and take collective action when there are common problems. Typically, these groups are only temporary and dissolve after the problem has passed. Their composition is determined by the nature of the dispute, patterns of acquaintance and propinquity in the neighborhood, and the special talents of particular residents. These temporary groups seem to serve the role of what Donald Schön has called "informal coping networks... through which individuals get what they want or need in order to cope with the problematic situations in which they find themselves..." (Shön, 1977).

In Johnson Square, coping networks form most commonly when a problem calls for sharing of information or the display of group action. For example, one network often mobilized for sharing information is located in two adjacent two-family houses each owned by a long-term occupant, but also occupied by transient tenants. The four households have no particularly strong social contacts, but they turn to each other often for information or advice about legal and medical assistance, how best to get someone to quiet a barking dog, and the like. Another more transitory network formed during one particularly hot summer when a fast-food outlet allowed garbage to collect in its dumpster. Following some initial, unsuccessful exchanges between individual residents and the owner, a group of neighbors came together and in short order planned and executed a response to the owner's negligence. Taking matters into their own hands, they scattered the garbage from the dumpster into the restaurant's parking lot, and then called the health department in the morning to insist that the restaurant be closed until the garbage was cleared away.

Similarly, residents may form coping networks when a problem troubling one of them is perceived as a community issue. Petitions to city agencies are constantly being circulated, and residents feel an obligation to share information and give support to neighbors who are asking for some form of municipal service. For example, when a landlord began to evict several elderly people so that he could convert his building to condominiums, nearby neighbors organized so successful a protest that he abandoned his plans, recognizing that the residents could effectively thwart his efforts by opposing him at City Hall hearings.

## Troubles

We asked our respondents to tell us what sorts of troubles they encountered in their daily lives in the Square. Based on much of the literature about disputing (e.g., Merry, 1981c) and the expectations of the designers of the NJC reform, we had anticipated that they would report a wide range of disputes—consumer problems, intrafamilial and neighbor-to-neighbor conflicts, petty criminal complaints, and the like. In fact, residents reported few consumer disputes, and those described did not generally involve neighborhood businesses. And those interpersonal disputes that were reported to us, whether intrafamilial or neighbor-to-neighbor, were usually regarded as minor—for example, a noisy party or smoky backyard grill.[6] A few residents did describe problems that involved criminal violations, though they rarely characterized them as such or called the police to report them. For example, one woman told us that an expensive car stereo system and tape deck had been stolen from her car and that her car had been damaged during the theft. She argued that since the equipment was easy to fence, and the police were not likely to identify or capture the thieves, she did not even report the incident. She did not, she said, want to "bother worrying about it." The majority of the residents we interviewed identified as their most frequent troubles matters that were more neighborhoodwide than interpersonal. These included annoyances about parking, rent, teenagers, and, in general, relationships between Johnson Square and "outsiders." When people would talk about such neighborhood problems, they usually began with a specific incident they had experienced ("The teenager two houses away from me parked in front of my driveway"), then quickly moved on to a more general description of the issue, ("Students don't respect private property here"), and often added a story which illustrated how residents dealt with it in the Square ("I will tell you what happened to the cars that parked in front of the house where a sick neighbor lived").

Parking-related complaints are a good example of what residents see as troubles, since they are the most frequent source of irritation in the Square. As many of our respondents see it, even though individuals take up their parking spaces, the ultimate sources of their parking troubles are the business establishments at the edge of the neighborhood— among them, a restaurant (The Cabaret), fast-food franchises, and a health spa—which attract large numbers of auto-driving clients. Because parking is at a premium anyway, patrons of these establishments become a major additional pressure on what few spaces are available, and our respondents must compete with them for on-street parking. Even those with private driveways or garages are not immune to this concern, since people frequently block their drives.

In the winter, these problems are exacerbated, since each space must be wrested at great physical effort from usually uncooperative snowbanks. Because one's space represents a major investment of time and effort, local residents generally—but not universally—acknowledge that whoever digs out a space "owns" it. Thus, from a number of residents, we heard the story of Mrs. H's sick father and her efforts to keep his parking space unblocked:

> One winter we did have that problem with father's parking space being taken, because we have a large apartment building up there and all the young people who live there, of course, most of them don't own shovels but they all own cars so, of course, if you've plowed out or shoveled your spot as soon as you've left they were in it. But you know it was nothing for someone to just get behind them and give them a shove up into the snowbank.... People wouldn't think anything about giving them a little nudge....

For the transients in Johnson Square's three apartment buildings, finding a parking space that does not "belong" to someone is a constant struggle, and for some it is a major constraint on their abilities to come and go as they please.

Other troubles in Johnson Square are also seen as large scale but even more strongly linked to outsiders—whether people coming into the neighborhood, the absentee-owners of the adjacent commercial establishments, or the city itself. Disputes with individual outsiders tend to focus on juveniles. The most frequently reported problem of this kind involves the clients of a pinball parlor—Gameland—which recently opened in the Square. Many residents complained that juveniles were louging on their porches and hallways, and that they were typically engaged in loud conversation, drinking beer, smoking pot, and occasionally causing minor vandalism. Since walking through the Square could constitute a shortcut to Gameland, it is assumed by our respondents that the juveniles are Gameland customers and thus, that their dispute is with Gameland as well as with the youths.

More generally, most (but not all) of the owners of businesses like Gameland are regarded as sources of trouble. Residents reported frequent conflicts with these people about garbage storage, attempts to convert residences to commercial use, and other types of changes the merchants propose from time to time. For example, The Cabaret burned down several years ago and was rebuilt next to its old foundation. Since then, many residents, especially those living next to The Cabaret, have had a running feud with the owner, who, they maintain, has violated city laws and agreements with them about how and when to fill in and landscape the old foundation and relocate his garbage.

Finally, many local problems involve claims against government. For example, many people identified cracks in their foundations, sewers, walls, and windows as having been caused by explosives used in a recent highway construction project nearby and were irritated that no city agency would even acknowledge the validity of their claims. Many saw this problem as a breach of their entitlement to city services. Some residents even saw their troubles with outsiders coming into the neighborhood as essentially disputes with the city, since in their view the troubles occurred because the police were not "keeping peace in the Square" as they should.

## Dispute Processing Mechanisms and Modes of Choice

Without the benefit of the stories that Johnson Square residents told us about their troubles, we would have been hard pressed to envision how they might have sought relief. There are no formally mandated dispute processors near the Square (e.g., citizen complaint bureaus), and—like the woman whose car stereo had been stolen—many residents were unwilling "to bother with" taking their disputes to the police or the courts. Given the ways in which some residents frame their troubles, moreover, it is difficullt to see how any of these dispute-processing mechanisms could come to their aid. While formal—but delayed—action might be taken against people who block driveways, nothing could protect the privacy of a parking space dug out of a snowbank, nor is there any clear way to reduce the tensions between residents and the customers of the commercial establishments.

Still, local residents are far from helpless to deal with a great variety of problems. The accounts of troubles in the Square contained some common themes about how problems were addressed. First, entitlement to services remains a strong principle in the neighborhood, and this feeling includes the right to have redress for grievances. Second, self-reliance in the handling of grievances is an important theme which seems to carry with it the belief that residents should initiate and control the process of resolving disputes, though they may turn to others (including those from whom they are entitled to receive services) for assistance. Finally, there is a strong sense that there is a proper order to be followed in the pursuit of redress for troubles—moving from use of self-help to invocation of official intervention.

Taken together, these views comprise what we call self-help justice. In practice, most residents try to approach their troubles either by handling a dispute alone, by mobilizing networks of friends and neighbors, calling on city services, or in some instances turning to a "neighborhood notable," and in that order. Only a few respondents reported that they looked for recourse in the courts or the City Council. Whether residents choose direct confrontation or help from third parties depends in large on two factors; how broadly they define their troubles ("My rent has been increased by my landlord" as opposed to "Rents in older buildings are higher than those with moden facilities") and how eager they are to pursue the dispute ("I would like the landlord to clean up the back yard" as opposed to "Can I still afford the rent here?").

Self-help justice in Johnson Square most often means direct confrontation with the source of the trouble. For example, one resident would wait outside, sometimes for long periods, in order to speak to the driver of an illegally parked car. Other neighbors, troubled by noise or smoke, were quite willing to contact the person who bothered them and usually reported mutually satisfactory solutions. The degree to which residents prefer direct confrontation is probably best summarized in the comments of R. K.:

> ...I was very close to, you know, checking off cockroaches on that form from the rent control board. I would have gone through that complaint process. But it's interesting...if you had your choice, you'd rather resolve things, you know, on your own...especially where we have this relationship with the landlord. ...I mean, I could barely have gone to the rent control board, 'cause I would rather just work things out with him.

Direct confrontation can, of course, also lead to more extreme measures, including violence—either verbal or physical. Indeed, self-help also includes what we might euphemistically call one-on-one nonconfrontation. Repeated misparking (especially in the winter) can result in a can of paint sprayed over the offending car. More violent measures are rarely used, but when they have been, serious property damages or personal injury has resulted.

Mobilizing networks of neighbors is often the successful route in the case of problems which, while individual at first, have the potential to affect others. For example, when Gameland's customers "hang out" in the area, residents in the apartment buildings, in which there are several single women, form groups to confront the teenagers or to call in an older man for reinforcement. Neighbors are sought out, too, when unexplained events occur which might be evidence of trouble (e.g., the sound of glass breaking nearby). Typically, neighbors assist each other by suggesting strategies, offering ties to other people or agencies, or occasionally just being available while a dispute is going on—to provide support or credibility to the person in trouble.

When self-help assistance from neighbors fails, residents may use their links with the city. They will, for instance, call upon the police to deal with loiterers, trespassers, noisy neighbors, and misparked autos. But, it should be noted, calls to these agencies are appeals not for mediation, but for support. And when residents call on other agencies, they use their aid in unusual ways. The group who called the health department after dumping garbage in the food outlet's lot were pushing the limits of that agency's function. Similarly, residents call the building department, zoning board, and the parks department, among others, to seek irregular support, either through action or by validating their sense of grievance. For example, when one neighbor could not convince the police to tow an illegally parked car, she called the fire department who obliged her by declaring it a fire hazard (which, strictly, it was not) and ordering the police to tow it.

Over the past several years, those who turn to outside agencies do so more often, and increasingly as part of a group action in the face of a large-scale dispute. One example is the response to plans for an auto repair shop to move into the area. Fearing that it might become a junkyard, one neighbor contacted her friends, and then they as a group confronted the new owner, who agreed to meet a number of their demands. Since this incident, residents have come to rely regularly on this approach when faced with property and land use issues, and have even begun to collaborate with nearby neighborhoods around this common interest.

As group action has developed, several residents of Johnson Square have emerged as "neighborhood notables"; that is, they have become known beyond their immediate circle of friends as being experts in some aspect of disputing. Mrs. M. is recognized as a talented organizer; if neighbors need a large number of people at a meeting or signatures on a petition, they will usually turn to her. Many of them believe that Mr. T. knows the law "like a book," and he has become a source of legal information on the myriad of city regulations and ordinances.

Mr. D., a city councilor who owns a nearby drugstore, plays two distinct roles in disputes involving the neighborhood. As a politician and civic official, he represents the neighborhood's interests (even though he is elected at large) and keeps neighbors informed of actions of the council. In these functions, he fulfills his formal mandate, but residents perceive him also as a particularly effective "neighborhood notable" who acts as an informal problem solver and advocate for neighbors. Some residents see his special talent as being expertise in "how to get the city to do what it should, even if the route is not quite legal."

Only as a last resort do residents use the city council or the courts as a dispute-processing mechanism, and even then, mostly for dealing with the abutting businesses and with city agencies. Typically, they go to the council when self-help and neighborhood resources have failed and they need official action. The courts were used by only two of our respondents, and neither case involved strictly local disputes.

## Summary and Conclusions

While Johnson Square is in many ways not the sort of neighborhood that NJC reformers had envisioned, it is clear that it does provide a social structure sufficiently strong to be influential in how residents experience and conduct disputes. Troubles and the disputing process exist in the larger context of neighborhood life, and many of their aspects can be understood in terms of the residents' ongoing relationships, their attitudes and values about disputing, and the collective history of the emergence and settling of disputes in the neighborhood.

The relationship between particular troubles and the social life of the Square occurs at both an individual and a collective level. For the individual with a dispute, the coping networks, besides offering support, shape the process by which a dispute will be conducted. For example, seeking advice on what to do about a blocked driveway, the resident is guided toward shaping the problem in terms that coincide with those that other neighbors have used. Similarly, the networks shape and reinforce a common sense of what is "worth the bother" and thus sufficient to be seen as trouble. Finally, the repeated appearance of a few stories (such as the response to the auto body shop) in our interviews suggests that these stories may act as a way for the networks in the Square to convey to newcomers how to respond to troubles.

Seen at the collective level, we believe that the networks may form a learning system. As troubles occur, groups of neighbors seem to gain new perspectives on how disputing can and should be conducted. For some residents each encounter seems to be handled more effectively than previous disputes. The community seems also to be becoming more differentiated, with particular individuals specializing in particular skills useful to dispute processing. And, to an extent, neighbors are becoming aware of the collective nature of their disputes and the effectiveness of group action to deal with them.

Despite what we see as important differences between Johnson Square and the type of neighborhood envisioned by proponents of NJCs, we do not conclude that there is no market at all for public intervention of this sort. In particular, it is clear that, if the NJC concept could be modified to fit the patterns of disputing and the values of the residents, there are active groups of people for whom it might represent an improvement in the nonjudicial processing of disputes. For example, it is clear that many residents do seek and value help with issues involving neighborhood change. They realize the need for collective action and particularly advice and information from specialized sources. An NJC which could fill this need would probably attract support, but even in this role, its effectiveness would be dependent on its ability to link with the existing structure of coping networks, in effect building on the strengths of the present system.

## Notes

1. Certainly, there are several kinds of studies which have influenced the many people who have participated in the planning of the NJCs. In particular, studies of mediation and similar informal dispute-processing mechanisms overseas have been influential—studies of *gasthaus* negotiation in Bavaria and systems of regaining lost sheep in Sardinia, for example, have been cited in the works of people seeking to develop the NJC movement (Nader and Todd, 1978). Similar studies of American experience with early examples of the NJC-style institutions have been useful (McGillis and Mullen, 1978).

2. Rowe (1980) describes her success in building organizational grievance mechanisms by locating and formalizing the existing networks of people who were already serving this purpose; the analogy to neighborhood settings seems powerful.

3. For us, "trouble" encompasses grievances, conflicts, disputes, discomforts, and so on. At this point we are not trying to distinguish among stages of disputing or extent of disagreements but merely to see what our respondents perceive as "trouble."

4. The research we are conducting looks at disputing in four "neighborhoods" (of a very small scale—say 100 households); this chapter discusses in detail the findings in one of those communities. Needless to say, the location and some identifying features of the neighborhood have been altered to preserve the anonymity of our respondents; the general features and specific descriptions of disputes and dispute processing are, however, accurate.

5. We began by interviewing residents to determine how they saw their neighborhood, both in general and with respect to disputes they had or could recall. In effect, we were recording "trouble cases" (Llewellen and Hoebel, 1941), asking our respondents to tell us about the relationships between troubles

they had encountered, whatever dispute-processing mechanisms they perceived as available, and Johnson Square. To date we have extensive interviews with 32 of the less than 100 households in the Square (better than 90 percent of those contacted). As often as possible we supported these interviews with participant observation in the community, by collecting descriptive and historical accounts of the·Square, and by discussions with others who know the community well.

6. While we have no reason in particular to mistrust our data, it is true that interpersonal disputes are difficult to elicit, and it is possible that they are there but unobservable by us. Our belief, though, is that unless such disputes become relatively public (e.g., because someone called the police to complain about noise or attempted to intervene personally), they are also unlikely to become a part of an NJCs caseload, for many of the same reasons that they are not reported to us.

# 6

# The Neighborhood Justice Centers Field Test[*]

**Janice A. Roehl and Royer F. Cook***

In the past decade, a number of programs designed as alternatives to courts for resolving minor disputes have emerged. In 1977, three such programs—known as Neighborhood Justice Centers (NJCs)—were created by the U.S. Department of Justice. They substituted mediation for adjudication as the means for resolving minor disputes between persons with ongoing relationships. These three centers are located in Atlanta, Kansas City, and Los Angeles. The Institute for Social Analysis, a private research organization, was asked to conduct an evaluation of these three centers in order to assess their impact on the disputants, the community, and the court system. This chapter draws on this evaluation. (For additional information the reader is referred to the interim and final reports of the project by Sheppard, Roehl, and Cook, 1979; and. Cook, Roehl, and Sheppard, 1980).

Dispute resolution programs have different, and at times opposing, goals; operate under a variety of sponsors, structures, and sociocultural environments; adhere to differing philosophies; are operated by staff with varying skills and experience; and process a wide variety of cases from many different referral sources. While no single program can be regarded as typical, the three NJCs are more or less representative of the various types of programs that have been created in recent years. There are also salient differences among these three centers, the most significant of which are their relationship with the criminal justice system and the community and their source of referrals. The Centers also had a healthy diversity of sponsorship, board involvement, and management style. Thus, while one can speak of the neighborhood justice movement

---

[*] This chapter was prepared especially for this volume. All references in the test of this chapter are found in the bibliography at the conclusion of this volume.

as a whole, it is important to recognize that different programs possess distinct purposes and processes.

The three original NJCs represent different models and lend themselves to a discussion of issues which continue to be debated by proponents and detractors of the neighborhood justice movement. One issue is whether an NJC should serve the criminal justice system or the community, and what such "service" should entail. Others deal with the role and background of mediators, communication between the parties, the mediator's ability to get at the underlying causes of a dispute, the effectiveness of mediation in reducing recidivism, and the appropriateness of different types of issues for mediation. Finally, a continuing concern of observers of the NJC movement is the degree to which mediation improves access to and enhances the quality of justice for participants.

This chapter describes the NJCs and then presents evidence on the appropriateness and effectiveness of mediation. While our observations are limited to the three Department of Justice NJCs, this experience also serves as a base for exploring the broader issues mentioned above.

## Goals of the Neighborhood Justice Centers Field Test

The purpose of the NJC Field Test evaluation was to study and assess the implementation, operations, and impact of the three experimental centers, as a way of providing information for developing future NJCs. To this end, the goals and objectives of the Field Test were identified and weighted by Department of Justice officials and NJC project directors themselves. Then evaluation resources were allocated to measure NJC progress toward each of these goals in proportion to their weighted importance.

Two goals were identified as most important through this initial procedure: the central concern was whether NJCs could provide relatively inexpensive, expeditious, and fair resolution of disputes, while at the same time enhancing the quality of justice delivered to the community. Operationally this was interpreted to mean that the Centers should be utilized by a cross section of the community; cost and speed of resolution should compare favorably to existing adjudication processes; resolutions of disputes should be fair, long lasting, and satisfactory; and the Centers should have a beneficial impact on the ability of the formal justice system to handle its workload. A second major concern was whether the Centers could attract civil and criminal dispute cases from a variety of sources within the community and criminal justice system. More specifically, program sponsors wanted to know whether NJCs could effectively handle various types of interpersonal disputes, including landlord-tenant disputes and consumer complaints as well as disputes both initiated by citizens themselves and referred from the justice system and social service agencies. The overriding concern here was to determine which types of issues, disputants, and referral sources are most appropriate for NJC mediation.

Project sponsors also identified four sets of secondary goals: (1) key elements of the community should have a positive view of the NJCs, (2) the NJCs should contribute to the reduction of tension and conflict in their communities, (3) the NJCs should be institutionalized in their communities, and (4) the evaluation of the NJCs should provide information to the National Institute of Justice that would be helpful to future planning.

## The Neighborhood Justice Centers

This chapter briefly describes the structure and functioning of the NJCs and then reports our findings on the two major and four secondary concerns of the program sponsors.

The Neighborhood Justice Centers in Atlanta, Kansas City, and Los Angeles were each provided with guidelines developed by the Department of Justice's Law Enforcement Assistance Administration, National Institute of Justice, and Office for Improvements in the Administration of Justice. As a result, the NJCs had certain characteristics in common, particularly the ways in which they were organized and staffed and the methods by which they resolved disputes. However, in keeping with the experimental nature of the Field Test, the NJCs had a healthy diversity in philosophy, sponsorship, case source and type, supervisory board structure and responsibility, and management style.

During their first two years the Centers each had an annual budget of approximately $135,000 and similar operating structures. Each NJC maintained a full-time staff of five or six, who were organized as follows: a Project Director with overall responsibility for the management and operation of the Center; a Deputy Director, typically in charge of scheduling mediations, contacting mediators, and coordinating other services such as follow-up and outreach; two or three intake workers responsible for all casework; and one or two secretaries. The daily operations of the NJCs—conducting intakes, contacting responding parties, scheduling hearings, conducting mediations and conciliations, and so forth—were basically the same for each Center.

The primary differences of the NJCs were referral procedures and the ways in which casework was handled (such as how respondents were contacted and encouraged to participate in mediation).

Each Center recruited community representatives as mediators. These mediators varied in age and ethnicity, and included students, retired professionals, homemakers, lawyers, social workers, and clerks, although they were overrepresented by people in the helping professions and those without full-time employment, and underrepresented by blue-collar workers and business professionals.

Initially mediators were trained by staff of the Institute for Mediation and Conflict Resolution (IMCR) [Editors' note: see Felstiner and Williams, included in this volume, pp. 111–153, for a discussion of the possible limitations of this approach], the American Arbitration Association (AAA), or local organizations, which followed IMCR's training approach. Later, NJC staffs developed their own training packages.

A typical NJC hearing proceeded as follows: the mediator made an opening statement to explain the mediator's role and describe the mediation process. Each disputant was asked to tell his or her side of the dispute without interruption, followed by clarifying questions by the mediator. The hearing would then continue as a joint session, with the issues discussed by both parties and mediator, or as a series of individual meetings in which the mediator would shuttle back and forth between the two parties. However organized, the job of the mediator was to gather facts and review issues in an attempt to move the parties to-

TABLE 6.1   NJC Caseloads from March 1978 to May 1979

| | Atlanta<br>Total = 2351 | | Kansas City<br>Total = 845 | | Venice/Mar<br>Vista<br>Total = 751 | |
|---|---|---|---|---|---|---|
| Disposition | *Percent* | | *Percent* | | *Percent* | |
| Mediation hearings held | 811 | 35* | 331 | 40 | 231 | 31 |
| Percent with agreements | 81% | | 95% | | 67% | |
| Resolved without a hearing | 381 | 16 | 153 | 18 | 106 | 14 |
| Remained unresolved, no hearing | 1146 | 49 | 350 | 42 | 402 | 54 |
| Referral Sources | | | | | | |
| Judges | 530 | 23 | 104 | 13 | 111 | 15 |
| Court clerks or prosecutors | 1039 | 44 | 270 | 32 | 83 | 11 |
| Police | 35 | 2 | 191 | 23 | 56 | 8 |
| Community agencies | 87 | 4 | 48 | 6 | 47 | 6 |
| Self-initiated | 200 | 9 | 101 | 12 | 378 | 51 |
| Legal aid | 133 | 6 | 35 | 4 | 26 | 4 |
| Government agencies | 175 | 8 | 49 | 6 | 17 | 2 |
| Others | 139 | 6 | 36 | 4 | 21 | 3 |
| Types of Cases | | | | | | |
| Domestic assault/harassment | 213 | 9 | 105 | 13 | 7 | 1 |
| Domestic settlement | 146 | 6 | 62 | 7 | 70 | 9 |
| Family dispute | 119 | 5 | 62 | 7 | 16 | 2 |
| Neighbors assault/harassment | 118 | 5 | 181 | 22 | 8 | 1 |
| Neighborhood nuisance | 90 | 4 | 121 | 14 | 70 | 9 |
| Disputes between friends | 278 | 12 | 86 | 10 | 34 | 5 |
| Landlord-tenant | 380 | 16 | 100 | 12 | 192 | 26 |
| Consumer-merchant | 553 | 24 | 61 | 7 | 226 | 31 |
| Employee-employer | 309 | 13 | 18 | 2 | 38 | 5 |
| Other | 129 | 6 | 45 | 5 | 87 | 12 |

* Cases with missing data on disposition, source, or type were excluded when computing percentages; information was missing from 1–2 percent of the cases.

ward an agreement. In a final joint session, if some resolution was reached, a written agreement was signed by both parties and witnessed by the mediator. Alternatively, the mediator might announce that no agreement could be reached and terminate the process. Of course, there were considerable variations in this process, depending on the type of case and parties and the individual style of the mediator. Some mediators, for instance, would actively question and lecture participants, while others would consciously refrain from such activities.

The original design for the NJCs required that each Center should conform to the needs and circumstances of the community it would serve. Thus, each local sponsor was given considerable leeway in structuring its program. The result was that each of the three programs was quite different from each other in terms of sponsorship, organization, and management. This in turn, affected their philosophies, referral systems, and size and nature of the caseload. Table 6.1 illustrates some of the consequences of these differences, as they pertain to the types of issues handled by the NJCs.

## Atlanta

The Atlanta NJC was a private, unaffiliated program, operating under the guidance of a Board of Directors composed of court officials, attorneys, and representatives from the police department and community agencies, and chaired by a popular local judge. This board, created specifically as a nonprofit organization to sponsor the NJC, remained very active in the Center's affairs and was instrumental in establishing its relationships with the courts.

Nearly half of all this NJC's cases were referred by court clerks in the State Court of Fulton County, the court which handles petty criminal and civil cases. Close to a quarter of its cases were referred by judges in the courts, usually at bindover hearings, the first step in processing criminal cases in the State Court. The remaining cases came from a variety of sources, including self-referrals, other government agencies, legal aid organizations, community service agencies, and the police. Cases were received from court clerks and by intake workers (volunteers, student interns, mediators, and staff members) who were stationed in the court's filing room. Primarily because of the large number of referrals from the civil warrants division, over one half of the NJC cases were disputes between landlords and tenants, consumers and merchants, and employees and employers. Interpersonal disputes between persons with a prior relationship (couples, neighbors, friends, families) made up approximately 40 percent of the cases.

The Atlanta NJC quickly came to handle between 150 and 200 cases each month. On average, 55 were mediated (with an agreement rate of 81 percent) and 25 were resolved through a conciliation process. Thus it was able to reach agreement about half the time. The Atlanta Center did not use arbitration, but occasionally it did refer cases to other agencies for assistance.

## Kansas City

The Kansas City NJC opened in 1977, as a program of the city's Community Services Department. Policy was officially formulated by the NJC project director, officials of the Community Services Department, and the city manager's office. Additional support and guidance were obtained from the NJC Advisory Board which included representatives of various community groups and city agencies. The Kansas City NJC was built on an earlier dispute resolution program which had briefly been operated by the Kansas City police department, and the NJC project director and several mediators had held similar positions in this earlier program. Furthermore, the Center continued to focus on the target area and referral relationships with the prosecutor's office and police department developed by the earlier program.

In sharp contrast to Atlanta, two-thirds of the cases in Kansas City involved criminal issues which were referred by (in order of frequency) the prosecutor's office, police department, and judges. Other sources of cases included (in order of frequency) the community (agencies made referrals and individuals came in on their own), government agencies, and legal aid organizations. Cases from the court came primarily from a staff member stationed in the prosecutor's office, and police referrals came from police officers themselves (many Kansas City officers had received information about the program), and a half-time police liaison specialist on the NJC staff. As a result of this work, the police increasingly became a source of referrals to the NJC.

Over 70 percent of the NJC cases involved disputes between couples, relatives, neighbors, and friends. The remainder involved a variety of civil issues, primarily landlord-tenant and consumer-merchant disputes.

During the 15 months of data collection of our Field Test, the Kansas City NJC handled an average of 60 cases each month. Approximately 22 were successfully mediated and 10 more were resolved without a hearing. A handful (8 percent overall) went to arbitration, and occasionally the Center would refer cases to another agency.

## Los Angeles (*Venice/Mar Vista*)

The Venice/Mar Vista NJC was sponsored by the Los Angeles County Bar Association, and its work was directed by a board composed of Bar Association officers and community and public agency representatives. In contrast to the criminal justice orientation in both Atlanta and Kansas City, the Venice/Mar Vista NJC was orientated to receive voluntary referrals from the community itself. To this end its staff engaged in an aggressive outreach campaign by making a great many presentations to local community groups, undertaking an extensive media campaign, and distributing literature in shopping malls, beach areas, and at meetings of community groups.

This effort, and particularly the media campaign, yielded results. Over 50 percent of the cases were brought by individuals on their own initiative, and other cases came from local community, legal aid, and government agencies. Only one-third of the cases were referred by court personnel or the police.

Nearly all the Venice/Mar Vista NJC cases were small claims disputes; over one-half involved landlord-tenant or consumer-merchant disputes. Even those of a criminal nature usually involved disagreements over money, property settlements, and other civil matters.

The NJC handled approximately 50 cases each month, on average successfully mediating 16 and conciliating 7. Because the Center relied so heavily on self-referral, not surprisingly it ended up referring a relatively large number of disputants to other agencies. In fact, because of its aggresive media outreach, it became something of a referral center for telephone callers as well.

## The Mediation Process: Case Characteristics and Individual Impact

The most important conclusion of our evaluation of these three Neighborhood Justice Centers is that *mediation can work*. The evidence we gathered showed that mediation is an effective and satisfactory method for resolving many types of minor disputes. During our two-year study, almost 4,000 varied cases from diverse sources were handled effectively by the Centers, and successful resolutions were reached in nearly half of them. Moreover, follow-up interviews six months later indicated that a substantial majority of disputants were satisfied with this alternative and were holding to the terms of their agreements. Furthermore, we found that mediation is more satisfactory to disputants and at least as effective in resolving disputes in the long term as court proceedings, and that the NJCs can resolve disputes much faster and at less cost than courts. Thus, with respect to their central goals, the NJCs were successful. This is not to say that they are flawless nor that mediation is useful for all minor disputes. However, it does strongly suggest this type of informal process has the potential for serving as a successful alternative to the courts. The bases for these conclusions are reported below.

### NJC Cases: *Number, Type, Source, and Disposition*

The Neighborhood Justice Centers collectively demonstrated that they could attract and process a sizable number of cases. During their first 15

TABLE 6.2   All NJCs Case Disposition by Referral Source

| | Judges (Bench Referrals) | Prosecuting Officer or Civil/Criminal Warrants Desks | Police | Community Agencies | Self | Legal Aid Organizations | Government Agencies | Others | Total |
|---|---|---|---|---|---|---|---|---|---|
| Cases with hearings, resolved (percentage) | 515 (69) | 279 (20) | 94 (33) | 33 (18) | 99 (15) | 29 (15) | 29 (12) | 46 (24) | 1124 (28.7) |
| Cases with hearings, unresolved (percentage) | 95 (13) | 68 (5) | 8 (3) | 7 (4) | 32 (5) | 18 (9) | 4 (2) | 17 (9) | 249 (6.4) |
| Cases resolved without a hearing (percentage) | 15 (2) | 260 (19) | 33 (12) | 34 (19) | 147 (22) | 39 (20) | 76 (32) | 36 (18) | 640 (16.4) |
| Cases unresolved, no hearing (no-shows, withdrawals) (percentage) | 89 (12) | 226 (16) | 48 (17) | 37 (20) | 106 (16) | 35 (18) | 42 (17) | 29 (15) | 612 (15.6) |
| Cases unresolved, no hearing (respondent refusals and no contacts) (percentage) | 31 (4) | 559 (40) | 99 (35) | 71 (39) | 295 (43) | 73 (38) | 90 (37) | 68 (35) | 1286 (32.9) |
| Total (Percentage) | 745 (19) | 1392 (35.6) | 282 (7.2) | 182 (4.7) | 679 (17.4) | 194 (5) | 241 (6.2) | 196 (5) | 3911 (100)* |

* Data missing on 36 cases.

TABLE 6.3  All NJCs Case Disposition by Type of Case

| | | | | | | | | | | | Total |
|---|---|---|---|---|---|---|---|---|---|---|---|
| Cases with hearings, resolved (percentage) | 181 (56) | 111 (40) | 88 (45) | 147 (48) | 86 (31) | 69 (43) | 77 (12) | 152 (18) | 31 (9) | 80 (31) | 1122 (28.6) |
| Cases with hearings, unresolved (percentage) | 20 (6) | 26 (9) | 12 (6) | 8 (3) | 18 (6) | 20 (5) | 25 (4) | 77 (9) | 19 (5) | 22 (8) | 247 (6.3) |
| Cases resolved without a hearing (percentage) | 23 (7) | 18 (7) | 16 (8) | 32 (10) | 47 (17) | 40 (10) | 176 (26) | 185 (22) | 87 (24) | 23 (9) | 647 (16.5) |
| Cases unresolved, no hearing (no-shows, withdrawals) (percentage) | 57 (18) | 57 (21) | 36 (18) | 38 (12) | 38 (14) | 80 (20) | 115 (17) | 103 (12) | 56 (15) | 35 (13) | 615 (15.7) |
| Cases unresolved, no hearing (respondent refusals and no contacts) (percentage) | 44 (14) | 66 (24) | 45 (23) | 82 (27) | 92 (33) | 89 (22) | 279 (42) | 323 (39) | 172 (47) | 101 (39) | 1293 (33) |
| Total (percentage) | 325 (8.3) | 278 (7.1) | 197 (5) | 307 (7.8) | 281 (7.2) | 398 (10.1) | 672 (17.1) | 840 (21.4) | 365 (9.3) | 261 (6.7) | 3924 (100)* |

* Data missing on 23 cases.

months, the Centers handled nearly 4,000 cases. Over a third of them reached a mediation hearing, and of these 82 percent resulted in a mutual agreement. Nearly one-fifth (17 percent) of all referred cases were resolved without a hearing taking place, usually through conciliation facilitated by the NJC. The primary reason for those unresolved cases was respondent refusal to participate after being contacted by the NJC.

Tables 6.2 and 6.3 provide a breakdown on NJC caseloads and report on the relationships between case disposition and referral source, and disposition and type of case. Reported here for the three NJCs as a group, similar patterns were found in each of the NJCs individually.

As a group, the majority of cases (62 percent) were referred from the criminal-civil justice system—from judges, court clerks, public attorneys, other court officials, and police officers. Over one-third of the NJC cases were self-initiated by individuals or referred by a variety of community, private, and government organizations. Self-initiated cases represented the largest source of cases outside the justice system, and half of these self-referrals learned of the NJCs through the media. One-quarter of the people first learned of the Centers by word of mouth or through family or friends, and still others were referred by a variety of local government, consumer and housing agencies, legal aid organizations, lawyer referral services, private attorneys, and the like.

The NJC cases were fairly evenly divided between interpersonal criminal disputes (45 percent), involving family members or other close relationships, and civil disputes (55 percent) between tenants and landlords, consumers and merchants, and employees and employers.

On the whole this reveals that informal dispute resolution centers can readily handle a variety of cases from a great many different sources. This conclusion is reinforced by caseload data from a recent study of alternative dispute settlement projects in Florida (Dispute Resolution Alternatives Committee, 1979), which found a similar diversity of issues and referral sources, and as well found a relatively high level of resolution (54 percent compared to 45 percent for the NJCs).

NJCs also fared well on the expeditious handling of cases. Hearings were typically held within one to two weeks of first contact, were scheduled within a day or two where necessary, and averaged two hours. The costs of handling these cases was equally as impressive, although here the cost per case varied dramatically in relation to caseload. In the Atlanta Center the average cost was $62 per case referred and $142 per case resolved, while in Los Angeles the figures were $202 and $589 respectively. While direct comparisons to court costs are impossible, available evidence (Felstiner and Williams, 1980; Hoff, 1974) indicates that the NJCs may become competitive with courts as their caseloads grow.

The characteristics of the disputants varied among the three NJCs, reflecting the different demographic compositions of the three cities.

The disputants reflected the racial composition of the communities which the NJCs served, but the Centers attracted a disproportionate number of lower-income people. Nearly half of the respondents in the Atlanta and Venice/Mar Vista NJCs were business people, usually owners of a small concern. These corporate representatives tended to have fairly high incomes and were almost always respondents, not complainants. A large proportion of cases in the NJCs were initiated by female complainants, who typically were involved in domestic conflicts. While these NJC disputant characteristics may revive concerns that the Centers offer "second-class justice" to powerless citizens (Hofrichter, 1977; Nejelski, 1980), it can also be argued that the NJCs provide an avenue for those who have had little or no access to justice institutions in the past (Cook et al., 1980; Singer, 1979a).

## Relationships Among Case Type, Source and Disposition

All three Centers experienced similar trends in the relationships among the source, type, and disposition of cases. Generally, interpersonal disputes were referred by criminal court officials and law enforcement officers, while civil cases were self-initiated or referred by small claims courts and community agencies. Most self-initiated cases involved complaints about money or property. Citizens do not bring other types of interpersonal problems to NJCs on their own. For instance, there were few self-initiated cases involving minor assault or harassment. Evidently people continue to turn to the courts or other social service agencies, avoid the issue, or deal with it themselves. Our hypothesis is that these types of interpersonal cases are not self-initiated at the Centers because of a lack of understanding and acceptance of the process, and not because of some inherent limits of mediation. Others, however, cite lack of coercion as a reason (Felstiner and Williams, 1980).

Referral source and type of case are both related to type of disposition. Source of referral had a strong effect on whether a case was mediated or not ($X^2 = 928$, p < .001). Judge-referred cases had a high mediation rate of 82 percent, while only 14–36 percent of the cases from other sources were mediated. Interpersonal disputes were more likely to reach a hearing ($X^2 = 310$, p < .001) than civil cases, and as well were more apt to be resolved ($X^2 = 97$, p < .001) by mediation or conciliation. Over half the interpersonal criminal cases were either mediated or resolved prior to a hearing (resulting in the resolution of 54 percent of all such cases), while only 38 percent of the civil cases either reached a hearing or were resolved prior to a hearing.

Interpersonal cases involving an ongoing relationship were more likely to reach a hearing than consumer complaints. This is probably due to the fact that interpersonal cases were usually referred by criminal justice officials, whose "referrals" are often perceived as coercion, a dimension that is lacking in most other types of referrals. Felstiner and Williams (1980) also suggest that for interpersonal disputes which might be of a continuing and damaging nature, there is often a greater sense of urgency to resolve the dispute. At hearing, interpersonal criminal cases are also more apt to result in an agreement (81–95 percent) than civil consumer cases (62–78 percent). The higher rate here is probably due in large to the fact that, unlike some issues, here there is substantial opportunity for compromise (which may be the most important aspect of mediation compared to winner-take-all adjudication). In contrast, consumer disputes often involve only one issue—money. Hence, the major problem is that respondents, and particularly corporate respondents, refuse to participate. Apparently landlords, merchants, employers, and the like feel little need to search for compromise. Intake and follow-up interviews support this interpretation; many respondents felt they could "win" by doing nothing, either because the complainant would eventually drop the issue or, if not, that a court would hold in their favor. Follow-up on unresolved cases revealed that only 40 percent of the complainants pursued other avenues if the NJC effort failed.

Informal coercion has long concerned those who feel NJCs may unwittingly compromise individual rights of participants (Snyder, 1978; Hofrichter, 1977). However, this is not in fact a critical problem. While informal coercion of official referral agents clearly operates, it is strongest in judge-referred cases and in arbitration, where proceeedings are formal. For the most part, the NJC staffs were conscientious in explaining that the mediation process was voluntary. Still, to a certain extent, NJC staff members did use strong persuasion in trying to convince respondents to participate, and it is difficult to envision an NJC which completely eschews all such forms of subtle coercion. (The San Francisco Community Board, which only mediates about 100 cases a year and does not receive justice system referrals, may be such a program).

## Impact on Disputes and Disputants

A major function of our evaluation was to explore the aftermath of the resolution process, to determine if it was satisfying to the disputants and resulted in lasting resolutions. To this end we conducted follow-up interviews with 1,642 disputants in over 1,300 cases, approximately six months after contact with the NJC. While recognizing the limitations of self-reported information, nevertheless we believe that disputants' perceptions of fairness and effectiveness of the mediation process are in themselves important measures of program impact. Here our interviews indicate overwhelming support for the NJCs. Respondents revealed that a high proportion of the agreements mediated or conciliated by the NJCs were still holding six months later and that most disputants reported having no more problems with the other party. Similarly, the vast majority of those we interviewed expressed satisfaction with the mediation process, mediator, and overall experience at the NJC. Most indicated they would return to the Center with a similar problem (see Tables 6.4 and 6.5).

The Atlanta NJC had the highest proportion of satisfied participants in mediated cases and the highest rate of stable agreements, while Kan-

TABLE 6.4 Disputant Satisfaction for Mediated Cases

| | | Disputant | | |
| --- | --- | --- | --- | --- |
| Index/Response | | Complainant (percent) | Respondent (percent) | Total |
| Satisfied with overall | Yes | 428 (88) | 347 (88) | 775 |
| experience at NJC? | No | 43 (9) | 30 (8) | 73 |
| | Somewhat | 18 (4) | 17 (4) | 35 |
| Satisfied with mediation | Yes | 414 (84) | 335 (89) | 749 |
| process? | No | 61 (12) | 41 (10) | 102 |
| | Somewhat | 15 (3) | 21 (5) | 36 |
| Satisfied with mediator? | Yes | 432 (88) | 348 (88) | 780 |
| | No | 39 (8) | 26 (7) | 65 |
| | Somewhat | 19 (4) | 21 (5) | 40 |
| Satisfied with terms of | Yes | 335 (80) | 296 (83) | 631 |
| agreement? | No | 65 (15) | 45 (13) | 110 |
| | Somewhat | 20 (5) | 17 (5) | 37 |

TABLE 6.5 Stability of the Agreement for Mediated Cases

| | | Disputant | | |
| --- | --- | --- | --- | --- |
| Index/Response | | Complainant (percent) | Respondent (percent) | Total |
| Have you kept all terms of | Yes | 316 (79) | 303 (87) | 619 |
| the agreement? | No | 9 (2) | 20 (6) | 29 |
| | Partially | 14 (3) | 21 (6) | 35 |
| | No terms | 63 (16) | 7 (2) | 70 |
| Has other party kept all | Yes | 287 (69) | 236 (67) | 523 |
| terms of the agreement? | No | 77 (18) | 47 (13) | 124 |
| | Partially | 49 (12) | 24 (7) | 73 |
| | No terms | 8 (2) | 47 (13) | 55 |
| Any more problems with | Yes | 135 (28) | 87 (22) | 222 |
| other party? | No | 341 (72) | 307 (78) | 648 |
| Where would you go in | NJC | 346 (72) | 285 (73) | 631 |
| future with a similar | Court | 79 (16) | 45 (12) | 124 |
| problem? | Attorney | 20 (4) | 17 (4) | 37 |
| | Nowhere | 15 (3) | 22 (6) | 37 |
| | Other | 20 (4) | 19 (5) | 39 |

sas City had the highest proportion of dissatisfied disputants and Los Angeles the lowest rate of agreement maintenance. Although these differences are significant, it should be noted that the vast majority of disputants interviewed in all three cities were satisfied and reported that their agreements were holding six months after disposition.

As a basis for comparison, we tracked a small sample of cases similar to those handled by the NJCs through the court system and then interviewed these disputants regarding their experiences. While the comparison is not perfect (only 66 complainants in the court cases were interviewed), the differences are nevertheless suggestive. While we found no substantial differences in the rates of reported dispute resolution between NJC and court complainants, we found dramatic differences in terms of reported satisfaction. NJC disputants were consistently more satisfied with the agreement, mediation process, and mediator than court complainants were with the verdict, court process, and judge. These findings on NJC resolution effectiveness parallel results from studies of other similar dispute resolution programs around the nation (Felstiner and Williams, 1980; Davis, Tichane, and Grayson, 1979; Dispute Resolution Alternatives Committee, 1979).

Although mediation was the primary resolution technique utilized by the NJCs, over one-third of all resolved cases were resolved prior to a hearing, suggesting that the NJCs also provide valuable services outside the hearing room. As a consequence, we collected follow-up data on these cases as well. Here too we found that such resolutions are effective. Interviewees reported satisfactory solutions, few further problems, and similar high levels of satisfaction with the NJCs. Clients of the Venice/Mar Vista Center had the highest rate of satisfaction, reflecting the greater time and effort the NJC staff spent on its far fewer cases.

Unresolved cases were also followed up and serve as a rough comparison group for mediated cases. The results contrast sharply with the mediated cases. Sixty percent of the complainants reported that their disputes remained unresolved, and the same percentage revealed that they had not sought additional assistance. However, most disputants reported that they were not having any more problems with the other party, although it is impossible to say whether this means continuing or additional problems beyond the precipitating one. However, in spite of the unresolved status of their cases, a large majority of both complainants and respondents reported satisfaction with the NJC, and 70 percent of the complainants said they would return to the NJC in event of a future dispute.

Overall these follow-up data indicate that from the disputants' points-of-view, the NJC mediation process is a satisfying and effective alternative to the courts. This conclusion is reinforced by the experience of the NJCs, each of which operated successfully despite differing locations, types of programs, and philosophies. These differences also shed some important light on the types of cases least and most likely to be handled by NJC-like programs. Interpersonal criminal disputes between couples and prior acquaintances appear to fare less well in the long term than do the civil consumer disputes. Disputants in interpersonal criminal cases are less likely to be satisfied with the NJC process, largely because they are more likely to continue to have problems with the other party after the hearing. This suggests the need for more detailed case classification and screening procedures, which match forum and issue more carefully, as well as more services in complex cases. For instance, in criminal cases, mediation programs may need to schedule more than one hearing and provide follow-up to insure that prescribed social service conditions, such as alcohol treatment or marital counseling, are complied with.

## Why does Mediation Work?

NJCs are effective. The question is, why? Our research suggests several answers. First, the nature of the issue and the process are important. Most resolved cases were not complex or deeply rooted and dealt with issues capable of resolution through compromise. In such cases, skilled third parties who treated disputes and disputants with care and respect and maintained control over the process were greatly appreciated by complainants and respondents alike. One advantage here is that in sharp contrast to most courts, disputants have an opportunity to state their stories in their own words and style and, in turn, listen to the other's version, a process which in itself participants find valuable.

A second set of factors had to do with the structure of the NJCs. NJC staff and mediators reflected the race, age, and occupations of the communities in which they were located, and they were often matched for particular cases (e.g., mediators were assigned to disputants of the same race, or both a male and female mediator are assigned in cases involving a domestic problem). Apparently these practices encouraged confidence and reduced the "distance" some people experienced in the courts. Also, the process and outcome of mediation was largely within the control of the disputants themselves, at all points, participation was voluntary and a disputant could stop or question the proceedings if desired. This control over the process and outcome was viewed positively by disputants.

## Conclusions: Implications of the NJCs

The NJCs are successful in pursuing their two major goals of providing inexpensive, expeditious, and fair resolution of disputes and attracting both civil and criminal cases from several types of referral sources. How then do they fare on their other goals of likelihood of achieving some beneficial impact on the justice system, permanent institutionalization, and community service? In this concluding section, we examine these NJC experiences in light of these concerns, and speculate on the future of similar such programs.

Impact on the justice system is, of course, a function of the number and types of cases referred to the Centers and the stages at which they are sent. Of the 4,000 cases handled by the three centers during the period of our research, only 745 were actually referred to the NJCs by a judge. Cases referred by other justice system officials were diverted before officially entering the system, and, of course, a great many cases were not referred by police or court officials at all. These referral patterns shed light on two important concerns, one dealing with reduction of delay and the other with reduction of congestion. Neither concern can be answered by our study, but our results are suggestive. Although it is conceivable that the NJCs might help in reducing backlogs and court delays, they are not now large enough to affect caseloads in courts significantly. Even in Atlanta, where the NJC had a sizable caseload and received a majority of its cases from the courts, it handled at best only one-fiftieth of the number of cases handled by the local lower trial courts, too few to make any appreciable impact.

A second concern was whether the NJCs would handle cases that otherwise would be dismissed or withdrawn prior to trial or would be real alternatives to adjudication. Here the picture is mixed. Both types of cases are handled by the Centers. Further, we found that even when the NJCs handled cases that might have dropped out, there are nevertheless some important benefits. These cases still require time and attention from intake clerks and public attorneys which is avoided when they are referred to the NJCs. Also, judges and court officials we interviewed in Kansas City and Atlanta were unanimous in their belief that the NJCs facilitated their work. By occasionally referring time-consuming cases to the NJCs, they reported that they were freed to devote more attention to the remaining cases. Mediation may also serve a preventive function by providing a remedy for the cases which typically drop out of the system but which are still effectively handled by third-party intervention.

The time NJCs take to handle their cases compares more than favorably with the courts. Courts in Kansas City and Atlanta take five to ten times longer to dispose of similar types of cases than the NJCs. Costs per NJC-resolved cases compare favorably to court system costs in Atlanta, and if the Centers become better known and utilized, their costs will decrease still further. And follow-up data indicate that the NJCs are at least as effective as the courts in resolving disputes on a long-term basis, and that disputants find mediation more humanistic, fair, and personalized than courts. In short, NJCs have the *potential* for easing the burden of the court system and offering an attractive resolution process to citizens. However, in order to have substantial impact on the court system, they must handle more cases.

## Serving the Community

NJCs were also designed to enhance local self-help in a defined community. Here they were not particularly successful. The Atlanta and Kansas City Centers rejected this idea from the outset and obtained cases from agencies which served the entire city. Only the Venice/Mar Vista NJC explicitly kept its community orientation and concentrated its outreach activities in the Venice and Mar Vista neighborhoods, although even then it did not restrict its jurisdiction to local residents. Instead it placed mediators and intake forms in small claims courts throughout a much larger area and aired public service announcements throughout the metropolitan region. Not surprisingly a great many of its cases (over half) came from outside the target area.

These secondary goals of the NJCs were expected to help reduce tension and conflict within the local communities. While it would be unreasonable to expect these small experimental programs to have any significant impact along these lines, we did spend some time examining this goal. Here too our findings are encouraging. The Centers did make some modest but demonstrable progress. According to our interviews, they enjoyed a very favorable reputation among the community leaders and the people they served, and were well regarded by staff members of key referral agencies. They also appeared to gain some small measure of success in informing the local community of their existence and services, no small achievement for a new program in the maze of urban social service agencies. A random sample survey of businesses and residences in the Venice/Mar Vista communities revealed that after just a few months of existence, 30 percent of the respondents were aware of the NJC, and most knew roughly what services it offered. While a few had learned of the NJC as a result of staff presentations to community organizations, most people learned about its work through public service announcements on radio, television, and the newspapers. It is, of course, difficult to judge the significance of a 30 percent recognition rate, but, on balance, it is probably more of a mark of achievement than of failure. Still some staff considered it disheartening given the considerable time and effort which went into their promotion campaign.

We also found the emergence of a drawback that is common to a great many social service programs. In interviews with NJC supervisory board members and community representatives, we discovered a "turf" problem that in all likelihood reduced the number of referrals from other community groups. Although they professed general support for the NJC concept, community programs were reluctant to refer their clients, and ultimate source of income, to the Centers. Instead they sought to "hold on" to their clients. Still, it is encouraging that on the whole, over one-third (38 percent) of the NJC cases came from sources *outside* the formal justice system, and in comparison to other similar recent "community" programs, the NJCs referral rate was quite respectable. For instance, Felstiner and Williams (1980) report a noncriminal justice system community referral rate of 7 percent in Boston, and the Florida study reports a rate of 30 percent, both lower than the NJCs. Furthermore, the rate of citizen-initiated cases in the NJCs was 17 percent, a figure that also compares favorably with other programs. For instance, the community-oriented Neighborhood Mediation Project in Portland, Oregon, had 19 percent of its cases initiated by citizens during the project's first year (Walsh and Splawn, 1979). Here too it is difficult to breathe much meaning into these figures, but they do suggest that such programs *can* successfully obtain referrals from community-based sources.

## Institutionalization

Still another, although minor, goal of the Field Test was to determine if the NJCs could be institutionalized, either in terms of generating their own alternative sources of funding or in terms of spreading NJCs to other communities. As to the first of these, the NJCs have been somewhat successful. After their pilot period, the Department of Justice continued to be the primary source of funding for all of the NJCs. As of January 1981, the Atlanta Center had received city and county funds to cover their annual operating costs, and the Venice/Mar Vista NJC had received some state funds facilitated by the passage of California's dispute resolution bill. However, the Kansas City Center was closed after efforts to obtain additional local support proved "nsuccessful. A combination of lack of visibility, diminishing funds, and increasing competition for the remainder, as well as poor refunding strategies, may have contributed to this difficulty in institutionalization.

On the other hand, the Field Test was very successful in encouraging adoption of the NJC concept in other communities. Since the Field Test, the number of alternative dispute resolution programs has mushroomed. In the past two years new Centers have opened in Honolulu, Houston, Washington, D.C., Chicago, Dallas, Denver, Portland, San Jose, and a host of other cities. Florida has developed a statewide network of at least 11 programs, and several states are planning or have already adopted legislation encouraging the development of such alternative mechanisms. NJC staff have frequently been called upon for advice and assistance. There is little doubt that this proliferation has been influenced in large by the experience of the NJCs and dissemination of information about them.

## Implications for the Future

While not without problems of both concept and execution, the NJCs have clearly demonstrated the value and potential of alternative dispute resolution programs, and while the three NJCs examined have faltered or may falter, their success must be seen in terms of the broader movement which is attracting support from a variety of sources at an accelerated rate. Indeed the neighborhood justice movement is now entering a stage of widespread acceptance and support. Although now a decade old, only recently has the movement emerged from embryonic form. Prominent judges and other leaders of the legal system are just now beginning to recognize the full value of mediation and alternative dispute processing, and these topics are now on the agendas of annual meetings of judges, bar associations, and other important forums. Similarly states are now beginning to adopt legislation to create alternative dispute programs, and a campaign to establish a National Academy of Peace and Conflict Resolution is well underway. At the national level, the Dispute Resolution Act of 1980 further encourages the creation of NJC-like programs, as well as providing for research, training, and technical assistance activities. Although funds for implementing the Act have not yet been allocated, other federal support has been forthcoming. Three new NJCs have been funded by LEAA, and a new community crime prevention program which fosters alternative dispute resolution services has been developed by ACTION and LEAA. It is all but certain that other such indications of support will be forthcoming in the near future.

Despite these successes, NJCs are not without their critics, many of whom, we think, have raised objections which stem from highly inflated expectations of the NJCs and the substitution of their own goals for those of the NJCs. For example, Tomasic [Editor's note: pp. 215–248.] has listed 18 assumptions about NJCs which he believes are implicit in the literature and goals of the movement and then proceeds to argue that NJC programs have failed on each of them. However, in fact, most of his assumptions do not coincide with the rather modest goals of the NJCs, and some of his intended negative conclusions (such as that mediation is appropriate for only a narrow band of disputes) are in fact inconsistent with most advocates' understanding of the value of mediation. Similarly others have criticized NJCs for not offering mediation as practiced in small-scale societies. Yet these critics are unduly harsh and interpret their evidence narrowly. Throughout this paper we have anticipated and made an effort to counter such criticisms. It is our firm belief that the NJCs should be judged primarily on the basis of their *own* articulated goals, rather than all the exaggerated rhetoric which is attached to the neighborhood justice movement. Having attempted the former, we believe we have found substantial evidence that shows mediation to be effective and satisfying.

This is not to say that NJCs are without considerable problems. The NJCs have had to work hard to attract cases and nurture referral sources. They have had difficulties convincing skeptical disputants of the value of their new and largely unknown service. They have had trouble in obtaining local support to continue their programs. They must handle more cases if they are to have a substantial impact on the justice system or community.

The roots of these problems lie in the lack of awareness and innate scepticism that is likely to accompany most new social service programs. But these are, we think, problems that can be overcome through public education and outreach. While this is not likely to be an easy task— among other things it requires disputants to orient themselves to acceptance of negotiation and compromise rather than a winner-take-all approach of adjudication—it is not impossible, and, as we have seen, the new process once used is highly valued. Still it is a long-term process, and definitive judgments of the NJC movement should not be based on the exaggerated rhetoric of its supporters or critics even on the successes or failures of the first few experimental programs.

# 7

# Community Mediation in Dorchester, Massachusetts*

**William L. F. Felstiner**
**Lynne A. Williams**

## Introduction

This chapter describes the mediation component of the Dorchester Urban Court—a program that substitutes lay mediation for criminal prosecution in cases where the victim and defendant are not strangers. It discusses the project's training program, the structure of mediation sessions, referral sources, caseload and caseload problems and compares the costs of mediation to court costs saved. Data for the report were gathered (1) by interviewing project staff and mediators and others knowledgeable about the project's origins and operation, (2) by analyzing the files of its first 500 cases, (3) by observing 34 mediation sessions, and (4) by conducting surveys of disputants and mediators. The purposes of the research were to describe the project's training and operation in detail, to identify operational problems and to explore the power of mediation as a form of social intervention into interpersonal problems.

Most of the cases referred to Dorchester mediation come from the Clerk or a judge of the local district court. If the defendant and complainant (victim) agree to mediation, a hearing is scheduled about a week later. At the hearing, two mediators try to get the disputants to settle past differences and agree upon the shape of future relations. If an agreement is reached, it is reduced to writing and signed. There is no pretense that the agreement is an enforceable contract. If it is not kept, however, the court process may start up again. If the agreement is kept, any pending prosecution is eventually dismissed. If no agreement is reached, the case is referred back to the clerk or a judge.

---

* All references in the text of this chapter are found in The Bibliography at the conclusion of this volume.

Mediation hearings are held in two-thirds of cases referred to the project. Agreements are reached in 90 percent of these cases. Twenty percent of the disputants report to the project that the agreement has broken down. Although property disputes proved comparatively difficult to get to mediation and to settle at mediation, they are more likely than interpersonal disputes to lead to stable agreements. The data suggest the more serious the dispute, the more likely agreement at mediation and the more likely that the agreement will break down. The explanation appears to be that serious disagreements have serious consequences if no agreement is reached. These cases then lead to vague agreements, easy to negotiate but hard to keep.

Our long-term follow-up confirms the project's data that improvement in the relations between the parties follows successful mediation. Slightly over one-half of the disputants we contacted attributed this improvement to mediation. The most common agreement failure concerned the payment of money and the most common response of a breakdown was to do nothing. Although most of the disputants believed that the sex or race of the mediators was irrelevant, one-half considered that co-residence of the mediators in Dorchester was important.

The original objectives of the mediation component were (JRI, 1974: 38):

- To resolve potential criminal disputes in a manner that (1) satisfies the parties and (2) prevents the recurrence of future problems by addressing the basis of the dispute. Strong emphasis will be placed on resolutions being effected as early as possible in the criminal justice process by providing intake capability at the Station House and the Prosecutor's Office as well as the Clerk's Office.
- To test the ability of community mediators to effect such resolutions and to compare their effectiveness with other methods of informal resolution now being employed in the District Courts and the Station House.
- To determine, through careful experimentation, which of a number of arbitration and/or mediation models and intake points is most effective in achieving fundamental resolutions of potentially criminal disputes.
- To build good will in the community toward the court, the police and the Prosecutor's Office.

These objectives have not stood the test of time well. No intake capability was ever developed at the Station House or Prosecutor's Office and the number of referrals from the Clerk has been disappointing. The project has made no attempt to compare its effectiveness with other informal methods of dispute resolution nor has it experimentally varied the model of mediation with which it began. In fact, so little energy was ever devoted to these objectives that it would be absurd to judge its performance in those terms. If one rather were to derive goals from actual efforts, we might say that the mediation program's objectives were:

- To process disputes between people who were not strangers to each other in such a way that (1) they better understood the nature of the conflict and the other party's perspective of it, (2) they were helped to explore arrangements which might eliminate or reduce similar conflict in the future, (3) they were able to agree on behavior or exchanges that mitigated the negative effects of past behavior.
- To provide such services through non-professional local citizens trained by the program in mediation.
- To develop a caseload of interpersonal disputes from the District Court and other referral sources that was large enough to reduce per case costs to a reasonable level.
- To act as a model for similar projects in Massachusetts and elsewhere and, to that end, to tolerate extensive research on their way of mediating interpersonal disputes.

## Mediator Training

The IMCR mediation model has two stated objectives:

- to resolve disputes in accordance with each disputant's sense of justice, and
- to prevent recurrence of conflict between disputants by "getting at" the underlying causes.

The trainers teach a specific series of maneuvers to be carried out by members of a mediation panel. But they stress that "mediation is an art, not a science," and that rules of order and timing are only basic guidelines.

Before specific techniques of mediation are taught, trainees are educated in basic attitudes and approach. The first goal is to earn the disputants' trust, both in the mediators themselves and in the process. Disputants will have to be ready to take the risk of making concessions. They will be willing to take risks only if they have confidence in the mediators who are in charge of the proceedings. Mediators are to earn the disputants' trust both through specific statements in a formally structured introductory speech which opens the hearings and by their ongoing attitude and behavior.

Trainees are taught to present seven specific topics in their introductory opening statement, which is made before the hearing gets under way.

- Words of welcome and introduction of panelists by name.
- Description of the mediation project and its rationale.
- Explanation of panelists' training and function.
- The rule of strict confidentiality—panelists are sworn to silence about the proceedings.
- The probability that the panel will want to meet privately without any of the participants or with one or two of them, at times.
- The fact that panelists will take notes for use during the hearing only and will destroy them afterwards.
- How the session will be conducted: panelists will listen to everyone, then work with the disputants to explore possible ways to resolve the problem. It will be the disputants themselves, not the mediators, who will fashion any agreement that may be made.

Mediators' principal attitudinal objectives are to be:

- Non-judgmental. A panelist's own value system is irrelevant. Any agreement will be made by and for the disputants. It is their values that count.
- Willing to be educated by the disputants. Intake staff may have gathered a lot of information, and the mediators may even have studied it. Nevertheless, there are two reasons why a mediator should adopt a receptive, listening attitude:
  - he will learn a lot about the disputants' sensitivities and priorities, and
  - the disputants feel a need to tell their story to a willing listener. Giving them time to vent their anger encourages them to trust the mediation process.
- Slow to come to conclusions. Mediators are to maintain a "provisional" feeling as long as possible, partly because "those who seem to know the answers tend to put others on their guard."

The behavior patterns specified for mediators are to:

- Listen without interrupting a disputant's flow of words. They are to start the session proper with an open-ended question directed to one of the disputants—usually the complainant–and let him talk until he "runs down." Giving him this freedom will encourage him to trust both the mediators and the process. Stopping the disputant's flow of words is to be avoided, as is anything even remotely resembling interrogation. This is one of many ways the trainers distinguish mediation from process in a courtroom.
- Make verbal responses. Trainees are to show they understand

what the disputant is expressing, as in "You feel this was un-
called for."

- Give non-verbal indications of attentiveness. Use body language, and "mm-hmm's" to encourage disputants to speak
freely.

A mediator's task as a fact-finder is different than it would be in a
courtroom or police station. Fact-finding in mediation means "Finding
out what the dispute is all about, and what facts are important to its
resolution." A basic premise is that mediators may not so much need to
know what happened as *why* it happened—the "underlying cause."
Mediators are, however, strongly warned against "interrogating" the disputants, even with "why" questions. "Why" questions may sound disapproving. Mediators are to try to limit themselves to what the trainers
call "overhead responses," such as: "Tell me more about it"; or "reflec-
tive responses," such as "You feel this shouldn't have happened."

In the main, the facts that are to be unearthed are not just what
happened, but what aspects of what happened are particularly aggravat-
ing to each disputant. Mediators are to listen closely for these points of
aggravation. They are told, "The disputants will educate you as to what
the issues are *for them*. If *they* don't make an issue of something, *it's not
an issue*." If a disputant states unequivocally that something is not an
issue or a sensitive spot, he is to be taken at his word, and the point is
not to be pressed.

After the mandatory introductory explanation, and when each disputant has had generous time to state his views and his "public position" on his wishes for resolution of the dispute (which mediators are to
be sure have been made clear), the panel will excuse the disputants
courteously and have a first private conference.

In the course of a typical hearing, the mediators will caucus together
several times. This is a time for taking stock ("What do we know and
what more do we need to know?") and planning ahead ("Whom shall
we call next, and why? What shall we say to him, and why?") After this
caucus, the mediation moves into a stage of shuttle diplomacy—a series
of interviews with one disputant at a time, interspersed with more panel
caucuses for stocktaking and tactical planning.

The mediators are now to find out what is most disturbing to each
disputant, while at the same time "building the will to settle" by finding
any small areas of agreement ("You both agree that there is at least a
possibility of resolving this problem through mediation") and narrowing
the gap between the disputants' positions. Trainees are instructed to
identify sensitive issues for one disputant, bring up these same issues
with the other and find some small area of agreement on the second's
part to take back to the first. An example: In a role-played case, a
tenant was angry at the superintendent of his building for "not keeping

the place up." In private session, however, the superintendent came back again and again to his powerlessness, his inability to keep up a large building with no support from the building's owner. He said "My family and I live in the building, too. We'd like to live in a decent building, too. But there's nothing I can do." Trainees are to carry this area of agreement (BOTH would like to have the building better kept up) back to the tenant.

In their caucuses with individual disputants, the important variables are *what* is to be transmitted from one disputant to another, and how it is to be presented. Facts and offers need not be transmitted at once. When they are transmitted, they can be shorn of negative comments and "shaped to appeal to the self-interest of the party you are addressing." The aim is to start the ball rolling with small areas of agreement, and use these to nudge the parties into other, increased areas of agreement. When an impasse is reached, the mediator is to act as an "agent of reality": that is, he is to focus the disputants' attention on what solution is realistically *possible* and "on the consequences of not reaching agreement."

Trainees are urged to be on the lookout for a sudden flash of agreement, to recognize it, and treat it as such. At this point, the mediators are to bring the parties together, announce "We have an agreement," and sum it up themselves. The role of the disputants is downplayed at this stage. The mediator is to "take over the proceedings and speak for the parties . . . . People are hesitant to make decisions. Letting parties verbalize an agreement as they see it may open the door to a new conflict."

Striking while the iron is hot, mediators are to present the disputants with a drawn-up agreement. Undertakings by all concerned are to be specifically operationalized. Not "No loud music at night," for example, but "Mr. Jones will not use his stereo after ten p.m." The disputants are asked to sign the agreement which has been written up by the mediators. Panel members are to thank the disputants for coming, and once again to stress the fact that none of the proceeding will ever be discussed by the mediators. If no agreement has been reached, the parties may agree to schedule a second attempt. Any referral for social services is left to the very end, after the session proper.

Using the IMCR model, Dorchester has been reasonably successful in transforming community people into paraprofessional mediators in the equivalent of one week of training. We do not mean to minimize this achievement by a critique which identifies some of the limitations and effects of this particular training program. Our reservations concern:

(a) The lack of attention to trainee motivation.
(b) The choice of the initial role-play.
(c) Ambivalence about manipulation.

(d)   The limited use of modeling.

(e)   Limitations of shuttle diplomacy.

( a ) Many training courses in helping skills begin with an effort to aid the trainees to understand their needs to be helpers (see Danish and Hauer, 1973). Presumably, mediators who have paid attention to and articulated their own motivation are less likely to be shaken by intractable disputes and disputants or to be defensive about their own sensitivities, and are more confident about their own legitimacy as mediators. IMCR training missed this opportunity.

(b) The initial role-play in IMCR training courses is the Hale case —a woman who wants to be separated from a man who neither wants the relationship to break up nor understands that that is what the woman wants. The Hale case is a powerful medium, because it is first, is pursued at great length and because the mediators are the trainers and therefore very smooth and manipulative. Presumably the Hale case was chosen to illustrate the difference between mediation and marriage counseling and to demonstrate that not every "marriage" can be saved. This choice may be unfortunate. It is easier for mediators to negotiate the terms of a separation than for them to help provide a more positive structure for a disintegrating relationship. The Hale material is not unambiguously a separation case. That it is so treated is a powerful model for mediators to treat most ambiguous living together cases as separation cases, and to push disputants earlier than they should in that direction. In Dorchester, we observed both the tenacity of the Hale case[1] and its influence in the direction of separation as THE solution to aggravated "marital" discord. Fortunately, perhaps, many disputants stoutly resisted the effort to dissolve their relationship.

(c) The training is ambivalent about manipulation and coercion. On the one hand, the trainers stress that free choice is a value—agreements last because they originate with the disputants. Yet, the trainers also indicate that disputants are to be maneuvered into an agreement by the use of ambiguities, by suppressing conflict in the later stages of a session, and by the coercion of the alternative to an agreement, whatever that might be. As we have suggested elsewhere (Felstiner and Williams, 1978), it is possible that a disputant who feels that his freedom of choice has been compromised by such manipulation may respond by subverting the agreement, by retaliating against the complainant outside of the agreement or by shifting his resentment toward himself or a third party. But this ambivalence may also have unintended consequences for the *trainees*. The contradiction between letting the disputants provide their solution to their problem and the mediator's responsibility to maneuver the disputants into making an agreement plagues many dispute processing programs and may be hard for trainees to assimilate when it is not confronted directly in training. We are concerned that trainees may resolve this conflict themselves by rejecting the mediative approach to problem solving and by falling back on the courtroom pattern ingrained through exposure to American culture. Although it would be hard to document such a shift, we suggest it because of the otherwise inexplicable reliance of Brooklyn trainees on interrogation as a mode of interaction.

(d) Most training courses for paraprofessionals in counselling use the same three techniques used by IMCR: 1) presentation of didactic material, 2) modeling by skilled practitioners, and 3) simulated practice sessions. But IMCR training is more heavily weighted toward practice. Didactic material is to be read through at home, but many trainees seem not to have bothered. Modeling consists almost solely of the initial mediation hearing videotaped by the trainers at the beginning of the course, before the trainees had been exposed to the basic principles and fine points of technique. There is little subsequent use of modeling by trainers.

Thus, each individual trainee does not have much exposure to "correct" mediation, by himself, his peers or the trainers. The instructional modality is chiefly the post-session critique by the trainers. "*You* made the agreement and sold it to them." "You weren't listening." "You missed the important point." This is essentially training by negative reinforcement, and delayed negative reinforcement at that.

Training can, however, be designed so that trainees *experience* use of correct responses or interventions, and are positively reinforced for such behavior. To produce this sequence, trainers must stop the role-play more often, model a better response, have the trainees do it themselves until their performance is tolerable and then tell them, "Good. That's right." (See, for example, Danish and Hauer, 1973; Carkhuff, 1969; and Truax and Carkhuff, 1967.) Obviously such a change would disturb continuity—letting the trainees run through an entire caucus or interview with a disputant without interruption. Our impression, nevertheless, is that improved trainee interventions are more important than improved trainee confidence that they can complete a mediation session without trainer assistance.

(e) The ideology of mediation, our data and common sense suggest that communication problems underlie many interpersonal disputes. Mediation can encourage disputants to tell each other about their complaints and what they want done about them. Yet the structure of mediation hearings incorporated in IMCR training—the strict adherence to shuttle diplomacy—is likely to minimize such interchanges.

Mediation project trainers would probably reply that neither the basic structure of IMCR mediation, nor any specific instruction given to the trainees, would prevent them from using direct, rather than indirect, communication when faced with a case in which it seemed appropriate. We believe that such a response would underestimate the power of mediation training as a socializing experience. Dorchester mediators are engaged in a process that was foreign to them before training, and their only model is what they have experienced as trainees. And the only model which they experience as trainees is one of indirect communication.

The indirect communication nature of mediation as taught at IMCR appears to reflect the prior experience of its founders. IMCR was organized and run by labor lawyers with extensive experience in labor mediation. The techniques of labor mediation were first shifted to use in community conflicts, and then to interpersonal conflicts (Nicolau and McCormick, 1972:99). We were told by the chief IMCR trainer that no explicit attempt was made to analyze the differences between labor and interpersonal disputes and, therefore, no attempt was made to adapt mediation methods devised in the labor situation to what might be different about interpersonal conflict.

Differences between the types of labor disputes which are mediated and some forms of personal disputes do exist. Labor mediation occurs when the parties to a prospective collective bargaining agreement cannot agree on its terms. Labor mediation is thus episodic, complete, impersonal and delayed. It is episodic in the sense that the disputes which it is mobilized to settle tend to stay settled during the period of the agreement. Terms are not re-negotiated and generally are followed. Although the differences in attitudes which form the basis of labor conflicts remain between points of mediation, the behavioral elements of those conflicts are fixed for a period of time, are generally uncontested for that period of time, and thus there is little need to pay attention to the parties' ability, or lack of it, to negotiate about those issues in the interim.

Labor mediation is complete in the sense that arbitration is available if any major issues are left for interim disposition. Labor mediation is impersonal in the sense that though the disputants' feelings about each other may be important, they are not crucial. They are not crucial because there is not necessarily any interaction between the parties' negotiating representatives in between mediator interventions and because substitutions can frequently be made among negotiators if aggravated problems in the interpersonal relations do occur. Labor mediation is a delayed process in that it occurs only after the parties have failed to agree upon contract terms after prolonged discussion of those very terms.

In the senses in which these terms are used, mediation of many interpersonal cases is not episodic, complete, impersonal or delayed. The disputants do not in mediation attempt to freeze the preponderance of their interaction for a substantial period. They are not writing detailed interaction contracts and they do not attempt to forecast and provide a response to the many turns that their relationship will take over time.

Substitutions are not possible. Parties to an interpersonal dispute that comes to mediation may well have tried for a long time to make their relationship more positive, but they may not have confronted directly the issues which prove to be, or ought to be, the gist of the mediation (see Felstiner and Williams, 1978). When labor mediators use indirect communication, they may be doing so because direct communication failed. When interpersonal mediators use indirect communication, on the other hand, they may be losing the opportunity for setting up direct communication for the first time. The stark consequence of all these differences from labor relations is that the ability of the disputants in interpersonal mediation to set the framework for continuing and important negotiations may be the core of what the mediation is about. Unfortunately, IMCR's adherence to a format of indirect communication limits the capacity of the process to lay the groundwork for improved direct communication in the future.

Richard Rosellen, a German sociologist, has suggested (1979) that the structure of IMCR mediation may also be based on a naive concept of the nature of conflict. This is Rosellen's argument: IMCR mediation appears to consider conflict as a disturbance in social relations. In this view, although conflict is socially and psychologically conditioned, it occurs only in intermittent, specific instances. On a practical level, if special consideration is given to these causes, the conflict can be resolved by an agreement. If the agreement is followed, the social relations will function well and without conflict (Weisbrod, 1977: 181; JRI 1974: ii, Wahrhaftig, 1977).

But Rosellen, and most social scientists, believe that a different understanding of conflict is more realistic. In this alternative view, conflict is seen as an integral part of social relations. Social relations function well not if they are undisturbed, but if they succeed in integrating diverging interests through continual confrontation and discussion of the issues, and if they control the explosive force of diverging interests through a continuous modification of the conditions of the relationship (see Coser, 1956: 47–48, 85; Deutsch, 1973; Ackerman, 1958: 85).

Rosellen is obviously referring to disputes between people who are involved in a continuous relationship rather than between people in a sporadic relationship, such as exists frequently between retailer and consumer or landlord and tenant. In continuous relationship cases, the conflict theory of normality suggests that mediation should downplay the utility of an agreement about a particular, concrete dispute and emphasize techniques and skills in conflict management and solving. Operationally, the shift in emphasis would stress direct communication between the disputants at the expense of shuttle diplomacy. It may be beyond the powers of lay mediators in a single two-hour session to employ the codified techniques developed by psychotherapists to improve communication skills between intimates (see Hoper et al., 1974; Saltmarsh, 1973). But we agree with Rosellen that a greater contribution could be made by a mediation process which would encourage direct communication between warring intimates instead of defining *the agreement* as the *sine qua non* of success in mediation. It is not entirely clear that the Dorchester project, with its highly structured relationship to the court, could make an appropriate adjustment. One does not know whether the judges would accept a statement from a complainant that a case should be dismissed, not because the presenting problem has been solved, but because the complainant feels better about his ability to get along with the respondent in the future without court intervention. But given the general propensity in Dorchester and elsewhere to throw out cases which the complaining witness does not want to press, the change may be feasible.

Neither Rosellen nor we ought to be surprised by the existence of a naive view of conflict. Folk perspectives are as current in the industrial world as they are in tribal society. The notion that social interaction is generally carried on in an undisturbed state, broken sporadically by conflict, and returned to a conflict-free equilibrium is twin to the myth that most people are constantly law abiding and that crime control is a matter of detecting and punishing the occasional deviant. That our myths are myths is not a secret. That our institutions continue to be based on these myths is also no secret. As Skinner has noted, "Antiquated theories that are ingrained in our language and our culture stand in the way of promising scientific alternatives" (1978: 86).

## Retraining

Retraining is to community mediators what supervision is to inexperienced psychotherapists, an opportunity to correct mistakes, to improve technique, to share frustrations and to be reassured about the value of the effort. Despite the benefits to be secured by retraining, it has been difficult to structure successfully in Dorchester.

The difficulties arise, in part, from a conflict in the goals of retraining. Is the process intended to rejuvenate and improve all mediators or is it primarily a device for performance evaluation, a chance to identify and weed out ineffective mediators? The staff tends to shy away from hard evaluation, but their reluctance to grade mediators and act on the basis of negative evaluations is a continuing source of annoyance to many of the better and more experienced mediators who resent serving on panels with those they consider incompetent. These mediators are concerned with the effect of the fumblers on the particular disputes the panel faces, on the reputation of the mediation program and, conceivably, on their own self-image as paraprofessionals. The result of this ambivalence is that the staff and the better mediators tend to have different expectations about retraining, and, when it is held, the mediators become even more distressed about the issue of competence because the staff does not use retraining to prune the ranks.

What the staff does do about inadequate mediators is to try to ignore them in forming panels. This effort is partially successful. For long stretches, a high proportion of mediation sessions are conducted by a small proportion of mediators. In June 1977, for instance, 6 mediators (11 percent) were scheduled to hear 15 cases (51 percent). Naturally, as the better mediators get most of the business, the gap in skill between mediators widens. This selection process caused a minor revolt in June 1977. The staff agreed to try to spread the burden evenly and in July an effort was made to use all mediators who had been ignored in the past. We had the impression as our fieldwork was finishing, that this effort had waned and that the old practice of distributing the work to those who were available, reliable and experienced had been re-adopted.

The significance of the work distribution practice for retraining is that it is difficult to get the mediators who most need retraining to come to the sessions. Their attendance is poor, first because there appears little profit in further training in a skill they are not given the opportunity to employ. Secondly, when they do attend a retraining session, the format may be intimidating. Retraining, like training, consists primarily in role-played mediation sessions. An inexperienced mediator, playing that role before experienced staff and highly experienced mediators (some of whom have now had experience as trainers), whose performance is analyzed for didactic purposes, is likely to be crushed by the experience. If they do not themselves undergo it, they witness the discomfort of others. In either event, attendance at the next retraining session is unlikely.

The staff had tried to counter the intimidation problem by dividing the mediators into small groups who would meet from time to time with a staff member to discuss and act out problems that they encountered in mediation. Most of the mediators did not show up for these sessions, nor were the staff resources adequate if the mediators had seized the opportunity, and this form of retraining was discontinued.

Retraining problems highlight the issue of the community dimension in community mediation. Whether half a dozen experienced mediators mediate the bulk of cases and do so with a high level of competence and professionalism or whether the caseload is met by 40 to 50 mediators each involved in an occasional mediation is a choice which ought to reflect a considered understanding of what the program is all about. If the basic concern is particular disputants and the failure of the criminal justice system to meet their needs, then mediation services ought to be provided by a small number of experienced, highly motivated, and closely supervised mediators. If, on the other hand, mediation is seen as an aspect of a community's struggle to settle its own quarrels, to take responsibility for its own social control and its own fate, then the base of mediators must be broad, even at the cost of less effective individual mediations. Otherwise one form of specialist catering to the needs of a passive clientele has simply been substituted for another. Many of the shortcomings of IMCR-type mediator training and of Dorchester's problems with retraining may then be the result of indecision about goals, of ambivalence about whether the program is basically a community program or a mediation program.

## Referral, Caseload and Follow-up

Thirty-four of the first 500 cases were referred to mediation by someone other than the Clerk, court or police. These other sources include social service agencies, truant officers, the welfare department, legal aid and other parts of the Urban Court program. There have also been several self-referrals. The important question concerning these referrals is not what they were like, but why there were so few. The problem can lie either with the lack of general awareness of or confidence in the program or with the lack of coercion exercisable against disputants advised by these non-criminal justice agencies to go to mediation. Two factors suggest that the problem is an absence of coercion rather than of public knowledge. First, social service agency personnel probably do know quite a bit about the project. It is a highly visible, storefront operation on the main street of Dorchester, two blocks from the courthouse. It has received substantial TV exposure. Its efforts to attract trainees for its mediation and disposition units have produced publicity in newspapers and on radio stations. More important than this activity directed toward general public awareness are the facts that the program is staffed by many people who have worked for local social service agencies, its social service referral activities are conducted directly with local social service agencies, and many of its community volunteers have social service agency ties. Yet that extensive network has produced only five social service referrals in 19 months.

Second is the general proposition that the no-show rate is a function of the level of coercion to which the respondent is subject: the less the cost of rejecting mediation (the less unpleasant the alternative), the less likely the respondent will be to agree to mediation. This logic seems both applicable and inapplicable to Dorchester. It is complicated, but worth exploring. If the respondent in a court or Clerk referral does not participate in a hearing or does not join in an agreement, the consequence may be continued criminal prosecution. Respondents referred by other sources are in no such jeopardy. If the coercion proposition is correct, we would expect to find a lower proportion of no-shows and of unsuccessful mediation in the court and Clerk conditions than when referrals are made by others. As can be seen in Tables 7.1 and 7.2 the hypothesis is supported by the no-show data, but not by the breakdown of successful mediations.[2]

TABLE 7.1   Referrals by Withdrawals

| Source of Referral | Frequency of Referrals | Withdrawals | Relative Frequency (Percent) |
|---|---|---|---|
| Court/Clerk | 413 | 120 | 29 |
| Other | 47 | 25 | 53 |

TABLE 7.2   Referrals by Outcomes

| Source of Referral | Mediation Held | Agreements Reached | Relative Frequency (Percent) |
|---|---|---|---|
| Court/Clerk | 291 | 258 | 88.7 |
| Other | 22 | 21 | 95.5 |

The small claims court is a potential source of cases. The reason why only an occasional small claims case has been referred to mediation is clear; the potential in a more favorable context is less certain. Small claims cases could be referred either when they are filed or when they are called for trial. Judge Dolan, who hears most small claims in Dorchester, wanted to give complainants the alternative of mediation at the time of filing. The Clerk refused on the ground that civil referrals must come from a judge, not a clerk. He apparently thought that shifting a case to mediation involved a discretionary, rather than an informative, function. If referral can only be made when a case is about to be tried, the postponement involved in going to mediation is a major disincentive. The parties are already in court and their case will be "settled" within a half-hour. Why wait for the less familiar process?

If the Clerk reversed his stand and offered these plaintiffs the alternative of mediation, the literature on small claims court indicates that it may have a major role to play. Yngvesson and Hennessey's (1975: 253) review of 56 small claims court analyses reports that "most observational studies suggest that formal atmosphere, judicial indifference or aloofness, presence of lawyers, and a crowded schedule, may hinder a full airing of grievances." The remedy frequently suggested for cases "in which the time dimension of the relationship is a deep one" (Yngvesson and Hennessey, 1975: 263) is mediation (McFadgen, 1972). Many small claims cases are collection matters or involve cut and dried factual issues. In many small claims cases at least one of the parties desires a normative outcome, a statement by an authority figure about what happened and what rules are applicable to what happened, even where they have a prior relationship to the other party. But the residual of prior relationship cases where the parties want to work out an accommodation for the future rather than receive an evaluation of the past may be substantial.

All caseload data in this section were collected from the case files at the mediation project. The files included information about intake, referral source, summaries of intake, interviews with the complainant and respondent, the charge or precipitating complaint, any communication between the case coordinators and the disputants, the agreements, if one was reached, and the results of the mediation project follow-up. Most of the files indicated the ultimate disposition of the case (e.g., whether the case was eventually returned to court), whether a weapon was used and what it was, and the problems underlying the presenting complaint.

TABLE 7.3   Coding of Dispute Level

|  | Frequency | Percent |
|---|---|---|
| Initial Phase: Independent Coding |  |  |
| Total Number of Disputes | 500 |  |
| Disputes Coded | 384 | 76.8* |
| Number of Agreements | 308 | 80.2† |
| Second Phase: Disposition of Disagreements |  |  |
| Number of Disagreements | 75 |  |
| Came to Agreement Through Discussion | 60 |  |
| Dropped Due to Insufficient Information |  |  |
| to Reach an Agreement | 15 |  |
| Final Frequency of Agreement | 368 |  |

* Percent of total caseload.
† Percent of total disputes coded.

The reliability of this information is difficult to determine. During the period studied six different individuals performed the case coordinator function. As one would expect, the amount of information and the degree of detail in the actual files varies between case co-ordinators. The variability lies not with the facts such as referral source, but with the specificity with which matters such as the ostensible dispute or the underlying problems are described.

The raw data were coded at two levels. Most of the data were recorded from the files and transferred directly to data processing format. The category "level of dispute" was coded at a later time, using various items of information about the dispute. Each individual dispute was categorized at one of three levels, varying in degree of seriousness and complexity. When sufficient information was not available, the dispute was not coded. The coding was done independently by two codes, and the initial rate of agreement was calculated. The coders then discussed the cases on which they disagreed and dealt with these cases in one of two ways: either one coder, in re-evaluating the case, decided to recode the dispute level and an agreement was reached or no agreement could be reached and the dispute level was left uncoded. (See Table 7.3.)

## Description of Criteria Used to Establish Dispute Levels

Level 1: One-shot dispute. There is no apparent underlying emotional and/or behavioral problem relevant to resolution at mediation, e.g., a small claim or security deposit dispute.[3]

Level 2: Not a single incident. Consists of escalating misunderstandings. There are no apparent underlying emotional and/or behavioral problems relevant to resolution at mediation, e.g., ongoing problems with neighbor's children leading to dispute between parents.

Level 3: Not a single incident. Dispute and resolution affected by underlying emotional and/or behavioral problems, e.g., ongoing husband/wife dispute involving chronic alcohol abuse and/or violent behavior.

TABLE 7.4 Dispute Level of Disputes Referred to Mediation

| Level | Frequency | Percent | Adjusted Percent |
|---|---|---|---|
| 1 | 99 | 19.8 | 26.9 |
| 2 | 115 | 23.0 | 31.3 |
| 3 | 154 | 30.8 | 41.8 |
| | | | 100.0 |
| Insufficient information to code | 132 | 26.4 | |
| | | 100.0 | |

TABLE 7.5 Presenting Complaint by Dispute Level

| Complaint | Dispute Level* | | |
|---|---|---|---|
| | 1 | 2 | 3 |
| Assault, assault and battery | 44 ( 25.6)[†] | 52 (30.2) | 76 (44.2) |
| Threats | 5 ( 14.3) | 12 (34.3) | 18 (51.4) |
| Harassment | 1 ( 6.7) | 7 (46.7) | 7 (46.7) |
| Breaking and entering | 1 ( 16.7) | 2 (33.3) | 3 (50.0) |
| Property damage | 13 ( 32.5) | 13 (32.5) | 14 (35.0) |
| Larceny | 12 ( 60.0) | 6 (30.0) | 2 (10.0) |
| Disturbing the peace | ( — ) | 4 (57.1) | 3 (42.9) |
| Contributing to delinquency of minor | ( — ) | 1 (20.0) | 4 (80.0) |
| Stubborn child, truant | 3 ( 14.3) | 9 (42.3) | 9 (42.3) |
| Dog bites, noisy dogs | 3 ( 50.0) | 3 (50.0) | ( — ) |
| Non-support | 6 ( 85.7) | 1 (14.3) | ( — ) |
| General family dispute | ( — ) | 2 (40.0) | 3 (60.0) |
| General money or property dispute | 6 (100.0) | ( — ) | ( — ) |
| Other | 5 ( 35.7) | 4 (35.7) | 4 (28.6) |
| | 99 | 116 | 143 |

\* Only 358 cases included both a coded dispute level and a presenting complaint.
† Row percent.

Tables 7.6, 7.7 and 7.8 demonstrate the clear relationship between dispute level and the course of a dispute. Table 7.6 indicates that the higher the level of dispute, the more likely it is to go to mediation. If, as we suspect, the higher the level, the more serious the dispute, the propensity to participate in mediation as the level increases is intuitively sound—the more serious the problem the more egregious the complainant's complaint, the greater the respondent's jeopardy and the more incentive both have to attend a mediation hearing.

TABLE 7.6   Disposition of Referred Cases by Dispute Level

| Disposition | Dispute Level* | | |
| | 1 | 2 | 3 |
|---|---|---|---|
| Withdrawal; Complainant No-Show | 18 (18.8) Column %<br>(31.6) Row %<br>( 5.0) Total % | 21 (18.8)<br>(36.8)<br>( 5.8) | 18 (12.9)<br>(31.6)<br>( 5.2) |
| Refused Mediation; Went Back To Court | 16 (16.7)<br>(43.2)<br>( 4.5) | 11 ( 9.8)<br>(29.7)<br>( 3.1) | 10 ( 7.1)<br>(27.0)<br>( 2.8) |
| Staff Settled | 1 ( 1.0)<br>(50.0)<br>( 0.3) | (—) | 1 ( 0.7)<br>(50.0)<br>( 0.3) |
| Mediation Session Held | 61 (63.5)<br>(23.2)<br>(17.0) | 80 (71.4)<br>(30.4)<br>(22.3) | 111 (79.3)<br>(42.2)<br>(30.9) |

\* Only 359 cases included both a coded dispute level and a disposition.

TABLE 7.7   Outcome of Mediated Cases by Dispute Level

| Outcome | Dispute Level* | | |
| | 1 | 2 | 3 |
|---|---|---|---|
| Dispute Settled at Mediation | 49 (80.3) Column %<br>(22.5) Row %<br>(18.6) Total % | 67 (83.8)<br>(30.8)<br>(25.5) | 101 ( 91.0)<br>( 46.5)<br>( 38.4) |
| Dispute Settled by Disputant After Mediation | (—) | (—) | 1 ( 0.9)<br>(100.0)<br>( 0.4) |
| Dispute Not Settled | 12 (19.7)<br>(35.3)<br>( 4.6) | 13 (16.3)<br>(38.2)<br>( 4.9) | 9 ( 8.1)<br>( 26.5)<br>(3.4) |

\* Only 359 cases included both a coded dispute level and a disposition.

TABLE 7.8   Mediation Project Follow-up Results by Dispute Level*

| Level | Agreement Working | Some Improvement | Agreement Broke Down |
|---|---|---|---|
| 1 | 41 (91.1)[†] | 1 ( 2.2) | 3 ( 6.7) |
| 2 | 40 (70.2) | 5 ( 8.8) | 12 (21.1) |
| 3 | 57 (54.8) | 20 (19.2) | 27 (26.0) |

\* Includes all successfully mediated cases in which a mediator project follow-up was conducted and for which there was a coded dispute level (N = 206).
[†] Row percent.

Table 7.7 suggests that the higher the level of dispute the more likely it is to be settled at mediation. However, Table 7.7 shows that the higher the level of a dispute the more likely it is that an agreement will break down. Measures of association (Tau b and Tau c) indicate that these three relationships are significant at the .01 level.[4]

Although the results shown in Tables 7.7 and 7.8 seem contradictory, they are not. Many of the agreements in Level 3 disputes are very vague. Rather than mandating specific behavior change, they tend to be worded in generalities, such as "Mrs. X will not nag Mr. X and Mr. X will drink less liquor." Because of their generality, these agreements are often more easily reached; however, they are difficult to keep because they involve broad changes in long-term behavior patterns, rather than changes in clearly defined behavior.

## Long-Term Follow-up

The most striking findings from the follow-up are:

1. Assaults are the most common precipitating incident of mediation, and alcohol abuse is the most common underlying problem it faces.

2. A substantial proportion (83 percent) of disputants report that the problem that led to a referral has improved. Slightly over one-half of disputants believe that the change in the problem was directly produced by mediation. The other party was reported to have fulfilled the mediation agreement in two-thirds of the cases.

3. The most common settlement failure concerned the payment of money.

4. In the case of a breakdown of the agreement, the most common response was to do nothing.

5. Most disputants believe that the sex or race of the mediators is unimportant. Among those who believe either factor is important, sex is more than three times as important as race. However, one-half of disputants believe that co-residence of the mediators in Dorchester was important.

6. More disputants believed that the mediators understood and respected their feelings than understood the situation of the disputants.

7. The mediators were responsible for producing agreements more frequently than the parties.

8. The mediation project failed to provide follow-up services one-half of the time they were promised.

9. Four-fifths of the disputants were pleased that they had been to mediation, although only two-thirds would use it again if faced with a similar problem.

10. The most common reason for agreeing to mediation was that court was considered inappropriate.

## Cost Analysis

This section presents information about the cost of operating the Dorchester mediation project, provides an estimate of the costs that the district court would have incurred but for the mediation project, and discusses the relevance of this cost data for mediation programs in general. It does *not* discuss the comparative benefits of mediation and orthodox court processing.

TABLE 7.9   Costs of the Mediation Project, July 1, 1976 Through June 30, 1977

| Item | Amount | | Percent of Total |
|------|-------|------|------------------|
| Personnel | | | |
| a) Mediation component | $57,020.13 | | |
| b) Central staff | 19,641.99 | $ 76,662.12 | 70 |
| Consulting & Contracting | | | |
| a) Temporary services | $    499.47 | | |
| b) Staff training | 1,902.50 | | |
| c) Mediator stipends | 4,394.50 | 6,746.47 | 6 |
| Office and Administration | | | |
| a) Rent | $ 1,703.33 | | |
| b) Heat | 660.10 | | |
| c) Alarm | 24.67 | | |
| d) Electricity | 655.82 | | |
| e) Supplies | 1,514.63 | | |
| f) Stationery | 1.00 | | |
| g) Postage | 575.41 | | |
| h) Reproduction | 1,761.42 | | |
| i) Telephone | 2,999.36 | | |
| j) Training materials | 116.69 | | |
| k) Advertising | 25.00 | 10,037.43 | 9 |
| Other | | | |
| a) Repair and maintenance | | 2,044.95 | 2 |
| Total Direct Costs | | $95,490.97 | |
| Indirect Costs (JRI)* | | | |
| a) Money raising (3%) | 2,864.73 | | |
| b) Grant management (6%) | 5,729.46 | | |
| c) Supervision (3.5%) | 3,342.18 | | |
| d) PR & develop. (2.5%) | 2,387.27 | 14,323.64 | 13 |
| Total Costs | | $109,814.61 | 100 |
| Adjustments to total cost to eliminate items unrelated to normal operations | | | |
| a) Research & eval. asst. | $ 4,079.61 | | |
| b) Money raising | 2,864.73 | | |
| c) PR & development | 2,387.27 | | |
| d) Racial violence mediation | 555.00 | $ (9,886.61) | |
| Total Adjusted Costs | | $ 99,928.00 | |

* Breakdown per N. Houston, former president of JRI.

## Costs of Mediation

Financial records of the Urban Court are not maintained for individual program components. Mediation cost figures were prepared by assigning undivided cost pursuant to time allocations reported by central staff, allocating rent and rental items in proportion to space used, and dividing the remainder of office and administrative items equally between the three program components. Indirect costs of 15 percent were actual charges by JRI. Costs were tabulated for the period July 1, 1976, through June 30, 1977, primarily because July–June is the fiscal year used by the district court.

Costs per unit of mediation activity are presented in the following table:

TABLE 7.10   Costs of Mediation per Referral, Mediations Conducted, and Agreements Reached 1976–77

| | | |
|---|---|---:|
| Total cost per | | |
| Referral | (330) | $332.77 |
| Mediation | (219) | 501.44 |
| Agreement | (183) | 600.08 |
| Total adjusted cost per | | |
| Referral | (330) | $302.81 |
| Mediation | (219) | 456.29 |
| Agreement | (183) | 546.06 |

## Court Costs Saved

The most reliable method for estimating the direct costs which the district court was saved from incurring because of the activities of the mediation project would be use of an appropriate control group.[5] In this procedure, cases qualifying for mediation would be randomly assigned into treatment and control groups. Victims in both groups would be made a tentative offer of mediation. Only victims indicating an interest in mediation after the tentative offer would be retained in the respective groups. Victims in the control group would then be informed that for some reason, such as an overdemand for mediation, their complaint must be processed as an ordinary criminal charge. Presumably most defendants in the treatment group would agree to mediation since refusal to agree might lead to continued prosecution.

The cases in the control group would be followed through the court process in detail. Every appearance before a clerk, prosecutor or judge would be monitored. The cases in the treatment group would also be observed as they were processed by the court system, presumably at less frequent intervals. The time consumed by each such event and the personnel in attendance would be recorded. With adjustments for clerical, supply and other support costs, these data would permit one to estimate fairly precisely the non-capital expenditures required from public funds to process these cases which were eligible for mediation, but were not referred to it. These costs would then be compared with the court and mediation costs of cases in the treatment group. The two sets of costs would constitute a cost/cost-savings comparison for mediation.

Such a research program was not possible in Dorchester for several reasons. One limitation was the relatively short period of time available for field work. But no matter how long a research period were available, a random assignment experiment was foreclosed in Dorchester by the low mediation caseload. During 1976–77, only 18 cases per month were mediated. In its second year of operation while field research was underway, the mediation project was engaged in an effort to develop credentials with the court and with the community, based upon performing services approved by its clientele, the personnel of the district court and the community. Diversion of a substantial number of prospective cases back into the criminal justice system without mediation would have subordinated program to research objectives. The research effort could have undermined the very program whose results it was trying to analyze. As a result, a second-best, but non-disruptive, research design was formulated.

The basic problem is to determine what the court careers of mediation cases would have been if they had not been referred to mediation. We begin with cases referred to mediation by the court. Upon referral, a case may not be mediated either because the victim and defendant at least allege that they have resolved the problem or because one or the other or both refuse to participate in mediation. Alternatively, the parties may participate in mediation, but not reach an agreement, or they may participate and reach an agreement. Only in the last instance has mediation altered the case's court career. Cases referred by the court are sent to mediation after arraignment, and the technical disposition is continued without a finding. Even after such referral, these cases are open criminal charges and cannot be terminated privately. This means that whatever their subsequent court careers, there is nothing to suggest that cases where no agreement is reached at mediation are treated any differently than if they had never been referred to mediation. Similarly, a mediation referral is not likely to have any impact on court processing for those cases in which the parties reach agreement on their own, or in which the claimant simply decides to drop the charges. In both instances, the case will probably be dismissed, with or without a mediation referral.

The questions then are: what would have happened to those cases which do not reach an agreement at mediation if they had not been referred; how many of such cases are there; and what are the costs of the court proceedings through which they would have been processed? We have estimated the hypothetical court careers in two ways. The simplest method was to assume that the distribution of careers for these cases was the same as the distribution of careers for all criminal cases in the district court during the period in question. Even this estimate could not be secured directly because the lag in preparation of court statistics required use of the case distribution for calendar year 1976, although cost figures are for fiscal year 1976–77.

Assuming that the career distribution of agreement cases would be the same as the distribution for all cases assumes that the population of agreement cases closely parallels the population of all cases. But we know that the latter assumption is wrong. In the first place, in almost all agreement cases there is a prior relationship between the victim and defendant, while studies in other courts indicate that such a relationship may exist in only one-half of cases generally (Vera, 1977: 19). In the second place, we know that the distribution of criminal charges is different for the two populations of cases. Table 7.11 shows those distributions.

TABLE 7.11   Distribution of Charges by Treatment, 1976 Defendants

|  | Number | District Percent | Court Percent w/o MV | Mediated Agreements Number | Percent |
|---|---|---|---|---|---|
| M/V | 3,594 | 58 | | | |
| Assaults | 558 | 10 | 23 | 107 | 59 |
| Larceny | 441 | 7 | 17 | 15 | 8 |
| Narcotics | 288 | 5 | 11 | | |
| B & E | 194 | 3 | 8 | 4 | 2 |
| Receiving | 152 | 2 | 6 | | |
| Dest. of prop. | 125 | 2 | 5 | 15 | 8 |
| Disorderly con. | 119 | 2 | 5 | 4 | 2 |
| Gaming | 103 | 2 | 4 | | |
| Threats & harrass. | 66 | 1 | 3 | 24 | 13 |
| Other (less than 100) | 455 | 7 | 18 (less than 4) | 14 | 8 |
| Total | 6,180 | 100 | 100* | 183 | 100 |

\* Total defendants minus those never arrested minus those bound over to Superior Court.
   Sources: Return of Criminal Cases in the Dorchester Court.

The differences in charges are striking. The most important court category, motor vehicle offenses, is not represented in the agreement cases at all. Although assault is an important category in both distributions, it accounts for nearly three times as high a proportion in the mediation context. Threats and destruction of property are important charges in mediation but not in court; the situation is reversed for narcotics charges and larceny. In general, it is possible that the court cases represent some that are regarded as more serious than the mediation cases (narcotics, breaking and entering) and also many less serious cases (motor vehicle violations).

Estimating the effect of these differences between the two populations of cases on court careers cannot be done with confidence. The more serious cases and the lower level of prior relationships involved in the all case group suggest that those cases would have more extended court careers: fewer would be dismissed because the prosecuting witness did not want to proceed and fewer would receive some form of *de minimus* treatment. On the other hand, the large number of motor vehicle cases in the all case population might produce a high level of summary treatment, thus truncating court careers.

Despite these differences, the profile developed from all cases in 1976 is useful in estimating the hypothetical court careers of mediated agreement cases. It is useful because it corresponds closely to an alternative profile described below.

As part of a recidivism study, we identified all the assault and battery and assault and battery with a deadly weapon cases which were filed in the district court in October 1975, the last month before mediation began to operate. In 27 of those cases, we could tell from the file in the Probation Department that a prior relationship had existed between the victim and the defendant. Court files were then searched to determine the disposition pattern of those 27 cases. That pattern and how it compares to the pattern of all cases in 1976 can be seen in Table 7.12.

TABLE 7.12   Disposition of Criminal Cases in District Court

|  | All Cases, 1976 Number | Percent | A & B, Prior Relationship Case October 1975 Number | Percent |
|---|---|---|---|---|
| Guilty |  |  | 6 | 23 |
| C. Rev/Pay | 1,624 | 22 |  |  |
| C/Disp. |  |  |  |  |
| Not guilty | 511 | 7 | 2 | 8 |
| Dismissed | 2,861 | 40 | 14 | 53 |
| Default | 1,516 | 21 | 1 | 4 |
| CWOF | 361 | 5 | 3 | 12 |
| On file | 343 | 5 |  |  |
|  | 7,217 | 100 | 26 | 100 |

The proportion of guilty findings in the assault and battery profile is virtually the same as the proportion of guilty, and functionally equivalent, findings in the all case profile. The level of not guilty findings is similarly close. Although a higher proportion of assault and battery cases was dismissed, and a lower proportion defaulted, the sum of these two summary dispositions in each profile are close (57 percent and 61 percent). The fraction of cases stayed without a finding or kept on file in both profiles is also nearly the same (12 percent and 10 percent).

Confidence in the use of these profiles is also generated by the large margin for error. Table 7.13 shows the court costs saved by each agreement case depending on what its disposition would have been in court if it had not been successfully mediated.

TABLE 7.13  Court Costs Saved by Type of Disposition

| Type of Disposition | Amount Saved |
| --- | --- |
| Guilty | $438.38 |
| C. Rev/Pay | 435.96 |
| CWOF | 435.54 |
| C/Disp. | 192.67 |
| Not guilty | 107.00 |
| Dismissal | 2.74 |
| Default | — |
| On file | — |

As far as cost savings go, errors in the correspondence between the profiles and the hypothetical court careers of agreement cases are unimportant among the first three dispositions listed. Only if the proportion of not guilty, dismissed, defaulted, continued for disposition or on file cases is significantly distorted would the court cost savings be affected. If these five categories were under-represented, if more agreement cases would have led to not guilty findings or been dismissed or defaulted or continued for disposition or placed on file than in the profiles, then the cost savings derived from the profiles would have been overstated. An error in that direction is probably unimportant from a policy perspective. A conclusion of this cost/cost-savings comparison is that the ratio of mediation costs incurred to court costs saved in Dorchester is about 2.7:1. If the court cost savings have been overstated, then the ratio will increase and mediation, which from a cost savings view does not appear particularly attractive, will simply appear less so.

An error in the opposite direction, overstating the bottom five categories and understating the top three would reduce the disparity between mediation costs and court costs saved. This reduction would have important policy implications if it were substantial. However, a major error in this direction is unlikely. The argument is simplest if one focuses on the assault and battery profile. On file, default continued for disposition, and not guilty cases cannot be seriously overstated since they total only 12 percent of all cases. The issue then is how likely is it that agreement cases, if not mediated, would be *dismissed* at a rate substantially lower than the general run of court cases? There are two reasons why such a result is unlikely. The reasons arise from the nature of the parties involved in these cases and from their inclinations toward settling their quarrel. In the first place, the parties in these cases have had a prior relationship and prior relationship is one of the chief causes of case dismissal (Vera, 1977: 20). Secondly, not only have the parties to these cases had a prior relationship, but their attitudes toward each other were sufficiently constructive that an agreement between them was concluded; hardly a signal that in the absence of mediation a greater proportion of these victims would have pressed for a court sanction than is generally the case.

Before court cost savings are calculated, one more threshold issue requires attention. The court costs include court personnel costs only. The costs of supplies and equipment, of capital investments such as the courthouse and of the few non-court personnel involved in maintaining the courthouse (janitors and cleaning persons) were neither identified nor included. Only the capital costs would have been significant. The costs of supplies and equipment in 1975–76, for instance, were equal to only 3 percent of the expenditures for personal services. The courthouse is more than 50 years old. Its value as carried on the books of the City of Boston is irrelevant to its market value, and its market value is unknown. Because estimating capital costs would have been either expensive or arbitrary, we have chosen to compare the cost savings in court personnel costs to the personnel costs of mediation, rather than attempt to compare the full costs of one program to the full costs of the other. In a way, this comparison may be unfair to mediation since mediation programs generally operate out of less pretentious and less costly quarters than courts. On the other hand, courthouses frequently represent sunk costs which will not be avoided in any way by the introduction of a mediation project, unless the volume of cases is such that, in the absence of the mediation program, additional courtroom facilities would be needed. In the last analysis, a personnel cost comparison may be more useful for mediation programs in general since personnel costs are less likely to vary widely from area to area than capital investments in real estate.

A detailed determination of court costs saved has been calculated. The following sequence of calculations was made:

- The average amount of time consumed by each of the events occurring in the profiles.
- The average amount of time consumed at different stages of the different forms of dispositions.
- The court personnel present at each of those stages.
- The personnel whose activities support the work of those present at court stages.
- The per minute costs of both types of personnel.
- The personnel costs for each form of court disposition.

The end product is a per case average of court personnel costs saved, and is illustrated in Table 7.14. This product (Table 7.14) provides a composite picture of the costs saved by each agreement case using both the all case and assault and battery profiles and the trial breakdowns from the Clerk's records and the Administrator's estimate. That is, depending upon the assumptions made, each agreement case referred by the court saved either $114.24, $118.25, $163.11 or $168.32.

So far, we have estimated the cost savings only for cases referred to mediation by the court. During 1976–77, 91 cases (28 percent) were referred by the Clerk after a section 35A hearing and 39 cases (12 percent) were referred by other sources. If cases referred to mediation by any of these sources would, in the absence of mediation, have been sent to court, then the savings in court costs per case would be in the range specified in Table 7.14 supplemented by the cost of an arraignment.[6]

TABLE 7.14   Costs Saved by Agreement Cases

| | | All Case Profile | | | Assault and Battery Profile | |
| | | | Admin. | | | Admin. |
| Disposition | Percent | Clerk's Data | Estimate | Percent | Clerk's Data | Estimate |
| --- | --- | --- | --- | --- | --- | --- |
| Guilty | 5 | $22.66 | $ 21.92 | 23 | $104.25 | $100.83 |
| Not guilty | 7 | 7.49 | 7.49 | 8 | 8.56 | 8.56 |
| CWOF | 5 | 22.52 | 21.78 | 12 | 54.5 | 52.27 |
| C/Disp | 5 | 10.38 | 9.63 | | | |
| C. Rev/Pay | 12 | 54.10 | 52.32 | | | |
| Dismissal | 40 | 1.10 | 1.10 | 53 | 1.45 | 1.45 |
| Totals | | $118.25 | $114.24 | | $168.32 | $163.11 |

The extra court costs of an arraignment are about $40.

TABLE 7.15   Arraignment Costs Over Costs Already Included

| | |
| --- | --- |
| Court personnel | $16.14 |
| Prep. of "Face Sheet & Past Record Information" | 4.05 |
| Continuances | .70 |
| Clerical costs | 18.83 |
| | $39.72 |

It is difficult to say whether the Clerk would have sent such cases to court. Section 35A hearings are conducted by the Clerk of the court, except when he is on vacation. The Clerk alleges that he sends to court all cases which he believes are appropriate for court action: that is, where a citizen is entitled to secure a complaint against another person, the Clerk will issue that complaint. Mediation cases, if this is true, would be cases where the Clerk would otherwise deny the complaint, either with or without trying to mediate the dispute himself. We observed the Clerk's hearings on nine days spread over four months. Table 7.16 shows the disposition of the cases that we observed.

TABLE 7.16   Disposition of Clerk's Cases

| | |
| --- | --- |
| Complaint issued | 18 |
| Complaint denied, complainant present | 1 |
| Complaint denied, complainant not present | 5 |
| Mediated by clerk | 6 |
| Referred to mediation | 1 |
| Complaint withdrawn | 4 |
| Other (continued or complainant sent elsewhere) | 7 |
| | 42 |

The one case referred to mediation would not otherwise have gone to court. The issue appeared to be who was terrorizing whose little sister or brother. The formal defendant was 11 years old.

Better evidence that referrals from the Clerk do not save court costs comes from observed cases that were sent to court, but that appeared appropriate for referral to mediation. Two examples are quoted from our field notes.

> The fourth case involved a 47 year old white man and a 21 year old white man. The older chap alleged that the younger one broke into his house and later broke his windows maliciously. The older fellow admitted tapping the younger one with a hammer, allegedly to protect his home. The 21 year old complained about the hammer attack: his wounds required 13 stitches. He said he was trying to contact a boarder upstairs in the other's house. The trespass claim against the young man was dismissed. Complaints were issued in assault and battery against the older chap and for property damage against the younger.

> The second case was a larceny case between a landlord and tenant. The landlord left a bureau on the porch of the house rented to the tenant, who either confiscated or disposed of the bureau. The landlord wanted the bureau back or the money for it. The complaint was granted.

The first of these cases was eventually referred to mediation by the court, but of course after the costs of an arraignment had been incurred. The second case was observed too late in our fieldwork to know what happened to it. Although the evidence is slim, our observations confirm that the Clerk sends to mediation only cases that he believes are inappropriate for court.

Table 7.17 reflects the disposition of the 39 cases referred to mediation in 1976–77 other than by the court and Clerk.

Inspection of the mediation project's files indicates that 15 of these 39 cases might have led to criminal charges against the respondent based on the presenting complaint had not the dispute been submitted to

TABLE 7.17  Disposition of Other Referrals by Source, 1976–77

| Source | Mediated to Ag. | Self-settled | Staff Settled | Pty(s) Refused Med. | Total |
|---|---|---|---|---|---|
| Police | 3 | 1 | | 4 | 8 |
| Walk-in | 4 | 1 | | 4 | 9 |
| Soc. serv. ag. | 3 | 1 | | 2 | 6 |
| Dispo. U.C. | 2 | | | 2 | 4 |
| Truant off. | 1 | 1 | | 1 | 3 |
| Legal Aid | | | | | |
| Comm. organ. | 1 | | | | 1 |
| Welfare | | | 1 | | 1 |
| Other | 5 | | | 2 | 7 |
| Total | 19 | 4 | 1 | 15 | 39 |

mediation. The charges would have been assault and battery (8), harassment (4), larceny, disorderly conduct and harboring a dangerous criminal. In 13 of these 15 cases, an agreement was reached at mediation. The other 2 "criminal" cases were settled by the parties before a mediation session was held. Assuming that all 13 "criminal" agreement cases would have gone to court but for the agreement, the maximum court costs savings for "other referrals" during 1976–77 would have been on the order of $2,700.[7]

Table 7.18 combines the court costs saved by agreement cases with the number of such cases. It indicates that, depending on the profile and the allocation of actual trial to guilty pleas used, the court cost savings allocable to mediation was somewhere between $15,384 and $21,386 in 1976–77.

TABLE 7.18  Court Costs Saved by Agreement Cases, 1976–77

|  | Per Case | Number of Cases | Total |
|---|---|---|---|
| Court referrals | $118.25 | 111 | $13,125.75 |
| All case, clerk | 114.24 | 111 | 12,680.64 |
| All case, admin. | 168.32 | 111 | 18,683.52 |
| A & B, clerk | 163.11 | 111 | 18,105.21 |
| A & B, admin. | 207.92 | 0 | 0.00 |
| Clerk referrals | 207.92 | 13 | 2,702.96 |
| Other referrals | — | — | — |

Before cost savings are compared to costs, we must face the preliminary issue of whether it makes sense to say that any court costs are saved just because the court was called upon to process fewer cases fully than would have been the situation if no mediation project existed. The argument against any savings is that court employees are already employed, most have a protected civil service status, and the effect of mediation will be to spread less work among the same number of employees, or permit the same number of employees to devote more time to the remainder of the caseload, rather than to enable fewer employees to provide the same level of services to a reduced caseload. This argument has even more force to the extent that the district court already has any excess capacity to process cases.

But we are not sure that what would actually happen in any particular setting when a mediation program is initiated ought for all purposes to determine whether cost savings are relevant or not. The effect of actual events may be crucial to a city council which has to decide how to spend finite resources over a limited period of time. But our charter is to consider mediation as a process of which Dorchester is an example, rather than to evaluate mediation in Dorchester for Dorchester's purposes. Political units must determine the kind and level of services that they will provide over a term longer than a few budgeting cycles. Whether they make such decisions explicitly, or let them be made by inertia, there will be a positive connection between the demand for a certain form of service and the resources which will be devoted to that service. If, in any setting in the long run, mediation produces a greater or lesser demand for court services, that change in demand will be reflected in the resources devoted to courts. It may not be reflected isometrically: every man-year saved may not mean one less person employed. Feather-bedding exists. Reductions in force may just mean no new employees are hired. But airline pilots replace railroad firemen and mechanical pickers replace farm workers and, given the demand, mediators and case coordinators will replace bailiffs and district attorneys.

The cost/cost-savings comparison presented in this paper, then, does not reflect what actually happened in Dorchester in 1976–77, but it does suggest what would happen over the long run in places which had court and mediation programs like Dorchester's. If you have or want to have this kind of mediation and this kind of court and you maintain these activities over many years, then this is what it is likely to cost you and this is what you may save.

Table 7.19 summarizes the annual personnel costs attributable to mediation.

TABLE 7.19   Personnel Costs Attributable to Mediation 1976–77

|  |  |
|---|---|
| Direct personnel | $76,662.12 |
| Consulting and contracting | 6,746.47 |
| Sub total | 83,408.59 |
| Less subsidy to court | 4,079.61 |
| Total | $79,328.98 |

Two forms of service are included in these costs that are not included on the court side of the comparison—fund raising and other developmental activities and bookkeeping. For purposes of comparison, expenses attributed to those activities will be deducted from mediation personnel costs.[8] The new total was $73,824.25 or $403.41 per agreement case.

These agreement cases in the 111 instances when referred by the court saved court costs per case of either $114, $118, $163 or $168, depending on the assumptions employed. The ratio then of mediation costs to courts costs saved was between 3.5:1 and 2.4:1. If costs and ratios are averaged, the court costs were $140.98 and the ratio was 2.9:1. The maximum cost savings for the thirteen cases referred by sources other than the court and Clerk was $207.92 per case and the ratio of mediation costs to that figure is 1.9:1. If cases from these two sources are weighted in proportion to their frequency, and if the average for court referrals is used, the weighted court costs saved would be $147.99 and the ratio between the costs of mediation and court costs saved would by 2.7:1.[9]

But it is perhaps unfair to compare mediation and criminal prosecution on a per case basis. The argument would be that the beneficiaries of mediation are all of the disputants involved, and thus two at a minimum. The beneficiaries of prosecution, in the sense that public resources are devoted to their assistance (the defendant gets a legal trial, a free lawyer, and perhaps counseling from a probation officer), are only one per case. Thus, comparing mediation costs and court cost-savings on a per recipient basis reduces mediation costs and the ratio between the two by at least one-half. One problem with this logic is that however persuasive it may be from the perspective of the participants, it makes no sense institutionally. From the point of view of a political unit in which both a criminal court and a mediation project are operating, two parties in mediation will always be required to replace one defendant in court unless the parties have levelled criminal charges against each other.

Even from the point of view of the participants, the argument must be shaded a bit. Many respondents in successful mediation receive little by way of compromise. It is not at all infrequent to encounter a mediation agreement in which the respondent agrees to cease some objectionable behavior and to pay some money while the complainant agrees only to drop the criminal charge. Functionally, such mediation is close to a court proceeding in which the case against a defendant is dismissed after he makes restitution and agrees not to pester the complainant. Nor is it always true that only defendants "benefit" from criminal trials. Victims in Dorchester regularly receive two kinds of returns directly from court proceedings—restitution and psychic satisfaction. For victims who have internalized a high level of rights consciousness, the emotional return for sanctions levied against the defendant may be substantial, legitimating both their complaint and their behavior.

Our cost/cost-savings comparison is, it must be remembered, a case study. Its conclusions cannot be automatically applied to other mediation projects or to other criminal courts. There are at least five characteristics of the Dorchester situation that have an important effect on costs and cost-savings which may not be typical of mediation projects— the form of mediation provided, the type of criminal cases referred to mediation, the extent of the caseload, the point at which cases are referred to mediation and the specific intake procedures used. Each of these characteristics warrants discussion.

From the point of view of cost, the salient features of mediation in Dorchester are the considerable time that is devoted to getting behind presenting complaints and the fidelity of mediators to a model in which they suppress fact finding and judgment formation in favor of disputant-initiated agreements about future conduct. These factors mean that Dorchester mediation is a "deep" variant requiring four times as much time per case as the more directive or more professional mediation used by projects in Columbus and Miami (McGillis and Mullen, 1977). Longer mediation is important financially primarily because it increases the amount of time spent by staff in directing the conduct of proceedings.

Two other dimensions of staff work in Dorchester are costly. First, an attempt is made to match the sex-race characteristics of the disputants with those of the mediators. This and a parallel effort to schedule sessions at the convenience of the disputants compounds an already difficult mediator scheduling problem and is a drain on staff time. Second, the staff's responsibility to keep in touch with the disputants after successful mediation so that the three-month report may be made to the judge in cases referred to by the court coupled to the staff's involvement in putting aspects of mediation agreements into effect—supervising property exchanges, arranging social service referrals, lecturing defaulting disputants—consume considerable staff time. Mediation programs which were neither saddled with nor assumed these responsibilities would operate with less staff, and obviously at less cost.

Most mediation projects process misdemeanors.[10] The jurisdiction of the Dorchester court extends to many crimes more serious than misdemeanors as they are generally defined. The court can try any criminal case for which the punishment does not exceed 5 years in prison. As a result, many of the cases referred to mediation reflect allegations of serious crimes—assault with a deadly weapon, low degree kidnapping, burglary, larceny. Several cases that we observed involved threats by, or use of guns, or attacks with weapons like tire irons. One of the reasons that deep mediation, despite its attendant costs, is appropriate in Dorchester is the gravity of the problems that it faces. But probably more important from a cost perspective is the relationship between the seriousness of many of the matters referred to mediation and the desire of the court's judges to continue to exercise some control over the cases that they refer to mediation. That control is expensive for the mediation project. It requires the staff to conduct follow-up and to make court appearances which could otherwise be avoided.

That mediation in Dorchester is pure mediation rather than mediation-arbitration has substantial negative cost consequences. Earlier in this chapter we argued that court cost-savings are produced only in agreement cases. If a mediation-arbitration process had been used in Dorchester instead of pure mediation, the number of agreement cases —that is, cases that would not require full court treatment—would have increased in 1976–77 from 183 to 216. In mediation-arbitration every case heard becomes an agreement case: none go back to court. This change alone would reduce the personnel cost per agreement case from $403 to $342 and the ratio of mediation costs to weighted court costs saved from 2.7:1 to 2.3:1.[11]

The third factor affecting cost is the caseload level. Mediation was provided to 219 disputes in Dorchester in 1976–77, an average of 18 cases per month. The first question is whether this caseload level is low, compared either to other mediation projects or to the ability of the Dorchester project to process cases with its existing staff and operating procedures. The question of inter-project comparison can be approached on the basis of cases mediated per staff person or of cases mediated per person in the population served by the project. On a hearings per staff person basis, Dorchester is low. McGillis and Mullen's data (1977: Table 1) indicate that the Columbus and Miami projects hear 268 and 309 disputes annually per staff person while the figure for Dorchester in 1976–77 was 54 hearings per mediation component employee. But this disparity simply reflects the differences in the type of mediation provided and in the type of dispute mediated. If Dorchester staff were not required to attend hearings, to attend court and clerk's sessions, and to provide follow-up for the court and with the disputants, then a smaller staff would be required.

A more important inquiry is whether the existing staff could process more cases in the Dorchester mode if more cases were available. We will look at availability first. It is not a question to which there is any easy answer. Table 7.20 shows the ratios between population served and hearings per month for the mediation programs surveyed by McGillis and Mullen (1977).

TABLE 7.20   Comparative Ratios of Hearings Held per Population Served for Five Selected Programs

| Program | Hearings per Month per 10,000 Inhabitants |
|---|---|
| Columbus, Ohio | 3.15 |
| New York, N.Y. | 2.00 |
| Dorchester, Mass. | 1.31 |
| Miami, Fla. | 1.27 |
| Rochester, N.Y. | .60 |

These ratios were determined from the population which McGillis and Mullen were told was served by these projects and the cases the projects estimate they heard. But one cannot rest entirely easy about Dorchester's caseload on the grounds that it serves a smaller population than the projects with markedly larger caseloads. The Miami program, for instance, hears a high number of cases, but has a low hearing to population ratio because it serves Dade County's 1,467,000 people. On the other hand, if the Miami project actually draws its clientele only from the 355,000 people in the City of Miami, it would hear proportionately four times as many cases as we have extrapolated from McGillis and Mullen's data and 3.8 times as many cases as Dorchester, if population were held constant. And, in fact, our analysis of the Dorchester intake process suggests that had relations between the local police and the First Justice of the court been better, the Clerk of the court been less anxious to mediate disputes himself and the project been able to develop referrals from the small claims court or police, it might have enjoyed a substantially higher caseload.[12]

The staff of the mediation component believes that they could process 40 referrals per month assuming that the proportion of referrals to hearings remained at its current level (62 percent). Supervisory personnel believe that an increase to 50 referrals would be workable. If we assume that the current staff could process a level of referrals midway between its and the supervisors' estimate (45 per month), how many of the 210 additional referrals might, given its current caseload, come from the court and thus produce additional cost-savings? As reflected in our discussion of intake problems, this query is difficult; the raw numbers suggest that there is adequate leeway. But the judges believe that few additional cases could be referred to mediation. If the proportion of court referred cases remained constant, an annual increase of 210 cases would reduce the mediation costs to court cost-savings ratio to 1.7:1 $\{73,824 \div [\frac{183}{330} \times 210) + 183]\} \div 148.$[13] If the current staff can handle 210 more referrals per year, but nothing near that number of new cases can be generated, then presumably a smaller staff can handle the current caseload since the excess capacity is somewhere between 33 percent and 46 percent.[14]

Cases in the criminal justice process in Dorchester are diverted late. The later the diversion, the less the cost-savings. If cases which eventually go to court were referred instead to mediation by the police, the costs of an arraignment, prosecutor and defender preparation time, and, in some instances, of a Clerk's hearing as well as trial and post-conviction expenditures would be saved. If the Clerk referred cases to mediation instead of issuing a complaint, arraignment costs would be saved. Mechanically, earlier diversion is feasible. The criteria used by ADAs to recommend, and the judges to make, referrals would not be particularly difficult for others to apply.

Despite its downstream referrals, Dorchester's loss of significant court cost-savings in comparison to other mediation projects is far from clear. Police referrals have been a problem for many mediation programs. Where, as in Dade County, a police connection has been institutionalized, some observers believe that the cases referred by the police would generally have been rejected rather than filed in court if the mediation project did not exist. In addition, upstream events are financially less important than post-conviction costs. In Dorchester, for instance, probation supervision for guilty findings averages ten times the cost of an arraignment and constitutes 64 percent of all costs including an arraignment. Even cases destined for dismissal where arraignment is the major cost, would have increased savings by only $3,200 in 1976–77 if they had been referred to mediation before, rather than after, arraignment.

The last local factor affecting cost is the mode of intake. Intake of court cases in Dorchester is based on staff attendance at court sessions and Clerk's hearings. Many other mediation projects are able to mobilize screening units in prosecutor's and Clerk's offices to make referrals without cost to the mediation project (McGillis and Mullen, 1977). Looking at the whole system, neither procedure is necessarily superior. Lesser mediation costs are traded off for greater court costs. The choice would be unimportant if the procedures were equally efficient, which they are not. Thus, the problem in Dorchester is not that intake processing is carried out by mediation, rather than court staff, but that so much time is wasted by mediation personnel in court and at the Clerk's hearings when nothing relevant to mediation is occurring.

## Cost Conclusions

Our cost data are fragile and the information available about other mediation projects is incomplete and tends to be somewhat self-serving. As a result, we are reluctant to propose flat conclusions in the cost/cost-savings area. With that caveat, we offer the following propositions:

- The costs of mediation can be substantial, particularly when deep mediation is not joined with arbitration and where a high level of intake and follow-up services are provided for the court.
- In Dorchester, mediation costs are 2 to 3 times the amount of court costs saved.
- That ratio could be reduced to roughly 1.7:1 if the caseload were increased to the maximum which current staff could handle: it would be 2.1:1 $[(57,500 - 183) - 148]$ if, given the current caseload, one less case coordinator were employed. The ratio could be further reduced if intake procedures were made more efficient and if the three-month follow-up were either eliminated or made the responsibility of the complainant. In other words, if the court expected less from mediation staff at intake and in follow-up, if it would tolerate some slight delays at intake and ambiguities in follow-up, then it would get more actual mediation for the resources devoted to mediation.
- The savings in court costs would be increased somewhat and the ratio of mediation costs to court costs saved could be reduced substantially if pure mediation were replaced by mediation-arbitration. The original choice of pure mediation was not made on ideological grounds, but because of supposed imperfections in the Massachusetts arbitration statute. That the statute is inadequate is unclear. Inadequate or not, whether the

statute should really be a concern is also problematic. Resort to court enforcement of awards made in mediation-arbitration sessions is extremely rare: it has only occurred twice in the entire experience of the New York Dispute Center. Nor do disputants with lawyers in New York appear to be scared away by the arbitration dimension of the process.

- Table 7.21 is a composite of the estimated mediation costs to cost-savings ratios that could result from various changes in Dorchester's operating procedures.

- Most of the court costs saved by mediation arise from reducing the need for probationary supervision. About one-half of mediated cases would, however, have resulted in dismissals if they had not been referred to mediation. One can then judge mediation as an alternative to cheap court processing (arraignment plus dismissal) in many cases and to expensive probation in significantly fewer cases.

- If mediation-arbitration were substituted for pure mediation and if the mediation staff was reduced by one, both steps that are within the power of the project to take, we estimate that the cost cost-savings ratio could be reduced to 1.8:1. Even with these changes the total costs of mediation would be $382 per hearing.

TABLE 7.21   Costs, Cost-Savings and Costs/Cost-Savings Ratios in Various Conditions

| Condition | Cost of Mediation (a) | Court Costs Saved (b) | Ratio (a) : (b) |
|---|---|---|---|
| Actual | $403 | $148 | 2.7:1 |
| Med-arbitration | 342 | 148 | 2.3:1 |
| Reduce staff by one | 314 | 148 | 2.1:1 |
| Reduce staff by one + med.-arb. | 263 | 148 | 1.8:1 |
| Max. caseload with current staff | 247 | 148 | 1.7:1 |
| Max. caseload with current staff + med.-arb. | 229 | 148 | 1.5:1 |
| Med.-arb. + 805 referrals per year | 148 | 148 | 1:1 |

## Conclusion

In this section we step back from the data and present our impressions as field workers on the Dorchester project and as researchers who have tried to follow the mediation movement in Europe as well as in this country (see Felstiner, 1974, 1975; Felstiner and Drew, 1978).

Our first reaction is that mediation's capacity to produce positive results is more a function of the level of emotional investment than of the
subject matter of a dispute. We earlier argued that property disputes because they are more firmly anchored in the past than relationship quarrels are more difficult to maneuver to agreement. Putting that reservation aside, it does not seem to us that mediation is more successful in
family than neighborhood disputes, in landlord-tenant than consumer
disputes, in dog bite than assault cases. The difference, rather, is between those cases where problems lie close to the surface, on the one
hand, and, on the other, disputes that reflect personal scripts, psychic
pre-dispositions or social conditions that have become part of an ingrained response to the dispute or the other disputant.

In the ideology of mediation, courts deal only with presenting complaints while mediation confronts underlying causes. Court dispositions
therefore tend towards irrelevance while mediation strikes for permanent solutions. The Dorchester training manual states that mediation
"prevents the recurrence of future problems by getting at the basic
reasons for the dispute" and "the purpose of mediation is ... to help
parties get at the root of their problems and devise their own solutions
to them." Our reservation is that "underlying cause" is a complicated
concept and mediation's power to identify and affect underlying causes
is a function of the kind of underlying causes that are present in a particular case.

Disputes submitted to mediation may be influenced by several kinds
of attitudes, events or conditions. There may, of course, be nothing
more at issue than the presenting complaint. The disputants may just
differ about facts or norms or values concerning a naked incident. There
may be no history to the disagreement nor behavior patterns related to
it. On the other hand, the dispute may have a past. It may be affected
by earlier incidents that disturbed the relationship between the parties so
that they interacted less or coped with each other in some maladaptive
fashion. Disputes may also be affected by general social conditions—
unemployment, racial hostility, inadequate housing, lack of recreation
facilities. All of these conditions may interact with personality dimensions which, although not originating in the dispute, underlie a party's
dispute-related behavior. And, of course, disputes may be affected by
chronic negative reactions to stress—substance abuse, resort to violence,
sexual inadequacy, etc.

These emotional and social conditions and the responsive behavior
to which they lead cannot be successfully addressed by mediation, and
many disputes that they generate are thus beyond the power of community mediators. But is it possible that we are giving the proponents of
mediation credit for trying to do something that they have never attempted to do and then criticizing them for failing to do it? Would it not be
correct to say that they do not allege that mediation is an adequate re-

sponse to underlying causes in the sense of substance abuse, negative coping patterns, poor housing or racial hostility? The objective rather is to expose these problems and to begin to get the parties talking about them. The deep problems are obviously related to the mediated dispute, but they are to be confronted by others after a social service referral. We do not doubt that this rationale is the private belief of the people who train mediators and run mediation programs. But the distinctions are blurred in the training program that we observed and are rarely made clear in public pronouncements about mediation. Trainers teach that "an agreement won't last if it hasn't dealt with the underlying cause." The Dorchester manual states that mediation will "help parties get at the root of their problems and devise their *own* solutions to them." It is true that mediation shares with most interpersonal psychotherapies the aim of uncovering emotional material underlying interpersonal problems and communicating this material to any intimately involved other. An attempt is made to help each disputant understand the other disputant's perspective, to get the feel of "the other man's moccasins." After this, however, mediation is content to deal with *overlying* material—a particular incident precipitated by underlying material. Moreover, the social service referral as the saving grace for deep problems is a myth in Dorchester. We were able to identify 79 instances of alcoholic abuse, chronic violence or severe psychological problems in the first 500 cases. Referrals to social service agencies occurred in 35 of these cases, but only 8 disputants kept even the first referral appointment.

Our point is not that mediation does not do enough, nor even that its proponents are not careful enough in distinguishing between what it can and cannot do. It is, rather, that mediation is not psychotherapy and that is what many of the disputes that come to mediation require, if any form of social intervention would be helpful. The problem, then, is not mediation as a process, but either its intake or referral when confronted with problems beyond its power to address. Our primary suggestion to projects that have experience parallel to Dorchester's, then, is to face up to the need to shift "deep" problems to psychotherapy and concentrate mediation efforts on sorting out the practical problems—the assistance in controlling pets, children and noise, in striking bargains over restitution for property damage and theft, in reducing the abrasive encounters of intimates who want to separate—that it does so well.

Our second general comment is related to the first. We do not mean to imply that the universe of interpersonal disputes is split into practical and deep problems and that any fool can easily tell the difference. On the contrary, practical problems may have complicated strands, deep problems can sometimes be helped by surface adjustments, and at the margins one type of problem shades gradually into the other. Whatever adjustments in intake and referral are made, mediation will often be operating in the gray area where practical problems have roots in social and intrapsychic conditions. In such cases, the mediation hearing should probably be viewed as an opening intervention rather than as the sole medium for providing service. What we are suggesting may be viewed as a more aggressive and structured follow-up than Dorchester and other mediation programs generally offer. That is, in those cases where the mediators believe that the agreement is incomplete or shaky, where lessons in improving communication may have been imperfectly grasped or where social services are obviously needed, the mediators should as a matter of course organize further mediation sessions or keep in contact with the disputants to monitor their interaction or help staff work with the disputants to keep the spirit of the mediation agreement intact. We believe that this active and persistent follow-up should be provided primarily by the mediators, rather than the staff, because it is the mediators that should have developed rapport with the disputants and should have acquired a broad and intimate feel for their conflicts. To the extent, moreover, that mediation projects are viewed as attempts by communities to take responsibility for their own lives by taking responsibility for their own conflicts (see Smith, 1978: 209), the more active and pervasive the role of community members the better. In sum, we suggest that mediation, if it is to be successful in terms of the lives of disputants rather than in terms of whether agreements were or were not reached, ought to be able to provide sustained support to disputants. The currrent model of a single intervention, after all, resembles in that respect the court process to which mediation is intended to be an improvement.

Our third conclusion concerns the influence of social organization on mediation. In an earlier paper (Felstiner, 1974: 79), one of us suggested that institutionalized mediation may require mediators who "possess as a matter of existing experience sufficient information about the particular perspectives and histories of the particular disputants to be able efficiently to suggest acceptable outcomes." Since the comparatively atomistic organization of social life in the United States implies low levels of general information about disputants, the prediction for the growth of mediation of interpersonal disputes was gloomy. This emphasis on the production function of mediation, on limitations to the ability of mediators to suggest workable accommodations, has been demonstrated by the Dorchester experience to be wrong. As Danzig and Lowy (1975) noted, production may be irrelevant since mediators may serve disputants primarily by structuring a process in which they provide solutions for themselves. Moreover, the level of information provided to mediators by disputants in Dorchester has been sufficient that they have generally been able to have a *direct* effect on outcomes.

We continue to believe, however, that social organization may have an inhibiting influence on the development of institutionalized mediation

TABLE 7.22  Mediation Hearings by Selected Referral Sources, NJCs (mid-March 1978 through September 1978)

|  |  | Referral Sources | | |
|---|---|---|---|---|
|  |  | *Self-ref.* | *Community Ag.* | *Total Hearings* |
| Mediation Hearings | Atlanta | 22 (7%) | 1 (·3%) | 305 |
|  | Kansas City | 4 (2%) | 8 (5%) | 172 |
|  | Venice/Mar Vista | 27 (55%) | 7 (14%) | 49 |

Source: Sheppard, Roehl, and Cook, 1979: Tables III.3; III.6, and III.9

in the United States. The old reservation was directed toward the process of mediation: the new is focused on caseload. Mediation programs generally derive cases from two sources—from the justice system (criminal courts, small claims courts, prosecutor's offices, legal aid), on the one hand, and from community agencies and directly through so-called self-referrals, on the other. Dorchester receives almost all of its cases from the justice system. Despite the project's high visibility, zero cost to the disputants, and record of successfully mediating many disputes, the citizens of Dorchester came unprompted to the project for mediation only four times in 1976–77. Dorchester's experience is not unusual. Table 7.22 reflects the small *number* of self-referrals that lead to mediation hearings in all three federal Neighborhood Justice Centers, regardless of their orientation toward the justice system.

Table 7.23 indicates that when compared to the populations served, mediation programs are not considered a useful resource by citizens with interpersonal problems unless they have been shunted in that direction by the justice system.[15]

TABLE 7.23  Self-Referrals per 10,000 Population per Month

| | |
|---|---|
| Atlanta | .50 |
| Venice/Mar Vista | .46 |
| Kansas City | .11 |
| Dorchester | .02 |

We do not know precisely how this low self-referral level compares to the use of mediation processes in Africa reported by anthropologists and proposed as models by American reformers (see Danzig, 1973). Observers of African mediation do not report rates (see, e.g., Gibbs, 1969a; Gulliver, 1963). It does not appear, however, that mediators in tribes such as the Kpelle or Arusha are only mobilized occasionally. When they are used, moreover, it is because a dispute is brought to their attention by the disputants, not by a formal institution of government. The key to the difference, it seems to us, is in the relationship between the disputants and the mediators. In both the African and American contexts, the disputants tend to be related and the supply of potential disputants is very large. But in the African situation, the disputants also are related to the mediators (see Gibbs, 1969a: 289; Gulliver, 1963). The mediators and disputants are part of a dense interpersonal network, part of each other's life experience. Our hypothesis, then, is that disputants are comfortable in mobilizing these mediators because they are familiar with them as people and with mediation as a process. Disputants are expected and expect themselves to use mediation as a response to conflict.

Very little of this is true for most Americans in most American communities. *Mediators are strangers*—their values and life experience are unknown. Institutionalized mediation is unfamiliar and its use is exceptional. It is thus life, not logic, that makes self-referred mediation viable in one context and not in another. For this reason, the fit between mediation and American social needs is not immutable. Americans may gradually become familiar with mediation untied to the justice system, but in the short term this form of mediation is likely to play only a small role at the margin of dispute processing behavior.

Finally, we will recapitulate the major insights gained in research on Dorchester that seem to us to be relevant beyond its case study borders.

- The key to the content of mediation hearings is the content of mediator training. Training programs should be designed for the kinds of disputes that mediators will hear. They should not assume that mediation techniques that work well for other kinds of conflict such as labor disputes will necessarily be effective in the interpersonal field.

- Many important mediation techniques are counter-intuitive to untrained personnel. Sustained mediation training is therefore critical regardless of the funding or philosophy of particular mediation projects. Whatever the training, mediation is a difficult task and there is a great range to the abilities of different people to learn and apply its techniques successfully. All mediation projects are thus faced with the problem of identifying and minimizing the poor work of a number of inept mediators.

- High volume mediation projects are likely to have important links to the criminal justice system. The connection to criminal justice means that domestic cases involving violence and harassment will constitute a prominent part of the hearing agenda—these cases are the most numerous category in Dorchester, in the Atlanta NJC and in the Brooklyn Vera-IMCR program. Where caseloads are markedly intra-family and violence related, mediation becomes a factor in community mental health rather than community dispute resolution and should be judged in comparison to other community mental health facilities as well as to court services.

- It is difficult to judge mediation programs on a cost basis. The means to measure the benefits of mediation in a systematic and adequate manner have not been developed so that even precise cost comparisons are naked of benefit information or coupled only to impressionistic benefit data. It is nevertheless useful to compare mediation costs to the costs of alternative services, including criminal court processing and other mediation programs. But the mediation to court comparison will generally be unfair to mediation because in most instances disputants in criminal court cases receive almost no services from the court. The most typical court career is several continuances and a dismissal while a significant proportion of mediation referrals lead to a hearing. Ultimately, then, what can be said about mediation as an alternative to criminal prosecution is that its per case costs can be substantial and may, in some instances, be more than those of lower criminal courts, while its benefits are almost surely likely to exceed those of criminal processing.

## Notes

1. "This is like the Hale Case," said a mediator in caucus more than a year after her training was completed.

2. The coercion hypothesis may not work within mediation hearings because "other" referrals who attend mediation, having come out of choice, are more motivated toward settlement than the Court/Clerk referrals.

3. Some of the disputes coded as Level 1 did involve serious underlying problems, such as drunkenness and racial animosity. However, these disputants had no ongoing relationship and in a few cases did not ever know each other. Consequently, those underlying problems, although contributing to the occurrence of the conflict, were not relevant to resolution of the dispute.

4. Level by Disposition (collapsing "withdrew" and "refused" categories as well as "staff settled" and "mediated"):

$$\text{Tau } c = .1514, \quad p. \ 001$$

Level by Outcome (collapsing "settled at mediation" and "settled after mediation"):

$$\text{Tau } c = .1045, \quad p. \ 01$$

Level by Follow-up:

$$\text{Tau } b = .2559, \quad p \ .00001$$

5. Mediation cases are referred by the court, the clerk and miscellaneous others—police, truant officers, social service agencies, self-referrals, etc. Estimates of the cost savings to the district court have been formulated for each referral source. It is not feasible to estimate the costs savings to other institutions. The efforts which truant officers or alcoholic treatment centers were

saved from making, minus the efforts they were mobilized into making, could not be tracked without the existence of a control group or otherwise reasonably estimated.

6. Public funds for personnel are consumed by more than time spent in court. ADAs and Massachusetts Defenders must prepare for cases as well as try them. These lawyers have told us, however, that cases referred to mediation by the court which return to court because no agreement was reached are scheduled for trial quickly. As a consequence the lawyers say that they are prepared to try a case after arraignment whether or not the case is referred to mediation, and the only time saved by successful mediation is time actually spent in court. The cost of case preparation would be saved when referrals to mediation eliminated arraignments. Such costs were not calculated since, as will be seen, few arraignments were avoided.

7. The maximum post-arraignment cost saving estimate is $168.20. Court costs of arraignment are $39.72. Their sum × 13 equals $2,702.96. Out of court lawyers' time is not included, but the difference between the maximum and minimum estimates is $54.06 which would pay for 3.2 hours of lawyer time or 1.6 hours assuming 50 percent overhead.

8. Slightly more than one third (35 percent) of the director's salary ($2,577.20), and the 25 percent of the bookkeeper's salary ($2,927.53) allocated to mediation.

9. For comparison purposes, Hoff estimates that the total direct costs saved the Philadelphia Municipal Court by diverting civilian complaint cases to the local 4-A project was $144 per case (1974: 43).

Another way to compare costs and cost-savings is to do just that. The personnel costs of mediation were $73,824. The maximum savings for court personnel were $21,386. The ratio between them is 3.5:1. This comparison is unfair to mediation, however, because it includes the costs of mediating cases with no criminal dimension, and thus no criminal court costs saved.

10. The IMCR-Vera felony project in Brooklyn is very recent, unusual and its costs are unreported.

11. A change to mediation-arbitration might, of course, have other consequences. Wary of arbitration by third parties whose provenance is unclear, fewer disputants might choose diversion in the first place. Facing arbitrated settlements that were imposed on them, fewer disputants might fulfil the terms of agreements. Mediation-arbitration may coerce the respondent to reach an agreement less than pure mediation where the result of failing to reach an agreement is the possibility of renewed prosecution rather than an award formulated by the mediator-arbitrators. In the absence of research on the issue, we do not know whether the consequences of any lesser coercion are fewer, better agreements or just better agreements or no consequences at all. We also suspect that mediator-arbitrators behave differently during sessions than pure mediators. Having the responsibility to decide the dispute if the parties cannot agree, mediator-arbitrators may make a greater effort to develop a factual background, may focus more on applicable norms and may be more concerned with questions of credibility than pure mediators. However, IMCR staff, who are familiar with both processes, are sceptical of the differences, particularly since imposed awards are infrequent (5–10 percent in New York) in mediation-arbitration (but

see Hoff, 1974: 21; McGillis and Mullen 1977: Table 1). Only comparative observation would settle the question.

A switch on mediation-arbitration would also have secondary cost consequences. In mediation-arbitration the criminal case is dismissed as soon as the parties agree to mediation-arbitration. All mediation costs associated with further court supervision would be eliminated and the court costs of such supervision would be saved.

12. Although an expanded caseload would reduce the per case costs of agreement cases, it would increase court cost-savings only to the extent that the increase in caseload came from cases which would otherwise be processed by the court. If, for instance, the number of agreement cases were doubled by the addition of police referrals in matters which currently are dropped by the police, the cost per agreement case would be halved, but not a penny more in court cases would have been saved. Thus, an increase in caseload would reduce the mediation costs to cost-savings ratio, but it would not reduce the total resources required to run both the court and mediation systems. Successful mediation might, of course, forestall behavior which ultimately would lead to a court case. Such a consequence is part of the ideology of mediation (see Weisbrod, 1977: 181–2), but it would require a difficult field trial to demonstrate.

13. Assuming a switch to mediation-arbitration, the ratio of mediation costs to court costs saved would become 1:1 when 805 referrals a year are made, an increase of 2.4 times the current level ($73,824 - 148 = .62x$).

14. A reduction of people performing case coordination functions from 3 to 2 would mean that court attendance and hearing coverage functions would have to be split and compensation time taken in the afternoons. Some help from central staff would be required at times of illness or vacation.

15. An alternative explanation, of course, is that the profile is simply not aware of the mediation programs' existence. A telephone survey by Sheppard, Roehl and Cook in Venice/Mar Vista revealed, however, that 30 percent of that population knew about the Venice/Mar Vista NJC.

# 8

# Mediation: The Brooklyn Experiment*

### Robert C. Davis

## Introduction

Mediation—a voluntary bargaining process in which parties to a dispute seek a mutually acceptable resolution under the guidance of a neutral third party (or parties)—has been gaining wide acceptance as a method of handling minor criminal offenses between acquaintances. In recent years, criminal court calendars in the United States have become overcrowded with cases, a large number of which stem from interpersonal disputes. Sander (1976) argues that police and courts have been expected to replace the church, family, and other traditional resources as mechanisms for resolving disputes.

But criminal courts are ill-equipped to handle this influx of interpersonal disputes, with the result that the quality of justice received by victims and defendants may suffer. Judges, prosecutors, and defense attorneys often complain of seeing incidents involving the same parties brought before them again and again. They feel that complainants in these cases often change their minds about testifying against someone with whom they have a continuing relationship, or just fail to show up. Even when complainants do want to prosecute, it may not be clear what to do with convicted defendants, short of incarceration—a response which, in these cases, is often inappropriate.

Consequently, court officials may be unwilling to give disputing parties the attention necessary to prevent an escalation of hostilities between them. Cases involving a prior victim-offender relationship are far more frequently dismissed than stranger-to-stranger cases (Vera Institute of Justice, 1977), ostensibly for lack of cooperation by the complainant,

* This research was supported by The New York Division of Criminal Justice Services. All references in the text of this chapter are found in the Bibliography at the conclusion of this volume.

but perhaps also because prosecutors simply do not feel it is appropriate to prosecute such matters in criminal court. Parnas (1973), in discussing the response of criminal courts to domestic disputes, states:

> ...there is a tendency on the part of those in a position to respond to ignore them altogether, or more usually, to respond in such a way as to get rid of such cases as quickly as possible (1973: 734).

Moreover, the time taken up by large volumes of cases arising from disputes may hamper the effectiveness of criminal courts in handling stranger-to-stranger cases—those that communities are most concerned about. The Vera Institute of Justice (1977) study points out that over-crowding of the courts with cases arising from interpersonal disputes has helped to produce long delays in the adjudication of serious stranger-to-stranger crimes and, in many instances, has "weakened the ability of the criminal justice system to deal quickly and decisively with the 'real felons', who may be getting lost in the shuffle." (1975: 15).

Concern about the ability of criminal courts to deal effectively with cases arising from interpersonal disputes and about the possibility that the large number of such cases prevented the courts from concentrating on serious stranger-to-stranger crimes helped foster a climate that encouraged experimentation with mediation as an alternative to prosecution. As early as 1973, Parnas argued for 'comprehensive" diversion of cases arising from domestic disputes from criminal courts to mediation. Paterson, Nicolau, and Weisbrod (1978) put the case for diversion of dispute cases out of the courts in the following terms:

> It seems an entirely appropriate goal to reserve to the courts those activities for which they are best suited and to avoid swamping and paralyzing them with cases that do not require their unique capabilities. This can be done by separating the private dispute settlement function from the criminal court structure and diverting such cases to a complementary dispute settlement mechanism specially designed to handle interpersonal conflicts (1978: 24).

During the last decade, social scientists proposed several models for the creation of decentralized community dispute resolution centers as alternatives to centralized and highly bureaucratized criminal courts. Danzig (1973) proposed one of the initial models for a community dispute resolution center, or moot. Interpersonal criminal and civil matters would be referred to the moot by social service agencies, police, courts, or individuals. Agreements reached through mediation would be upheld voluntarily by the disputants; that is, agreements would not be enforceable by the courts. He feels that community pressure brought to bear upon the disputants would be sufficient to uphold the agreement.[1] Danzig stresses the importance of mediation as a therapeutic process, citing studies of police response which suggest that many times complainants want police officers to act in the capacity of a mediator rather than to make an arrest.

Fisher's (1975) concept of community courts is drawn from the Beth Din in Israel. A community court, in a relatively small area such as an apartment complex, would be provided for by the legislature and would have exclusive jurisdiction over certain matters. Mediators would be elected from the community. Decisions might involve solutions such as restitution, or punitive measures, including depriving disputants of use of community property or evicting them. In contrast to Danzig's model, verdicts would be binding and any violations would be enforceable in the formal courts.

Sander (1976) has recommended the formation of dispute resolution centers operated by the government, which would have the capabilities of mediating, arbitrating, or simply fact-finding. If necessary, cases would be referred to the courts for adjudication. All decisions would be open for court appeal. Sander's model represents a compromise position between the noncoercive moots proposed by Danzig and the highly coercive community courts espoused by Fisher.

Once the concept had been articulated, mediation programs sprang up rapidly across the country. In 1971, the Columbus Night Prosecutor's Program began using mediation to resolve bad-check cases, and by 1979, over 30 cities had set up community mediation programs which mediate and/or arbitrate civil and criminal matters arising from interpersonal disputes.[2]

In 1976, under the joint sponsorship of the American Bar Association, the Judicial Conference of the United States, and the Conference of Chief Justices, the National Conference on the Causes of Popular Dissatisfaction with the Administration of Justice (which has come to be known as the Pound Conference) was held. A Task Force appointed by the conference subsequently stressed the need for alternative forums for processing disputes, including mediation and arbitration. Shortly thereafter, the U.S. Department of Justice initiated an experimental program of Neighborhood Justice Centers in three communities.

Although there is much diversity among mediation programs (see McGillis and Mullen, 1977, for a comparative description of six mediation programs), they share a common assumption that criminal offenses arising from interpersonal disputes are often better resolved in mediation than in the courts. Courts are seen: (1) as being unable to devote sufficient time to these cases, (2) as being constrained in their scope of inquiry by rules of evidence, (3) as ascribing to one disputant the role of complainant and to the other the role of defendant—designations which may often be quite arbitrary, (4) as rendering "winner-take-all" decisions, and (5) as excluding the disputants themselves from an active part in the adjudication process. In contrast, mediation is seen as a process which stresses: (1) the need to probe the underlying causes of incidents; (2) the need to promote disputants' participation in the dispute settlement process; and (3) the need to encourage both disputants to accept responsibility for their interpersonal problems and to recognize a common interest in resolving them (see, for example, Paterson, Nicolau, and Weisbrod 1978).

The case for mediation as an alternative means of resolving criminal cases between acquaintances is compelling. And early evaluation studies have lent empirical support to the arguments in favor of mediation by providing data which suggest that most disputants are satisfied with solutions reached in mediation, that disputants tend to feel that mediation alleviates tensions in relationships, and that mediation programs help to reduce court caseloads (e.g., Anno and Hoff, 1975; Connor and Surette, 1977; Moriarty, Norris, and Salas, 1977; Bush, 1977). But, to date, there has been little empirical evidence to suggest that mediation more effectively resolves interpersonal disputes than prosecution.

Thus, however attractive mediation may seem in theory, it must also be assessed through empirical study. Pretrial diversion was also an appealing and widely heralded concept ten years ago, but when diversion programs were finally subjected to empirical scrutiny, they were found wanting (see, e.g., Baker and Sadd, 1979; Fishman, 1973). Today as public support for the idea of mediation continues to mushroom, this bandwagon effect should not obscure the need as well for critical evaluation and that decisions about the types of cases appropriate for mediation and styles of mediation be informed by empirical data. This study hopes to contribute to this empirical inquiry.

Specifically this study seeks to determine if mediation is a more effective method of resolving interpersonal disputes involving criminal acts than standard prosecution in the courts. Although at least two other recent studies have addressed this same issue (Felstiner and Williams, 1979; Sheppard, Roehl, and Cook, 1979, and extracted in this volume), the advantage of this study is that it employed an experimental design which randomly assigned either mediation or criminal court. To our knowledge it is the first such experimental test of a mediation program, and as such it is our hope that it will provide an especially useful basis for discussing mediation programs in general, as well as encourage others to employ experimental designs in their own research on mediation programs.

## The Program

The Brooklyn Dispute Center was established in July 1977 by the Institute for Mediation and Conflict Resolution (IMCR) in conjunction with the Victim/Witness Assistance Project (now the New York Victim Services Agency) of the Vera Institute of Justice.

At the time of the evaluation, all cases considered for mediation came from custodial felony arrests.[3] Cases were screened in the District Attorney's complaint room by program staff..If a case met the standards for mediation[4], contact was attempted with the victim (in person if the victim was present in the complaint room, or by phone if he or she was not present) to see if he or she was interested in mediation. If the victim agreed, or if the staff member was unable to contact the victim, approval for mediation was sought from the screening prosecutor. If the prosecutor approved the case, it was tentatively scheduled for a mediation hearing within two weeks. At arraignment—provided that the defendant had not been found to have a serious prior record, and that he or she agreed to mediation—the court approved the case for mediation. If approved, the case was either adjourned in contemplation of dismissal[5] (if the complainant had signed a mediation consent form) or adjourned for three weeks (if the complainant was not present to sign the form) pending the outcome of mediation.

Mediators were community members trained in a 50-hour program which included role playing, lectures, and group discussions. All agreements were written as arbitration awards and were enforceable in Supreme Court, civil term. When a case had been mediated, it was dismissed in court on the motion of the prosecutor's office.

Mediation sessions began with an introduction by the mediator(s) describing mediation to the disputants, telling them of their rights, and informing them that if one of them failed to live up to the agreement they reached, the Center would prepare papers for civil court action on behalf of the aggrieved individual. In the next stage, disputants were each given an opportunity to present their point of view, that is, to describe the nature of their relationship, and the events that led up to police intervention. Emphasis on the criminal incident itself was minimized. Parties were allowed as long as they wanted to develop their point of view, with the stipulation that they could not interrupt each other. In a third stage, each party was asked in private if there was something he or she wished to share with the mediator(s) in confidence. At the end of each private interview, the mediator(s) asked if he or she could share the information with the other disputant. This stage sometimes was prolonged if the mediator(s) decided to see each party in several private sessions, either to attempt to verify information or to help a party work through difficult feelings, in order to gain the best settlement for both. In the final stage, the disputants were brought back together and the mediator(s) explained what he or she thought each party wanted in the written agreement. Parties were free to object to provisions or change wordings. After the agreement had been written, each party was given a copy to take home.[6] Both individuals were instructed to contact the Center in the event that the agreement was broken.

# Method

The present paper is based upon an evaluation of the Brooklyn Dispute Center by the Vera Institute in conjunction with the New York Victim Services Agency (readers who wish to examine the full report are referred to Davis, Tichane, and Grayson, 1979). The primary question addressed in the study was whether mediation of felony cases arising from interpersonal disputes was an improvement over the traditional method of handling interpersonal disputes in the courts. That is, does mediation result in greater satisfaction of disputants with the adjudication process and case outcome, and does it reduce the likelihood of continuing interpersonal problems?

To answer these questions, a randomly selected control group was chosen from those cases which had been approved for mediation by the screening prosecutor and by the complainant (if he or she was present in the complaint room at the time mediation screening occurred).[7] Complainants who had agreed to mediation but whose cases were selected as controls were informed (as they had been warned earlier) that there was not enough room in the mediation program for their cases. This explanation was essentially true. If it was not for the fact that the control group syphoned off one-third of the cases approved for mediation, the Center would not have been able to handle all of the cases referred to it; in fact, midway through the intake period, the proportion of cases assigned to the control group was increased from one-third to one-half at the request of the Center. All together, 465 cases (259 cases referred to the Dispute Center and 206 control cases) were sampled between August 15 and December 15, 1978.

Because the evaluation of the Brooklyn Dispute Center was a part of a larger evaluation of Vera's Victim/Witness Assistance Project, the focus was on victims' (rather than defendants') perceptions of the two different adjudication processes and on the results they achieved. Complainants in both experimental (referred to mediation) and control (referred to court) groups were interviewed three times by evaluation staff. The first interview (conducted in the complaint room or by phone if the complainant was absent from the complaint room) asked about his/her history of problems with the defendant, the nature of the incident and his/her relationship to the defendant, and the objectives he/she sought from the criminal justice system. The second interview (conducted after case adjudication in court or in mediation) asked complainants about their participation in the adjudication process and about their satisfaction with the outcomes of their cases in mediation or in court. The final interview (conducted four months after case adjudication) asked complainants about changes in the frequency with which they saw the defendant, about their perceptions of improvement or worsening of the defendant's behavior towards them, about new problems that had arisen with the other, and about new requests for intervention of the criminal justice system in the dispute. At the time of the follow-up interview, a check was made of official records to determine whether either party to the dispute had been arrested for a crime against the other during the four-month interval since case adjudication.

Davis, Tichane, and Grayson (1979) also report on the results of interviews with defendants, who were contacted once, at the time of the complainants' final interview four months after case adjudication. (The interview with defendants was essentially a combination of material covered in the second and third interviews with complainants.) The results of the defendant interview, which essentially parallel those based on the complainant interviews (although trends tend to be less pronounced), are not discussed here; the interested reader is referred to the original report.

## Results

### Volume and Types of Cases Referred to the Dispute Center

Screening of prior relationship felony arrests for mediation eligibility was performed in the complaint room by V/WAP staff and by prosecutors. A few cases were also eliminated from consideration because either complainants or defendants refused to have their case mediated or because the arraignment judge refused to send the case to mediation. But in spite of the rigorous screening process, ultimately, 30 percent of prior relationship felony arrests or 10 percent of *all* felony arrests involving a civilian complainant were referred to the Dispute Center during the intake period for the evaluation.

Over three-quarters of referred cases were second-degree assaults or burglaries, although cases ranged from first-degree robbery to criminal mischief (see Table 8.1). Seventy percent were D felonies, which carry a maximum penalty of seven years in prison and a $5,000 fine.

Although cases referred to the Center involved serious charges, for the most part they were not cases in which defendants would otherwise have run the risk of serious sanctions in court. In the control group of cases which were prosecuted, 73 percent of defendants whose cases were not disposed at arraignment were released on their own recognizance, and 70 percent of all control cases were ultimately dismissed or adjourned in contemplation of dismissal. Conversely, only 3 percent of defendants in the control group were sentenced to jail terms (of less than one year) after pleading to misdemeanor charges and only 1 percent had their cases transferred to the grand jury (and who, depending on the grand jury's action, must subsequently have to stand trial on or plead to felony charges in Brooklyn Supreme Court).

TABLE 8.1   Top Arrest Charge in Cases Referred to Mediation

|  | Percentage |  |
|---|---|---|
| **Violent Offenses** |  |  |
| Assault | 51 |  |
| Assault 1st degree (C Felony) |  | 1 |
| Assault 2nd degree (D Felony) | 6 | 50 |
| Robbery |  |  |
| Robbery 1st degree (B Felony) |  | 1 |
| Robbert 2nd degree (C Felony) |  | 2 |
| Robbery 3rd degree (D Felony) |  | 3 |
| Rape | 1 |  |
| Rape 1st degree (B Felony) |  | * |
| Rape 3rd degree (E Felony) |  | * |
| Other | 2 |  |
| Reckless Endangerment 1st degree (D Felony) |  | * |
| Unlawful Imprisonment 1st degree (E Felony) |  | * |
| Criminal Possession of Weapon 3rd degree (D Felony) |  | * |
| **Property Offenses** |  |  |
| Burglary | 29 |  |
| Burglary 1st degree (B Felony) |  | 1 |
| Burglary 2nd degree (C Felony) |  | 13 |
| Burglary 3rd degree (D Felony) |  | 14 |
| Criminal Trespass 1st degree (D Felony) |  | 1 |
| Grand Larceny | 7 |  |
| Grand Larceny 2nd degree (D Felony) |  | 2 |
| Grand Larceny 3rd degree |  | 5 |
| Criminal Mischief | 3 |  |
| Criminal Mischief 2nd degree (D Felony) |  | 2 |
| Criminal Mischief 3rd degree |  | * |
| Forgery | 1 |  |
| Forgery 1st degree (C Felony) |  | * |
| Forgery 2nd degree (D Felony) |  | * |
| Possession Forged Instrument 1st degree (C Felony) |  | * |
|  | 100 | (N = 465) |

* Less than one percent

## Rates of Complainant Participation in Dispute Settlement Processes

Many complainants failed to participate in formal dispute settlement processes. Only 56 percent of cases referred to the Dispute Center were actually mediated, because complainants refused to participate when they arrived at the Center 12 percent of all cases referred) or because one or both parties failed to appear (32 percent of all cases referred).

Among cases not mediated because one or both parties failed to appear at the Dispute Center, the most frequent cause was complainant failures to attend (19 percent of all cases referred). The next most common occurrence was for both parties to be absent (9 percent of all referrals). In only 3 percent of all referrals did the defendant alone fail to appear. The finding that victims were far more likely to fail to appear at mediation sessions than offenders contradicts results reported in several other evaluation studies (Anno and Hoff, 1975; Connor and Surette,

1977; Moriarty, Norris, and Sulan 1977). The unusually low rate of defendant no-shows observed in the present study is likely a result of the fact that these defendants had pending court cases at the time of their mediation date. Charges had been filed by the prosecutor, and their cases had been arraigned and adjourned pending the outcome of mediation. Therefore, there was a very real possibility of sanctions if defendants did not attend the mediation session.

Many of the complainants whose cases were not mediated later went to court (the Center referred cases not successfully mediated back to the court for prosecution); in fact, in 45 percent of cases which were not mediated, complainants later attended court on at least one occasion.

In the control group, 19 percent of the complainants never came to the complaint room and never attended a court proceeding. These complainants, therefore, never received the intended exposure to the criminal court dispositional process.

The many disputants in both experimental and control groups who were not exposed to the intended treatments posed a problem for the original study design. The design, which drew its strength from random assignment of cases to treatments, called for comparing all experimental (mediation) cases to all control (court) cases. Yet because many complainants in the experimental group were not exposed to the mediation process (and many complainants in the control group were not exposed to the disposition process in court), any effects of the treatments would have to be very large, indeed, to show up. Because of the high rates of attrition in both experimental and control groups the critical comparisons on recidivism presented below are made in two ways: all experimental cases are compared with all control cases, and cases which were actually mediated are compared with cases in which complainants attended court (including the complaint room) at least once.

## The Impact of Dispute Settlement on Disputants' Relationships

In agreement with the results of previous work, the study found that the process of mediation was perceived positively by complainants: 94 percent of complainants whose cases were mediated believed the mediator had heard their version of the incident, while 65 percent of complainants in the control group who attended court believed that the judge had heard their side of the incident (chi-square = 22.09, p < .01); 88 percent of complainants whose cases were mediated believed the mediator had conducted the case fairly, while 76 percent of complainants in the control group who attended court believed that the judge had conducted their case fairly (chi-square = 3.94, p < .05); and, over the entire experimental group, 73 percent of complainants reported being satisfied with the resolution of their cases while, over the entire control group, only 54 percent of complainants were satisfied with the outcomes of their cases (chi-square = 11.16, p < .01).

There was also evidence that, after their cases had been concluded, complainants whose cases were referred to the Dispute Center had more positive perceptions of the defendants in their cases than complainants whose cases were referred to court for prosecution: Among cases referred to the Dispute Center, 23 percent of complainants reported still feeling anger toward the defendant upon conclusion of their case, compared to 48 percent in the control group (chi-square = 117.65, p < .01); and 21 percent of complainants whose cases were referred to the Dispute Center still feared that the defendant would seek revenge against them for reporting the crime, compared to 40 percent in the control group (chi-square = 12.30, p < .01). Moreover, four months after their cases had been concluded, 62 percent of complainants whose cases had been referred to the Dispute Center and who still saw the defendant reported improvement in the defendant's behavior toward them; only 40 percent of control group complainants who had maintained contact with the defendant saw a change for the better in his or her behavior (chi-square = 6.71, p < .01).

Taken together, these data strongly indicate that the mediation process is perceived more positively by complainants than the court process and that going through mediation enhances complainants' perceptions of their relationships with defendants to a greater degree than does going through the court process. The differences are all the more striking when it is remembered that the effects are diluted because many complainants in the experimental group never went to mediation.

Yet, in spite of the improvement in complainants' perceptions of their relationships, there was little evidence that mediation was more effective than court adjudication in preventing recidivism during the four-month follow-up period. Table 8.2 shows that there were only small differences between cases referred to mediation and cases referred to court in: (1) the frequency of new problems reported by complainants, (2) complainants' calls to ask the police to intervene again, or (3) new arrests of either party for a crime committed against the other. While the differences that did exist were in the expected direction (that is, recidivism tended to be less frequent among cases referred to the Dispute Center), they did not approach statistical significance. Moreover, this was true even when comparisons were confined to only those cases in which complainants had actually been exposed to the mediation or the court process.

However, in both experimental and control groups new interpersonal hostilities were the exception rather than the rule. Over both samples, only one in five complainants reported continuing problems with the defendant, only 12 percent of complainants called the police in response to a problem with the defendant, and in only 4 percent of the sampled cases was a disputant arrested for a new crime against the other. Much of the reason for the reduction in friction between disputants seemed to

TABLE 8.2  Four-Month Recidivism According to Treatment Group and Participation in Dispute Settlement Processes

| | Proportion (Percentage) of Complainants Who Reported Continuing Problems with Defendants** | | Proportion (Percentage) of Complainants Who Reported Calling Police** | | Proportion (Percentage) of Cases Involving New Arrests of Either Party for a Crime Against the Other | |
|---|---|---|---|---|---|---|
| **All Cases Referred to Mediation** | | | | | | |
| • Cases mediated (n = 145) | 24* | | 14* | | 3* | |
| • Cases not mediated: complainant later attended court (n = 51) | 10 | 19* | 9 | 12* | 8 | 4* |
| • Cases not mediated: complainant did not attend court (n = 63) | 0 | | 0 | | 2 | |
| **All Cases Referred to Court** | | | | | | |
| • Cases in which complainant attended court (n = 166) | 30* | | 15* | | 5* | |
| • Cases in which complainant did not attend court (n = 40) | 26* | 28* | 7 | 13* | 3 | 4* |

* No differences between (a) all cases referred to mediation versus all cases referred to court and (b) cases actually mediated and control cases in which complainant attended court were significant at the .10 level or better by chi-square test.

** NS for these measures are smaller than those reported in the table. They are based upon 47 percent of the entire sample for whom follow-up interviews were completed.

be that the defendant's arrest often occasioned a reassessment of the relationship by disputants; over the entire sample, 68 percent of complainants reported seeing the the defendant less often than before the defendant's arrest, and only 60 percent of complainants reported having any regular contact with the defendant.

Perhaps the most surprising thing about the data presented in Table 8.2 is that, according to each recidivism measure, in both experimental and control groups recidivism was less in cases in which complainants *failed* to participate in formal dispute resolution processes. This result is particularly pronounced in the experimental group, but the trend holds for control cases as well. On its surface, this anomalous finding would appear to suggest that disputants are better off staying home than taking their problems to either mediation or court!

But the types of disputes in which complainants elected not to participate in formal dispute resolution processes were very different from the types of disputes in cases in which complainants did participate. In particular, among cases in which complainants did participate, disputants were more likely to have strong interpersonal ties (defined as immediate family members, lovers, and ex-lovers) and complainants were more likely to have called the police previous to the sampled incident (see Table 8.3). And these cases with complex antecedents had a far higher likelihood of recidivism (see Table 8.4). Among cases in which interpersonal ties were strong and complainants had called police previous to the sampled incident, complainants were more likely to report continuing problems (44 percent for cases with these characteristics compared to 14 percent in all other cases), complainants were more likely to call upon police to intervene again (27 percent for cases with these characteristics compared to 4 percent for all other cases), and one of the parties was more likely to be arrested for a crime against the other (12 percent in cases with these characteristics compared to 1 percent in all other cases).

Complainants who chose not to avail themselves of formal dispute resolution processes may have perceived themselves as having little to gain by doing so. With relationships that tended to be less involved (according to the strength of interpersonal ties and dispute history), these complainants may have felt a less compelling need to seek a reconciliation with the defendant than complainants who did go to court or mediation. Instead, they often chose avoidance as their solution. As Table 8.5 shows, most complainants who did not go to mediation or court simply reduced contact with the defendant. Nearly four in five of these complainants reported less contact after the defendant's arrest, and only 12 percent reported seeing the defendant daily during the follow-up period. Complainants' decisions not to participate in dispute settlement processes seemed to be rational ones which—measured by the standard of recidivism—seemed to be successful.

TABLE 8.3  Complainants' Participation in Dispute Resolution Processes According to Strength of Disputants' Interpersonal Ties and Whether Police Had Been Summoned on a Previous Occasion

| | Proportion (Percentage) of Cases in Which Disputants Had Strong Interpersonal Ties* | | Proportion (Percentage) of Cases in Which Complainant Had Called Police Previous to Sampled Incident |
|---|---|---|---|
| **All Cases Referred to Mediation** | | | |
| • Cases mediated (n = 118)** | 59 | | 38 |
| • Cases not mediated: complainant later attended court ( n = 29) | 41 | 51 | 21 | 30 |
| • Cases not mediated: complainant did not attend court (n = 31) | 32 | | 10 |
| **All Cases Referred to Court** | | | |
| • Cases in which complainant attended court (n = 101) | 54 | | 34 |
| • Cases in which complainant did not attend court (n = 34) | 41 | 50 | 29 | 31 |

* Strong interpersonal ties is defined to include family members, lovers, and ex-lovers.
** Ns based on portion of sample who received initial interview (68 percent of total sample).

TABLE 8.4    Risk of Recidivism by Nature of Disputants' Relationship and Previous Calls Made to the Police

| | Moderate/ Weak Ties | Strong Ties |
|---|---|---|
| *Percent of Complainants Who Report Problems with the Defendant During the Follow-up Period* | | |
| Police called previously | 27 (n = 15) | 44 (n = 48) |
| Police not called previously | 11 (n = 73) | 15 (n = 46) |
| *Percent of Disputants Who Called Police During Follow-up Period* | | |
| | Moderate/ Weak Ties | Strong Ties |
| Police called previously | 0 (n = 15) | 27 (n = 48) |
| Police not called Previously | 4 (n = 73) | 7 (n = 46) |
| *Percent of Disputants Arrested for Crime Against the Other During Follow-up Period* | | |
| | Moderate/ Weak Ties | Strong Ties |
| Police called previously | 0 (n = 20) | 12 (n = 78) |
| Police not called previously | 1 (n = 133) | 1 (n = 81) |

But, while avoidance worked for some complainants, it was not a viable option for others, whose relationships were closer and whose disputes had more involved histories. For the latter complainants, it was not as easy to extricate themselves from relationships on which they may have been emotionally or financially dependent, even when the relationship had become counterproductive and threatened the safety of one or both parties. While these complainants were more likely to seek the aid of dispute resolution processes, the cases of a substantial minority were not successfully resolved in either court or in mediation. These may be the sorts of dispute cases which Wilt et al. (1977) found to escalate into homicides.

## Conclusion

The results of this study are consistent with other research which has also found that disputants feel better about their experience in the criminal justice system and about each other after mediation than after the traditional court process. For this reason, and because court officials often express reservations about becoming involved in cases arising from interpersonal disputes, mediation has an important role to play in the resolution of these types of interpersonal disputes.

TABLE 8.5 Complainants' Reports of Contact with the Defendant During the Follow-up Period, According to Participation in Dispute Settlement Processes

| | Proportion (Percentage) of Complainants Who Reported Seeing Defendants Less Often | Proportion (Percentage) of Complainants Who Reported Seeing Defendants Daily |
|---|---|---|
| All Cases Referred to Mediation | 65 | 27 |
| • Cases mediated (n = 89)* | 76 | 18 |
| • Cases not mediated: complainant later attended court (n = 22) | 69 | 22 |
| • Cases not mediated: complainant did not attend court (n = 16) | 80 | 0 |
| All Cases Referred to Court | 61 | 30 |
| • Cases in which complainant attended court (n = 61) | 66 | 26 |
| • Cases in which complainant did not attend court (n = 27) | 77 | 18 |

* Ns based on portion of sample who received follow-up interview (47 percent of total sample).

But mediation is not, nor should it be expected to be, a panacea for all the problems of people in relationships that have deteriorated to the point of criminal acts of aggression. Our findings suggest that mediation is no more effective than prosecution in preventing recidivism and, moreover, that a great many people in cases arising from interpersonal disputes prefer not to use mediation as the means of coping with their problems. While these conclusions are necessarily limited to only one mediation program, the findings are consistent with results of others' research in other jurisdictions (Felstiner and Williams, 1979; and Sheppard, Roehl, and Cook, 1979). Taken together these studies suggest the need for closer examination of the types of cases that can most benefit from mediation.

For example, Felstiner and Williams (1979) suggest that mediation (because of the brief time involved) is not an appropriate means of dealing with deep-seated, underlying problems that give rise to hostile acts between individuals. Still they believe it may be useful in cases in which disputants' problems lie close to the surface. Data from the present study lend at least partial support to their argument.

Cases we found to be least amenable to mediation involved disputes between intimates where there was also a "deep-seated" pattern of serious hostilities. Here people were likely to continue to maintain regular contact after the precipitating incident, and, hence, the probability of continued friction between the disputants remained high. But where there was greater "relational distance" between the disputants, complainants were more likely to desire reconciliation, a finding that is consistent with the research of others (Black, 1973a; Gluckman, 1955; Sarat, 1976). But, unfortunately, the complex etiology of these disputes and the irrational habits of a great many people caught up in the web of dispute and anger make them extremely resistant to change. In order to make a real difference for these people caught up in these kinds of relationships, a more sustained form of intervention is likely to be needed. Still even here mediation may be an effective step toward resolving problems, but only if it is followed up with more intensive and appropriate social services.

Conversely, less complex cases, where disputants have only "surface" problems may—as Felstiner and Williams argue—be the most appropriate for mediation. Yet (based on what happened in the present study in cases in which interpersonal ties were weaker and there was no previous history of criminal justice involvement) it should be recognized that these disputants may often choose simply to avoid each other rather than to avail themselves of the opportunity for mediation. Moreover, avoidance in these cases is usually successful (as judged by the standard of recidivism), because the relationship is often expendable.

If there is anything to be learned from the present study, it is that people need or want different things from dispute resolution, depending on the nature of their particular dispute. For those who *want* to talk things through with each other, mediation is appropriate, especially if followed up by additional services when problems are deep seated. For those who do not want to reconcile or negotiate a settlement, mediation is not likely to work, and prosecution may be the more appropriate response. And for still others who want nothing more than to be left alone, simple avoidance may be more appropriate than either mediation or prosecution. The challenge to the justice system is, of course, to make available a variety of dispute settlement options that meet the various and variable needs of disputants, a task which, as we have seen, is not easy.

## Notes

1. Felstiner (1974), however, believes that community moots are not viable within a mobile, atomistic society. In smaller, simpler societies, group ostracism is an effective threat to induce individuals to comply with mediation agreements. However, in technologically advanced societies, which lack stable social networks within communities, such sanctions would not be effective.

2. Reported in Sheppard, Roehl, and Cook (1979).

3. The Brooklyn Dispute Center now accepts misdemeanor and summons cases as well, but the bulk of its caseload remains felonies.

4. Major reasons for exclusion from consideration include: (1) nature of charge (murder, attempted murder, first-degree assault, first- and second-degree rape, arson, and attempted arson are excluded), (2) evidence that a gun was used in commission of the crime, (3) drug addiction of either party, (4) cases involving prostitutes and/or pimps, (5) cases involving disputes between a parent and a child under 18 years who is living with the parent, (6) cases involving retarded or other incompetent individuals, (7) cross complaints (cases where both parties are defendants), and (8) cases in which a minor is hospitalized or an adult is hospitalized in critical condition.

5. Cases adjourned in contemplation of dismissal are dismissed in six months if the defendant is not rearrested within that time.

6. If parties fail to reach an accord, the hearing is adjourned and the same mediator renders an arbitration decision on a later date. The Center's staff estimates that arbitration is necessary in only five percent of their cases.

7. If complainants were not present, cases were still scheduled for mediation if the prosecutor approved, and therefore, were also eligible for the control group. The selection of the control group is flawed by the fact that selection occurred before the judge or defendant in arraignment had a chance to consider the possibility of mediation. In practice, however, this did not turn out to be a major problem since only 4 percent of cases scheduled for mediation in the complaint room were later disapproved by the judge or defendant.

# Part III

## Assessment

# 9

## Defining "Success" in the Neighborhood Justice Movement*

Sally Engle Merry

### Introduction

Resolving minor, interpersonal disputes through mediation rather than adjudication, an innovative and potentially powerful idea for American society, is in danger of appearing a disappointing failure despite its initial enthusiastic reception. Its possible demise is caused by two factors: (1) the underlying processes and social organization of mediation have been insufficiently understood, and (2) the idea has been implemented in ways very different from the intentions of the original proponents. Throughout the twentieth century, the courts have assumed a burgeoning share of interpersonal domestic, friend, and neighbor disputes. The recent enthusiastic adoption of the notion of formal mediation centers both within the United States, where at least 100 centers are now in operation (Cook et al., 1980: 5), and in Canada and Australia, represents a reaction to this trend in dispute management and testifies to the attraction of a more humane, just, and responsive mode of settling disputes under the control of local communities rather than the centralized organs of the state. The effort to create new forums for resolving disputes represents an important part of the "third wave" in the "access-to-justice" movement (Cappelletti, 1978: xi).

Yet, the form in which such centers are being implemented differs significantly not only from the ideas of the original proponents, but also

* Many of the ideas presented here were developed in discussions with Susan Silbey, and I am grateful to her for many insights and suggestions. All references in the text of this chapter are found in the bibliography at the conclusion of this volume.

from the prototypes of mediation in societies where it serves as the predominant mode of settling disputes. This has occurred primarily because community mediation in the industrialized societies is being asked to serve too many conflicting and contradictory interests. In order to understand mediation and its potential role in American society better, this paper provides: (1) an examination of the prototypes of mediation and the social settings in which it occurs naturally, (2) an analysis of the impact of the social context and the surrounding social structure on the way mediation functions, and (3) broader definitions of effectiveness and success which describe more fully what Neighborhood Justice Centers (NJCs) can provide in the American context. I will compare the present models of NJCs with their major prototypes, pointing to substantial differences in organization and social context which raise critical issues for evaluating the neighborhood justice movement.

## Prototypes of Community Mediation

Early proponents of the introduction of mediation into American society (Danzig, 1973; Lowy, 1973; Danzig and Lowy, 1975; Fisher, 1975; Nader and Singer, 1976; Sander, 1976) drew their inspiration from three situations in which mediation serves as the predominant mode of dispute settlement: nonindustrial, small-scale societies reported in the anthropological literature (Gibbs, 1963; Nader, 1969), socialist people's courts and comrades' courts (Lubman, 1967; Cohen, 1967; Berman, 1969; Canter, 1974; Crockett and Gleicher, 1978; Li, 1978; Spence, 1978), and labor and commercial arbitration in the United States (Mentschikoff, 1961; Macaulay, 1963; Fuller, 1971; Fisher, 1975; Getman, 1979). Danzig, for example, envisioned a community moot modeled after village moots in Liberia, functioning as a therapeutic, conciliatory, and noncoercive forum located within local communities to handle minor criminal disputes between friends and family which raise no larger social problems (1973: 45–48). Yet, this view of mediation in small-scale societies is idealized and somewhat misleading, emphasizing the role of conciliation and voluntary cooperation and ignoring the very important roles of coercion, power, and custom (Merry, 1981a). Evidence from the way mediation functions in each of these prototypes suggests the need to examine more carefully the conditions under which mediation serves as an effective mode of handling disputes (see also Felstiner, 1974; Getman, 1979).

Anthropological prototypes, for example, rely extensively on the power and coercion of the mediator and the surrounding social structure. Mediators tend to be powerful and influential political leaders who enhance their position through successfully mediating cases. Agreements focus on exchanges of property and the payment of damages rather than

the restoration of harmonious relationships and promises of good behavior. Mediators are neither strangers nor indifferent, and are neutral
only insofar as they have competing loyalties to both sides. A mediator
is preeminently a representative of the moral code of his or her society
and is never thought to function without reference to the dominant
value system or previous decisions in similar cases. Further, the process
of settling cases itself plays a crucial role in redefining and enunciating
the rules of the society (Merry, 1981a).

Socialist people's courts are often explicitly committed to implanting
a new ideology and value system as well as resolving disputes (e.g.,
Yang, 1945; Cohen, 1967; Lubman, 1967; Canter, 1974; Crockett and
Gleicher, 1978; Spence, 1978). They are often backed by the substantial
coercive powers of the state and manned by party cadres. Judges in
Cuba's Popular Tribunals, for example, frequently give moral lectures
(Berman, 1969; Canter, 1974). They are laypersons, elected within local
areas of 4,000 to 5,000 residents, and may be acquainted with the disputants before the case. Trials are public and settlements typically consist of damages, restitution, or punishment. Penalties range from public
admonition, mandatory education, and relocation of workplace, to a
maximum of 180 days of confinement to the house (Berman, 1969:
1325). In Chinese Peoples' Mediation Committees, mediators are
elected by representatives of the residents and are expected to be "politically upright" (Lubman, 1967). They are to educate the people about
national policies and laws. Mediation committees are located in urban
neighborhoods, factories, and farms. In urban areas, mediators tend to
be politically active homemakers; in organizations and rural areas, they
are closely linked to the administration. Since they are one of the means
adopted to construct a new socialist society, they operate within a clear
moral system and often deliver lectures on moral virtue and new ways of
thought. Although decisions are subject to a court appeal, the committees have extensive authority and autonomy (Crockett and Gleicher,
1978). In urban neighborhoods, they have the power to invoke sanctions
through the police and other cadres and in factories and rural communes
control work situations, demotions, reduction in salary, transfers, or entry of demerits in employees' dossiers (Lubman, 1967: 1349).

Labor arbitration characteristically occurs between two parties who
are heavily interdependent, who negotiate through a pattern of economic trade or exchange, who formulate a set of shared rules and understandings for future relationships, who negotiate through agents, and
who act as equals during the negotiation process although in the daily
operation of the enterprise they are not (Fuller, 1971: 309–312.) Other
studies of labor and commercial arbitration and negotiation emphasize
the formality of the process, the explicit reference to rules, the emergence of shared understandings over the period of combined negotiation,
the inherent incentive to settle built into the structure of ongoing indus-

trial and commercial relationships, and the importance of the equality of the parties (Eisenberg, 1976; Getman, 1979). Macaulay notes the flexibility, informality, and absence of legal sanctions common in business contracts where the parties are guided by a body of custom and practice, linked through crosscutting personal and business ties, and anxious to maintain commercial exchanges in the future (1963: 63–67). Lawsuits are most common when a dealer's franchise has been cancelled and the commercial relationship consequently terminated (1963: 65).

## The Social Context of Mediation

A careful examination of the social contexts surrounding mediation in these prototypes reveals significant differences from the social structure enveloping American NJCs which may have important implications for the ability of these centers to function as they were intended. The social features of American neighborhods differ from the characteristics of situations in which mediation emerges naturally in three important respects (Merry, 1981a). First, village and pastoral societies are generally stable, closed, and bounded social systems, particularly in settings where connections with the larger economic and political order are minimal. Here, individuals cannot escape from their local communities without sacrificing much of their social lives and often their economic livelihood. Where cash crop production for the national market or wage labor are becoming more important aspects of economic life, however, these conditions are beginning to change (Pitt-Rivers, 1971; Starr, 1978; Yngvesson, 1976), and mediation appears to be declining in significance as a mode of dispute resolution (see Collier, 1973; Ayoub, 1965). Even American cities, in contrast, contain more stable and homogeneous enpermanent relationship with one another and who share significant similarities in their notions of how to achieve settlements (Getman, 1979). American cites, in contrast, contain more stable and homogeneous enclaves, while the surrounding tissue is mobile and avoidance of disputes is common (Felstiner, 1974; Merry, 1979c).

Second, societies that commonly rely on mediation are often more homogeneous in norms and values than American neighborhoods. Under these conditions, dispute resolution can rely on shared expectations and customs to resolve disagreements and is less dependent on explicit, state-enacted laws and formally coercive mechanisms such as adjudication. Mediation in socialist states is embedded in an explicit set of norms and values stemming from the revolutionary ideology which the state is endeavoring to implement. American labor and commercial negotiation similarly builds on a set of customs and past negotiations which create rules and precedents for future discussions. However, the social fabric of the American urban neighborhood rarely provides these conditions. This poses a dilemma for mediation programs. Since they generally cannot rely on a body of shared understandings about appropriate and offensive behavior, they can either restrict their operations to settings where substantial consensus on relevant rules and precedents exists or use mediation itself as a forum for developing a consensus between disputants about the rules governing their conflict (Thibaut and Walker, 1975; Eisenberg, 1976).

A third difference between village and pastoral societies, socialist states, and American society is the prevailing legal culture. The American belief in individual rights, which are at least theoretically protected by the court, is quite different from the situation in stateless societies where an individual's legal rights depend on his or her ability to marshall allies and extract damages from an opponent, or in socialist states where the rights of the individual are often subordinated to the needs of the family, group, class, or state. In isolated, small-scale societies, even if a court is available, it is often remote, inaccessible, expensive, and unpredicable, so that the mediator is, in effect, the final recourse (Collier, 1973; Jones, 1974; Cantor, 1978; Nader and Todd, 1978; Merry, 1981a). Cultural values about disputing in American society present an obstacle to mediation. In Chinese society, for example, mediation and conciliation are the approved and respected ways of dealing with conflict and are used in roughly 90 percent of all disputes (Yang, 1945; Wolf, 1972; Cohen, 1967; Crockett and Gleicher, 1978; Li, 1978). Chinese culture places much less emphasis on the individual's possession of legal rights, which can be asserted and defended in a court, than American society. In the urban United States, even if individuals do not expect to receive satisfaction in court, they continue to believe in their legal right to go to court and often regard compromise and conciliation as letting the other party take advantage of them. One program evaluation reports persisting difficulties in persuading its suburbanite users to try mediation rather than the court, and often finds that they are willing to try mediation only after they have been told by the prosecutor that they must try mediation instead of court (Evaluation Group, 1980).[1] Introducing the new cultural values of compromise and conciliation in place of asserting legal rights and winning may require long-range experimentation with the idea, well beyond the 12- to 18-month periods which mediation programs are generally given in order to justify themselves.

The notion of a community as a cohesive, locally based social system with shared values and a sense of belonging is not the most useful way to conceptualize the complex textures of urban social systems. Communities in this sense do occur in cities, yet many urbanites live in areas which do not resemble the traditional community. A more useful analytic concept is the social network, the pattern of social relationships linking individuals to one another (Bott, 1957; Mitchell, 1969; Jacobson, 1971; Boissevain, 1974). Urbanites' networks of enduring relationships may be restricted to a local area or may extend to a wide geographical space yet include few neighbors. Similarly, a local area may contain a single, interconnected social network (Whyte, 1955; Gans, 1962) or several discrete, unconnected social networks which coexist in the same space (Merry, 1979; 1980). An individual's social network can be close-knit (highly interconnected) or loose-knit (unconnected (Bott, 1957). The ease of avoiding disputes by exiting from local social systems, the interconnectedness and durability of social networks, the degree of consensus on moral norms, and cultural values about disputing all influence whether mediation is appropriate in a particular social context (see Felstiner, 1974). Where escape from a local social system and avoidance of a dispute are costly, the incentive to settle is greater. The more close-knit the social networks joining the two disputing parties, the greater the pressure they feel to resolve their quarrel rather than to continue the battle (Bott, 1957; Epstein, 1969; Wheeldon, 1969).

This analysis suggests the need to transplant community mediation into American society with more sophistication and greater awareness of the impact of the surrounding social structure. The extent and condition of ongoing relationships, the role of consensus and shared values, the need to settle, and the availability of avoidance and court as culturally acceptable and socially possible alternative solutions to conflict all seriously influence the way mediation functions. Perhaps community mediation could be more effective in settings where conditions such as urban ethnic villages, organizations, workplaces, professional associations, and institutions exist rather than in neighborhoods where the underlying structure of community is fragmentary and brittle. Mediation may be able to harness informal social pressure only in those pockets of American society which retain the social characteristics of urban villages, where it can build on preexisting community structures and patterns of informal social control.

## The Role of Coercion

In the prototypes discussed above, mediated settlements are usually backed by a range of forms of coercion and pressure exerted on disputants both to engage in discussions and to abide by an agreement. This pressure assumes a variety of forms. The social pressures of the community are generally of paramount importance in small-scale societies. The intransigent or noncompliant disputant faces the risk of gossip; loss of reputation; diminished political influence; loss of favors from powerful persons who can dispense loans, rights to land, or contacts to persons in high places; difficulties in finding marriage partners for his children; social ostracism; and ultimately expulsion from the community (Pitt-Rivers, 1971; Campbell, 1964; Bailey, 1971; Merry, 1981b). Mediated settlements are commonly backed by violence as well in small-scale, stateless societies. An aggrieved disputant, his kin group, or the mediator may directly assault an intransigent disputant or launch an insidious, indirect attack through witchcraft or sorcery, which produces misfortunes and wasting diseases (Evans-Pritchard, 1937, 1940; Barton, 1919; Hoebel, 1954; Barth, 1959; Colson, 1953, 1974; Collier, 1973).

Another form of pressure to settle common to all the prototypes of mediation is the need to restore peace inherent in the structure of the situation. In labor and commercial arbitration, for example, the interdependence of labor and industry or buyer and seller provides an intrinsic need to forge an agreement (Fuller, 1971: 310; Macaulay, 1963). When the disputants are involved in an ongoing relationship which they both wish to or are forced to maintain into the future, they may choose to compromise and settle rather than to press for victory in court. Neighbors who cannot easily move away, spouses who do not wish to separate, and residents of small-scale, isolated villages all feel the need to come to an agreement and restore peace because they must deal with one another in the future (Collier, 1973; Yngvesson, 1976; Nader and Todd, 1978). In these situations, it is the expectation of a future to the relationship which is critical (Jacobson, 1971, 1973). When a relationship has a long future, disputants tend to seek peace, but if they can or expect to terminate it soon, victory may seem preferable. Disputants may also share a desire to settle if they wish to break off a relationship, as in the case of separating or divorcing spouses or businesses severing a contract (Fuller, 1971: 308). More generally, Sarat suggests that the critical variable is the ease of substituting one relationship for another (1980). Where costs of substitution are low, the incentive to settle is less. Where they are greater, there is more inherent interest in arriving at an agreement.

Another form of pressure to settle is the desire of each disputant to behave in a form he or she considers morally acceptable and respectable. Insofar as mediation functions with reference to norms, some disputants in some situations may be persuaded to settle in the interest of maintaining their moral profile. If hearings are public, this internal desire is powerfully buttressed by the desire to appear virtuous in front of one's fellows (Gibbs, 1963; Epstein, 1958). This outcome assumes consensus on values, however, and does not apply either to situations where disputants have conflicts of norms or where they have diametrically opposed interests (Fuller, 1971).

Finally, mediated settlements may rely on the coercion of the court. Disputants who know that failure to arrive at an agreement will return them to court clearly face particular pressures to settle. The prospect of court can encourage a settlement in two ways: first, because the process of going to court is so protracted, expensive, and unpredictable that there is little hope of winning, as occurred in prerevolutionary China (Cohen, 1967: 1212) and contemporary India (Cohn, 1959; Kidder, 1974); or second, because one or the other party expects to lose in court. The party weaker in court may be more eager to mediate. As Galanter points out, relative strength in court depends not simply on legal rights, but also on a whole series of bargaining chips related to resources, exclusion of evidence, and ability to tolerate delay, uncertainty, and increasing costs (1979a: 7).

The role court coercion should play in American NJCs is a recurring and vexing problem. Although the original proponents of mediation advocated a voluntary, noncoercive process (Danzig, 1973; Danzig and Lowy, 1975) and mediation program personnel continue to pay lip service to the principle that mediation is noncoercive, elements of coercion are subtly entering into the process through the back door in the form of court referrals, continuations of cases in court, and even "reminders" by mediators that if the disputants cannot reach an agreement, the case will return to court (Snyder, 1978: 120; Evaluation Group, 1980: 49). A serious problem for mediation programs trying to generate large caseloads is the reluctance of respondents to participate. In the first 15 months of operation, the Neighborhood Justice Centers were unable to resolve half their referrals, and in half of these cases, the reason was the respondent's refusal to cooperate (Cook et al., 1980: 26). A mediation program in affluent, white, suburban Suffolk County, New York, reports similar rates of respondent refusals: 40 percent of cases were not resolved, and over half (22 percent of all cases) were not resolved because of respondent refusals (Evaluation Group, 1980: 80). On the other hand, a Brooklyn program to mediate felony cases pending before the court had a strikingly different pattern: 32 percent of the cases were not mediated because of "no-shows," but in only 3 percent of the cases did the defendant alone fail to appear (Davis et al., 1979: 95). Under pressure of a serious charge, defendants apparently are willing to cooperate, while it is complainants who choose to drop the case.

In general, rates of appearance for hearings seem to vary with the coercive powers of the referral source. The same Neighborhood Justice Center study reported that 82 percent of cases referred by judges lead to a hearing and 71 percent were resolved, in comparison to only 14–36 percent of referrals from other sources which reached a hearing and 35–45 percent ultimately resolved (Cook et al., 1980: 23, see also Snyder, 1978: 129–130). Some program personnel are clamoring for more legal clout such as subpoena powers and legal enforcement (Moriarty et al., 1977: 79), while others have adopted the use of court or courtlike stationery to summon respondents to hearings.

Evidence from the prototypes of mediation suggests that some form of coercion is clearly necessary to arrive at settlements which will be kept, but mediation programs could be more creative in developing non-court forms of pressure. Ironically, since one of the fundamental goals of the mediation movement was improving the quality of justice available to disputants in interpersonal conflicts by replacing court coercion and legal remedies with mechanisms more appropriate to those situations, this drift towards increasing reliance on court sanctions in order to generate referrals and resolutions flows against the current.

Because of the need for pressure behind settlements, some kinds of disputes may not be amenable to mediation. Where the parties have no inherent interest in settling, where they have diametrically opposed interests, where they do not share similar norms along which an agreement can be forged, where they are not linked into any form of ongoing social network which could impose pressures on them to restore peace, or where customs and laws prohibit recourse to witchcraft or violence, disputants may be unwilling to compromise without external pressures. These disputes may require adjudication in court. For example, specific disputes that center on concrete issues, such as payment of damages or debts, seem to be more susceptible to mediation than general ones evolving out of complex, tangled webs of insult and rivalry, abuse and counterabuse, and intense emotional involvement. The first category can be resolved by a concrete agreement to pay while the second requires promises of behavioral changes stretching into the future. In the first six months of operation, the caseloads of the Neighborhood Justice Centers fell about half and half into these categories (Sheppard et al., 1979: 33).

Specificity and generality affect the ability of a dispute settlement forum to produce an agreement which can in some way be supported and enforced by center staff. It is more feasible to monitor a concrete transfer of goods than an improvement in behavior. In a study of five Florida dispute settlement centers, concrete disputes were less likely to come to a hearing, but had much higher rates of long-term resolution than those which involved behavioral change (Dispute Resolution Alternatives Committee, 1979: 35, 54, 56–57).[2] The Brooklyn Dispute Resolution Center handling felony arrests found cases involving intimate relationships and a history of calls to the police most likely to flare up into new violent conflicts requiring further police and court intervention (Davis et al., 1979: 65). In the anthropological prototypes of mediation, agreements are usually concrete and involve an explicit and often immediate transfer of goods, marking of a boundary, or delivery of a public apology which can be observed and enforced by the assembled spectators (Gulliver, 1963; Yang, 1945; Barton, 1919; Merry, 1981a). Thus, interpersonal disputes, which are perceived as particularly appropriate for mediation, are less likely to produce a long-term resolution than concrete disputes, despite the assumption that mediation is less effective here.

## Implementing Mediation in American Communities

### Expectations of Community Mediation

During their implementation, community mediation programs have subtly shifted in basic features of organization and design in an effort to respond to a wide range of conflicting and contradictory political goals and
interests. The movement has created strange bedfellows: those concerned with court congestion and overload (American Bar Association,
1976; Bell, 1978b), those concerned with the quality of justice and access to justice (e.g., Danzig, 1973; Lowy, 1973; Danzig and Lowy, 1975;
Cappeletti 1978; Singer, 1979b), and those concerned with the death of
community who hope that community mediation centers will provide an
avenue to strengthen and empower local communities by decentralizing
social control functions and providing community residents with an en-
hanced sense of their ability to handle legal and political problems on
their own (Danzig, 1973; Wahrhaftig, 1981). In examining both the implementation and the evaluation of neighborhood justice centers, it
appears that in this uneasy compromise, the judicial definition of need
(the first set of goals), has taken precedence over the second two (see
Cook et al. 1980:9). Centers are restructured in order to generate large
caseloads and reduce costs while evaluations stress the number of cases
handled and the potential reduction of demands on the criminal and
civil justice systems (Cook et al. 1980; Dispute Resolution Alternatives
Committee n.d.; Moriarty 1977).

Other goals for neighborhood justice centers have been virtually
ignored, both in the planning process and in the bulk of evaluation studies. Although it appears that community mediation has failed since it
does not appear to substantially reduce judicial caseloads (Cook et al.
1980), this failure is simply an artifact of the limited slice of goals stressed in the implementation and evaluation process. The pressures of
funding, of adapting to bureaucratic settings, and of justifying a program
in a short space of time in terms of caseloads and costs per hearing have
driven neighborhood justice centers to seek justice system referrals, to
expand the size of the area they serve, and to use the threat of court to
press for hearings and agreements.

Further, in an effort to generate and maintain caseloads, many
programs have expanded beyond their original mandate. Rather than
restricting their scope to interpersonal disputes between equals such as
neighbors and friends, they are increasingly handling disputes between
non-equals such as landlords and tenants, merchants and customers, employers and employees, and other organizations and individuals. In the
first 15 months of operation, 55 percent of the caseloads of the three
neighborhood justice centers fell into the category of civil disputes of the
latter kind, while only 45 percent were interpersonal disputes in domes-

tic, neighbor, and family relationships (Cook et al., 1980: 22). While mediation appears to be tremendously valuable in disputes between equals, in the available prototypes it appears that in disputes between nonequals, it simply replicates existing power relationships. Successful collective bargaining, for example, is contingent on the rough equality of the parties (Getman, 1979: 933–934). Logically, the weaker party will settle for the best he or she can get, while the stronger party will be unwilling to accept a settlement which he or she does not feel is the most advantageous. Here, mediation may be inappropriate. It can be argued that in spite of these difficulties mediation is still better than what the courts provide, but if this is the case, the solution is not to create an alternative of questionable utility, but to launch a renewed effort to reform the courts.

## Evaluating Neighborhood Justice Centers

These observations have important implications for evaluations of Neighborhood Justice Centers. Clearly, any evaluation is rooted in a set of standards against which performance is measured, yet the range of possible standards used has heretofore been quite narrow. A survey of several recent evaluation studies reveals that they have focussed on the judicial goals of the NJC movement, but, with some exceptions, virtually ignored quality of justice issues and entirely neglected community development concerns (McGillis and Mullen, 1977; Moriarty et al. 1977; Dispute Resolution Alternatives Committee, 1979; Snyder, 1978; Sheppard et al., 1979; Cook et al., 1980; Evaluation Group, 1980; Davis et al., 1979). Evaluations typically focus on caseload data with minimal discussion of the processes of mediation, the nature of the community within which it occurs, and the impact of a mediation center on community organization and functioning.

These evaluation studies place primary emphasis on the caseloads of the centers, their sources of referral, case type, and case disposition: goals which were enunciated at the 1976 meeting of the National Conference on the Causes of Popular Dissatisfaction with the Administration of Justice (the Pound Conference) (Cook et al., 1980: 7,8). Yet, the caseloads of Neighborhood Justice Centers have been disappointing. Despite energetic media campaigns, cultivation of a wide range of referral sources, and substantial commitment of limited program resources to intake, caseloads have remained small, particularly in proportion to the caseloads of courts. The Dorchester Urban Court, for example, conducted 438 hearings in its first two years of operation (Snyder, 1978: 130), but the local lower court handled 6,000 non-motor-vehicle law violations a year in the same period (Felstiner and Williams, 1978). Particularly surprising is the continued low number of voluntary referrals.

For example, the 15-month evaluation of the Neighborhood Justice Centers reports that only 17 percent of their referrals were voluntary "walk-ins" (Cook et al., 1980: 27). Referrals from social service agencies were also low, representing only 16 percent of the total (Cook et al., 1980: 27). Referrals from an established source within the court system, such as the clerks' or prosecutors' office or the bench, appears to be the most reliable route to a respectable caseload. The Atlanta and Kansas City Neighborhood Justice Centers, for example, which used these sources for two-thirds of their cases, received more referrals than the Los Angeles center which, endeavoring to avoid dependence on justice system referrals, received only one-third from criminal or civil justice sources. Of the total caseload of the centers, Atlanta handled 60 percent, Kansas City 21 percent, and Los Angeles 19 percent (Cook et al., 1980: 25–39). The evaluation report finds the low caseload of the Kansas City Center puzzling given its justice system referral source since such programs generally handle a larger volume.

Furthermore, it is not clear whether mediation programs are having any significant impact on the caseloads of the courts. Interviews with justice system personnel in the Neighborhood Justice Center cities indicated that they did not perceive the centers to be reducing caseloads although they did free the judges from some of the most difficult and time-consuming cases (Cook et al., 1980: 83). An evaluation of a suburban program indicated that since the bulk of their referrals came from the police and the prosecutor's office, substantial justice system resources had already been expended in processing these cases before they received them (Evaluation Group, 1980). No research has determined whether the cases coming to NJCs would all have been handled by the courts or whether they represent a group of disputes which would otherwise simply have been endured, avoided, or "lumped" (Felstiner, 1974: Merry, 1979c), although three evaluations suggest that the cases mediation handles would not have been prosecuted (Moriarty et al., 1977; Evaluation Group, 1980: 64; Davis et al., 1979).

A second measure commonly used to evaluate NJCs is speed. Centers generally perform well by this standard, hearing cases within a week to ten days after the referral (McGillis and Mullen, 1977). A study of the Suffolk County program estimated the average lapse between referral and closure of case in mediation at one month in comparison to four to five months in court (Evaluation Group, 1980: 85–86). The Neighborhood Justice Centers held a hearing an average of nine days after intake (Cook et al. 1980: 34), while the court in Atlanta took an average of 63 days between initial filing and final disposition (Cook et al., 1980: 74). However, Tomasic notes that court figures are not that different if all cases are considered, not just those which are adjudicated (Cook et al., 1980: 40–42). In Atlanta, for example, 77 percent of court cases are dropped for various reasons after six days. Although it takes

98 days to come to a trial, only 14 percent of cases go this far (Cook et al., 1980: 76).

A third measure is costs in comparison to courts. Although cost figures are easy to manipulate, it appears that Neighborhood Justice Centers, because of substantial staff time and low caseloads, show relatively high costs per hearing. Costs can be measured either per referral or per hearing, a difference which can shift the figures by 50 percent (Cook et al., 1980: 101). Costs vary greatly with size of caseload, ranging from $4.18 per hearing in 1979 in one program, which processes numerous routine bad check cases, to $589 per hearing in another program with a small caseload (Cook et al., 1980: 101). Clearly, these figures do not accurately describe the quality of service, only the ratio of caseload to program budget. It is notoriously difficult to estimate the costs of a hearing in court, but a few rough estimates indicate that mediation programs are generally more expensive per case than courts (Felstiner, and Williams, this volume, and Hoff, 1974, cited in Cook et al., 1980: 101–102). However, another estimate, similarly based on sketchy figures from the courts, suggests the opposite (Evaluation Group, 1980: 109).

Three other measures are used to assess quality of services provided. One is case disposition: the proportion of cases which are resolved in any way, either through a hearing or before the hearing, often because of the intervention of mediation center personnel. Here again, the record is disappointing. Only 45 percent of the NJC referrals resulted in an agreement or resolution (Cook et al., 1980: 26). However, it is difficult to interpret this figure. We need to consider comparative rates of resolution of cases in court as well as the fact that cases may be settled at the Neighborhood Justice Center which would otherwise never have been resolved. My own study of a small urban neighborhood suggests that many disputes fester unresolved and that even when they are taken to court, the court does little or nothing to settle them (Merry, 1979). A small comparative study of courts in the NJC evaluation reported that 50 percent of court cases were dismissed before going to a hearing or trial (Cook et al., 1980: 79). Even initiating legal action appeared to help the disputants, however. The controlled comparison study of the Brooklyn Dispute Resolution Center in which cases were randomly assigned to mediation or court found that 72 percent of court referrals were dismissed or adjourned and only 28 percent were forwarded for prosecution (Davis et al., 1979: iii). A 1971 Vera Institute study found similarly high rates of deterioration even for felony arrests: 44 percent resulted in dismissal or acquittal and only 15 percent ended in a conviction for a felony (1977: 1).

A second measure of quality of services is disputant reports of satisfaction with the process. Typically, disputants are contacted by phone six months after the hearing and asked whether they found the process satisfactory and whether they were satisfied with the mediator, the agreement, and the overall experience (e.g., Cook et al., 1980: 132–135). Rates of satisfaction with neighborhood justice centers are impressively high: between 75 percent and 90 percent, an average of 88 percent, responding affirmatively in all the centers (Cook et al., 1980: 47, 54). Other studies report similarly high levels of satisfaction. Moreover, a comparison with a small cohort of court users in Atlanta and Kansas City suggests that rates of satisfaction in court are lower (Cook et al., 1980: 100). For example, in Atlanta, only 33 percent of complainants felt that the adjudicated sentence was fair, in contrast to 86 percent of complainants who said that they were satisfied with the terms of the mediated agreement (Cook et al., 1980: 100). Eighty-eight percent of disputants were satisfied with the mediator in the NJC study, while 64 to 69 percent said they were satisfied with the judge (Cook et al., 1980: 100). The Brooklyn controlled comparison of court and mediation found many more complainants who felt that they had had an opportunity to tell their side of the story in mediation (94 percent) than court (65 percent), but a much smaller discrepancy in perceived fairness of the mediator (88 percent) and the judge (76 percent) (Davis et al., 1979: 50). The same study revealed that more respondents thought mediated outcomes were fair (77 percent) than adjudicated ones (56 percent) (Cook et al., 1980: 51). It is intriguing that with the exception of the Brooklyn study, questions about mediation focus on the quality of the experience, not on the sense of justice done. Clearly, the experience is more personalized, humane, pleasant, and less bureaucratic and routinized than the court and, Starr points out, affords greater dignity to the disputants (1978), but we know little about whether disputants also think it is fairer or more just.

A third aspect of the quality of services measured is rates of long-term resolution or agreement stability. Here again, rates of agreement stability appear high, with over 30 percent of complainants and respondents stating that they have kept the agreements in the three neighborhood justice centers (Cook et al., 1980: 56–57). The Florida study reports a somewhat lower rate of long-term resolution, with 52 percent of complainants who had a hearing reporting the problem totally resolved 6 to 12 months later (Dispute Resolution Alternatives Committee, 1979: 33). Yet, we have virtually no comparable figures from court, nor any idea of what rates of resolution would be a realistic goal. The Brooklyn study found no difference in the rate of recurring problems and future demands on police and courts between cases that were adjudicated and those which were mediated (Davis et al., 1979: 60–61).

Nor do we know how the content of the dispute affects what rate of resolution is desirable. The rate of long-term resolution for concrete, specific cases which are susceptible to negotiation and can be resolved through a single transaction appears to be much higher than for general cases requiring behavioral change. In Florida, complainants seeking material or monetary items were most likely to perceive their problem as totally resolved 6 to 12 months later, while those involved in domestic/child welfare cases were least likely to perceive total resolution in the long run (Dispute Resolution Alternatives Committee, 1979: 56). Similarly, agreements involving immediate transactions, such as payment or return of property or disengagement, were more likely to be perceived as totally resolved by the complainant in the long run than those involving repairs to be made, the obligation to establish cooperative relationships, or the promise to control animals or alter past behavior (Ibid.). Similarly, we should probably expect higher rates of resolution where disputants have outcome correspondence (a mutual interest in coming to a resolution with shared gains and losses) than in disputes where outcomes are noncorrespondent (interests are diametrically opposed, and the gains of one party are losses for the other) (Thibaut and Walker, 1975: 8). Lynne Williams suggests that rates of resolution vary according to the number of issues at stake and the level of divergence between the disputants in what they are seeking (1980).

This list of measures for evaluating Neighborhood Justice Centers focuses on judicial goals and ignores many other ways of judging their effectiveness. I will describe a range of other ways of evaluating Neighborhood Justice Centers arising, first, from quality of justice goals and, second, from community development goals.

It is clearly important to evaluate whether Neighborhood Justice Centers improve access to justice. Although users of NJCs are roughly similar to the communities they serve in race, they appear to be disproportionately low income (Cook et al., 1980: 23). In Atlanta and Kansas City, complainants were disproportionately black and female (Cook et al., 1980: 152–157), and in Brooklyn, the majority were young, black or Hispanic, poor (56 percent unemployed), uneducated (52 percent without high school diploma), and female (63 percent) (Davis et al., 1979: 32–33). In Suffolk County, complainants were generally white and middle income, as is the community, but were largely (58 percent) female (Evaluation Group, 1980: 75). Since 62 percent of the caseload consisted of neighbor-neighbor disputes, this may simply reflect the greater involvement of women in the local neighborhood (Evaluation Group, 1980: 78). However, as Tomasic points out, Neighborhood Justice Centers serve largely as points of exit from the justice system, not entry into it (1980). Centers which rely heavily on justice system referrals are not providing a service for people who would otherwise find the legal system inaccessible. My research on a low-income urban community suggests that such people are already users of the court, although the quality of justice they receive is poor (Merry, 1979b). Neighborhood Justice Centers may be more successful in removing unwanted cases from court dockets than in providing a superior or more accessible form of justice (see Abel, 1979).

A second issue is how Neighborhood Justice Centers affect the quality of justice. Some critics argue that existing mediation programs simply provide second-class justice for the poor and underprivileged (Hofrichter, 1977; Singer, 1979b). Surprisingly, no study has investigated disputants' perceptions of fairness and justice, although experimental (Thibaut and Walker, 1975) and empirical (Casper, 1978) research on such questions exists, nor has any study questioned the impact such a center has on citizens' dissatisfaction with the legal system. Sarat suggests that citizen participations in the legal system other than jury service leads to disenchantment and diminished respect rather than increased confidence (1980: 55). It is important to determine whether NJCs will counteract this awareness or simply increase alienation from the legal institutions of American society.

A quite different series of goals for Neighborhood Justice Centers emerges from the community development field, suggesting further measures of success. Although important, most of these measures are not easily susceptible to quantification. Community mediation could provide a means to counteract a state of anomie, isolation, alienation, and fear in a community by facilitating communication between people who would otherwise remain distant acquaintances, even locked into relationships of hostility and conflict. Particularly in areas where substantial differences in class, life-style, and values divide residents, the inevitable conflicts of daily life are exacerbated by misunderstanding and, often, group and ethnic prejudice (see Merry 1980; 1981c). Disputants in these situations may deal with their differences through avoidance, endurance of a state of ongoing conflict, or "lumping it," while the conflict swells feelings of ethnic hostility. Mediation could provide a valuable means to counteract this social isolation by providing a mechanism for people to communicate with each other, breaking down hostilities founded on misunderstanding. Even if the number of disputes resolved is small, the improvement in the quality of neighborhood life could be great. If one goal of mediation is to facilitate communication and forge shared understandings, however, the continued reliance on the caucusing procedure, derived from the very different context of labor arbitration, seems questionable. Felstiner and Williams cogently argue that withdrawing for private caucuses with the mediator interrupts the flow of communication between the parties (1978).

In such heterogeneous communities where the need to find a way of dealing with one's neighbors or associates nonetheless exists, mediation could provide a process by which the settlement of disputes itself engenders a discussion of relevant and underlying norms and values, particularly if mediation programs abandon their ostrichlike approach to the issue of values. At the moment, mediators are instructed to be nonjudgmental and not to let their moral views affect the course of the mediation process. Although it is clearly not the place of the mediator to decide which party is right and which wrong or to provide ready-made solutions, it is not realistic to eliminate values from the process. Each disputant phrases his or her position in moral terms, thus providing a justification for his or her actions. Part of the discussion in mediation concerns which justification of conduct is morally superior. Starr describes insightfully the ways values do in fact enter into the mediation hearings she observed in Brooklyn (Davis et al., 1979: 43–44). In the anthropological prototypes, the process of settling a dispute leads to the clarification and enunciation of relevant values. Similarly, mediation in American settings could provide a means for disputants to recognize differences in their standards concerning the allocation of scarce resources, moral and appropriate behavior, family life, and neighborly responsibility, ideally forging a common set of standards by which to arrive at a solution. Thibaut and Walker find that the process of discussing standards is possible within the framework of mediation (1975). Whether this can happen in American communities is clearly debatable at this point, but the question needs to be considered in Neighborhood Justice Centers.

The emergence of at least some level of common understanding about appropriate and offensive behavior would not only solve the presenting problem but also forge a set of rules by which future conflicts could be handled, analogous to the process in labor arbitration (Fuller, 1971). For example, a recent study of disputing in an American neighborhood suggests that common understandings about right and wrong parking behavior ease the stresses associated with limited parking space and heavy snowfalls (Buckle and Buckle, 1980). The development of shared understandings could also reduce the anomie and alienation which often leads to distrust and hostility between different groups.

Another way of measuring the success of neighborhood justice centers is to investigate the extent to which they increase local autonomy in dealing with social control problems, reducing their reliance on the coercive powers of the state. Galanter points to the drawbacks of "legal centralization" which vests the control of behavior more extensively in the court system, expanding the net of centrally created laws tossed over the average citizen (1979a). Decentralizing social control not only limits state power over the lives of individual citizens, but also enhances their sense of mastery and control over their environment and provides them with a greater ability to cope with their own problems.

Many of the important disputes affecting Americans do not concern their relationships with family, neighbors, and friends but with organizations, government, and outsiders (Abel 1979; Buckle and Buckle, 1980). Although the value of mediating such unequal disputes is questionable, mediation can provide a mechanism through which the settlement of individual disputes leads to a transformation of that dispute from an individual grievance to a collective problem susceptible to political action (a concept suggested by Yngvesson and Mather). Wahrhaftig provides an example of such a transformation occurring in the process of mediation in the San Francisco Community Boards' programs, which use public hearings (Wahrhaftig, 1981). Community mediation could thus become a vehicle for social change rather than simply a dispute-processing service.

Finally, mediation programs can contribute to the development of local leadership and dispute settlement skills which can be applied outside the centers. In the anthropological prototypes, mediators are powerful and influential community leaders who develop their competence in dispute settlement and translate their success into political power. In the American context, both mediators and users will gain experience in an alternative mode of handling differences. Ironically, a measure of the success of this learning experience could be fewer cases returning to mediation. Where mediators are placed on a board controlling the program, as they are in the San Francisco Community Boards, this may enhance their ability to assume unofficial roles as community leaders. Such leadership can channel discontent and contribute to the transformation of individual disputes into collective political action. Obviously, mediation programs may not foster leadership or lead to any changes in cultural values about disputing, but these are possible benefits which should not be overlooked.

The criteria of success discussed above all concern the policy questions of whether or not Neighborhood Justice Centers should be implemented and how they should be structured. Perhaps of greater significance is the unique opportunity offered by the NJC movement to expand our theoretical understanding of the role of law in society. These centers offer a setting in which we can gain a greater understanding of local dispute settlement processes and the ways mediation functions in urban, industrialized societies. An anthropological approach is particularly valuable here. Anthropologists have been in the forefront of a shift in focus in the study of law and society from legal institutions to the processes of handling disputes. Based on extensive research on disputing in nonindustrialized societies, they suggest analyzing the range of ways disputes are handled in varying social contexts (e.g., Abel, 1974; Nader and Todd, 1978). Anthropologists have also emphasized the existence of multiple legal systems (Pospisil, 1967), "semi-autonomous social fields" (Moore, 1973), and legal pluralism, in the broadest sense: multiple modes of resolving disputes which coexist in every society. Actors make choices between these modes, some of which are embodied in formal structures such as courts, while others are based on local kin groups, village political organizations, religious bodies, or simply influential individuals with personal respect. These dispute resolution forums are attuned to different forms of dispute and to differing relationships between the parties. Covillagers might seek out one forum while members of related but separate villages would turn to another. The essense of the anthropological perspective is an understanding of the functioning of all these forums and their interrelationships, not only those which fall under the auspices of the state. The critical questions for legal anthropology in the future may be the articulation of legal modes of resolving disputes with nonlegal ones (Rosen, 1980).

Adopting this perspective with reference to Neighborhood Justice Centers raises a number of empirically and theoretically interesting questions. How do people in local neighborhoods resolve the range of disputes they confront, and what forums do they use? What kinds of disputes erupt for which there is now no recourse, and how are they handled? Is there a widespread perception that the court is the preferred location for resolution, but is avoided because it is too expensive, time consuming, formal, and inaccessible, as the access-to-justice movement assumes? Do disputants perceive mediation as a valuable mode of resolving their differences either before or after they have tried it? How does mediation relate to other modes of resolving disputes, particularly legal ones? Does mediation already occur within other structural arrangements? What other effective modes of dispute resolution now exist at the local level? Can mediation function within the fragmented social structure typical of urban neighborhoods?

These questions take the vantage point of the actor/disputant, asking where his or her needs lie, where lacunae in dispute settlement mechanisms exist, and what sorts of institutional arrangements he or she prefers to use. In contrast, much of the previous discussion of Neighborhood Justice Centers springs from the perspective of the system, from the needs of courts and from systemic notions of a lack of equal access to justice. Mediation programs provide an ideal opportunity to examine the range of dispute settlement mechanisms used at the local level and to consider the potential of noncourt settings to deliver dispute resolution which citizens view as legitimate and just. A broader understanding of the range of ways disputes are handled and the kinds of forums which can provide justice from an actor's perspective is critical in light of persisting, intractable issues of ineffective criminal justice, public disillusion with the judicial system, overwhelming demands for rapid, effective dispute resolution by an expanding body of citizen disputants, and the cry for a judicial system which furthers rather than obstucts progress towards social justice.

## Conclusions

Evaluations of Neighborhood Justice Centers have focused on the judicial definitions of need and standards of success, neglecting issues of quality and access to justice as well as community development goals. If the benefits as well as the failures of the NJC movement are to be accurately understood, we must expand the range of standards by which they are to be judged. Although there is some evidence from cross-cultural research that efforts of this kind to revive indigenous law gradually die out from disuse (Galanter, 1979a), a fair assessment of the successes and failures of the NJC movement should take into account all the goals, both those of the right and the left, which it is expected to serve. However, Neighborhood Justice Centers are also not a panacea which can reverse the implacable drift toward greater centralization, bureaucratization, and dissolution of community characteristic of American society.

The NJC model now in use does not really reproduce either indigenous patterns of dispute settlement through mediation or ideal images of community moots. It is rather a new hybrid, forged and twisted by the conflicting pressures of the need for institutionalization, funding, the need to justify a program in terms of a limited set of values, and the political pressures of right and left. Despite its origins in compromise and accommodation, the present model of the Neighborhood Justice Center is being replicated throughout the country even though it is by no means the only possible model for community mediation. It is puzzling that despite the burst of enthusiasm for Neighborhood Justice Centers, there has been very little experimentation with alternative forms of social context and definition of "community," types of mediator, roles of mediator, processes of mediation, involvement of values, public versus private hearings, sources of referral, nature of agreements, restrictions on the types of cases which can be handled, uses of coercion and social pressure, or relationship to the court. Perhaps the wide appeal of community mediation is precisely that it purports to serve so many different interests. Yet, unless we think more broadly about what mediation can and cannot do in the American social context, we risk prematurely pronouncing it a failure.. The poor showings on measures of caseloads and costs must be stacked against the need for a long trial period to test the acceptability of a radically different mode of dispute settlement to the American public. Further, the discrepancy between the original prototypes and the kinds of Neighborhood Justice Centers now being established suggests the need for more creative experimentation on the ways mediation can be adapted to American society.

## Notes

1. One police officer in Suffolk County alluded to this difficulty in the following quote:

> The problem is not sending cases to CMC (the mediation program), the problem is sending enough cases directly to CMC. If our workload is to

be saved, we are going to have to send many more cases to mediation than are now sent. We are going to need on-the-spot agreement with the D.A.; without it, nothing is saved—without it mediation isn't that important. I would like to send more of my cases to CMC. The problem is people want to go to court . . . they want to talk to the judge. (Evaluation Group, 1980: 66)

2. The neighborhood justice center evaluation reported only slight differences in satisfaction and long-term resolution by case type (Cook et al., 1980: 50). However, in cases unresolved by the Neighborhood Justice Centers, 47 percent of the interpersonal/criminal cases were later resolved in comparison to only 27 percent of civil/consumer cases. The agreements in the former were less stable, with 33 percent reporting more problems in the future, in comparison to only 18 percent of the latter (1980: 62–65).

# 10

# Justice Centers Raise Basic Questions[*]

### Richard Hofrichter

Significant changes are emerging in alternatives to courts for the resolution of a wide range of citizen disputes and grievances.[1] Most of these quasi-judicial and non-judicial forums and procedures have existed for many years and include arbitration, mediation, conciliation, upgrading the quality of small claims courts, community courts, pre-trial intervention, community complaint centers, and administrative tribunals, to name but a few. The federal government currently funds about twelve community justice projects of varying models.

Recently, however, the scope and pace of government activity has increased. For example, the Courts Division of the Law Enforcement Assistance Administration (LEAA) in the Department of Justice has recently funded three experimental Neighborhood Justice Centers (NJCs) in Los Angeles (bar association sponsor), Kansas City (city manager), and Atlanta (the courts). These groups, with guidelines from LEAA,[2] will plan the centers from scratch, and all expect to begin operations by early 1978. LEAA also plans funding research on "the state of the art" nationwide.

The Consumer Controversies Resolution Act (S957), a bill recently introduced in the Senate, proposes "to assist in the development of innovative concepts and approaches for the resolution of [citizen] controversies" in order to "resolve disputes effectively, fairly, inexpensively, and expeditiously."[3] The bill, as amended, would establish a resource center within the Office for Improvement in the Administration of Justice in the Department of Justice.

By surveying operating mechanisms and evaluating them, the resource center, in its first year of activity, would function as a clearing-

* Reprinted with permission from 2(6) *New Directions* 168–172, copyright © 1977 National Resource Center for Consumers of Legal Services.

house for the exchange of information and provide technical assistance in improving or creating dispute resolution mechanisms. The results of research would be used to establish priorities and set guidelines on a nationwide basis. In the second year, seed grants would be made available for improving or creating projects funded directly through the Department of Justice rather than a state agency. Any non-profit organization, business, bar association, municipal agency, etc. could establish a program and receive funding.

What is the significance of these developments from the perspective of low and middle income parties who use or will use NJCs, particularly for consumer and minor criminal matters? Will they signify revitalized forums for the same character of justice available in the courts? May they systematically favor the long run interests of powerful groups in the jurisdictions served?

Many of the programmatic issues associated with specific models have been described elsewhere.[4] Future evaluations will determine whether NJCs work well on their own terms as defined by sponsors or funders. This article raises a few general but major issues about the interests and values potentially promoted by NJCs. It relates these issues to varying interpretations of the problems that have led to the new emphasis on non-judicial community justice. Essentially, these issues concern (a) differentials in economic bargaining power among disputants, (b) social control, and (c) community participation in planning new forums.

## Competing Interpretations of the Legal System Crisis

A variety of explanations exist for the emergence of the current interest in alternatives to courts. These explanations are closely allied with basic policy issues surrounding the criteria by which to evaluate NJCs. Issue definition partially depends on whether the interpretation of the problems which give rise to alternatives is presented from the perspective of federal bureaucrats, social scientists, and legal professionals or within a broader contextual framework which includes, among other things, the needs of clients or client groups. Each view shares certain assumptions about the role of the legal system, its internal crises, and the values endemic to legal justice.

Generally, the conception of bureaucrats and professionals functions in a tradition of legal reform and technocratic solutions to what may constitute essentially political problems. In this view, LEAA, for example, identifies as one of its basic concerns the elimination of forces that threaten efficiency, such as an overload of cases, understaffing, delay, and fiscal crisis, rather than the realization of specific values associated with a more substantive idea of justice, whatever its elements.

Indeed, justice becomes equated with efficiency and rationality of procedures. An effective project is thus one which successfully (a) processes cases without violating measures of fairness and due process, and (b) eliminates "junk" cases from the courts without relinquishing control over disputes which could escalate into costly cases for the courts or even organized social protest. Goals and strategies translate into cost-benefit models committed to caseload reductions and bureaucratic reorganization.[5]

This is not to deny the importance of these questions or the value of seeking flexibility and informality. Yet such an instrumental approach, which assumes shared values among disputants and the avoidance of controversy as a goal, ignores other fundamental political dimensions of social conflict that cannot be easily remedied by bureaucratic, therapeutic, or legal formulas.

The resolution of disputes and the quality of justice does not depend entirely either on the rule of law or the efficiency of procedure. The organized power and resources of the disputants prior to reaching a public forum also influences the nature of the process and its outcomes. The perspective of NJC planners sometimes neglects important changes in the character of contemporary conflict (organizations v. individuals) which may hamper efforts to impose models of community justice where no real community exists, except in jurisdictional terms.

An alternative framework for analyzing the movement toward Neighborhood Justice accepts, as does the above view, the general consumer dissatisfaction with justice based on the high cost of legal service; the inaccessibility and complexity of the courts; problems enforcing small claims; the absence of fairness; and the need for appropriate remedies not dependent on findings of guilt or fault. The limitations of the adversary system are not in dispute.

However, in the alternative framework, the crisis in the legal system is also explained within the context of social order transformations such as (1) the growing centralization and concentration of corporate power resulting in restrictions on challenges to corporate control of society's resources and how they should be used, (2) the breakdown of traditional conflict resolving and socializing institutions, such as the family, school, church, and political clubhouse, and (3) the expanded role of government into more activities of everyday social life. Large scale bureaucracies emerge which in turn create new demands for rights in relation to the benefits conferred by those bureaucracies.[6] At the same time, demands for equality and participation expand. What is the crisis in the legal system produced by these changes?

The standards of rationality and formality in the courts become inapplicable for managing new forms of social conflict and dislocation arising from these occurrences. The rule of law and the structure of legality fails to account for the differentials in material and authoritative resources possessed among a new order of disputants with predetermined powers and rights. Individuals increasingly dispute with institutional entities and strangers such as chain stores and landlords. If, as much legal and historical analysis suggest,[7] conceptions of order and law derive from material relationships between those who possess property (in the broadest sense) and those who do not, then the effects of these changes cannot easily be concealed in the daily operation of the legal system through its usual symbols and practices.

The legitimacy of formal legal order is in danger of being undermined in light of new demands made upon it, its revealed biases preserving inequality and protecting those with great resources, as well as its sluggish and inefficient operations. The prevention of social breakdown where traditional institutions fail requires a constant revision of social forms for the protection of established order (for purposes of sustaining stable processes of production and consumption), while, at the same time, seeking popular support through symbols and procedures that mask substantive inequalities.

Neighborhood Justice Centers may represent a classic example of the ongoing attempt to neutralize demands and resolve these inherent tensions in the legal system by means of various models of quasi-legal and administrative apparatuses, designated as a form of voluntary community conciliation. Finally, the replacement of courts by NJCs for certain kinds of problems parallels similar movements by government toward what is commonly referred to as deinstitutionalization (replacing asylums) in the mental health system and community based corrections (replacing prisons) in the criminal justice system. This is a central context in which NJCs must be understood.

From the perspective of low and moderate income, unorganized complainants and respondents of the new forms of community justice, given the framework described above, a number of issues emerge suggesting divergent directions for NJCs. These issues will require further research but appear endemic to NJCs, regardless of the model.

## Disputant Differentials in Resources

Theoretically, NJCs will resolve disputes between parties known to each other and having contact on a regular basis. But the social reality of conflict in a modern industrial society and preliminary indications from NJC planners suggest their applicability for a very broad range of problems and grievances.

This means that the NJCs may indirectly weaken the rights of low and moderate income groups and their ability to use the regular courts as protection against the increasingly institutionalized and concentrated power of organizations with vast resources, e.g., landlords, creditors, and government bureaucracies.[8]

Why? First, NJCs are likely to limit the scope of client demands and remedies since, by definition, they operate without the trappings of formal legal proceedings. Second, cases which might have appropriately entered the regular courts may now be channeled, initially, into NJCs. While the NJC forum is itself accessible, the cost of instituting a case in court at a later time may be costly. Third, many disputes, such as those involving regular patterns of activity, may require collective action or non-judicial responses. NJCs may deflect attention from this fact. Even though outcomes generally will depend on the ability to generate binding settlements, the relation of NJCs to the formal legal system, and the scope of dispositions available, the need for a collective response or policy transformation cannot be achieved through individualized dispute resolution.

The prevention of repeated fraudulent activities, for example, housing code violations or excessive rates charged by finance companies, requires a substantive reordering of property rights. The political dimension of these injustices is excluded when translated into a misunderstanding resolvable by negotiation and the avoidance of conflict. Where consumers are complainants, resolution by accommodation conceals the inequality between parties in bargaining power and does nothing to restrict repeated fraudulent activity against the same or other complainants, while actually satisfying an individual's monetary claim of the moment.

Such informal systems provide the sense of having had one's day in court without challenging the wrong committed at a more general level or confronting the problem in another arena.

Query: will the NJCs be used by landlords for non-payment of rent? Probably not. Landlords need not be accommodating or informal in promoting their claims most of the time. Consumers cannot as easily shape the structure of conflict. An important question is whether the users will essentially be those without education or resources to employ the civil courts.

## Social Control

Another major issue involves the implications of NJCs as new modes of social control by local elites for disapproved conduct or violations of social norms. The reach of NJCs is more expansive than the courts, most notably when (1) employed as (a) an instrument of social pressure for the restriction of morally undesirable behavior or (b) a means for containing and deflecting large scale grievances that might erupt as social protest, and (2) integrated with an extensive variety of other public service agencies to which parties are routinely referred. The intensity, scope, and duration of supervision by the State increases. Large numbers of people may get caught in the system, regardless of due process protections. Peer pressure in homogeneous communities with parochial values present formidable obstacles to impartiality. All types of non-criminal deviant behavior may be sanctioned and given general support, mediated through the informal atmosphere of a local citizen dispute center.

The accessibility of NJCs allows for an over-inclusion of cases and the institutionalization of conflicts that might never have entered the courts. They thereby pose threats to individual liberty, even if the disputant ultimately obtains a positive outcome. The trauma of further penetration into the criminal justice system is avoided but at a high price. Efficient forms of social control of deviant populations may arise without the visible onus of the State. The regulation of social life can be as oppressive as any other kind, especially when the source of control is obscured through the seemingly autonomous apparatus of the NJC.

For example, in minor criminal or borderline criminal cases where social norms are violated rather than laws and where the sanctions stipulate referral to some form of treatment as opposed to punishment, the danger of overcontrol by the State, disguised as an apolitical helping agent, looms large. The distinction between treatment, service, and punishment is sometimes very fine.

What kind of protections can be built in when NJCs assume the characteristics of ordinary bureaucracies? Bureaucratic rationality substitutes for legal rules rather than a hoped for idealized "living law," transmitted through voluntary agreements arrived at by means of personalized rules of human interaction. Under these circumstances, the contrast articulated by planners between externally imposed law (in the regular courts) and spontaneous conciliation through voluntary agreements (in NJCs) breaks down. How far can a seemingly informal system go in limiting freedom without a legal determination of guilt?

This question raises another social control issue: the character of the connection of NJCs with the public agencies to which disputants may be referred. Will referrals be voluntary or coercive? Apart from which rights may be waived and the application of formal sanctions for non-compliance, what pressures might exist, for example, in intrafamily disputes or minor criminal matters where either party fears escalation of the case into the courts for non-compliance? What will be the values and interests of the new mediator bureaucrats, as agents of the community replacing legal bureaucrats, in applying norms, rules, and sanctions? What spheres of private action resulting in conflict will not be of interest to the jurisdictions with NJCs?

The issue of privacy is also related to the voluntary-coercive aspects of NJCs,[9] as well as to the efficiency of an effective referral process. On the one hand, an effective NJC requires systematic coordination with all of the appropriate referral agencies in a given jurisdiction and a comprehensive record-keeping system.[10] Will the use of records be restricted to the immediate dispute situation or may they be activated in future incidents—such as if one party decides to initiate proceedings at a later date? Will information be kept that would not normally be maintained at all?

While the information on file in referral agencies is obviously not the same as a criminal record, it does create a serious privacy issue since the range of agencies accumulating data increases access and potential use of such information. Citizens should expect that government agencies will not intrude without an explicit violation in a provable case. What links will referral agencies have with agencies of criminal justice? What kind of conduct ought to be considered beyond the realm of interest to the State and be excluded?

## Community Planning and Participation

As noted earlier, the legal system in many cities reflects the interests of the major property holders, legal professionals, and other organized interests who use the courts on a regular basis.[11] In the new NJCs, the issue of popular control is central. Who will plan and design them? It is not yet clear what role community representatives have had or will have in planning the models devised for the three LEAA demonstration projects in Los Angeles, Kansas City, and Atlanta. Program guidelines provide for a project board which "should contain people who are part of the community being served. The board may include representatives of public and private agencies or lay persons active in the community." The interpretation of this element may vary widely as it affects the client population.

The report accompanying S 957 clearly indicates a requirement for participation of low-income consumers in any state plan. The application for an agreement to provide financial assistance for upgrading or developing consumer controversy mechanisms must include comments of consumers. The meaning of participation in practice is, of course, an open question. It certainly does not mean control. But community justice must be accountable to its customers and offer the opportunity for making an effective contribution.

Decisions regarding types of disputes handled, eligibility of users, and overall monitoring and priority setting should not be left in the hands of local elite civic groups, legal system experts, bar associations, or federal planners. To do so discourages the idea promoted by NJCs that social conflict resolution remains the responsibility of all segments of society rather than bureaucratic planners. The latter typically seek to impose principles of conflict management, derived from abstract conceptions of justice and guided by instrumental values and attentiveness to existing community power relations.

## The Potential

What about the positive aspects of NJCs from the point of view of the unorganized individual in conflict with organized interests? First, the opportunity arises for questioning the foundations of the legal system— its structure, processes, procedures, and the role of professionals, as well as technical weaknesses and system actor abuses. The involvement of non-professionals and the public debate over the elements of NJCs from their roots enhances this probability. Nothing need be taken for granted; every system characteristic may be questioned and evaluated.

This questioning can be accomplished not only at the level of cost and productivity or programmatic effectiveness, but in more qualitative terms which can lead to the beginning of a re-evaluation of property rights. As Roberto Unger of Harvard Law School explains, the minimizing of formal rationality in the effort to achieve substantive justice erodes existing entitlements and obligations thereby revealing the true under pinning of such entitlements.[12] The demystification of law and professionalism begins with a totalistic form of evaluation. Such an analysis reveals the social meaning of conflict. It penetrates the fundamental claims of legalism to neutrality, autonomy, and impartiality, distinguishing substantive from procedural rights and their source within the context of the non-legal resources and position of conflicting parties.

At the same time, community residents can learn skills of negotiation, mediation, and advocacy which enhance their general competence to use the legal system more effectively. Lay mediators are not likely to become a special class, alienated from their peers. Moreover, experience with dispute resolution systems that limit formal procedures and abstract legal jargon heightens awareness of the economic and political character of legal rights and their development through struggle.

## Conclusion

The attempt to simplify conflict resolution in an increasingly complex and diversified environment by means of informal, decentralized NJCs raises some crucial political and legal questions. At the same time, new forms of local justice offer an unprecedented opportunity for rethinking the foundations of our legal institutions.

An assumption of NJCs that disputing parties will know each other or have contact on a regular basis, in many instances, denies the fact that conflicts increasingly occur between strangers and organized bureaucracies, public and private. A community model cannot be easily superimposed where no real community exists, except in jurisdictional or ethnic terms. The pretension of informal neighborly justice disregards the political nature of conflict and the danger of indirect elite control.

Thus, what on the surface appears as a movement toward a more personalized, decentralized, and community controlled justice, may actually represent a new form of State bureaucracy, extending the purview of State authority well beyond that of conventional courts. As anthropologist Laura Nader has noted:

> Informal methods of [dispute resolution] are more accessible, less formidable, less expensive but not necessarily more likely to produce equitable results or to eliminate future complaints.[13]

As long as alternatives to courts are conceived primarily as responses to managing caseloads, achieving formal equality through procedures, and minimizing legal system costs to the State, they cannot truly transform the quality of justice. Power is not easily challenged through law.

Future directions may depend in no small part on the organizing capability of community groups in the struggle over the specific characteristics of NJCs. If social justice is to be informed by community experience and participation rather than represent new symbolic forums controlled by privileged organized elites, then the issues raised above must remain central to the coming debate over transformations in our legal order.

## Notes

1. See Earl Johnson, Valerie Kantor & Elizabeth Schwartz, *Outside the Courts—A Survey of Diversion Alternatives in Civil Courts*, National Center for State Courts, Denver, 1977; Joseph Stulberg, "Programs for Mediating Neighborhood Disputes: A Perspective," paper presented at the National Conference on the Causes of Popular Dissatisfaction with the Administration of Justice, St. Paul, Minn., 1976, reprinted in 70 F.R.D. 79, 1976; Laura Nader and Linda Singer "Dispute Resolution" Cal. State Bar Jl.51, No.4, July 1976.

2. Memorandum to Proposed Neighborhood Justice Center Program Grantees, *Grant Application Guidelines & Procedures*, Training & Testing Division, Office of Technology Transfer, LEAA, Dept. of Justice, Washington, D.C., August 3, 1977.

3. Senate report to accompany S 957, Consumer Controversies Resolution Act, Committee on Commerce, Science, & Transportation, 95th Congress, 1st Session, May 16, 1977. As of this writing the legislation is still being revised and amended.

4. J. Mullen, *Neighborhood Justice: An Analysis of Potential Models*, submitted to Office of Technology Transfer, National Institute of Law Enforcement & Criminal Justice, LEAA, Cambridge, Mass., Abt Associates, June 1977; Research Institute On Legal Assistance, Legal Services Corporation, "The Development of Alternatives to Formal Dispute Mechanisms," *Clearinghouse Review* Vol. 11, No. 3, July 1977, 226.

5. See, for example, "Proposed Mission & Functions Statement for NILE-CJ" LEAA, Washington, D.C., nid.; National Advisory Commission on Criminal Justice Standards and Goals, Task Force on Courts, *Courts*, Washington, D.C.: LEAA, 1973, passim.

6. See Charles Reich "The New Property," *Yale Law J1*, 73, April 1964, 778.

7. See Morton Horwitz, *The Transformation of American Law*: *1780–1860*, Cambridge, Mass., Harvard University Press, 1977; Michael Tigar and M. Levy, *Law & the Rise of Capitalism*, N.Y., Monthly Review Press, 1977.

8. See Marc Galanter "Why the 'Haves' Come Out Ahead: Speculations on the Limits of Legal Change," *Law & Society Review* 9, No. 1, Fall 1974, 95.

9. Supra, Note 2, *Grant Application Guidelines & Procedures,* p. 7, state that there must be "a briefing process to ensure the disputants understand the voluntary nature of the process."

10. Id., p. 7.

11. See David Caplovitz, *The Poor Pay More*, N.Y., Free Press, 1967; James Eisenstein, *The Politics of the Legal Process*, N.Y., Harper & Row, 1973.

12. *Law & Modern Society*, N.Y., Free Press, 1975, 199.

13. Supra, Note 1.

# 11

# Alternatives to the Criminal Court System

## William Clifford*

## Law and Behavior

Some years ago Gulliver studied social control in a remote branch of the
Arusha tribe, living in Tanzania on the shores of Lake Victoria, because
this was a small group of people living together so simply that they had
no formal political organization.[1] There were very few clans living
together and when disputes arose between the clans, the elders would
gather very informally to try to settle the matter, be it an alleged breach
of contract, a tort, or a criminal offence. As is usual in such circumstances, the sanction was invariably a form of compensation, the offending person or his clan giving a number of animals to the offended, as
might be decided by the ad hoc meeting of local elders. Most disputes
were settled amicably in this way. But Gulliver was interested in what
happened when the offender did not pay. After all, there was no one
filling the role of police officer, bailiff, or court officer to enforce the
judgement, no one group dominating the others and no formal procedure for redress of default.

He discovered that the conventional way for a dissatisfied "litigant"
to get his rights was for him to wait for the next meeting of the elders.
Then, as they gathered, he began to shout as loudly as he could so as to
make it quite impossible for the meeting to discuss anything else until
they had heard his complaint. They couldn't do anything, of course, because they had no enforcement procedure. But neither could they move
on to any other business, because his shouting was designed to prevent
this. If he kept it up long enough, the clan of the defaulting offender

* Director, Australian Institute of Criminology. Modified version of an
address delivered to the Western Australian Conference of Stipendary Magistrates on October 1, 1980.

would eventually be pursuaded by the others to prevail upon the miscreant to pay his dues. This having been done, the meeting could proceed to other business.

Compare now that little, inconspicuous gathering on the shores of Lake Victoria to the newsworthy General Assembly of the United Nations in New York. The procedures are not so different. However complicated and technologically sophisticated it may be, our so-called civilization is still rather simple in its approach to the settling of disputes. If you want attention in New York, you have to shout—and keep on shouting. The international scene is still seeped in rudimentary customary law and has to deal with many problems in a way probably no more effective than the Arusha principle.

The moral of this comparison is that efficiency in solving problems is not necessarily a function of legal sophistication—though we are often misled into believing so. However comprehensive and precisely drafted our modern statutory law, it has really much less real effect upon people's behavior than has some of the unwritten expectation of customary law on the societies it serves. Legislators wax furiously about drug abuse, obscenity, even organized and corporate crime, but the growing libraries of statutes have less and less effect on behavior. We can punish for stealing, murder, and rape, but we are not terribly effective in preventing it by new laws and sanctions.

Yet, as is well known, social controls are remarkably effective. To illustrate this, in the years before police cars were ubiquitous and a police officer frequently had to march his arrested suspect to the police station, it was possible for the most recalcitrant habitual criminal to be marched along by simply removing his belt. Hardened offenders with no respect for the law would be far more concerned with holding up their trousers so as not to appear in ridiculous contravention of social custom (Of course it would not work so well today when such conventions are scorned). One of the reasons why modern laws have so little effect on delinquent gangs is the strength of the internal discipline and strict codes implicit in an essentially lawless organization. And as we continue to train children for "the challenge of change" rather than "conformity" we must expect deviant social cultures with a variety of different norms and values to emerge. These internal pressures will be stronger than external laws. In fact, we positively encourage deviation by our lack of direction and guidance in a plural society. We reward it when it leads to the fierce independence which breaks new ground; we penalize it when it leads to crime and we are surprised to find our prisoners not only unrepentant but convinced that they are victims of a system with double standards. The fact is that we trust our statute law and formal court procedures too much. This is not to argue for an abolition of all law, but for less faith in its capacity for affecting behavior and greater discrimination in legislation.

## The Unification of Complexity

We have spent two hundred years or more fashioning a complex society, open, liberal, and strikingly diverse in its fundamental values. It is tolerant to a fault of varied standards of behavior. At the same time we have been covering this social variety in society with a mass of detailed legislation on fairly uniform principles which no longer find the general acceptance they should, because our laws and morals diverge. As we have stoutly defended the freedom of the individual—even against community interests—and sought to control our increasingly atomized society with remote bureaucratic power and a veritable deluge of legislation, that legislation has become, of necessity, indifferently enforced and progressively more ineffective in controlling—or for that matter even guiding—public behavior.

It should not come as a surprise that the amount of crime recorded in a democratic society is in inverse proportion to the number of statutes and professional personnel. Looking across the world at the rates of crime, it is possible to demonstrate that these rates are highest where there are more written laws, more lawyers, judges, magistrates, and criminologists. It is also possible to show that crime is not even perceived as being a problem where there are no written laws and where there are no professional services for its enforcement. This global anomaly surely provides a lesson for those not too hypnotized by the glitter of modernity and the decorum of our legal systems. It is a situation not easily dismissed as a coincidence or simply a question of better recording. About half of our crime in economically developed countries is never recorded: there is a dark figure for crime: but in close-knit tribal societies, individual misbehavior cannot be so easily hidden. In other words, we know that crime is controlled there, even if it is not formally recorded.

## The Decline in Group Rights and the Rise of Legislation

Over the past two centuries, at the same time as society has been processing the cause of individual liberty from the Stoic's natural law through Rousseau's natural rights to its modern guise of international human rights, there has been a concurrent devaluation and even emasculation of family, group, and community influence. As individuals have been guaranteed more and more independence—not only legally but politically, economically, and socially—they have been concentrated (very rapidly in historical terms) into sprawling urban collectivities with the atomized personal units so dependent upon interrelated support services. So that millions of people are now quite vulnerable not only to the winds of political, economic, or social change, but to any small ruthless terrorist group or even to a single determined individual prepared to hold a large city to ransom. Western society has, in effect, destroyed its family and community rights—the ultimate sources of all behavioral control—for the precious benefits of a relatively untrammeled individuality and the public right to deviate. Then in its desperation to control this mass of individuals devoid of their natural family and community constraints, modern society has rushed into voluminous legislation and strengthened its bureaucracies.

All this has meant the courts intruding ever further into areas previously left to informal controls. The thrust of formal proceedings has not only taken over much of the responsibility which was community, family, or private but as these groups become undermined and ineffective by the changes in society, the law is rarely slow to fill the gaps. So a kind of paradox emerges that the more emancipated the individual becomes from his or her social grouping, the more regulated he or she becomes by a more remote authority which, since it cannot be uniformly successful in its attempts to control, is unfairly manipulatable by the shrewd and intelligent. And, of course, with so much legislation, there has to be discretion in its application. Without this discretion we would literally be unable to move. Only a few years ago in the United Kingdom, every police officer could fall back upon certain by-laws for the control of public behavior which the police officers themselves used to call 'Breathing Acts," that is, even breathing might be construed as an offense. This is to exaggerate of course: but there are few people today unaware of the extent to which they are regulated by the modern state. And studies abound to demonstrate the amount of social bias which (perhaps necessarily) creeps into law enforcement. In no other way can we explain 30 or 40 percent of prisoners in many countries belonging to minority groups—or the majority of those charged coming from the lower-income sections of society. The laws are not only discriminatory in application. They are now so numerous and complex that it may soon be necessary to rethink the adage that ignorance of the law is no excuse. These days one can excuse even lawyers their ignorance of those branches of law in which they may not be practising.

So, if all the laws were to be enforced, people would not be able to move. They can do so only because the police and the courts use discretion. It is this informality permeating formality which makes the system work at all. Discretion should not be allowed to become discriminatory, but legislation to eliminate all discretion could paralyze the system or make it intolerably oppressive.

Since the police hear of only about 50 percent of all the crimes committed and since they exercise their discretion to reduce the percentage passed on to the courts, the sad procession which magistrates process every day may be only a fraction of the total number of offenders, that is, so many more are at large. This tends to make them the ones who were caught—the scapegoats for the major problem of crime in a society. In this sense we can see that the court system may be labeling people as criminal, as different to other people: and that the selection for this labeling could be so haphazard as to be unfair—no matter how fair we may try to be in dealing with the individual case. The sense of unfairness amongst offenders when they are punished for what they know so many other people are doing unmolested is very marked—and it tends to increase. Yet imagine the opposite situation, with everyone caught for every infringement of existing law and no one being allowed to escape prosecution. It is doubtful if any existing system could survive such pressure—and certainly few liberties for the citizen would remain.

Again, our technical laws and adversary procedure may mean rewarding, in court, forensic skills more than merit. Being impartial and legally correct may not always be consistent with fairness. Magistrates can, and sometimes do, find opportunities to stretch the law to cover unforeseen circumstances: but this is a limited discretion. As legal aid extends, more and more cases which might have been settled out of court in the past are now formally litigated. The discretion of the magistrate is likely to be limited not only by statute but by what the parties themselves will allow.

## The Real Costs

It is an old maxim of lawyers that "hard cases make bad law": but it is a maxim which has gone unheard for years now. At every new twist and turn statutes increase and we have still not learned to appreciate, it seems, that however effective they may be as declarations of rights and obligations they have been proved to be dismally inefficient in controlling behavior. Not only do they fall into disrepute by their number and complexity now beyond the range of the traditional "reasonable man." They lose further status when it is appreciated by the public that a lawyer's ability for presenting a case in court may have more real meaning than a law which serves best those most capable of manipulating it. As mentioned, the traditional ability of the magistrate to use his or her discretion to redress this balance is now reduced to the extent that legal representation extends.

So there are many reasons for seeking to avoid court procedure when this is possible. First is the tradition of public participation in English legal systems which have lost much of their public involvement character as they have professionalized. There is nothing wrong with voluntary informality if it will work—a fact we cannot afford to overlook. Secondly the statutes and the legal system applying them are progressively and even notoriously ineffective in really controlling behavior. Thirdly there are the obvious questions of cost and the growing need to find less expensive alternatives. But paradoxes abound: and we should not overlook the fact that the modern search for alternatives to the criminal justice system coincides with an increasing recourse to the courts to vindicate personal rights as people become better educated, more conscious of their rights and as they are provided with more access to lawyers and the legal process. Perhaps it is the second trend—this flooding of the courts—which makes the search for alternatives more urgent.

We are often told that costs alone dictate the need for alternatives, so a few facts here may be of interest. The cost of law courts and legal services in the Australian states, adjusted for inflation, has risen from $8.7 million in 1906–1907 to $43.1 million in 1977–1978, that is, a five-fold increase in expenditure over about 70 years (the costs have doubled every 13 years or so). In Western Australia over the same period this cost has increased more than six-fold from $.8 million to 5.3 million. That is to say it doubled every 12 years. During 1978–1979 the *actual* expenditure on the administration of Western Australia's courts was $6.6 million—this included the costs of the Supreme Court ($1.38 million), the District Court ($.57 million), Courts of Petty Sessions ($3.48 million) and the Family Court ($6.62 million).

Unfortunately it is not possible at this stage to identify the cost of criminal, as distinct from civil, cases in Western Australia's courts but some figures from Victoria may be of interest. In that state during 1978–1979 the average cost of a criminal trial was about $10,200 in the Supreme Court and $6,700 in the County Court. These costs were, however, very much higher than those in Magistrates' Courts where the average cost of a traffic or minor prosecution heard in Chambers was $14. We are not sure, however, whether these figures include judges' and magistrates' salaries.

Now these costs have to be related to income, and in New South Wales the fines collected pay for *most* of the administration of the law, that is, mainly the court work. In 1977–1978 the Attorney-Generals and Justice Office in N.S.W. cost A$63.3 million—and this included a cost for the police employed collecting fines. Revenue was A$61.6 million, so there was a rough balancing out. In Western Australia the courts showed a profit. For A$5.7 million spent on the Supreme, District, and Magistrates Courts, the revenue was A$8.7 million. Therefore, if alternatives are being preferred on grounds of costs alone, it may be difficult to get them much cheaper.

In terms of cases heard, Dr. Mukherjee of the Australian Institute of Criminology has determined that the number of criminal cases heard by District and Supreme Courts—per rate of population—has not increased since early in the century. The rate in the Magistrates Courts was also fairly static until traffic and property crimes proliferated after the Second World War. There were jurisdictional changes to account for the fact that the Magistrates Courts heard most of the cases—less than 2 percent of all criminal cases being referred to District and Supreme Courts.[2]

So, it is likely to be less the amount of work than the changes in the system which increase the total costs per taxpayer: but assuming that these real costs continue to double every 12 or 13 years, we can expect that a zero population growth in Australia will find the costs of formal court hearings disproportionate. It is all right to speak of revenues covering these costs, but it should not be overlooked that, for the public generally, both the court costs and court revenues represent payments to be made for the total system.

## Limits of Alternatives

There has been a traditional search in English law for ways of avoiding the time of judges being taken up unnecessarily. In Anglo-Saxon countries the legal system has always depended upon people serving voluntarily or being obliged to give time to the subject of law and order. Watchmen, constables, justices of the peace have all been devices for involving the public in keeping local order.

In applying laws, national and local, there was always a wide range of discretion. This sometimes became too wide, however, and the notion of the "King's Peace" was essentially a device to *limit* local discretion in certain types of cases. We can find the survival of peer group judgment and local discretion in the practice of compurgation and in the development of the jury. The sacred principle of English law was always the right to be tried by one's peers: and there are many examples of those peers deliberately frustrating formal legal rules when they thought them to be unfair in the given case. When hundreds of offenses carried the death penalty, juries devalued stolen property to a level below the capital liability, and they have acquitted in the face of undeniable evidence if they have felt an acquittal to be appropriate. Local legal history in Australia is replete with examples of juries opting for decisions that served local interest rather than abstract law.

On the other hand, public participation in the law can go too far. Lynching is a negative form of public participation and the arbitrary judgments of the mob are an abomination. In fact, the criminal law was originally a device to limit the excesses of vengeance and untrammeled public participation. So when we seek alternatives we have to take care that in our quest for cheaper, more effective, and less remote remedies than are provided now by our criminal courts we do not submit the persons involved to a kind of justice which suffers from the virtues of its simplicity: and from an informality which permits both bias and irrelevancies, vested interests and jealousies to intrude to an impossible extent.

There are, of course, a great many systems of justice across the world which are not formal in the sense of belonging to a regular legal and court system. The best known of these is the customary court found in Africa, Asia, Melanesia, among Aborigines in Australia, and in many of the Latin American countries among the Indians. However the customary court is a *substitute* rather than an *alternative* if it happens to exist in conditions in which there are no formal courts to hear the cases. And an analysis of the customary tribunals among the Barotse in Central Africa by Max Gluckman showed nearly 30 years ago that there was a great deal more precision and formality involved than might appear on the surface. He identified in the Barotse tribal process most of the fundamental principles of English law (though I believe he was stretching his evidence here and there). His work was a warning about being too patronizing to the customary court procedures.[3]

The little known but most effective use of the customary courts to act as an indigenous alternative to the regular formal tribunals was in Zambia where, for years, the Urban Native Courts had a concurrent jurisdiction by statute with the regular courts—unless, of course, the offences were serious. There were Native Courts in the country districts operating for each tribe under the supervision of the District Officer who was also the local magistrate. But the Urban Native Courts were more general, serving people from many tribes living in towns. Here the elders from various tribes were selected to deal in the most appropriate tribal fashion with disputes and offences occuring in town. They were effective and in their work were evolving what amounted to a new form of integrated customary law, applicable to all tribe member—of any tribe— living in the town.[4] But again they had their disadvantages. The writer, investigating these courts some years ago, found that police able to get enough evidence to satisfy a formal court took the case there. When they did not have enough evidence, they took the case to the Urban Native Court, where formal rules of evidence did not apply. So the informality often served the prosecution more than the defence.

The United Kingdom Courts of Equity in the seventeenth century grew out of a need to depart from the technicalities and delays of Common Law but they themselves eventually became so technical and bureaucratized that they were reintegrated with Common Law in a single system in the nineteenth century. The infamous Star Chamber may be regarded as another way to get round the formality of the Common Law Courts, but for this reason it was not popular. The Western countries' later development of a series of administrative tribunals to cut through the formality of the law has had an anticipated result. As professional judges were often chosen to chair such attempts at informality—as an appeal to ordinary courts was allowed to applicants and as each side sought legal advice and professional representation—there has arisen a variety of administrative tribunals which can hardly be called informal. They are just as formal as any of the regular courts. This development towards precedent and set rules of procedure seems to serve the professional. Also, as already observed, this preoccupation with alternatives or the interest in deformalizing the courts goes hand in hand with a greater public consciousness of rights and a greater demand for access to legal advice and representation. So there should be no surprise at the tendency to formalize the informality which is pursued.

This formalization has not yet happened to the pretrial juvenile panels set up in some states of Australia which are intended to divert many juveniles from the courts. Here police officers and social workers sit to advice parents and young people referred by the police for acts that could have led to a prosecution. However, even here more formality could well develop if such panels were to make decisions which the parties might begin to regard as detrimental. At the moment they have little power and this may be why they have escaped the intrusion of the law for so long and have kept their "welfare" character. If there should be citizen advocacy to motivate feelings to the extent that those called fail to appear or else become concerned with the extent to which their rights may be affected, we may still see a descent to the familiar legal form. This is what eventually happened to the Child Welfare Councils in Sweden—but it must be acknowledged that the Swedish councils had power to decide upon the child's future. The point is that the search for informality will always be limited by the sense of rights in a given community. Discretion can be regarded as a necessary lubricant for any set of rules—or as an open door to discrimination. The extent to which we formalize or informalize the courts will depend on our attitude to discretion.

In the Philippines there are informal tribunals, known as the Barangay Courts, for settling disputes in the rural areas. These have the local Barangay captain as chairman and have 10–20 members. They hear all civil cases and criminal cases punishable by imprisonment of 30 days or a fine of not more than 200 pesetas. Presidential Decree 1508 of 1978 institutionalizes these courts—from which lawyers are specifically barred! It seems to work. In India there are the panchayats or local councils which are really concerned with local government but which have a section for dealing with disputes and minor offences. And Sri Lanka has its conciliation tribunals.

In the socialist world there is a reliance upon comrades courts, and on a wide range of factory, street, school, neighborhood and courtyard committees not only to deal with disputes and minor forms of deviation but to encourage conformity and to interpret government policy about behavior at the most local levels. These have become such a regular part of local life that they are generally respected and are extremely effective. They have power and can be expected to be backed up by the authorities should they be defied. In those socialist countries where there is a formal legal system in addition to these local courts, however, it has been interesting to discover that there is a preference for the formal and less immediate rather than the informal and immediate kinds of trial—whenever the offense is more than trivial.

## The Exercise of Discretion

To avoid discrimination at all costs, is to formalize. To regard the exercise of discretion by the police and by those who have to make a decision to prosecute as the oil which makes modern legal machinery work smoothly is to extend the scope for informality. Actually, discretion is difficult to exclude completely. As already shown, discretion is necessary to avoid the mass of laws becoming oppressive. Why not extend it so as to reduce the numbers of those who appear before the courts? Why should not cases which can be settled between victim and offender be settled by the prosecutor instead of always being brought to court? It is a device which we do not use very much in the Anglo-Saxon system but which is used extensively in civil law systems—in Holland, the Philippines, and Japan for example.

To a limited extent countries like Australia are using this already —but to a very limited extent. Police discretion avoids a great many neighbors' quarrels and minor assault cases being brought to the court. Traffic offenders are warned and it is well known that so many cases of shoplifting or stealing from work places are never prosecuted. And, of course, there is the negotiation on a plea which, while not so extensive as plea bargaining in the United States, does still seek to determine the issues for a court hearing. In the other countries mentioned, however, this exercise of discretion is literally wholesale. No case is allowed to take up the time of the court unless it is considered necessary because of the circumstances of the offence or its inherent gravity. A great deal more could be done to avoid court hearings and reduce the number of cases in Australia by exercising this wider kind of discretion. The Australian Institute of Criminology has already convened meetings of Chief State Prosecutors to discuss the possibilities of widening the discretion for diverting cases from the courts. In Australia, problems may, however, arise from the reduction of the present police monopoly (or virtual monopoly) of prosecutions. There, as in the United Kingdom, the police prosecute their own cases in court and some police become qualified lawyers to qualify more appropriately for this work. Only when a case reaches the highest courts do the police seek legal representation. If, therefore, discretion to prosecute were vested in a legal prosecutor, this would reduce police involvement. But it should be noted that a system of this kind already operates in the Australian Capital Territory, where police hand over prosecutions to Crown Council.

A very important factor in any change of system is the need for those to be trusted with the exercise of discretion gradually to earn public confidence. In Japan, for example, the reason the public prosecutor system works so well is the extent of public support for and trust in the system.[5] Obviously, there must be provision for an objection to be raised by those who feel themselves badly served by the discretion being exercised—and this provision for appeal permits increased formalization. In the countries already mentioned, such appeals (not to courts but to other public bodies) have been minimal because of the reliance on the public prosecutors. It may be that wherever systems are changed, it would be impossible to expect such uniform public support for some time.

## Conclusions

There is a need to be extremely cautious about proposals to circumvent the criminal justice system or about suggestions that virtue lies only in diverting offenders. Anglo-Saxon countries have struggled for centuries to achieve the standards of fairness, impartiality, and justice which they rightly esteem. On the other hand, society itself has changed, and the formal system which is so highly valued may well become even more effective with rather less automatic use. Many cases that would never have been expected to reach the courts in earlier generations are now commonly heard. The recourse to courts is more common. So many more cases are defended vigorously. So many cases which would have been disposed of in minutes are taking hours and days, if not weeks. With legislation overflowing and courts having to be multiplied, the process has to be simplified if the taxpayer is ever to afford the mounting costs.

With appropriate precautions then, it is reasonable to explore alternatives—not in the simplistic way that has often been suggested so that neighborhood, factory, or street committees become questionable informal substitutes for a fair, impartial, and qualified hearing, but with due regard to all the negative, as well as positive, features of change. After all, there was a time when London magistrates sat for an hour before their official courts opened every morning to hear applications from anyone with a grievance. This one they sent to social workers, the other to the police, a third they directly counseled not to be foolish or hasty. Only to the fourth did they allow an application for a summons. That was surely a dispensing of justice informally, efficiently, and with common sense and compassion.

## Notes

1. P. H. Gulliver, *Social Control in an African Society*, (Boston: Boston University Press, 1963).

2. S. K. Mukherjee, *Crime in the Twentieth Century* (London: Allen and Unwin for the Australian Institute of Criminology, in course of publication).

3. Max Gluckman, *The Judicial Process Among the Barotse of Northern Rhodesia* (Manchester, England: Manchester University Press, 1955).

4. Arnold Leonard Epstein *The Administration of Justice and the Urban African: A Study of Urban Native Courts in Northern Rhodesia* (London: HMSO, 1953).

5. See W. Clifford, *Crime Control in Japan* Lexington, Man.: Heath, 1976).

# 12

## Mediation as an Alternative to Adjudication: Rhetoric and Reality in the Neighborhood Justice Movement[*]

**Roman Tomasic**

### Introduction

A number of diverse and yet somewhat related developments led me to want to look more closely at the current enthusiasm that many reformers seem to have for greater lay participation in the legal system and, in particular, in the areas of dispute resolution and judicial administration.

First, there has developed in recent years an increasingly large literature on the crisis that courts in the Western world have been seen to be facing. Thus, we have seen phrases such as "judicial overload" (Marcus, 1979); the "legal explosion" (Barton, 1975); "hyperlexis" (Manning, 1977); the "court crunch" (Lasker, 1977); "legal pollution" (Ehrlich, 1976); and the "plague of lawyers" (Auerbach, 1976). These and many other similar expressions of alarm with the current state of the administration of justice[1] have led reformers to begin to experiment with alternatives to traditional models of adjudication.[2] A major feature of this experimentation has been the emergence of the neighborhood justice movement. Before looking at this movement, a number of other background developments need also to be reviewed to help us understand the emergence of this movement.

The 1960s and 1970s saw a concerted attack from many quarters on the notion of professionalism in the legal system. One example of this was the criticism that tended to be made of lawyers for complicating le-

---

[*] All references in the text of this chapter are found in the Bibliography at the conclusion of this volume.

gal service delivery and for creating many cost barriers to access to justice. The growth of a demand for legal services delivered by nonlawyers, as well as the greater regulation of the activity of lawyers and legal services delivery by nonlawyers, has been an expression of this supposed flight from professionalized ways of delivering services (see, e.g., Illich, 1977; Haug, 1973). This has also been linked to the so-called 'revolt of the client' (see, e.g., Rosenthal, 1977, and Tomasic, 1978a: 117–134). This attack on the exclusive competence of lawyers, as well as upon their unresponsiveness and dominance, needs also to be seen in the context of other movements such as consumerism (Nader, 1976) and the stress that has once again begun to be placed upon the notion of community.

The "quest for community" (Nisbet, 1962) has a long pedigree. Sociologists such as Ferdinand Tonnies (1974) and Emile Durkheim (1933) long ago stressed the virtues of community control. However, Durkheim's call for a community-based morality has failed to be taken up, and many have seen this call, like the current fears concerning court overload, as being based upon an essentially conservative view of reality. As Abel (1974: 303) has noted, both Max Weber and Roscoe Pound saw these types of calls as illustrations of inevitable fluctuations in society between such poles as "abstract formalism" and "real substantive goals" (Weber, 1967: 226) and "justice without law" and "justice according to law" (Pound, 1922: 54; see also Friedman, 1978). The attack upon "abstract formalism" or upon the notion of "justice according to law" has in recent years also been linked with fears related to the cost of these approaches as well as to the realization that many of the systems of control built into the legàl and criminal justice systems were not achieving goals that had been held out for them.[3] This led to the so-called community-based corrections movement, decarceration (Scull, 1977; Tomasic, 1979b; and Tomasic and Dobinson, 1979), and diversion programs. All of these developments have been seen as having serious problems (Mullen, 1975; Nejelski, 1976). One of these has been the fact that more often than not "community control" has either meant "no control" or unnecessary control (see also Hofrichter, 1978). Moreover, these attempts to graft community mechanisms upon the legal system or parallel to the legal system have generally been quite superficial in their impact, in that they have not sought to bring about basic structural changes in the community, in keeping with the aspirations that are inherent in the ideology of community, as seen, for example, in the work of Durkheim. Very few, if any, of these community-based programs have been adequately evaluated. Where they have, they have not been found to be the panacea that many reformers have had in mind. It should however be noted that programs such as diversion have been quite successful in diverting attention from continuing inequities that are to be found in the legal system.

To some extent, the "access to justice" movement and the stimulus which this has given to the neighborhood justice movement has served to compound the illusion that real and substantial court reform is both possible and underway. I would argue that this is quite illusory, as is evident after closer scrutiny of these attempts to institutionalize lay justice.

A related movement is evident in the emergence of court administrators as an increasingly powerful and pivotal group in the overall court structure. The office of the court administrator has been perceived as the center for the management of the tension between the needs of the judiciary and the demands for community participation (Nejelski, 1977c: 17; see also Nejelski, 1977a). This wide-ranging movement for popular participation in the legal system clearly goes far beyond the specific area of Neighborhood Justice Centers (NJCs). Antecedents to the notion of community justice can be seen in the juvenile court movement (Nejelski, 1979: 3), as well as in the small claims court movement (see, generally, Ruhnka and Weller, 1978: 3; Yngvesson and Hennessey, 1975). Despite all these initiatives in the fields of court reform and alternatives, it is important to take heed of the warning that we "should guard against the creation of new, unnecessary administrative entities. We should not be caught up in the 'catch words' and fund projects simply because they are the latest fad. We need to ask hard questions" (Nejelski, 1979: 12).

The next section will consist of a general description of the neighborhood justice movement. This will be followed by an assessment of some assumptions underlying this movement. The final section will seek to discuss some of the implications of the movement and will offer some suggestions as to what direction this movement might take if it is to be of greatest value.


## The Neighborhood Justice Movement

It has been argued that the "distinctively populist cast of the movement for alternative dispute resolution rests on an implicit belief in neighborhoods, private bargaining and decision makers less detached than judges and lawyers; but it may also stem from growing distrust of accumulated centers of power, especially governmental power. The emphasis placed upon negotiation, bargaining and compromise elevates party control of the process by the disputants and reduces the importance of preestablished authority and rules" (*Yale Law Journal*, 1979: 907–908). The roots of the neighborhood justice notion have been described by Felstiner and Williams (1978) as alien to Anglo-American jurisprudence. They are to be found in models provided by African moots (Gibbs, 1963; Danzig, 1973), by socialist comrades' courts (see, e.g., Kurczewsky and Frieske, 1978; Fisher, 1975), and by psychotherapy and labor mediation (Felstiner and Williams 1978: 1). The evaluators of the U.S. Department of Justice's three Neighborhood Justice Centers observe that "the foundation for the concept" of the Neighborhood Justice Center "...was laid by Danzig (1973) in his proposal to establish community moots..." (Cook et al., 1980: 4). This concept was taken up by Sander (1976), whose model of the dispute resolution center may be seen as a compromise between Danzig's community moot and Fisher's (1975: 1287–1288) model of coercive community courts modeled on socialist comrades' courts (see further McGillis and Mullen, 1977: 28–29; Davis et al., 1979: 4; and Cook et al., 1980: 4). Sander's conception was then developed by the U.S. Department of Justice under Attorney General Griffin Bell with the assistance of a hurriedly produced concept document prepared by Daniel McGillis and Joan Mullen.[4] This development followed the recommendation of the Follow-up Task Force of the 1976 National Conference on the Causes of Popular Dissatisfaction with the Administration of Justice (the Pound Conference), which recommended that NJCs be developed to "make available a variety of methods of processing disputes, including arbitration, mediation, referral to small claims courts as well as referral to courts of general jurisdiction" (McGillis and Mullen, 1977: 29). Significantly, the Task Force was chaired by Attorney General Griffin Bell, who selected three locations for the testing of models of the Neighborhood Justice Center that he had been instrumental in evolving. Not unexpectedly, one location was to be Atlanta, whilst the others were Kansas City and Venice/Mar Vista in Los Angeles.

In their study of potential models for the NJC, McGillis and Mullen examined six innovative programs that were dealing with minor disputes.[5] They examined 12 dimensions of these programs for purposes of comparison.[6] These dimensions have remained central to subsequent evaluations of these types of dispute processing mechanisms. Although a number of techniques were being relied upon in these vastly different projects, mediation seems to have become the dominant technique relied upon[7] and the justice system has become the main source of cases for most NJCs.[8]

The Federally funded "model" NJCs draw together key aspects of the debate surrounding minor-dispute resolution, and as such it is useful to look closely at this program and the "final" evaluation report. For purposes of contrast and elaboration of various themes it is also helpful to draw from a number of other recent evaluation reports. In particular, the reports that have emerged from the experience of the Dorchester Urban Court Program (Felstiner and Williams, 1978, 1979; Snyder, 1978), the Brooklyn Dispute Resolution Center (Davis et al., 1979) and the evaluation of the five Citizen Dispute Settlement Programs in Florida (Dispute Resolution Alternatives Committee, 1979) will be looked at. In the establishment of Neighborhood Justice Centers as "model" programs by the U.S. Department of Justice, a number of arguments have been repeated, almost ad nauseam, although the conclusions drawn from these arguments are not always as obvious as those advancing them would like us to think. Griffin Bell had stated that the "traditional procedures of the courts are generally too slow and costly to be useful in resolving relatively minor disputes." In addition, it tends to be argued, as Bell did, that the "adversary process . . . is not always the best mechanism for resolving these disputes" (1978a: 53). If this is so, one might expect the reformer to argue that we need new, nontraditional procedures and courts which do not rely upon adversary proceeding. One possible example of this is the small claims court which often relies upon mediation or conciliation. However, instead of developing the existing small claims court model, reformers like Griffin Bell have gone on to argue that these courts are not meeting the "need", as "many people are *unaware* of the formal mechanisms that have been created, such as small claim courts . . ." (Bell, 1978a: 53, emphasis added). It tends to be argued that Neighborhood Justice Centers will be able to do better, although no adequate reason is given why people will be more aware of these centers than of courts such as small claims courts. It should also be noted, however, that the centers were seen as places from which persons could be referred to "the agency or court best suited to deal with the problem" (Bell, 1978a: 54). This seems to assume that disputants will come directly to the center *from* the community. In fact, this has not been the case and was not so in those centers existing prior to the establishment of the three Department of Justice model programs. At present, most cases are referred *to* the centers *from* the courts, the police, or the prosecutors, that is, from the justice system. Thus, rather than providing an appropriate mechanism for obtaining access to the justice system, the Neighborhood Justice Centers actually seem to be exit points from the justice system.

Although there have been a number of evaluations of dispute resolution centers in the United States in recent years, the evaluation of the Department of Justice's three "model" Neighborhood Justice Centers completed by the Institute for Social Analysis is among the most ambitious. Moreover, it is presented as a "final" evaluation report and, although it is often a little vague, it does conclude with some very strong recommendations. As these three centers were seen as "models" for further such programs, this evaluation and its often problematic conclusions need to be critically assessed and not overlooked or excused.

The first thing to be said about this study is that it has, as it itself points out, a deliberate policy bias (Cook et al., 1980: 103). Its aim is to facilitate governmental decision making and not necessarily to provide an exhaustive or definitive understanding of a particular problem or series of problems. Thus, the conclusions contain firm recommendations, although these are all too often based on expressions and formulations themselves quite problematic. Thus the NJC is seen to meet "a clear public need" (Cook et al., 1980: 104–105) and to appear to handle most minor disputes more efficiently that the courts. Throughout the report, many formulations are presented very tentatively, far more so than the conclusions would seem to imply. The point of these observations is simply to point out that it is extremely dangerous to rely upon this "final" report on these "model" projects as a definitive guide. As the report is quite overoptimistic about the effectiveness of the NJC, it should be contrasted to findings such as those obtained recently by the Vera Institute in its study of the Brooklyn Dispute Resolution Center. Contrary to suggestions contained in the final report of the three NJCs by Cook and his associates, the Vera Institute report as well as the evaluation of the Dorchester Urban Court Program, by Felstiner and Williams, cast serious doubt on many of the conclusions and recommendations made regarding Neighborhood Justice Centers by the Institute for Social Analysis.

This paper does not aim to provide a detailed description of the workings of the diverse range of Neighborhood Justice Centers currently in existence. While some such descriptions are already available elsewhere, we really need much more detailed research on these centers before this can be done, or for that matter before there is any further expansion in the number of these centers as a result of government initiatives. Each of the assumptions to be discussed below could well be the subject of a separate research study. Especially where comparisons are being made, such as with the courts, every effort should be made to include random assignment as part of any evaluative research design, even though this may somewhat inhibit the growth of some of these centers (see further Baunach, 1980). Nevertheless, the NJC movement has become sufficiently institutionalized to allow the identification of widely shared assumptions that are held by proponents of Neighborhood Justice Centers. A discussion of these assumptions will be the subject of the next part of this paper.

## Some Assumptions Underlying the Neighborhood Justice Center/Alternate Dispute Resolution Center Movement

At the present time there are over 120 community dispute resolution centers in the United States (McGillis, n.d.). Although many of these have very similar features, there are also some major differences among them. These differences are most often based on differing assumptions held by those instrumental in establishing these centers. Linda Singer (1979: 12) has noted that there are "varied and sometimes conflicting objectives" held by supporters of nonjudicial dispute resolution forums. She also suggests (1979: 10) that supporters of these forums may "... have different, sometimes unstated objectives." Thus, judges may support such alternatives in an effort to make their courts more efficient by helping to reduce caseloads, costs, and delays; politicians may provide support out of a belief that they are less expensive to operate than the courts; community organizers may have yet another set of objectives. The evaluators of the U.S. Department of Justice's NJCs isolated six major goals and four objectives of these centers (Cook et al., 1980: 117–118), while Linda Singer (1979a: 10–12) has identified five objectives of people supporting nonjudicial dispute-processing forums. Some of these objectives are similar to the stated goals of the Office for Improvements in the Administration of Justice within the U.S. Department of Justice (Bell, 1978a: 53).

The objectives of the NJC as outlined in the NILECJ design contained the following:

1. To establish in the community an efficient mechanism for the resolution of minor criminal and civil disputes which stresses mediation and conciliation between the parties in contrast to the findings of fault or guilt which characterize the traditional adjudication process.
2. To reduce court caseload by redirecting cases that are not appropriate for the adversarial process.
3. To enable the parties involved in the disputes to arrive at fair and lasting solutions.
4. To serve as a source of information and referral for disputes that would be more appropriately handled by other community services or government agencies (quoted in McGillis and Mullen, 1977: 196).

It is therefore possible to isolate a range of assumptions that are present in all this debate. Some of these are related, and there may well be others. The assumptions that will be discussed here may be divided into three broad categories. First, there are those that relate mainly to disputes and disputants; secondly, there are those that relate mainly to qualities associated with mediation and mediators; and, finally, there are those assumptions that make comparisons between mediation and court processing. While these categories are by no means rigid or mutually exclusive, I have isolated 18 such assumptions in the academic literature, evaluation, and policy statements. These are as follows:

1. Mediation is able to deal with the *roots of problems*.
2. Mediation improves the *communicative capacities* of disputants.
3. Mediators are not *"strangers"* but are *"friends"* of the disputants.
4. Unlike adjudication, mediation is *noncoercive*.
5. Mediation is *voluntaristic* as it allows disputants to solve their own problems themselves.

6. Mediation centers provide *easier access to the legal system.*
7. *Disputants want to get away from the courts* and into mediation centers.
8. There is such a thing as a *sense of "community."*
9. Unlike judges, mediators *"represent"* the community and share its values.
10. The use of mediation is a means of *reducing tension* in the community.
11. Mediators are *not professionalized* and do not require long periods of training.
12. Mediation centers are *nonbureaucratic* and are flexible and responsive.
13. Mediation is able to deal with a *wide range of disputes.*
14. Mediation is *speedier* than adjudication.
15. Mediation is *less costly* than adjudication.
16. Mediation is *fairer* than adjudication.
17. Mediation can reduce *court congestion and delay.*
18. Mediation is *more effective* than adjudication in dealing with *recidivism.*

Each of these assumptions are in fact the hypotheses upon which mediation centers have been based. The discussion presented below of each of these assumptions should not be seen as an attempt to provide either a definitive confirmation or rejection of the hypotheses underlying them. Instead, the discusssion of each assumption is only intended to provide tentative conclusions on their adequacy. More definitive conclusions must await the appearance of studies that specifically seek to test the hypotheses to be found here. We do, however, already have some such attempts, although these are extremely limited. Lest it be thought, from the approach that I take to each of these assumptions, that I am setting up a lot of straw men only to knock them down, it should be stressed that each of these assumptions represents a key feature of the ideology or rhetoric of the neighborhood justice movement. Even though no one person or agency would necessarily share all of these assumptions, together they would all be endorsed somewhere in the movement, at some time.

## 1. Mediation Is Able to Deal with the Roots of Problems

One of the key assumptions concerning mediation centers is that they are able to deal with problems far more extensively than are courts and, as a consequence, are able to come to terms with the roots of these problems. Danzig and Lowy (1975: 678–682), for example, argue that mediation is able to deal with the causes of problems or conflicts. They add that unlike disputes dealt with by official agencies, such as the police, which "tend to fester and break out again" (1975: 684), mediation is more successful. This is because disputants are encouraged to think "about the root causes of their disputes and beyond this about the role social organization plays in causing, defining, and resolving such matters" (Danzig and Lowy, 1975: 691–692). Felstiner and Williams (1979: 27) point to the fact that in mediator training programs, a ". . . basic premise is that mediators may not so much need to know what happened as why it happened—the underlying cause." One training manual for mediators states that mediation ". . . prevents the recurrence of future problems by getting at the basic reasons for the dispute" (quoted by Felstiner and Williams, 1978: 234). Research that has been undertaken on the Dorchester Urban Court Program's mediation component by Felstiner and Williams (1978 and 1979) suggests that such mediation is at best only successful in dealing with superficial aspects of disputes (1978: 232). These researchers found that mediation confronts only ". . . those causes that lie close to the surface and which do not involve three or more parties." However, Felstiner and Williams found that Dorchester mediators were reluctant to get involved with disputes between the respondent and third parties. They concluded that ". . . this narrow exercise of jurisdiction . . . hobbles the power of mediation to reach underlying causes . . ." (1978: 235), so that successful mediation seems to be limited to "the shallow end of maladaptations" (1978: 236). In theory, deeper problems are supposed to be referred to social service agencies, but such referrals seem to be nonexistent or somewhat limited in Dorchester (Felstiner and Williams, 1978: 236–237). Concerning the issue dealing with the social structural or organizational aspects of disputes raised by Danzig and Lowy, it appears that far from confronting social structural causes of disputes, community mediators seem merely to induce disputants to accept these structural inequalities.

## 2. Mediation Improves the Communicative Capacities of Disputants

Proponents of mediation centers like Danzig and Lowy (1975: 689) argue that mediation facilitates communication between disputants. For them, mediation becomes an "educational process" (1975: 692) by bringing the component of the dispute to the surface. Felstiner and Williams (1978: 237) note therefore that the ". . . ideology of mediation states that unlike court processing mediation hearings improve the parties' capacity to communicate. . . ." They confirm that ". . . communication problems underlie many interpersonal disputes" (1979: 32). This is by no means a new revelation however. Social theorists have long seen communicative problems as explaining deviance and conflict in society. Habermas (1970) has, for example, developed the concept of "distorted communication" which helps to explain disputes in society. However, for Habermas, distorted communication has social structural roots and as such cannot be readily remedied simply through mediation sessions. In fact, it seems from the research reported by Felstiner and Williams that mediation in fact only reinforces the existence of distorted communication. In Dorchester, the structure of mediation hearings involved a form of "shuttle diplomacy" or "indirect communication"—the separate caucusing of mediators with disputants did not facilitate direct communication between disputants (1979: 32–33). Although they argued that this defect arises out of the reliance in the Dorchester mediative model upon techniques drawn from labor mediation, it is doubtful whether the removal of the device of "shuttle diplomacy" would solve this problem. One reason for this would be the fact that third parties, and particularly powerful third parties, are not part of this dialogue. Snyder, in his study of the Dorchester program, notes that instead of the "strong internal pull toward cohesion" that Lon Fuller saw as mainly arising from mediation, avoidance "was found to be frequent" (Snyder, 1978: 771). If, therefore, we agree with Danzig and Lowy (1975: 689) that the process rather than the outcome ought to be the basis for assessing mediation, it seems far removed from the ideal communicative processs.

## 3. Mediators Are Not "Strangers" but Are "Friends" of the Disputants

Presumably one reason why mediation is seen as facilitating communication between disputants is because mediators are seen to be "friends" and not "strangers." Thus we find some observers arguing that the ". . . average citizen does not view the urban court as an integral, valued element of his neighborhood or community, staffed by recognizable friends and neighbors" (Cook et al., 1980: 3). They add that ". . . any sense that justice has been delivered [in the court setting] is often overwhelmed by feelings of frustration and powerlessness; that one has been *dealt with* by strangers rather than *served* by a segment of the community" (Cook et al., 1980: 2, emphasis added). The assumption that mediators are less strangers than court officials to disputants ignores the fact that mediators are themselves often drawn from the court-affiliated bureaucracy, such as the probation service. Then, of course, there is the spurious contrast between being "dealt with" and being "served." From their Dorchester study, Felstiner and Williams concluded that in fact *"mediators are strangers . . .* their values and life experiences are unknown. Institutionalized mediation is unfamiliar and its use is exceptional" (1979: 166, emphasis added; see also Merry, 1979b).

Another issue raised here is the values that mediators apply. Presumably friends and neighbors would apply the same values as those of the disputants. The evaluators of the Brooklyn Dispute Resolution Center found that mediators actually tried to reinforce dominant societal values such as the value of kinship and the avoidance of violence (Davis et al., 1979: 42–43). Although apparently contrary to the NJC rhetoric, it seems to be an inevitable feature of the role of the mediator. This has been described by Gulliver (1969: 213–214) as follows: "He not only affects the interactions but, at least in part, seeks and encourages an outcome that is tolerable to him in terms of his own ideas and interests." If this is accepted, then the findings of Davis and his colleagues should not be surprising. The Brooklyn evaluation also revealed that the mediators tended to adopt a quasi-judicial role and gave legal advice to disputants. Mediators were perceived by the evaluators as seeking to act as "role models" and sometimes sought to make authority statements (Davis et al., 1979: 43, 46). If this is to be a normal feature of the role of mediators in the NJCs, then the problem of the lack of due process that some observers have pointed to arises (Snyder, 1978: 780–781). This is particularly important as mediators really lack the power to provide broad-ranging remedial relief, which is implied by their assuming judgelike roles. This is partly because, as Singer (1979a: 36–37) notes, "settlements achieved through negotiation or mediation between the parties cannot serve as precedents for settlements between other parties." Disputants are also critical of NJCs on the grounds that they lack enforcement powers (Cook et al., 1980: 68). Hofrichter (1977: 169) sees all of this as having the potential to neutralize demands for justice as well as to mask substantive inequalities (see, however, Singer, 1979: 24). The same criticism has also been made by the U.S. Solicitor General (Lawscope, 1977: 1190), who has suggested that a large sector of society may well be being deprived of access to the courts as a result. It is curious that this tends to be the group which most recently seems to have been given the hope of access through reforms such as improved legal services (Abel, 1978: 8).

## 4. Unlike Adjudication, Mediation is Noncoercive

Danzig and Lowy (1975: 691–692) have argued that mediation is "... neither coercive nor threatening." They (1975: 686–687) also point to the "... noncoercive style" of models for dispute resolution centers, such as the community moots that Danzig (1973: 46–48) had earlier proposed. On the basis of what seems to be a misinterpretation of the anthropological evidence, they argue that as "... the moot has no power of compulsion and does not preempt regular court action, a complainant has nothing to lose by turning first to it..." (1975: 687). Felstiner (1974: 74) had earlier argued that "... since the outcomes it produces are consensual, are generally compromises, mediation *need not* be backed by coercive power" (emphasis added). Developing this theme, Frank Sander (1976: 121) asserted "... there is a world of difference between a coerced or semicoerced settlement of the kind that so often results in court and a voluntary agreement arrived at by the parties." Thus mediation is to be distinguished from "...the coercive quality of the typical adjudicative intervention" (Sander, 1976: 122). While most commentators suggest that in an ideal setting mediation is noncoercive, studies of American applications of mediation need to qualify this view considerably, if it ever had much basis in the first place. From their Dorchester study, for example, Felstiner and Williams (1978: 230) provide evidence to suggest that disputants do not agree that mediators are noncoercive. They note (1978: 244) that the Dorchester experience shows that "mediation is ambivalent about manipulation and coercion." Furthermore, Felstiner and Williams (1979: 31) observe that the type of training provided by the long-established institute for Mediation and Conflict Resolution for Dorchester mediators promotes this ambivalence. They add that this may have unintended consequences because the "... contradiction between letting the disputants provide their solution to their problem and the mediators' responsibility to maneuver the disputants into making an agreement may be hard for trainees to assimilate when it is not confronted directly in training" (1979: 31). They go on to express concern that trainee mediators may actually try to resolve this contradiction by "...rejecting the mediative approach to problem solving by falling back on the court room [coercive?] pattern ingrained through exposure to to American culture." Felstiner and Williams argue that so few cases were referred to mediation in Dorchester by sources other than the judge, the court clerk, or the police, basically because these other sources, such as social welfare agencies, did not possess the power of coercion, although the existence of the urban court program was well known to these nonofficial or noncoercive agencies (1979: 57–58). The high no-show rate for referrals from community agencies was also seen to be "a function of the level of coercion to which the respondent is subject" (1979: 58). This suggests that coercion is clearly built into Neighborhood Justice Centers, despite the claims concerning noncoercive mediation that have issued from reformers.

Felstiner and Williams (1979: 120) also found that, while mediation "...is designed to be a non coercive process through which the disputants reach a mutually satisfactory agreement, and the mediator's stated role is to help them reach that agreement...," in actual fact three-quarters of the Dorchester mediators surveyed by them "...find no problem with nudging the disputants, especially the respondent, towards agreement." Similar findings from the Dorchester program were earlier reported by Frederick Snyder who noted that "...the mediators frequently 'remind' recalcitrant parties that the case will reenter the criminal justice process in district court in the absence of a negotiated agreement" (1978: 756). Also paralleling Felstiner and Williams, Snyder (1978: 766) observes that disputes are more likely to lead to mediation where the option is presented by authorities because these authorities are in a position to bring subtle coercive pressure to bear on the parties to the dispute.[9]

The experience of the three Department of Justice Neighborhood Justice Centers once again confirms the important place that coercion plays in mediation programs, especially where links with the justice system are strongest. The evaluators of these centers admit that "... it is difficult to envision a program which receives referrals from the justice system completely eschewing all forms of subtle coercion" (Cook et al., 1980: 102). Although they quickly add that this is not seen to be a threat to the rights of citizens, it has been suggested that many cases which would never have been processed by the justice system are nevertheless dealt with by mediation centers (Hofrichter, 1978). This raises the criticism that was often made of diversion and the community corrections movement, namely, that such alternatives simply served to widen needlessly the net of coercive social control. It seems that the same criticism may perhaps be applicable to Neighborhood Justice Centers which are based upon justice system referrals (see, further, Silbey, 1979: iv, 42).

Finally, regarding the nature of this coercion, the Brooklyn study by Davis and his colleagues (1979: 43–46) revealed that mediators attempted to impose dominant societal values, seemed to adopt a quasi-judicial role, and, like judges, seemed to be acting as "role models." There is therefore little doubt of the nature and existence of coercion in the mediation programs that have so far been evaluated. This therefore calls this key assumption into question and raises the issue of whether disputants are receiving a form of second-class adjudication or justice (see, further, Nejelski, 1977b; Lawscope, 1977). These questions are by no means new and were being raised at the time when NJCs began to get established. This clearly stems from ambiguities present in the anthropological literature on mediation, for, as Gulliver (1979: 212) has noted, the "... ghost of the neutral (or impartial or disinterested) mediator tends to haunt the scene, even where that is probably a myth in practice." Much the same kind of reservations need to be made about the next assumption of voluntarism. Finally, however, regarding Davis's finding that mediators tend to impose dominant societal values, it could be argued that the very fact that mediators are playing this role suggests that these values may well be breaking down or losing their legitimacy and so are seen to be in need of reemphasis. Barkun (1964 and 1968: 106) has suggested that where "system-preserving values" exist they have the effect of *"an implied third party,"* even though a mediator is not physically present (see, further, Gulliver, 1969: 230). This has important theoretical implications concerning the social control and legitimizing aspects of mediation, which yet remain to be fully explored.

## 5. Mediation Is Voluntaristic as It Allows Disputants to Solve Their Own Problems Themselves

One observer has noted that the objective of "increased self-sufficiency ... without heavy reliance upon representatives of the legal system" is evident in individual orientations to the community justice movement (Singer, 1979a: 11–12). A manual for mediators points out that through mediation, disputants can "... devise their own solution" to their problems (quoted in Felstiner and Williams, 1978: 236). It has been argued that this "... elevates party control of the process by the disputants and reduces the importance of pre-established authority and rules" (*Yale Law Journal*, 1979: 907–908). Frank Sander has speculated that come the millennium, and his model of the Dispute Resolution Center which relies upon a variety of techniques, "... there will be ample opportunity for everyone to play a part" (1976: 131). There is clearly a voluntaristic vein underlying all this comment. However, it is evident from current programs that, like the presence of coercion, a fully voluntaristic process of mediation is yet to be achieved. Felstiner and Williams (1978: 236), for example, point out that many mediation agreements may work "... not because ... [they had] been formulated by the disputants, as the ideology alleges, but because a mediator was alert to a feasible adjustment in a destructive cycle of interaction." Furthermore, when Dorchester disputants were followed up, only 18.3 percent thought that they had been responsible for producing the agreement; 33.3 percent attributed responsibility to the mediators, whilst 26.7 percent felt that everyone involved had been responsible (Felstiner and Williams, 1979: 100). These figures hardly convey the overwhelming impression of voluntarism. In the Brooklyn study, however, the complainants participating in mediation were found to appreciate the "sense of participation and control" (Davis et al., 1979: 51). It needs however to be said that in the court process, complainants also possess considerable degree of choice and control, as is evident from the very high percentage of charges that tend to be dropped due to the failure of complainants to appear or to press charges.

## 6. Mediation Centers Provide Easier Access to the Legal System

It has been argued that those who support Neighborhood Justice Centers see them as a means of providing greater access for the community to justice as well as being a means of furthering the political and economic struggle for equal justice (Singer, 1979: 10–11). Thus, the U.S. Department of Justice (1977: 2–5) saw Neighborhood Justice Centers as "... a point of entry into the entire justice system for residents of the community with any type of grievance" or for "... problems that they cannot resolve themselves." These centers were also seen as points of referral to "... the most appropriate public agency or court to deal with the problem." Attorney General Griffin Bell (1978a: 63) saw Neighborhood Justice Centers as providing "... an avenue of justice for many persons now shut out of the legal system."

Many of these objectives have failed to be achieved to any significant degree. Due to their close association with the justice system, these centers seem to be more points of "exit" rather than of "entry" into the legal system. Some critics have even suggested that what has resulted is a kind of second-class justice. The U.S. Solicitor General, Wade H. McCree (Lawscope, 1977: 1190), has been reported to have said that Neighborhood Justice Centers have the potential of cutting off access to the court system to the poor, an "underclass" that looks to the courts as its only hope. The fact that most complainants in Neighborhood Justice Centers seem to be poor, females, and blacks seems to provide support for this fear.

Concerning the argument that the justice centers provide referrals to social service agencies, the Dorchester experience seems to clearly show that this is far from being so (Felstiner and Williams, 1979: 101). In Los Angeles, the Venice/Mar Vista NJC was seen by social service agencies to be in competition with them (Cook et al., 1980). In addition, Snyder (1978, 780–781) has pointed to the dangers of serious threats to the security of individuals referred to mediation due to the lack of due process.

## 7. Disputants Want to Get Away from the Courts and into Mediation Centers

Many commentators have argued that there is a public demand for community mediation centers. The evaluators of the Department of Justice's NJCs argue that these centers seem to meet "... a clear public need" (Cook et al., 1980: 104). There tends to be a slippage between the assertion that there is supposedly a scarce supply of dispute resolution services and the conclusion that this means that there is a demand for them and even more extravagantly a "need" for them. For example, Danzig and Lowy (1975: 68ff.) note that while much mediation occurs in society, such as is evident in the work of lawyers and government agencies, the poor tend to be inadequately supplied here. They also point to the amount of police time that is used to settle disputes and go on to suggest that this implies a demand for mediation centers. This conclusion seems to be unjustified. For example, Felstiner and Williams (1978: 233) note that in fact "... disputants have a mental set toward dispute processing which is dominated by a courtroom model." The fact that so many of the Neighborhood Justice Centers spend a great deal of their resources trying to create interest in their work among residents is an indication of the lack of a spontaneous demand for mediation services from the community. The Venice/Mar Vista NJC in Los Angeles tried very hard to create a community awareness of its activities, but only about 30 percent of the population sampled knew of its existence. But even this is far from a demand. The San Francisco Community Board Program, which undertakes intensive community work and seeks cases solely from the community, manages to process only about 100 cases a year. In Dorchester, Felstiner and Williams (1979: 8-9) highlighted the extremely artificial community demand for the services of the mediation component. They found that the program was used by the judiciary in Dorchester "to defuse local crises" and was seen by it as "an adjunct of the district court; its purpose is to improve the performance of the regular court." From the point of view of the judiciary this is then a court program controlled and operated by and for the court. If this is so, then it suggests that disputants are not getting away from the influence of the courts at all, even if they wanted to do so.

## 8. There Is Such a Thing as a Sense of "Community"

This raises the old issue whether it is realistic to talk about the existence of a sense of community. Laura Nader (1979b: 47) has noted that our legal system has roots in a much smaller society in which public opinion was "an important mechanism of social control," although she adds that we now live in a society characterized by anonymity. Similarly, William Felstiner (1974: 87) has pointed to the absence of group cohesion and a strong respect for authority in the United States and has also argued that it is unlikely that any mediator "will possess as a matter of existing experience sufficient information about a particular perspective and the histories of the particular disputants to be able efficiently to suggest outcomes" (1974: 79). Although Danzig and Lowy (1975: 676) disagree with this, it is notable that NJCs have tried very hard, but somewhat unsuccessfully, to *recreate* a sense of community. Ironically, by far the vast majority of cases received by NJC tend to come from the justice system. One wonders whether it is realistic to talk of a sense of community when cases come to NJCs from large urban areas and mainly from outside the target areas selected for the various NJCs (see Cook et al., 1980: 41). The rhetoric of community needs to be appraised by reference to the practice of the NJC. Sander (1976: 128), however, saw mediation centers as "the last hope of a sense of community..." despite the existence of "our alienated and divisive society." If, as Felstiner and Williams (1979: 7) suggest, "community" should be appraised by reference to "the role of the community in policy direction and to the backgrounds of the mediators," it appears from the Dorchester experience that the emergence of sense of community is a forlorn hope. Also, the evaluators of the U.S. Department of Justice's NJCs suggest that they have little faith in the existence of a community as a base for these centers (Cook et al., 1980: 106) and, instead, stress the importance of a justice system connection if high caseloads are to be achieved. When they refer to "key elements in the community" being motivated to support these centers, they seem to suggest that these realistically comprise only justice system personnel. In fact, they argue that "... the notion of restricting services to a neighborhood or section of the city does not seem feasile or desirable for NJCs..." (Cook et al., 1980: 94). This signals a turning away from a search for a sense of community.

## 9. Unlike Judges, Mediators "Represent" the Community and Share Its Values

As mentioned above, it has been suggested that one way of testing the sense of community is by looking at mediators. It has been argued, or assumed, that mediators should be seen as "community representatives" (Snyder, 1978: 739). It is difficult to determine in what sense mediators are representatives. For example, Felstiner and Williams (1978: 226) found that in Dorchester most mediators came from a limited sector of society,—62 percent were homemakers, students, and social and community workers. Furthermore, they also found (1979: 38–39) that the bulk of disputes tended to be mediated by only half a dozen out of the 40 to 50 mediators, further highlighting the tenuous nature of the representation assumption. Also, 45 percent of a sample of mediated disputants in Dorchester did not think that mediators had to live in Dorchester (Felstiner and Williams, 1979: 97). This highlights once again the ambivalent attitude to whether mediation ought to be seen as a community program. In the final analysis, the stress upon judicial control (Erickson, 1978: 51) of such centers runs in the face of any possibility of the NJCs representing anything other than the justice system. This illustrates once again the danger of attempting to transplant concepts from one social context to another. In the Kpelle Moot in Liberia, for example, the "mediator will have been selected by the complainant. He is a kinsman who holds an office such as town chief or quarter elder, and therefore has some skill in dispute settlement. It is said that he is chosen to preside by virtue of his kin tie, rather than because of his office" (Gibbs, 1963: 3; see also Gulliver, 1979: ch. 7). In contemporary mediation centers in the United States, few if any of these features of mediation in small-scale societies are to be found. This has been emphasized by the anthropologist Sally E. Merry (1979b). She concludes that if the small-scale society model of mediation is to be consistently followed, NJCs "must serve very small populations rather than districts containing several thousand residents who do not know one another nor expect to deal with one another in the future" (1979b: 39). Unless strategies such as these are adopted for NJCs, the capacity of mediators to be representative in anything but a most superficial way will be severely limited. However, if high caseloads are to become a primary objective of the NJC, the notion of representativeness must be seen as impossible to satisfy.

## 10. The Use of Mediation Is a Means of Reducing Tension in the Community

One commentator (Singer, 1979: 10) has observed that one of the objectives of those who support community mediation centers is to attempt to reduce social conflict before it escalates into violence. For example, Danzig and Lowy (1975: 687) have noted that the "mediator might be able to suggest future conduct by both parties to reduce tensions. . . ." Similarly, Snyder (1978: 774) has argued that mediation helps disputants to reshape their thinking about each other and to recognize ways to minimize their mutual hostility. However, it should be pointed out that in Dorchester, it was not felt to be feasible "to mediate cases between parties greatly unequal in power" (Felstiner and Williams, 1979: 13–14). Nevertheless, one of the six major goals of the NJC program was to "contribute to the reduction of tension and conflict in the community" (Cook et al., 1980: 17). This consensus orientation seems to ignore the social purposes and value of conflict in society (Coser, 1956). Hofrichter (1978: 7) had noted that the approach to be adopted by NJCs is based upon the assumption of "a social order with harmonious values. It assumes the desirability of accommodation, and the avoidance of serious controversy as an implicit goal." While the reduction of tension might be seen necessary in small-scale societies where disputants are in continuous relationships with each other, it is far from being an essential or even a desirable objective in highly urbanized societies where avoidance tends to be as common as it is (see, further, Felstiner, 1975). The experience of NJCs suggests that avoidance is an extremely common approach adopted by disputants to each other. While the reduction of tension would be seen by law enforcement agencies as facilitating their efforts directed at improving social control strategies, it is questionable whether it facilitates the resolution of disputes. While the introduction of third parties has been seen as "cooling out" the disputant, as Parsons (1962) argues in his discussion of the role of lawyers in their dealings with their clients, the purpose of this is often to investigate what further action can be taken, such as by litigation. However, it might also lead to a "lumping it" response where the costs of further action might be seen as prohibitive. This does not however remove the basic cause of the tension. While NJCs may be able to reduce tension in neighborhoods, we need to ask whether this is at all desirable, and who benefits from this most.

## 11. Mediators Are Not Professionalized and Do Not Require Long Training

While it is true to say that mediators require far less training than judges, lawyers, court officials, or police, some serious questions have been raised concerning the quality of most mediators. Not only do many

require retraining, the reluctance to undertake such training has generally led to a high turnover of mediators. There is clearly a need for an
experimental comparison of the effectiveness of a program using volunteer mediators with one that relies upon paraprofessional full-time
mediators. It seems that social processes at work within NJCs are cir-
cumventing the rhetoric of deprofessionalization and moving to an informal recognition of the need for more specialized, experienced, and well-
trained mediators. In the Venice/Mar Vista NJC, the volunteer
mediators were not even used during the evaluation period. In Dorchester, the majority of mediators criticized the incompetency of many of
the volunteer mediators (Felstiner and Williams, 1979: 113) and 57 percent of the cases were dealt with by 11 percent of the mediators (Felstiner and Williams, 1979: 37). Just as the enthusiasm for delegalization
can be seen as an overreaction to the excesses of legalism, and vice versa (Abel, 1978: 39), so too, the deprofessionalization movement is an
overreaction to the frequent absurdities executed in the name of professionalism (see, generally, Sussman, 1959, and Haug, 1969 and 1973). It
needs, however, to be remembered that in our highly professionalized
societies there can be little escape from some degree of professionization
and the reliance upon experts and technique. If this is so, then it raises
serious doubts—the NJC experience seems to emphasize—concerning
continuing adherence to the ideology of deprofessionalization. However,
this then raises the dilemma of the extent of professionalization and the
criticism that, by depriving disputants in NJCs of the best possible professional assistance, they may receive second-class justice. Inevitably,
the balance between formal and informal procedures, complex and simple procedures, and professional and nonprofessional services becomes a
political question (see, further, Friedman, 1978).

## 12. *Mediation Centers Are Nonbureaucratic and Are Flexible and Responsive*

Related to the issue of deprofessionalization is another catch-cry of the
alternatives movement, namely that, unlike courts, mediation centers
are nonbureaucratic and, thus, flexible. Snyder (1978: 775) has, for example, stressed the view that in Dorchester "mediators are not professionals operating within a government bureaucracy." This however does
not apply to the main coordinators and full-time staff of the Dorschester
center, who tend to be drawn from sectors of the court bureaucracy—
such as the probation service—and who tend to conduct a disproportionately large number of mediation sessions. Nevertheless, there is a
conscious attempt in mediation to be "antilegal" and "ahistorical" (Felstiner and Williams, 1979: 1).

Critics of alternatives such as NJCs point to what they see as ". . . a
constant danger of bureaucratization and the accretion of rules and cere-

monies" (Singer, 1979a: 47). A stress on high caseloads would seem to encourage this as an inevitable by-product. Others argue that in the context of the NJC, "bureaucratic rationality" is inevitable as it "substitutes for legal rules rather than an idealized 'living law,' transmitted through voluntary agreements, arrived at by seemingly personalized rules of human interaction" (Hofrichter, 1978: 49). The seeming inevitability of such a "bureaucratic rationality" appears to be implicit in the goal adopted by the U.S. Department of Justice of seeking to institutionalize its model NJCs (Cook et al., 1980: 93ff.). Pressures deriving from obtaining suitable sources of funding and case referral—as well as the location of these centers within wider bureaucracies such as city governments and the courts—increase the likelihood of bureaucratization and inflexibility. This seems an inevitable by-product of NJC attempts at survival. In looking at Soviet comrades' courts, Smith (1974) has usefully highlighted the bureaucratic trend that characterizes dispute settlement ideologies which have led to greater control over these courts. Legislation setting up NJCs in the United States includes a range of controls over these centers that are essentially bureaucratic and difficult to separate from the day-to-day operations of these centers.

The close connection of the mediation centers to the courts raises the greatest danger to the nonbureaucratic ideology. The strict guidelines for referrals that have been established in the Brooklyn dispute resolution center, as well as in other centers, highlights this. Also, the fact that if the mediation agreement is not kept, the threat of referral of the case back to the court (Felstiner and Williams, 1979: 12), illustrates that the mediation centers are already an extension of an existing bureaucracy. Also, the permanent staffs of mediation centers are very sensitive to the needs of the court bureaucracy, with their own career histories often being intimately associated with this. Felstiner and Williams (1979: 11), for example, point to "the increasing propensity" of the local Dorchester judge "to juggle personnel between the urban court and the district court's probation department." Personnel were often transferred into the better paid probation department from the mediation center as a reward, or transferred in the opposite direction as a punishment, at the direction of the judge (Felstiner and Williams, 1979: 12). This seriously calls into question the relationship between the antibureaucratic ideology and reality.

## 13. Mediation Is Able to Deal with a Wide Range of Disputes

One frequently hears that mediation can be applied to dealing with a wide range of disputes in society. Cook and his colleagues (1980: 105) noted, for example, that NJCs ". . . appear to handle most minor disputes more efficiently than the courts." A closer examination of the type of cases most often handled, and those handled successfully, by mediation centers suggests that such assertions are somewhat optimistic and and that it may be desirable to narrow even further the scope of problem types dealt with in mediation centers.

Laura Nader (1979b: 59), for example, argued that it is rare to find third-party complaint handlers dealing with consumer problems without the force of law to back them up. Similarly, Abel has observed that where disputants are enmeshed in multiplex relationships, the case which is the crux of the dispute is often an expression of a long-standing antagonism (1974: 230). Felstiner and Williams (1978: 243) therefore add that since the cognitive orientations of disputants will influence success in disputing, "mediation will fail where adjustments are unfeasible." Similarly, Abel had earlier pointed to the importance of status relationships in disputant choices. This led him to conclude that in affectual status relations, disputants will seek to avoid the external control of coercion and attempt to maintain control of their dispute, while finality or a decision favoring one party will be avoided where social relations are enduring and irreplaceable (Abel, 1974: 294). How then does this affect the dispute mediation centers?

The experiences of various NJCs suggest that a rather narrow profile of disputants and of dispute tends to be found there. This narrowness may be attributed to the narrow social base from which most referrals are made (Felstiner and Williams, 1979: 76). The NJCs tend to possess a preponderance of relatively powerless people and few organizations and businesses. The individuals tend mainly to be female, black or Hispanic, and poor. This is particularly so in the case of complainants.

The fact that most NJCs were not set up to deal with disputes between individuals and organizations has led some observers, like Linda Singer, to conclude that this ". . . limitation prevents community dispute centers from being a solution to many of the most acute problems of dispute resolution" (1979a: 24).

Regarding individual disputants, in the Brooklyn center the majority of those referred to mediation were blacks or Hispanics (Davis et al., 1979: 32). In the Atlanta NJC, 70 percent of complainants were black, as were 76 percent of respondents (Cook et al., 1980: 40–42).

Singer has noted that NJCs predominantly tend to serve low-income groups (1979a: 19). This has been confirmed by the model NJC evaluators who concluded that the NJCs appear to attract a disproportionately high number of lower-income people (Cook et al., 1980: 23). The Brooklyn evaluation found that 56 percent of the individuals in cases referred to mediation were unemployed, 4 percent had part-time jobs, and most had not completed high school (Davis et al., 1979: 32). While it is optimistic to suggest that higher-income people "should" be recipients of NJC justice (Cook et al, 1980: 87–88), it seems unlikely that this will happen, mainly because the type of case mediated is a function of the type of case that the courts want to refer out. Felstiner and Williams (1979: 76) argue, therefore, that cases should be sought from beyond the justice system. This objective, if seriously pursued, would undercut judicial control of NJCs.

One of the most startling features of the narrowly based caseloads of the mediation centers is the greater likelihood NJCs have of dealing with female complainants. For example, during the first six months of the Dorchester Urban Court program, 63.9 percent of complainants were adult females, while only 22.5 percent of respondents were adult females (Felstiner and Williams, 1979: 64). In Atlanta, 57 percent of complainants were females, while 69 percent of respondents were males (Cook et al., 1980: 40–42). In Brooklyn, 63 percent of cases referred to mediation were women. In the case of domestic disputes, 87 percent of complainants were women, while only 38 percent of the complainants in nondomestic disputes were women.

If one turns to the type of case that tends to be brought to dispute mediation centers one finds a preponderance of disputes involving violence (78.9 percent in Dorchester) and long-term ongoing disputes. One-shot disputes accounted for only 26.9 percent of cases in Dorchester (Felstiner and Williams, 1979: 66–68). Although I will look at recidivism later, it is notable that property disputes and those involving long-standing relationships are most difficult to solve by resort to mediation (Felstiner and Williams, 1979: 79, 84) although the Florida Citizen Dispute Settlement study found that public order and neighborhood disputes were least likely to be totally resolved in the long term (Dispute Resolution Alternatives Committee, 1979: 54). The resolution rates for these two types of disputes were 43.2 and 36.9 percent respectively. In contrast, this Florida study found that disputes involving property and those involving personal disputes were most likely to be resolvable in the long term, 64.9 and 55.7 percent respectively. It was also reported that neighborhood and public order disputants had the least regard for the effectiveness of the mediator. This further illustrates the irrelevance of the rhetoric of community, as does the Florida finding (1979: 55) that disputes involving strangers could most easily be resolved in the long term, unlike those involving neighbors, husbands and wives, divorced spouses, and males and females in cohabitation. It is interesting to note that the San Francisco Community Board Program, a most atypical NJC although one without justice system ties, rarely deals with intimate interpersonal disputes such as the above (Cook et al., 1980: 6).

This rather limited treatment of the caseloads of various NJCs suggests that mediation as practised in these centers tends to deal with a very limited range of disputants and problem types. While this is partly a function of referral networks, it is also evident that not all types of problems that are referred can be dealt with adequately since many disputes are heavily embedded in the social structures from which they come. Moreover, proponents of alternatives have exaggerated the possible achievements of mediation—partly to be able to attract the support of funding sources—and, in doing so, have created easily shattered expectations about the legal system. Because of such shattering of expectations, the reform movement in this area may become somewhat superficial, so that significant and longer lasting reforms will be more difficult to achieve. Also, it is likely that interest in NJCs will very quickly wane after this initial period of exaggerated enthusiasm. Reforms based upon fads rather than upon well thought out and researched proposals are less likely to succeed in the long term.

## 14. Mediation Is Speedier than Adjudication

One problem with a series of assumptions based upon comparisons with the courts is that it is very difficult to come up with useful conclusions without controlled studies that rely upon random assignment of cases to the court and to the mediation program. To date, only the Vera Institute's evaluation of the Brooklyn Dispute Resolution Center has relied upon random assignment.[10] However, because such issues as speed, cost, fairness, and recidivism are key variables seized upon by reformers, the tendency has been to decry the absence of truly experimental studies, but nevertheless to abandon virtually all sense of caution and then to proceed to make rather strong conclusions or speculations about the advantages of mediation when compared with court processes.

For example, while Sander (1976: 126) has pointed to the need for "a controlled experiment," he also asserts that "...it is generally assumed—rightly, I believe—that arbitration is speedier than litigation...." He would presumably also say the same thing about mediation. The question of speed is difficult to assess as it also needs to be tied to the quality of outcome. Also, comparisons tend to be made between the whole court process, rather than just between the length of the adjudication and the time that it takes to reach a mediation agreement from the time of referral. It would be more appropriate to compare cases from the time that they first enter the justice system. That most court cases never reach adjudication is often ignored in these comparisons, which only look at adjudicated cases. This is important, if we accept that most mediated cases would also never have been adjudicated, had they not been referred to mediation.

Thus although it took 98 days to process a court case in Atlanta from filing to trial, only 14 percent of cases reached a hearing, and of these less than half were found guilty (Cook et al., 1980: 76). It is notable that 77 percent of cases were dropped after six days, and those resolved without a mediation hearing were processed in an average of eight days. In the NJCs, a hearing was held, on the average, nine days after intake and second hearings occurred 11 days after the first hearing (Cook et al., 1980: 34). In Atlanta, 16 percent of NJC cases were resolved prior to a hearing. The average time between intake and closing was found to be ten days (Cook et al., 1980: 34). About 60 percent of all cases handled by the three model NJCs came from Atlanta, so these figures are particularly meaningful. They certainly do not show that mediation is any faster than court processing for the vast majority of complainants. This is important if it is argued that most complainants never intended to pursue a case to adjudication and simply use arrest and early court processing for symbolic purposes (see, generally, Black, 1971).

## 15. *Mediation Is Less Costly than Adjudication*

Another major, yet problematic, assumption concerns the cost of mediation. It has been noted that alternatives like mediation are "intended to alleviate the persistent inaccessibility of judicial relief for the poor and middle class . . . by providing cheaper . . . . methods for resolving disputes" (*Yale Law Journal*, 1979: 906; see also Singer, 1979a: 10). This seems clearly to have been one aim of the Department of Justice in establishing NJCs (see Cook et al., 1980: 117). Earlier, Danzig and Lowy (1975: 691) had pointed to what they saw as ". . . the extraordinary costs that the members of our society are now paying due to the paucity of interpersonal dispute resolution mechanisms in America." Felstiner had previously argued that avoidance is probably less costly than either mediation and adjudication (1974 and 1975: 695), and he speculated that mediation would be more costly and difficult to operate in America than in poorer, less technologically complex societies. However, Sander (1976: 125) went on to argue that ". . . until better data become available one can probably proceed safely on the assumption that costs rise as procedural formalities increase." While the cost issue is also rather complex, it seems clear that for those centers for which evaluations are now available (like Dorchester, Brooklyn, Atlanta, Kansas City, and Venice/Mar Vista), mediation costs more than court processing. Then there is also the issue of social costs, although this is probably even more difficult to calculate at present.

In Dorchester, Snyder (1978: 791) found that at a cost of between $300 to $400 a case mediation was operationally very expensive. Similarly, Felstiner and Williams intimated that in Dorchester, "mediation costs are 2 to 3 times the amount of court costs saved" (1979: 153). It seems that most cost "savings" came from a reduced need for probationary supervision. Felstiner and Williams argue, however, that it would be possible to lower these higher costs if greater coercion were used, such as by adding arbitration to mediation (1979: 153–154).

Taking another approach to the issue of comparative costs in this area, the Brooklyn evaluation found that mediated cases actually involved a greater number of court appearances than did cases which were adjudicated without resort to mediation (Davis et al., 1979: 66). It is no wonder therefore that the number of court referrals has not been as great as some NJCs would like to see. Similarly, it is not surprising then that NJCs seem to have made very little impact on overall court case-loads. This suggests that unless NJCs get more cases they will be unable to reduce their costs per case, but the larger the number of cases refer-red out to NJCs by the courts, the greater will be the increase in addi-tional court work as a result of the need for post-referral appearances in court by disputants. This is really a major dilemma.

## 16. Mediation Is Fairer than Adjudication

Then we come to the issue of fairness. The U.S. Department of Justice saw NJCs as helping to enhance the quality of justice by providing more responsive and lasting solutions (1977: 2–3) than the courts were able to provide. While there is need for much more research on this point, it is useful to note, as Felstiner and Williams have done (1979: 113), that at present ".. . there is a great danger of a *false comparison* between crim-inal and civil action on the one hand, and mediation on the other . . . lacking adequate field research on mediation, the tendency is to com-pare an ideal form of mediation with the reality of the court process . . . a comparison very much, weighted in mediation's favor." Bearing this in mind, it is interesting to note the Vera Institute's Brooklyn evaluation findings, which show that while 88 percent of mediated complainants thought that the mediation was fair, 76 percent of the control group thought that the judge was fair. Although this difference was found to be significant, the evaluators were surprised by it and noted that it was ". . . smaller than might have been expected" (Davis et al., 1979: 50). Yet, over 70 percent of court cases had been dismissed (Davis et al., 1979: 52).

## 17. Mediation Can Reduce Court Congestion and Delay

One of the more widely articulated cries of court reformers over the years has related to fear that there is excessive and unnecessary conges-tion in the courts which produces needless delays in dealing with dis-putes. Reference has already been made to the veritable flood in recent years of writing stressing this concern with emotional expressions such as "the law explosion" and "hyperlexis." While being a little skeptical of these "dire predictions," proponents of alternatives, such as Frank San-der, still give some credence to these predictions. Sander, for example, suggests that a "way of reducing the judicial caseload is to explore alternative ways of resolving disputes outside the courts. . . ." He goes on (1976: 112ff.) to develop this theme at some length. Sander (1976:

114) adds, "quite obviously, the courts cannot continue to respond effectively to these accelerating demands—it becomes essential therefore to examine other alternatives." Other proponents of NJCs have been a little more direct in stressing this theme as a justification for the development of neighborhood mediation centers. Thus, one Department of Justice official saw the aim of the model NJCs as being to "reduce court caseloads by redirecting cases that are not appropriate for the court process" (Lively, 1971; see also Department of Justice, 1977: 2–3). The third aim of the U.S. Department of Justice (1977: 3) in establishing NJCs was stated to be to "reduce the caseloads of local courts and other justice system agencies..." (see also Cook et al., 1980: 117). Similarly, Snyder (1978: 766) has observed that NJCs are meant to assist in the speedier handling of cases by the courts by freeing the time of judges to deal with more "serious" problems. Snyder does however point out that they have not had much impact, particularly on the work of court clerks and prosecutors.

Snyder's findings in this regard have been echoed in later evaluations. The almost negligible impact of NJCs on court congestion and delay is far from the provision of "substantial relief to...local court" (McGillis, 1980b: 5) that some proponents of mediation centers had hoped for. In Dorchester, Snyder (1978: 768) found that about three days a month of judges' time were saved through the use of mediation, although he added (1978: 778) that the Dorchester program had very little impact on the operation of the criminal justice system. However, Felstiner and Williams (1979: 46) did not find that the Dorchester District Court was overloaded, although they suggested that the probationary service might be. The evaluators of the three NJCs found that they had no effect on court caseloads (Cook et al., 1980: 83). In Brooklyn, Davis and his colleagues (1979: 66) found that the experimental mediation group, as a group, required more court attendances than did the control group, as a group. This is far from being the endorsement of this assumption that many had hoped for. A final point regarding court overload has been suggested to me by Malcolm Feeley, who points out that NJCs assume that there is a finite number of disputes in the community so that all that is needed is a sufficient number of new mechanisms for dispute processing to allow all disputes to be dealt with. It is equally possible that the creation of new forums will lead to an increase in the number of disputes that people articulate or discover that they have. The result of this, Feeley suggests, is that increasing public access to more and cheaper forums may simply serve to increase problems seen to be caused by backlog and overload. This can be linked to the argument that many cases that are referred to NJCs would previously have been dismissed by the courts. Davis's findings seem to confirm that the effect of this referral may be to increase court congestion, as Feeley also suggested.

## 18. Mediation Is More Effective than Adjudication in Dealing with Recidivism

While it has been argued that the success of mediation should be assessed by the "process by which the outcome has been reached and generated," and not by the outcome (Danzig and Lowy, 1975: 689), it is impossible to ignore long-term outcomes. All mediation programs therefore have follow-up procedures, and the monitoring or assessment of recidivism has been seen to be important enough to be part of most evaluative strategies. One of the most important objectives of the three model NJCs established by the U.S. Department of Justice was to agree upon "resolutions which are fair, *long-lasting*, satisfactory to the disputants" (Cook et al., 1980: 117, emphasis added). To ignore this assumption regarding recidivism would be tantamount to acknowledging that NJCs and mediation seek only to leave the disputants with a "good feeling," a result often associated with mediation (see Smith, 1978), highlighting the psychologism in this movement (cf. Simon, 1980).

In assessing the available statistics, one needs to distinguish resolution rates obtained immediately after mediation and long-term follow-ups regarding recidivism. Thus, the three "model" NJCs seem to have achieved an overall "resolution rate" of about 45 percent, with 28.6 percent of all cases being resolved as a result of a mediation hearing. However, this 45 percent figure was partly due to the higher figure for the Kansas City NJC, which used arbitration in addition to mediation (Cook et al., 1980: 24–25). Nevertheless, the follow-up figures are far less glowing in the picture that they present. Although some follow-up data are available in the evaluation report on the three model NJCs (Cook et al., 1980: 45–69), these are largely impressionistic and based upon attitudinal data. Such data are of little value in assessing recidivism rates to contrast with "resolution" rates. The Vera Institute study, using random assignment of cases in Brooklyn, does provide us however with a useful comparison. That study found that there was no significant difference between court processing and processing through mediation in "reducing the actual incidence of subsequent hostilities between the parties" when both experimental and control groups were compared (Davis et al., 1979: 59–64). This study found that 12 percent of the mediated cases called the police again during the follow-up period, while only 13 percent of the control group of court cases did likewise. Similarly, while 4 percent of either of the mediated parties were subsequently arrested for a crime against the other, this was also the case with 4 percent of the court control cases (Davis et al., 1979: 62).

Similarly, Felstiner and Williams also reached a negative conclusion in their Dorchester follow-up. They found no support for the hypothesis that mediation is more effective than adjudication in reducing recidivism and went on to report that "exposure to full court treatment appears to have a more positive effect than successful mediation for subjects who had committed assaults prior to the 'experimental' intervention (Felstiner and Williams, 1979: 157)." They also noted that there was no significant difference in the recidivist behavior of mediated when compared with court-processed cases (Felstiner and Williams, 1979: 158). Once again, this is far from showing the overwhelming superiority of mediation that many of its proponents have suggested.

## Discussion

While much of the above analysis is admittedly incomplete, that such a relatively superficial analysis can nevertheless raise so many questions about the neighborhood justice movement, only serves to highlight the gulf between rhetoric and reality in this area. How is one to explain this apparent gap? It is clear that while the language of NJC proponents has been quite successful in prompting the establishment of new programs, the same cannot be said for the success of programs. A number of general observations regarding this situation have been hinted at earlier. One possible explanation for the failure to match more closely rhetoric and reality can be attributed to the enthusiasm of policymakers for action, based more on perceived political necessities rather than on intellectual justifications. The manner in which mediation has, for example, been seized upon has often meant that it has had to be imposed upon social structures which have had little experience with it. The manner in which the Kpelle moot, for example, has been adapted to American circumstances is a good example of this. Richard Danzig's argument along these lines highlights the leap of faith that is so common in the neighborhood justice movement. Danzig (1973: 43) ended his argument for the relevance of this particular model of mediation to American society by exclaiming, "Despite the differences between a tribal culture and our own, isn't there a place for a community moot in our judicial system?" More than 20 years after Gibbs's fieldwork for his study of the Kpelle Moot was completed, Phillip Gulliver (1979: 210), who directed the dissertation that arose out of Gibbs's fieldwork, was able to observe that ". . . mediation still remains a poorly understood process." Interestingly enough, in his survey of the anthropological and other literature on mediation, Gulliver neglected to mention Gibbs's article even in passing. Yet, despite our relative ignorance, there is little comparative research on the dynamics of mediation in urban America, and policymakers seem to proceed blindly upon the assumption that there is abundant clarity in this area. The mushrooming growth of NJCs is a very good illustration of this. In Gulliver's words ". . . quite strong cultural stereotypes and subjective, dogmatic assumptions have been proffered as fact and analysis" (1979: 211). Gulliver also notes in regard to the supposed impartiality of the mediator that one "...should maintain a healthy cynicism here and inquire what is in it for the man in the middle" (1969: 217). This brings us to our next point, namely the benefit that the justice system obtains through its support of and involvement with mediation centers.

One of the paradoxes of the neighborhood justice movement is its heavy reliance upon the justice system for case referrals, on the one hand, and its attempt to sustain a commitment to the ideology of community in an effort to preserve its independence from the justice system, on the other. Needless to say, these are two somewhat contrary situations. A commitment to high caseloads necessitates strong ties to the justice system, while total commitment to the notion of community will necessitate low caseloads and uncertain sources of funding for NJCs. Moreover, cases referred to NJCs from the justice system are more likely to be resolved in a way that is perceived as adequate by the NJC, due largely to the coercive backdrop of the courts, while the few cases that are referred from community sources are far less likely to be seen as satisfactorily resolved. As a consequence, there is an incentive for NJCs to concentrate upon improving their justice system networks, as these seem to provide the best hope for ensuring the survival, success, and institutionalization of the NJCs. Despite the apparent obviousness of this strategy, which seems to run in the face of a commitment to community, the retention of the community ideology may be explained as a legitimating device, which need bear no relation to reality, and may simply serve to mask the reality of the expansion of justice system bureaucracies in society.

While the NJC was originally conceived as "a point of entry into the public sector for citizens with problems that they cannot resolve themselves" (U.S. Department of Justice, 1977), it seems that actually the opposite has happened in the vast majority of cases. In other words, most cases are referred to the NJCs from "the public sector," rather than coming directly from the community. As noted above, this highlights the paradox in the foundations of the NJC movement. On the one hand, there is a largely superficial attempt to recreate a sense of community and citizen participation in dispute processing, while, on the other hand, the NJCs are seen as a convenient place into which many of the more difficult, insoluble, and time-consuming problems of the courts can be diverted. The contradiction between these two bases of the NJC movement have been noted by both those within the movement and apparently impartial or uncommitted evaluators. For example, the Community Board Program in San Francisco has resisted involvement with the court system and insisted instead upon building a community base, even though this only produces a comparatively small caseload of about 100 cases a year. The evaluators of the three model Department of Justice NJCs also identified the paradox of attempting to combine both a justice system and a community perspective when they concluded that "Neighborhood Justice Centers with connections to the local justice system will attract and resolve more disputes than centers without such referral sources" (Cook et al., 1980: 106). Furthermore, they noted that where the NJC has justice system referral networks it is not necessary to limit the services of the NJC to a particular community at all (Cook et al., 1980: 94). Of the Atlanta NJC disputants, only 12 percent of respondents and 17 percent of complainants lived in the original target area. The Atlanta NJC dealt with 60 percent of all the three model NJC cases (Cook et al., 1980: 33). Based upon the experience of the Venice/ Mar Vista NJC in Los Angeles, which had especially tried to create an impact upon the local community, they went on to add that "... such a community oriented stance increases the difficulty of attracting cases" (Cook et al., 1980: 106). In this particular center it also seems to have created several management problems for the center coordinators. Nevertheless, the evaluators went on to conclude that NJCs "... need to develop more effective ways for improving public awareness about NJCs." This call is based upon the disappointing finding that "even after a year of public service announcements, television appearances, and several other community outreach efforts, approximately 70 percent of the Venice/Mar Vista residents had not heard of the Neighborhood Justice Center. But even these outreach efforts were sporadic and limited by meager resources..." (Cook et al., 1980: 104). It is difficult to imagine more resources being available from government in the future than were available for these model programs. Moreover, research on community attitudes would suggest that information campaigns have the greatest impact upon better-educated, wealthier people, a very different type of person from the type that tends to be drawn into the NJCs. Unfortunately, no data are presented in the model NJC evaluation on the backgrounds of the 30 percent of people who were aware of the existence of the NJC in Venice/Mar Vista.

Although many proponents of NJCs stress the originality of this alternative, it is clear that, in its present form, it is in many respects simply a "repackaged" version of the earlier diversion programs, which were based upon the now largely discredited rehabilitationist ethos. Curiously, many of the same people who previously operated diversion programs now operate NJCs. Even the concept of diversion is to be found in the literature of the NJC movement. The Department of Justice (1977), for example, saw NJCs as providing relief to overburdened courts "by diverting matters" that do not require a full court hearing. McGillis (1980b: 5) has also referred to "... the diversion benefit..." of NJCs in providing "... substantial relief to... local courts." (Davis et al. (1979: 11) refer to "diversion" to mediation (see also Singer, 1979a: 9–10). It seems that mediation has become simply one more diversionary alternative. While diversionary programs tend to be therapeutic in nature, it has been argued that NJC mediation is not therapeutic (Cook et al., 1980: 91), suggesting that NJCs are nondiversionary. It should, however, be recalled that in his case study of the Kpelle Moot, Gibbs (1963: 1) saw mediation as practised there as "a therapeutic model for the informal settlement of disputes." In any case, Cook et al. (1980: 109) observe that mediation is to be found on a continuum between court processing and long-term therapy and counseling. This sounds very much like diversion as it also included a variety of degrees of therapy. Also, like diversion, mediation programs run by NJCs often require that disputants return to the court for a final decision on their charge after the conclusion of mediation. For example, in Atlanta, the court sought to keep control of the cases that it had referred to the NJC by requiring disputants to return to the court (Cook et al., 1980: 82). Most programs require at least some kind of feedback to the court. Once it is accepted that the differences between NJCs and diversion programs are not as great as some have argued, many of the criticisms of diversion will also be applicable to mediation programs (see, further, Nejelski, 1976; Mullen, 1975).

As noted earlier, it is important to avoid overenthusiasm for untested or fad reforms (Nejelski, 1979: 12). One reason for this is the argument that one needs first to understand the nature of the society in which we live and the character of the legal system with which we have to work. As noted earlier, the anthropologist Laura Nader has, for example, argued that our legal system has its "... roots in a much smaller society" in which public opinion was "... an important mechanism of social control." She goes on to argue that we now live in a society characterized by anonymity and that "... our law is no longer appropriate for an industrial society in which most real and potential complaints occur between strangers of unequal power" (Nader, 1979b: 46). This suggests that one may need to do more to our legal institutions than mere tinkering or grafting limbs on a body that remains the same. This strategy has the potential of producing a kind of Frankenstein monster.

This type of caution has been urged by other anthropologists of law. Katherine S. Newman, for example, warns similarly regarding the development of community-based dispute settlement programs relying upon mediation. She observes that "... it is an open question ... whether institutional forms of this sort can be made effective in the context of modern industrial societies. We need to determine more precisely those aspects of the 'social context' which encourage or discourage the effectiveness of alternative institutions" (quoted by Selznick, 1980: 217). A fuller development of this theme is to be found in the work of another anthropologist, Sally Merry (1979b; see also 1979a), when she compared the use of mediation in simpler and more complex societies and suggested that there were major differences in the social organization and assumptions of each which needed to be taken into account by reformers.

A number of important points emerge from the above warnings and can be applied to assist us to understand the neighborhood justice movement. First, as we have seen, this movement is based upon the premise that it is possible to recreate a sense of community by emphasizing communication and the reduction of tension between people. In this way it is hoped that the individual will more readily be prepared to accept what might otherwise be regarded as an outmoded part of the legal order. Thus, the neighborhood justice movement clearly can be seen as serving a legitimizing function and consequently deflecting or diverting criticism of the formal legal system with its significant inequalities. Rather than urge the recreation of the formal legal system, arguments such as Nader's suggest that the alternatives movement neutralizes reform efforts by its attempts to foster the ideal of community. In reality, however, something very different is occurring which brings us to a second point arising from the above. This concerns the issue of unequal power and the inability of the existing legal system to deal with this problem satisfactorily. While inequalities of power are by no means new, it can be argued that these have become more damaging to the individual due to the failure of our systems of law and social control to provide access for the powerless. By shunting the poor in particular into Neighborhood Justice Centers, this whole problem is further accentuated. Mediation, as the principal technique of such centers seems to successfully induce the powerless to accept their condition of powerlessness, but is completely unable to force the powerful to comply with the wishes of the powerless, or to equip the powerless with tools for obtaining greater access to the legal system.

It is clear that there is an intimate relationship between the existing legal system and the emerging system of neighborhood justice. Moreover, I would suggest that the latter could not exist but for the continued existence of deficiencies in the formal or official legal system. To argue that these alternatives can humanize the legal system by drawing into it a greater "community" orientation is somewhat problematic, as these alternatives actually serve as mirrors of that formal system and so may do no more than reflect inequalities found within it. I would suggest that panaceas, if they are to be found at all, are *not* to be found in the mythical "community," but in the legal system itself. If this is correct, then it is imperative to concentrate reform efforts within the legal system itself and not upon outside efforts, even though there may be some very attractive rhetoric for such outside endeavors. It is interesting to note that in contrast to the United States, there has been little enthusiasm for notions like Neighborhood Justice Centers in Europe. Instead, reformers have concentrated upon court procedures and structures. This seems to be a far more realistic strategy, although it is true to say that there have been American proponents of reform strategies with primarily a court orientation. Cratsley's (1978) concept of a community court is more in keeping with this approach, as is the recent experimentation with court-annexed arbitration currently being evaluated by the Federal Judicial Center (1979).

In concentrating reform efforts within the justice system, a priority area would be the ideology of the system itself (see, further, Griffiths, 1970), such as that perspective which stresses official intervention in the lives of individual disputants. The justification of such intervention needs to be questioned by reformers far more so than it has been to date. This is particularly important if it is true that intervention simply expands the absolute number of disputes in society at any one time. It could be argued, as many judges seem to assert by their action of referring such cases out of the courts, that the courts simply cannot play any useful role and should therefore have nothing at all to do with certain disputes. The reliance upon the rhetoric of community seems to be a half-hearted acknowledgment of this fact, although this has been fatally flawed by the irrelevance of the notion of community for most people.

Another strategy might be to place more emphasis on the earlier phases of the court process, as many cases never proceed to adjudication, and the filing of a complaint seems to be seen as sufficient retaliatory action by most disputants. This part of the court process should receive much more attention from reformers. Another approach might be to develop other models already in existence within the justice system, such as the small claims court, the family court, and the juvenile court, as well as the office of the court clerk.

If one thing is clear from the neighborhood justice experience, it is that neighborhood justice or dispute processing needs to be entirely independent of the justice system, as well as far less grandiose in its structure. NJCs seem to be treated at the present time as a parallel but subservient justice system. As a consequence, they tend to fall between two stools, court processing and a genuine local mechanism, so that as Cratsley (1978: 5) has said in another context, it is "neither a truly alternative mechanism nor a real court." This is really quite fatal.

Finally, I should finish on a positive note regarding mediation, as the impression may have been conveyed that I might see it as a completely foolhardy exercise. Such an impression would be unfortunate as third-party intervention using mediation has far more applications than those discussed here. It is clear that there are many varieties of mediation and that we have yet to explain the ramifications and applications of these. It is desirable that this experimentation not be halted, although the rather too narrow form of mediation that is being institutionalized in NJCs shows that the technique is often otiose and sometimes even pernicious and undesirable. Nevertheless, with a greater emphasis on the localization of disputing, whether in the neighborhood, between consumers and retailers, in bureaucracies, among businesspersons, and in the workplace, it seems that mediation will continue to play an important place in dispute processing, provided it is not confused with adjudication. Mediation should not therefore be dismissed after this current wave of enthusiasm for NJCs has passed but, rather, should be looked at closely to assess the range of other applications that it may have in the field of dispute processing. This may need to be preceded by research on the nature and existence of informal dispute-processing mechanisms already in society.

## Notes

1. See also Rifkind (1976); Goldman et al. (1976); Gillespie (1976); Freeman (1977); Adams (1977). Bell (1978b).

2. Of course none of these have been *experiments* in the strict scientific meaning of this term.

3. It has been argued that "reformers alternate between building institutions and taking them apart, between urging regulation and calling for deregulation" (*Yale Law Journal* 88: 906, 907).

4. Mullen (1975) had earlier pointed to the dilemma of diversion, so that it was somewhat ironic to find her advancing the NJC concept.

5. These were The Boston Urban Court Program, The Columbus Night Prosecuter Program, The Miami Citizen Dispute Settlement Program, The New York Institute for Mediation and Conflict of Resolution Dispute Center, The Rochester American Arbitration Association Community Dispute Services Project and the San Francisco Community Board Program.

6. These 12 dimensions were: (a) the nature of the community served, (b) the type of sponsoring agency, (c) project office location, (d) project case criteria, (e) referral sources, (f) intake procedures, (g) resolution techniques, (h) project staff, (i) hearing staff training, (j) case follow-up procedures, (k) project costs, and (l) evaluation.

7. McGillis (1980b: 12) states that the designation of the Columbus Night Prosecutor Program as an Exemplary Project by LEAA in 1974 led to mediation becoming the dominant technique relied upon.

8. It needs to be stressed that the notion of a Neighborhood Justice Center is used here to cover a wide range of different types of organizations, although strictly speaking it applies only to the three U.S. Department of Justice projects.

9. See also Linda Singer (1979a: 37–41) for a discussion of problems of coercion in mediation. Also see Hofrichter (1977: 170–171).

10. I understand that researchers from SUNY-Buffalo are currently evaluating another NJC upon the basis of the random assignment of cases.

# Bibliography

Aaronson, A., et al. (1975) *The New Justice: Alternatives to Conventional Criminal Adjudication*. Washington, D.C.: Law Enforcement Assistance Administration.

Abel, Richard (1972) *Toward Comparative Social Theory of the Disputing Process*. New Haven: Yale University Press.

—— (1974) "A Comparative Theory of Dispute Institutions in Society." *Law and Society Review* 8: 217–347.

—— (1978) "From the Editor." *Law and Society Review* 12: 189–198.

—— (1979) "Delegalization: A Critical Review of Its Ideology, Manifestations, and Social Consequences," in E. Blankenburg, E. Klausa, and H. Rottleuthner, eds. *Alternative Rechtsformen und Alternativen zum Recht*, pp. 27–47. *Jahrbuch fuer Rechtssoziologie und Rechtstheorie*, Band VI. Opladen: Westdeutscher Verlag.

—— (1980) "Informal Alternatives to Courts as a Mode of Legalizing Conflict," unpublished paper.

——, ed. (1982) *The Politics of Informal Justice: The American Experience*. New York: Academic Press.

Abelson, Robert P. (1968) "Psychological Implications," in Robert P. Abelson et al., eds., *Theories of Cognitive Consistency: A Sourcebook*. Skokie, Ill.: Rand McNally.

Abner, Willoughby (1969) "Conflict in a Free Society." Presented at the University of Massachusetts, Amherst, mimeo.

Ackerman, Nathan W. (1958) *The Psychodynamics of Family Life*. New York: Basic Books.

Adams, Bert N. (1971) *The American Family: A Sociological Interpretation* Chicago: Markham.

Adams, William H. (1977) "Would We Rather Fight than Settle? The Litigation Explosion: Two Fundamental Causes". *Florida Bar Journal* 51: 496–499.

Afton, Robert J. (n.d.) "Citizens Dispute Settlement Project, Minneapolis City Attorney's Office" (Description of program; Judith A. Jackson, Project Director, Marry Ann Stark, Diversion Counselor).

Alexander, Christopher (1966) *The City as a Mechanism for Sustaining Human Contact*. Berkeley: Institute of Urban & Regional Development, University of California.

American Bar Association (1976) *Report of the Pound Conference Follow-up Task Force*. Chicago: American Bar Foundation.

American Bar Association Special Committee on Resolution of Minor Disputes. *Dispute Resolution*, Issue No. 3–4 (Fall 1979).

American Bar Association (1980) *Dispute Resolution Program Directory*, *Washington*, D.C., ABA Special Committee on Minor Disputes

Anno, B. J., and B. H. Hoff (1975) "Refunding Evaluation Report on the Municipal Court of Philadelphia 4A Project." Washington, D.C.: Blackstone Associates.

Aubert, Vilhelm (1963) "Competition and Dissensus: Two Types of Conflict Resolution." *Journal of Conflict Resolution* 7: 26–42.

—— (1967) "Courts and Conflict Resolution." *Journal of Conflict Resolution* 11: 40–51.

—— (1969) "Law as a Way of Resolving Conflicts: The Case of a Small Industrialized Society," in Laura Nader, ed., *Law in Culture and Society*. Chicago: Aldine.

—— (1979) "On Methods of Legal Influence," in S. Burman and B. E. Harrell-Bond, eds., *The Imposition of Law*. New York: Academic Press.

Auerbach, J. (1976) "Plague of Lawyers." *Harpers* 253 (October 1976): 37.

Axelrod, Morris (1956) "Urban Structure and Social Participation." *American Sociological Review* 21: 13–18.

Ayoub, Victor F. (1965) "Conflict Resolution and Social Reorganization in a Lebanese Village." *Human Organization* 24: 11–17.

Bailey, F. G., ed. (1971) *Gifts and Poisons: The Politics of Reputation*. Oxford: Blackwell.

Baker, Sally, and Susan Sadd (1979) *Court Employment Project Evaluation Final Report*. New York: Vera Institute of Justice.

Balderman, Evelyn (1974) "Jewish Courts." Unpublished manuscript in the custody of the UCLA Law School Library.

Bard, Morton (1973) "The Role of Law Enforcement in the Helping System," in John R. Snibbe and Homa M. Snibbe, eds., *The Urban Policeman in Transition*. Springfield, Ill,: Thomas.

Bardach, E. (1978) *The Implementation Game: What Happens to a Bill After It Becomes Law*. Cambridge, Mass.: MIT Press.

Barkun, M. (1964) "Conflict Resolution Through Implicit Mediation." *Journal of Conflict Resolution* 8: 121–130.

—— (1968) *Law Without Sanctions*. New Haven: Yale University Press.

Barnes, J. A. (1961) "Law as Politically Active," in Geoffrey Sawer, ed., *Studides in the Sociology of Law*. Canberra: Australian National University Press.

Barth, Frederick (1959) *Political Leadership Among the Swat Pathan*. Monograph N. 19 London: London School of Economics.

Barton, John H. (1975) "Behind the Legal Explosion." *Stanford Law Review* 24: 567–584.

Barton, R. F. (1919) *Ifugao Law*. University of Chicago Publications in American Archaeology and Ethnology No. 15. Berkeley: University of California Press (reprinted 1969).

Baunach, Phyllis Jo (1980) "Random Assignment in Criminal Justice Research: Some Ethical and Legal Issues." *Criminology* 17: 435–444.

Baxi, Upendra (1974) "Comment: Durkheim and Legal Evolution: Some Problems of Disproof." *Law and Society Review* 8: 645–651.

Beals, Alan R. (1961) "Cleavage and Internal Conflict: An Example from India." *Journal of Conflict Resolution* 5: 27–34.

Becker, Calvin (1975) "Conflict and the Users of Adjudication," in *Studies on Diversion*. Toronto, Canada: East York Community Law Reform Project.

Bell, Griffin B. (1977) Foreword to McGillis and Mullen, *Neighborhood Justice Centers: An Analysis of Potential Models*. Washington, D.C.: U.S. Government Printing Office.

Bell, Griffin B. (1978a) "New Directions in the Administration of Justice: Responses to the Pound Conference—Responses of the Justice Department." *American Bar Association Journal* 64: 53–59.

—— (1978b) "Crisis in the Courts: Proposal for Change." *Vanderbilt Law Review* 31: 3–15.

—— (1978c) "The Pound Conference Follow-up: A Response from the United States Department of Justice." *Federal Rules Decisions* 76: 320.

Bell, Wendell (1968) "The City the Suburb, and a Theory of Social Choice," in Scott Greer et al., eds., *The New Urbanization*. New York: St. Martin's Press.

——, and Marion D. Boat (1957) "Urban Neighborhoods and Informal Social Relations." *American Journal of Sociology* 62: 39–398.

Bellow, Garry (1977) "Turning Solutions into Problems: The Legal Aid Experience." *NLADA Briefcase* 34: 106–110, 117–125.

—— (1979) "Legal Services to the Poor: The 'First Wave' in the Access-to-Justice Movements, an American Report." (Paper presented at the colloquium on Access to Justice After the Publication of the Florence Project Series: Prospects for Future Action, Florence.

Berman, H. (1972) "The Educational Role of the Soviet Court." *International and Comparative Law Quarterly*. 21: 81–94.

Berman, Jesse (1969) "The Cuban Popular Tribunals." *Columbia Law Review* 69: 1317–1354.

Best, Arthur, and Alan R. Andreasen (1977) "Consumer Response to Unsatisfactory Purchases: A Survey of Perceiving Defects, Voicing Complaints and Obtaining Redress." *Law and Society Review* 11: 701–742.

Bethel, Charles A., et al. (1978) "Conflict Resolution in High Schools: A Modest Proposal." *National Association of Secondary School*

*Principals Bulletin* 62: 22–27.

Black, Donald (1971) "The Social Organization of Arrest." *Stanford Law Review* 23: 1087–1111.

——— (1973a) "The Mobilization of Law." *Journal of Legal Studies* 2: 125–149.

——— (1973b) "The Boundaries of Legal Sociology," in Donald Black and Maureen Mileski, eds., *The Social Organization of Law*. New York: Academic Press.

——— (1976) *The Behavior of Law*. New York: Academic Press.

———, and M. P. Baumgartner (1978) "Self-Help in Modern Society." *Law and Human Behavior* 2: 223–244.

Blankenburg, Erhard, and Udo Reifner (1979) "Beyond Legal Representation: Dispute Processing, Non-Judicial Alternatives and the 'Third Wave' in the Access-to-Justice Movement, A European Report," unpublished paper, Florence: October 1979.

Blumer, Herbert (1969) *Symbolic Interaction: Perspective and Method*. Englewood Cliffs, N. J.. Prentice-Hall.

Bohannan, Paul (1957) *Justice and Judgement Among the Tiv*. London: Oxford University Press.

——— (1965) "The Differing Realms of Law." *American Anthropologist—Special Issue: The Ethnography of Law*. Laura Nader, ed. Vol. 67 (6) (December 1965).

Boissevain, Jeremy (1974) *Friends of Friends: Networks, Manipulators and Coalitions*. New York: St. Martin's Press.

Bott, Elizabeth (1957) *Family and Social Network*. London: Tavistock.

Boyer, Barry B., and Roger C. Crampton (1974) "American Legal Education: An Agenda for Research and Reform." *Cornell Law Review* 59: 221–297.

Brandt, Victor S. R. (1971) *A Korean Village Between Farm and Sea*. Cambridge, Mass.: Harvard University Press.

Bridenback, Michael L., Kenneth P. Palmer, and Jack B. Planchard (1979) "Citizen Dispute Settlement: The Florida Experience." *American Bar Association Journal* 65: 570–573.

Bruff, Harold H. (1973) "Arizona's Inferior Courts." *Law and the Social Order* 1973: 1–48.

Buckle, Suzann, and Leonard Buckle (1977) *Bargaining for Justice*. New York: Praeger.

——— (1980) "Bringing Justice Home: Some Thoughts About the Neighborhood Justice Center Policy." Paper delivered at the 1980 Meetings of the Law and Society Association.

Budnitz, Mark (1977) "Consumer Dispute Resolution Forums." *Trial* 13(12): 45–49.

Burgess, Ernest W., Harvey J. Locke, and Mary Margaret Thomas (1963). *The Family: From Institution to Companionship* 3rd ed. New York: American Book Company.

Bush, Robert A. (1977) *San Francisco 4A Project Arbitration as an Alternative*. American Arbitration Association.

Cahn, Edgar S. and Jean C. Cahn (1970) "Power to the People or the Profession?—The Public Interest in Public Interest Law". *Yale Law Journal*. 79: 1005–1067.

California Law Review (1964) "The California Small Claims Court". *California Law Review* 52: 876–898.

California Legislature (1977–1978) Regular Session. *Assembly Bill No. 2763*.

Campbell, J. (1964) *Honour, Family and Patronage*. Oxford: Clarendon.

Canter, Richard S. (1973) "Consequences of Legal Engineering: A Case from Zambia." Presented at the 72nd Meeting of the American Anthropological Association in New Orleans.

——— (1974) "Law Without Lawyers: Cuba's Popular Tribunals." *Juris Doctor*. 4: 24–27.

——— (1978) "Dispute Settlement and Dispute Processing in Zambia: Individual Choice vs Societal Constraints," in Laura Nader and Harry F. Todd, Jr., eds., *The Disputing Process and Law in Ten Societies*. New York: Columbia University Press.

Cappelletti, M., ed. (1978–1979) *Access-to-Justice*. 4 vols. Milan: Guiffre and Alphen aan den Rijn: Sijthoff and Noordhoff.

Cappelletti, M. and Garth, B. (1978) "Access to Justice: The Newest Wave in the Worldwide Movement to Make Rights Effective." *Buffalo Law Review*. 27: 181–292.

Carkhuff, Robert R. (1969) *Helping and Human Relations*. New York: Holt, Rinehart and Winston.

Carlin, Jerome, and Jan Howard (1965) "Legal Representation and Class Justice." *UCLA Law Review* 12: 381–437.

Carrington, Paul D. (1977–1979) Report at Conference: "Current Developments in Judicial Administration: Papers Presented at the Plenary Session of the American Association of Law Schools, December 1977." Reprinted in the Joint House Hearings on the Dispute Resolution Act, 1979, pp. 632–636.

Carstairs, G. Morris (1967) *The Twice Born*. Bloomington: Indiana University Press.

Carter, Leif (1977) *Reason in Law*. Boston: Little Brown.

Cartwright, Bliss, Marc Galanter, and Robert Kidder (1974) "Introduction: Litigation and Dispute Processing." *Law and Society Review* 9: 5–11.

——— (1975) "Conclusion: Disputes and Reported Cases." *Law and Society Review* 9: 369–384.

Casper, Jonathan D. (1978) "Having Their Day in Court: Defendant Evaluations of the Fairness of their Treatment." *Law and Society Review* 12: 237–253.

Clifford, David, and Donald Warren (1976) "Community Studies."

Summary of presentation to "Informal Service Networks" working group. Cambridge, Mass. Mimeograph.

Clifford, W. (1976) *Crime Control in Japan*. Lexington, Mass.: Lexington Books.

Cohen, Jerome Alan (1967) "Chinese Mediation on the Eve of Modernization." *Journal of Asian and African Studies* 2: 54.

Cohen, Percy S. (1968) *Modern Social Theory*. London: Heinemann Educational Books.

Cohn, Bernard S. (1967) "Some Notes on Law and Change in North India," in Paul Bohannan, ed. *Law and Warfare*. Garden City: The Natural History Press; Austin: University of Texas Press.

——— (1965) "Anthropological Notes on Disputes and Law in India." *American Anthropologist*. 67(2): 82.

Collier, Jane Fishburne (1973) *Law and Social Change in Zinacantan*. Stanford: Stanford University Press.

Colson, Elizabeth (1953) "Social Control and Vengeance in Plateau Tonga Society." *Africa* 23: 199–212.

——— (1974) *Tradition and Contract: The Problem of Order*. Chicago: Aldine.

Columbia Journal of Law and Social Problems (1970) "Rabbinical Courts: Modern Day Solomons." *Columbia Journal of Law and Social Problems* 6: 49–75.

Comment (1975) "Pretrial Diversion: The Threat of Expanding Social Control." *Harvard Civil Rights—Civil Liberties Law Review* 10: 180–214.

Conard, Alfred (1971) "Macro-Justice: A Systematic Approach to Conflict Resolution." *Georgia Law Review* 5: 415–428.

Connor, Ross, F. and Ray Surette (1977) *The Citizen Dispute Settlement Program—Resolving Disputes Outside the Courts, Orlanda Florida*. Washington, D.C.: American Bar Association.

Cook, Royer F., Janice A. Roehl, and David I. Sheppard (1980) *Neighborhood Justice Centers Field Test—Final Evaluation Report*. Washington, D.C.: American Bar Association.

Coser, Lewis A (1956) *The Functions of Social Conflict*. New York: Free Press.

Cover, Robert M. (1979) "Dispute Resolution: A Foreword." *Yale Law Journal* 88: 910–915.

Cox, Bruce, and Gordon S. Drever. (1970–71) "Some Recent Trends in Ethnographic Studies of Law." *Law and Society Review* 5: 407–415.

Cratsley, John C. (1978) "Community Courts: Offering Alternative Dispute Resolution Within the Judicial System." *Vermont Law Review* 31: 1–69.

Crockett, George W., and Morris Gleicher, (1978) "Teaching Criminals a Lesson: A Report on Justice in China." *Judicature* 61: 278–288.

Crowe, Patricia Ward (1978) "Complaint Reactions to the Massachusetts Commission Against Discrimination." *Law and Society Review* 12: 217–286.

Danish, Steven J., and Allen L. Hauer (1973) *Helping Skills: A Basic Training Program*. New York: *Behavioral Publications*.

Danzig, R. (1973) "Toward the Creation of a Complementary, Decentralized System of Criminal Justice." *Stanford Law Review* 26: 1–54.

———, and M. J. Lowy (1975) "Everyday Disputes and Mediation in the United States: A Reply to Professor Felstiner." *Law and Society Review* 9: 675–694.

Davis, Robert C., Martha Tichane, and Deborah Grayson (1979) "Mediation and Arbitration as Alternatives to Prosecution in Felony Arrest Cases—An Evaluation of the Brooklyn Dispute Resolution Center." New York: Vera Institute of Justice.

Dawson, John P. (1960) *A History of Lay Judges*. Cambridge, Mass.: Harvard University Press.

Deutsch, Morton (1973) *The Resolution of Conflict*. New Haven: Yale University Press.

Diamond, Stanley (1978) "The Rule of Law Versus the Order of Custom," in Charles Reasons and Robert Rich, eds., *The Sociology of Law—A Conflict Perspective*. Toronto, Canada: Butterworths.

"Dispute Resolution" (1979) *The Yale Law Journal* 88: 905–909 (Introduction to Series of Articles on Dispute Resolution).

Dispute Resolution Alternatives Committee (1979) (J. W. Hatchett, Chairman). *The Citizen Dispute Settlement Process in Florida—A Study of Five Programs*. Office of the State Court Administrator, Florida Supreme Court.

Dolbeare, Kenneth M. (1967) *Trial Courts in Urban Politics: State Court Policy Impact and Function in a Local Political System*. New York: Wiley.

——— (1969) *The Federal District Courts and Urban Policy: An Exploratory Study*. New York: Wiley.

Doo, Leigh-Woo (1973) "Dispute Resolution in Chinese-American Communities." *American Journal of Comparative Law* 21: 627–663.

Durkheim, Emile (1933) *The Division of Labor in Society*. New York: Free Press.

Eckhoff, T. (1966) "The Mediator, the Judge and the Administrator in Conflict Resolution." *Acta Sociologica* 10: 148–172.

Edelman, Murray (1964) *The Symbolic Uses of Politics*. Campaign: University of Illinois Press.

——— (1978) *Political Language: Words That Succeed and Policies That Fail*. New York: Academic Press.

Ehrlich, T. (1976) "Legal Pollution." *New York Times Magazine*, February 8, 1976, p. 35.

Eisenberg, Melvin A. (1976) "Private Ordering Through Negotiation:

Dispute Settlement and Rule Making." *Harvard Law Review* 89: 637–681.

Eisenstein, J., and H. Jacob (1977) *Felony Justice*. Boston: Little, Brown.

Emmett, Isabel (1964) *A North Wales Village*. London: Routledge & Kegan Paul.

Engel, David M., and Eric H. Steele (1979) "Civil Cases and Society: Process and Order in the Civil Justice System." *American Bar Foundation Research Journal* 1979: 295–346.

Epstein, A. L. (1953) *The Administration of Justice and the Urban African: A Study of Urban Native Courts in Northern Rhodesia*. London: HMSO.

——— (1958) *Politics in an Urban African Community*. Manchester: Manchester University Press.

——— (1969) "Gossip, Norms and Social Network," in J. Clyde Mitchell, ed., *Social Networks in Urban Situations*, pp. 117–128. Manchester: Manchester University Press.

Erickson, William H. (1978) "New Directions in the Administration of Justice: Responses to the Pound Conference—Responses of the American Bar Association." *American Bar Association Journal* 64: 48–53.

Evaluation Group (1980) "An Evaluation Report on the Suffolk County Community Mediation Center." Unpublished.

Evans-Pritchard, E. E. (1937) *Witchcraft, Oracles and Magic Among the Azande*. Oxford: Clarendon.

——— (1940) *The Nuer*. Oxford: Oxford University Press.

Falke, J., G. Bierbrauer, and K. F. Koch (1978) "Legal Advice and the Non-Judicial Settlement of Disputes: A Case Study of the Public Legal Advice and Mediation Center in the City of Hamburg," in M. Cappelletti and J. Weisner, ed., *Access to Justice: Volume II, Promising Institutions*, pp. 103–152. Milan/Leiden: Guiffre/Sijhoff.

Federal Bureau of Investigation (1977) *Uniform Crime Reports for the United States, 1976*. Washington, D.C.: U.S. Government Printing Office.

Federal Judicial Center (1979) *Interim Evaluation Report on Court-Annexed Arbitration in Three Federal Judicial Districts*, June 1979.

Feeley, Malcolm (1976) "The Concept of Laws in Social Science: A Critique and Notes on an Expanded View." *Law and Society Review* 10: 497–523.

——— (1979) *The Process in the Punishment: Handling Cases in a Lower Criminal Court*. New York: Russell Sage Foundation.

———, and Austin Sarat (1980) *The Policy Dilemma: The Crisis of Theory and Practice in the Law Enforcement Assistance Administration*. Minneapolis: University of Minnesota Press.

Felstiner, William F. (1974) "Influences of Social Organization on Dispute Processing." *Law and Society Review* 9: 63–94.

———— (1975) "Avoidance as Dispute Processing: An Elaboration." *Law and Society Review* 9: 695–706.

————, and A. B. Drew (1979) *European Alternatives to Criminal Trials and Their Applicability in the United States.* Washington, D.C.: U.S. Government Printing Office.

————, and Lynne Williams (1979/1980) "Community Mediation in Dorchester, Massachusetts." Washington, D.C.: U.S. Government Printing Office.

Fetter, T. (1978) *State Courts: A Blueprint for the Future.* Williamsburg, Va.: National Center for State Courts.

Fisher, E. A. (1975) "Community Courts: An Alternative to Conventional Adjudication." *American University Law Review* 24: 1253–1291.

Fishman, Robert (1973) "An Evaluation of the Effect on Criminal Recidivism of New York City Projects Providing Rehabilitation and Diversion Services." Report to the New York City Criminal Justice Coordinating Council.

Ford Foundation (1978) *Mediating Social Conflict.* New York: Ford Foundation.

Foster, George M. (1960) "Interpersonal Relations in Peasant Society." *Human Organization* 19: 174.

Frank, J. (1949) *Courts on Trial: Myth and Reality in American Justice.* Princeton, N.J.: Princeton University Press.

Freeman, Richard C. (1977) "Crisis in the Federal Courts: A District Judge's Analysis." *Georgia State Bar Journal* 13: 130–131.

Friedmann, Karl A. (1973) "Complaining—Comparative Aspects of Complaint Behavior and Attitudes Towards Complaining in Canada and Britain." Presented at the Annual Meeting of the Canadian Political Science Association in Montreal.

Friedman, Lawrence M. (1973) *A History of American Law.* New York: Simon & Schuster.

———— (1978) "Access to Justice: Social and Historical Context," in M. Cappelletti and J. Weisner, eds., *Access to Justice,* vol. 2, pp. 3–36. Milan/Leiden: Guiffre/Sijhoff.

———— (1979) "Access to the Legal System and the Modern Welfare State: An American Report." (Paper prepared for the Colloquium on Access-to-Justice. After the publication of the Florence Project Series: Prospects for Future Action, Florence.

————, and Robert V. Percival (1976) "A Tale of Two Courts: Litigation in Alameda and San Benito Counties." *Law and Society Review* 10: 267–301.

Fuller, Lon (1963) "Collective Bargaining and the Arbitrator." *Wisconsin Law Review* 1963: 1–46.

———— (1969) "Human Interaction and the Law." *The American Journal of Jurisprudence* 14: 1–36.

———— (1971) "Mediation—Its Forms and Functions." *Southern California Law Review* 44: 305–339.

———— (1979) "The Forms and Limits of Adjudication." *Harvard Law Review* 92: 353–409.

Furer-Haimendorf, Christoph von (1967) *Morals and Merit*. London! Weidenfeld and Nicholson.

Galanter, Marc (n.d.) "Private Alternatives to Official Dispute Processing: Newspaper Source Materials." Buffalo: Faculty of Law and Jurisprudence, SUNY

———— (1968) "The Displacement of Traditional Law in Modern India." *Journal of Social Issues* 24(4): 65–91.

———— (1974) "Why the 'Haves' Come Out Ahead: Speculation on the Limits of Legal Change." *Law and Society Review* 9: 95–160.

———— (1975) "Afterword: Explaining Litigation." *Law and Society Review*. 9: 345–368.

———— (1977) "Delivering Legality: Some Proposals for the Direction of Research." *Law and Society Review* 11: 225–246.

———— (1979a) "Justice in Many Rooms." Working Paper, Disputes Processing Research Program. Madison: School of Law, University of Wisconsin.

———— (1979b) "Beyond Legal Representation: Dispute Processing, Non-Judicial Alternatives and the 'Third Wave' in the Access-to-Justice Movement " Paper presented to Colloquium on Access to Justice, Florence, Italy.

Galaway, B., and J. Hudson (1978) *Offender Restitution in Theory and Action*. Lexington, Mass.: Lexington Books.

Gans, Herbert (1962) *The Urban Villagers: Group and Class in the Life of Italian-Americans*. New York: Free Press.

Garafalo, James, and Kevin J. Connelly (1980) "Dispute Resolution Centers Part I. Major Features and Processes." *Criminal Justice Abstracts*, September 1980.

Gellhorn, Walter (1966) *When Americans Complain*. Cambridge, Mass.: Harvard University Press.

Getman, Julius (1979) "Labor Arbitration and Dispute—Resolution." *Yale Law Journal* 88: 916–950

Gibbs, James L., Jr. (1962) "Poro Values and Courtroom Procedures in a Kpelle Chiefdom." *Southwestern Journal of Anthropology* 18: 341–350.

———— (1963) "The Kpelle Moot: A Therapeutic Model for the Informal Settlement of Disputes." *Africa* 33: 1–10.

———— (1967) "The Kpelle Moot," in P. Bohannan, ed., *Law and Warfare*. Garden City New York: The Natural History Press.

———— (1969) "Law and Personality: Signposts for a New Direction," in

Laura Nader, ed., *Law in Culture and Society* Chicago: Aldine.

Giles, F. T. (1949) *The Magistrates' Courts*. Baltimore: Penguin Books.

Gillespie, Robert W. (1976) "The Production of Court Services: An Analysis of Scale Effects and Other Factors." *Journal of Legal Studies* 5: 243–265.

Gluckman, M. (1955) *The Judicial Process Among the Barotse of Northern Rhodesia*. Manchester: University Press for the Rhodes-Livingstone Institute.

——— (1965) *Politics, Law and Ritual in Tribal Society*. New York: New American Library.

Goldbeck, Willis B. (1975) "Mediation: An Instrument of Citizen Involvement." The Arbitration Journal 30: 241–253.

Goldman, Jerry, Richard L. Hooper and Judy A. Mahaffey (1976) "Caseload Forecasting Models for Federal District Courts." *Journal of Legal Studies* 5: 201–242.

Goldman, Sheldon, and Austin Sarat (1978) *American Court Systems: Readings in Judicial Process and Behavior*. San Francisco, Freeman.

Gough, E. Kathleen (1955) "The Social Structure of a Tanjore Village," in McKim Marriott, ed., *Village India*. Chicago: University of Chicago Press.

Grace, Roger (1970) "Justice, Chinese Style." *Case and Comment* 75: 50.

Greason, A. (1980) "Humanists as Mediators: An Experiment in the Courts of Maine." *American Bar Association Journal* 66: 576.

Greer, Scott (1956) "Urbanism Reconsidered." *American Sociological Review* 21: 19–25.

——— (1962) *The Emerging City*. New York: Free Press.

Greuel, Peter J. (1971) "The Leopard-Skin Chief: An Examination of Political Power Among the Nuer." *American Anthropologist* 73: 1115–1120.

Griffiths, John (1970) "Ideology in Criminal Procedures, or a Third 'Model' of the Criminal Process." *Yale Law Journal* 79: 359–417.

Grossman, Joel B., and Austin Sarat (1973) "Courts and Conflict Resolution: Some Observations on the Choice of Dispute Settlement Forum and Its Political Impact." Presented at the IX World Congress of the International Political Science Association in Montreal.

Gulliver, P. H. (1963) *Social Control in an African Society*. Boston: Boston University Press.

——— (1969) "Dispute *Settlement Without Courts:* The Ndendueli of Southern Tanzania," in L. Nader, ed., *Law in Culture and Society*, pp. 24–68. Chicago: Aldine.

——— (1973) "Negotiation as a Model of Dispute Settlement: Toward a General Model." *Law and Society Review* 7: 667–691.

——— (1977) "On Mediators," in J. Hamnett, ed., *Law and Social Anthropology*. New York: Academic Press.

———— (1979) *Disputes and Negotiations—A Cross-Cultural Perspective* New York: Academic Press.

Habermas, Jurgen (1970) "Toward a Theory of Communicative Competence," in Hans Peter Dreitzel, ed., *Recent Sociology II*. London: Macmillan.

Hager, Philip (1972) "Neighborhood Court Judges Its Own Juvenile Offenders," *Los Angeles Times*, Dec. 25, 1972.

Hahm, Pyong-Choon (1969) "The Decision Process in Korea," in Glendon Schubert and Daniel J. Danielski, eds., *Comparative Judicial Behavior*. New York: Oxford University Press.

Handler, J. F. (1978) *Social Movements and the Legal System: A Theory of Law Reform and Social Change*, New York: Academic Press.

Haug, Marie R. (1973) "Deprofessionalization: An Alternative Hypothesis for the Future," in Paul Halmos, ed., *Professionalization and Social Change*. pl. of pub.: University of Keele. *The Sociological Review*, Monograph No. 20.

———— (1969) "Professional Autonomy and the Revolt of the Client." *Social Problems* 17: 153–161.

Herman, M. S., P. C. McKenry, and R. E. Weber (1979) "Mediation and Arbitration Applied to Family Conflict Resolution: The Divorce Settlement." *Arbitration Journal* 34: 17.

Higginbotham, Honorable A. Leon (1976) "The Priority of Human Rights in Court Reform." 70 *Federal Rules Decisions*, 79.

Hirschman, Albert (1970) *Exit, Voice and Loyalty*. Cambridge, Mass.: Harvard University Press.

Hitchcock, John T. (1960) "Surat Singh, Head Judge," in Joseph B. Casagrande, ed., *In the Company of Man*. New York: Harper & Row.

Hoebel, E. A. (1954) *The Law of Primitive Man: A Study in Comparative Legal Dynamics*. Cambridge, Mass.: Harvard University Press.

Hoff, Bert H. (1974) *Arbitration as an Alternative to Criminal Courts*. Philadelphia: Blackstone Associates.

Hofrichter, R. (1977) "Justice Centers Raise Basic Question." *New Directions in Legal Services* 2(6): 168–172.

———— (1978) "Neighborhood Justice and the Social Control Problems of American Capitalism: A Perspective." Mimeo, Paper presented at the Second National Conference of Critical Legal Studies, Madison, Wisconsin.

Holleman, J. F. (1973) "Trouble-Cases and Trouble-less Cases in the Study of Customary Law and Legal Reform." *Law and Society Review* 7: 585–609.

Hoper, Claus, et al. (1974) *Awareness Games*. New York: St. Martin's Press.

Houseman, Alan W. (1978) "Legal Services and Equal Justice for the Poor: Some Thoughts on Our Future." *NLADA Briefcase* 35: 44–49, 56–64.

Howell, P. O. (1954) *A Manual of Nuer Law.* London: Oxford University Press.

Hufstedler, Honorable Shirley M. (1971) "New Blocks for Old Pyramids: Reshaping the Judicial System." *Southern California Law Review* 44: 901–915.

Hunt, Eva, and Robert Hunt (1969) "The Role of Courts in Rural Mexico," in Philipock, ed., *Peasants in the Modern World.* Albuquerque: University of New Mexico Press.

Illich, Ivan O. (1977) *Disabling Professions.* London: M. Boyers.

Institute for Social Analysis (1979) *National Evaluation of the Neighborhood Justice Centers Field Test—Final Report* (First Draft) November, 1979.

Jacobson, David (1971) "Mobility, Continuity and Urban Social Organization." *Man* 6: 630–645.

——— (1973) *Itinerant Townsmen: Friendship and Social Order in Urban Uganda.* Menlo Park. Calif.: Cummings.

Johnson, Earl (1978) "Courts and the Community," in T. Fedder, ed., *State Courts: A Blueprint for the Future.* Williamsburg: National Center for State Courts.

——— (1979) "Beyond Legal Representation: Dispute Processing, Non-Judicial Alternatives and the 'Third Wave' in the Access to Justice Movement." Colloquium on Access to Justice after the Publication of the Florence Project Series: Prospects for Future Action, Unpublished paper. Florence: October, 1979.

———, Valerie Kanter, and Elizabeth Schwartz (1977) *Outside the Courts: A Survey of Diversion Alternatives in Civil Cases.* Dênver: National Center for State Courts.

———, and Elizabeth Schwartz (1978) *A Preliminary Analysis of Alternative Strategies for Processing Civil Disputes.* Washington, D.C.: U.S. Government Printing Office.

Jones, Edgar A., Jr. (1964) "Power and Prudence in the Arbitration of Labor Disputes: A Venture in Some Hypoteheses," *UCLA Law Review* 11: 675–791.

Jones, H. W., ed. (1965) *The Courts, The Public and the Law Explosion.* Englewood Cliffs, N.J.: Prentice-Hall.

Jones, Schuyler (1974) *Men of Influence in Nurinstan: A Study of Social Control and Dispute Settlement in Waigal Valley, Afghanistan.* London: Seminar Press.

Judicial Council of California (1973) *History of the Role of Arbitration in the Judicial Process.* Sacramento: Judicial Council of California.

Judicial Resource Institute (1974) *The Urban Court.* Boston: Judicial Resource Institute.

Kastenmeier, Robert W. (1977) *State of the Judiciary and Access to Justice.* Hearings before the Sub-Committee on Courts, Civil Liberties, and the Administration of Justice, Committee on the Judiciary,

House of Representatives (June 20, 22, 29; July 20, 21, 28 and 29, 1977). Washington, D.C.: U.S. Government Printing Office.

——— (1979) *Resolution of Minor Disputes*. Joint Hearings before the Sub-Committee on Courts, Civil Liberties and the Administration of Justice of the Committee on the Judiciary and the Sub-Committee on Interstate and Foreign Commerce, House of Representatives (June 6, 7, 14 and 18, 1979) Washington, D.C.: U.S. Government Printing Office.

Kaufman, Michael T (1971) "Abbie Hoffman Accused Before a 'Court' of Peers," *New York Times*, Sept. 2, 1971.

Kawashima, Takeyoshi (1963) "Dispute Resolution in Contemporary Japan," in Vilhelm Aubert, ed., *Sociology of Law*. Baltimore: Penguin Books.

Kidder, Robert L. (1973) "Courts and Conflict in an Indian City: A Study in Legal Impact." *Journal of Commonwealth Political Studies* 11: 121–140.

——— (1974) "Formal Litigation and Professional Insecurity: Legal Entrepreneurship in South India." *Law and Society Review* 9: 11–37.

——— (1975) "Afterword: Change and Structure in Dispute Processing." *Law and Society Review* 9: 385–391.

Kilpatrick, James (1977) Article on Chief Justice Berger, *Boston Globe*, June 1977.

Knowles, William H. (1958) "Mediation and the Psychology of Small Groups." *Labor Law Journal* 9: 780.

Kreps, Gary, and Dennis Wenger (1973) "Toward a Theory of Community Conflict: Factors Influencing the Initiation and Scope of Conflict." *The Sociological Quarterly* 14(2): 158–174.

Kurczewsky, Jacek, and Kazimierz Frieske (1978) "The Social Conciliatory Commissions in Poland: A Case Study of Non-Authoritative and Conciliatory Dispute Resolution as an Approach to Access to Justice," in M. Cappelletti and John Weisner, eds., *Access to Justice*, Vol. II, Promising Institutions. Milan/Leiden: Guiffre/Sijhoff.

Ladinsky, Jack, Stewart Macaulay, and Jill Anderson (1979) *The Milwaukee Dispute Mapping Project: A Preliminary Report*. Working Paper 1979–3, Disputes Processing Research Program. Madison: University of Wisconsin Law School.

Landes, William M. (1971) "An Economic Analysis of the Courts." *Journal of Law and Economics* 14: 61.

Landy, David (1965) "Problems of the Person Seeking Help in Our Culture," in Mayer N. Zald, ed., *Social Welfare Institutions*, pp. 559–574. New York: Wiley.

Lansing, John B., and Nancy Barth (1964) *Residential Location and Urban Mobility: A Multivariate Analysis*. Ann Arbor: University of Michigan, Institue for Social Relations.

Lasch, Christopher (1980) "Life in the Therapeutic State." *The New*

*York Review*, June 1980.

Lasker, M. E. (1976) "Court Crunch—The View from the Bench," *Federal Rules Decisions* 70: 245–257.

Lawscope (1977) "Neighborhood Justice Plan Rapped by McCree." *American Bar Association Journal* 63: 1190–1191.

Lazerson, Mark (1982) "In the Halls of Justice the Only Justice Is in the Halls," in Richard Abel, ed., *The Politics of Informal Justice: The American Experience*. New York: Academic Press.

Legal Services Corporation (1977) "The Development of Alternatives to Formal Dispute Mechanisms." *Clearinghouse Review* 11: 226–228.

Lempert, Richard (1972) "Norm-Making in Social Exchange: A Contract Law Model." *Law and Society Review* 7: 1–32.

——— (1976) "Mobilizing Private Law: An Introductory Essay." *Law and Society Review* 11: 173–189.

——— (1978) "More Tales of Two Courts: Exploring Changes in the 'Dispute Settlement Function' of Trial Courts." *Law and Society Review* 13: 91–138.

Leslie, Gerald R. (1967) *The Family in Social Context*. New York: Oxford University Press.

Levi, E. (1976) "The Business of Courts: A Summary and a Sense of Perspective." *Federal Rules Decision* 70: 212–223.

Levin, Martin (1977) *Urban Politics and the Criminal Courts*. Chicago: University of Chicago Press.

Lewin, K. (1948) *Resolving Social Conflict*. New York: Harper & Row.

Lewis, Oscar (1965) "Further Observations on the Folk-Urban Continuum and Urbanization with Special Reference to Mexico City," in Philip M. Hauser and Leo F. Schnore, eds., *The Study of Urbanization*. New York: Wiley.

Li, Victor H. (1978) *Law Without Lawyers: A Comparative View of Law in China and the United States*. Boulder, Colo.: Westview.

Liebman, Donald A., and Jeffrey A. Schwarts (1973) "Police Programs in Domestic Crisis Intervention: A Review," in John R. Snibbe and Homa M. Snibbe, eds., *The Urban Policeman in Transition*. Springfield, Ill.: Thomas.

Litwak, Eugene (1960a) "Occupational Mobility and Extended Family Cohesion." *American Sociological Review* 25: 9–21.

——— (1960b) "Geographic Mobility and Extended Family Cohesion." *American Sociological Review* 25: 385–394.

Lively, G. Martin (1977) "Memorandum to Proposed Neighborhood Justice Center Grantees," August 3, 1977, mimeo. Training and Testing Division, Office of Technology Transfer, U.S. Department of Justice.

Llewellyn, Karl N., and E. Adamson Hoebel (1941) *The Cheyenne Way*. Norman: University of Oklahoma Press.

Lowy, Michael J. (1973a) "Modernizing the American Legal System:

An Example of the Peaceful Use of Anthropology." *Human Organization* 32: 205–209.

——— (1973b) Review of Leopold Pospisil, *Anthropology of Law. American* Anthropologist 75: 953–957.

Lubman, Stanley (1967) "Mao and Mediation: Politics and Dispute Resolution in Communist China." *California Law Review* 55: 1284–1359.

Macaulay, Stewart (1963) "Non-Contractual Relations in Business: A Preliminary Study." *American Sociological Review* 28: 55–67.

Manning, Bayless (1977) "Hyperlexis, Our National Disease." *Northwestern University Law Review* 71: 767–782.

Marcus, Maria L. (1979) "Judicial Overload: The Reasons and the Remedies." *Buffalo Law Review* 28: 111–114.

Marks, F. Raymond (1976) "Some Research Perspectives for Looking at Legal Need and Legal Services Delivery Systems: Old Forms or New?" *Law and Society Review* 11: 191–205.

Mather, Lynn M. (1977) "Ethnography and the Study of Trial Courts," in John A. Gardiner, ed., Public Law and Public Policy. New York: Praeger.

———, and Barbara Yngvesson (1981) "Language, Audience, and the Transformation of Disputes." *Law and Society Review* (forthcoming).

Mayer, Adrian C. (1960) *Caste & Kinship in Central India.* Berkeley: University of California Press.

Mayhew, Leon M. (1975) "Institutions of Representation: Civil Justice and the Public." *Law and Society Review* 9: 401–429.

McFagden, Terence (1972) *Dispute Resolution in the Small Claims Context.* Unpublished LL. M. Thesis, Harvard University.

McGillis, Daniel (1979) Testimony for House Hearings on the Dispute Resolution Act, June 14, 1979.

——— (1980a) "Recent Developments in Minor Dispute Processing, *Dispute Resolution* (ABA Special Committee on Resolution of Minor Disputes), Issue No. 5, pp. 12–14.

——— (1980b) *Policy Briefs: Neighborhood Justice Centers.* Washington D.C.: U.S. Department of Justice.

——— (1980c) "Dispute Processing Projects: A Preliminary Directory," Mimeo, 74 pages.

——— (n.d.) *Proposals for a Study of Dispute Processing Networks.*

———, and Joan Mullen (1977) *Neighborhood Justice Centers: An Analysis of Potential Models.* Washington D.C.: U.S. Government Printing Office.

McGongale, John J., Jr. (1972) "Arbitration of Consumer Disputes," *Arbitration Journal* 25: 65–84.

Meador, D. (1974) *Appellate Courts: Staff and Process in the Crisis of Volume.* St. Paul, Minn.: West Publishing Company.

Mentschikoff, Soia (1961) "Commercial Arbitration." *Columbia Law Review* 61: 846–869.

Merry, Sally Engle (1979a) "Can Community Dispute Settlement Centers Work? A Comparison with Anthropoligical Models of Mediation." Unpublished paper, Wellesley College.

—— (1979b) "A Plea for Rethinking How Dispute Resolution Works," *The Mooter* 2(4): 37–40.

—— (1979c) "Going to Court: Strategies of Dispute Management in an American Urban Neighborhood." *Law and Society Review* 13: 891–925.

—— (1980) "Racial Integration in an Urban Neighborhood: The Social Organization of Strangers." *Human Organization* 39: 59–69.

—— (1981a) "The Social Organization of Mediation in Non-Industrial Societies: Implications for Informal Justice in America," in Richard Abel, ed., *Informal Justice*. New York: Academic Press.

—— (1981b) "Toward a General Theory of Gossip and Scandal;" in Donald Black, ed., *Toward a General Theory of Social Control*. New York: Academic Press.

—— (1981c) *Urban Danger: Life in a Neighborhood of Strangers*. Philadelphia: Temple University Press.

Metzger, Duane (1960) "Conflict in Chulsanto." *Alpha Kappa Deltan* 30: 35.

Miller, Walter B. (1955) "Two Concepts of Authority." *American Anthropologist*, 57: 271–289.

Mitchell, J. Clyde, ed. (1969) *Social Networks in Urban Situations*. Manchester: Manchester University Press.

Mnookin, Robert H., and Lewis Kornhauser (1979) "Bargaining in the Shadow of the Law: The Case of Divorce." *The Yale Law Journal* 88: 950–997.

Mohr, J. (1976) *"Organizations, Decisions and Courts." Law and Society Review* 10: 621–642.

Moore, Sally Falk (1970) "Politics, Procedures and Norms in Changing Chagga Law." *Africa* 40: 321–344.

—— (1973) "Law and Social Change: The Semi-Autonomous Social Field as an Appropriate Subject of Study." *Law and Society Review* 7: 719–746.

*The Mooter* (1978–9) "Homespun Mediation" and "Disputes that Divide a Neighborhood" 2: 1–2.

Moriarty, William F. Jr., Thomas L. Norris, and Luis Salas (1977) *Evaluation: Dade County Citizen Dispute Settlement Center*. Dade County Criminal Justice Planning Unit, Florida.

Mukherjee, S. K. (1981) *Crime in the Twentieth Century*. Sydney: Allen & Unwin.

Mullen, Joan (1975) *The Dilemma of Diversion*. Washington D.C.: U.S. Government Printing Office.

Nadel, S. F. (1951) *The Foundations of Social Anthropology.* London: Cohen & West.

———, and Duane Metzger (1963) "Conflict Resolution in Two Mexican Communities." *American Anthropologist* 65: 584–592.

Nader, Laura (1965) "The Anthropological Study of Law." *American Anthropologist, Special Issue: The Ethnography of Law*; 67(6).

——— (1969) "Styles of Court Procedure: To Make the Balance," in Laura Nader, *Law in Culture and Society*, ed., Chicago: Aldine.

——— (1972) "Up the Anthropologist—Perspectives Gained from Studying Up," in Dell Hymes, ed., *Reinventing Anthropology*, New York: Pantheon.

——— (1979a) "Disputing Without the Force of Law." *Yale Law Journal* 88: 998–1021.

——— (1979b) "Complainer Beware." *Psychology Today* 13(7): 46–60, 98.

———, and Linda Singer (1976) "Dispute Resolution in the Future: What Are the Choices?" *California State Bar Journal* 51: 281–286.

———, and Todd H. E., Jr. eds. (1978) *The Disputing Process and Law in Ten Societies.* New York: Columbia University Press.

———, and Barbara Yngvesson (1973) "On Studying the Ethnography of Law and Its Consequences," in John J. Honigmann, ed., *Handbook of Social and Cultural Anthropology.* (Skokie, Ill.: Rand McNally.

National Institute of Law Enforcement and Criminal Justice (1974) *Citizen Dispute Settlement: The Night Prosecutor Program of Columbus, Ohio.* Washington, D.C.: U.S. Government Printing Office.

——— (1978) *Exemplary Project Supplementary Validation Report: Citizen Dispute Settlement Program, Miami, Florida.* Washington D.C.: U.S. Government Printing Office.

Nejelski, Paul (1976) "Diversion: The Promise and the Danger." *Crime and Delinquency* 22: 393–410.

——— (1977a) "Judging in a Democracy—the Tension of Popular Participation." *Judicature* 61: 166–175.

——— (1977b) "Do Minor Disputes Deserve Second-class Justice?" *Judicature* 61: 102–103.

——— (1977c) "The Federal Role in Minor Dispute Resolution." Mimeo, address given before the National Conference on Minor Dispute Resolution, Columbia University School of Law, May 26, 1977.

——— (1979) "Thoughts About Courts, Their Alternatives and the Dispute Resolution Act," Mimeo.

——— (1980), "The 1980 Dispute Resolution Act." *The Judge's Journal* 1980: 33–35, 44–45.

Nelson, Douglas (1949) "The Small Claims Court." *Wisconsin Bar Bulletin* 22: 237.

Nicolau, George, and Gerald W. McCormick, (1972) "Community Disputes and the Resolution of Conflict: Another View." *Arbitration Journal* 27: 98–112.

Nimkoff, M. R., and Russell Middleton (1968) "Types of Family and Types of Economy," in Robert F. Winch and Louis Wolf Goodman, eds., *Selected Studies in Marriage and the Family*, 3rd ed. New York: Holt, Rinehart and Winston.

Nimmer, Raymond T. (1978) *The Nature of System Change: Reform Impact in the Criminal Courts*. Chicago: American Bar Foundation.

Nisbet, Robert A. (1962) *The Quest for Community*. New York: Oxford University Press.

Nonet, Philippe, and Philip Selznick (1978) *Law and Society in Transition: Toward Responsive Law*. New York: Harper, Row.

Packer, Herbert (1968) *The Limits of the Criminal Sanction*, Stanford: Stanford University Press.

Palmer, J. W. (1975) "Pre-Arrest Diversion—The Night Prosecutor's Program in Columbia, Ohio." *Crime and Deliquency* 21(2): 100–108.

Parnas, Raymond I. (1973) "Prosecutorial and Judicial Handling of Family Violence." *Criminal Law Bulletin* 9: 585.

Parsons, Talcott (1951) *Towards a General Theory of Action*. New York: Harper & Row.

––––––– (1962) "The Law and Social Control," in W. M. Evan, ed., *Law and Sociology Exploratory Essays*. New York: The Free Press.

––––––– (1965) "The Normal American Family," in Seymour M. Farber, Piero Mustacchi, and Rober H. L. Wilson, eds., *Man and Civilization: The Family's Search for Survival*. New York: McGraw-Hill.

Paterson, Basil, George Nicolau, and Ann Weisbrod (1978) "An Alternative to Criminal Justice Process." *New York Law Journal* January 11, 1978.

Pickett, Neil (1979) "Neighborhood 'Courts' Working, LEAA Reports." *The National Law Journal* 1(23): 9.

Pitt-Rivers, Julian (1971) *The People of the Sierra*. 2nd ed. Chicago: University of Chicago Press.

Podgorecki, Adam (1969) "Attitudes to the Workers Courts," in Vilhelm Aubert, ed., *Sociology of Law*. Baltimore: Penguin Books.

Pospisil, Leopold (1964) *Kapauku Papuans and Their Law*. New Haven: Human Relations Area Files Press.

––––––– (1967) "Legal Levels and Multiplicity of Legal Systems in Human Societies." *Journal of Conflict Resolution* 11: 2–26.

––––––– (1971) *Anthropology of Law: A Comparative Theory*. New York: Harper & Row.

––––––– (1973) "Anthropology of Law: A Rejoinder to Lowy." *American Anthropologist*, 75: 1170–1173.

Pound, Roscoe (1922) *An Introduction to the Philosophy of Law.* New Haven: Yale University Press.

President's Commission on Law Enforcement and Administration of Justice (1967) *Task Force Report: The Courts.* Washington, D.C.: U.S. Government Printing Office.

Randolph, L. L (1973) *Third Party Settlement of Disputes in Theory and Practice.* Dobbs Ferry, N.Y.: Oceana.

Reiss, Ira L. (1971) *The Family System in America.* New York: Holt, Rinehart and Winston.

Reiss, Paul J. (1962) "The Extended Kinship System: Correlates of and Attitudes on Frequency of Interaction." *Marriage and Family Living* 24: 333.

Rifkind, S. (1976) "Are We Asking Too Much of Our Courts?" *Federal Rules Decisions* 70: 96.

Roberts, John M. (1965) "Oaths, Autonomic Ordeals and Power." *American Anthropologist* 67(2): 186.

Rosellen, Richard (1979) "Mediation: Verfahren swischen Gesprachstherapie und Hard Selling." *Jahrbuch fur Rechtssoziologie und Rechstheorie,* vol. 6.

Rosen, Lawrence (1980) "Making Justice More Accesible." *American Ethnologist* 7: 567–571.

Rosenberg, Maurice (1965) "Court Congestion: Status, Causes and Proposes Remedies," in H. W. Jones, ed., *The Courts, The Public and the Law Explosion.* Englewood Cliffs, N.J.: Prentice-Hall.

——— (1971) "Devising Procedures that are Civil—to Promote Justice that Is Civilized." *Michigan Law Review* 69: 797–820.

——— (1972) "Let's Everybody Litigate?" *Texas Law Review* 50: 1349–1368.

Rosen, Keith S. (1971) "The Jeito: Brazil's Institutional Bypass of the Formal Legal System and Its Developmental Implications." *American Journal of Comparative Law* 19: 514–549.

Rosenthal, Douglas E. (1977) *Lawyer and Client: Who's in Charge?* New York: Russell Sage Foundation.

Ross, H. Laurence (1975) "Insurance Claims Complaints: A Private Appeals Procedure." *Law and Society Review* 9: 276–292.

——— and Neil Littlefield (1978) "Complaint as a Problem-Solving Mechanism." *Law and Society Review* 12: 199–216.

Rossi, Peter Henry (1955) *Why Families Move.* New York: Free Press.

Rothenberger, John E. (1970) *Law and Conflict Resolution, Politics and Change in a Sunni Moslem Village in Lebanon.* Unpublished Ph. D. dissertation, University of California, Berkeley.

Rubin, J. Z., and B. R. Brown (1975) *The Social Psychology of Bargaining and Negotiations.* New York: Academic Press.

Rudolph, Lloyd, I., and Susanne Hoeber Rudolph (1967) *The Modernity of Tradition.* Chicago: University of Chicago Press.

Ruhnka, John C. (1979) *Housing Justice in Small Claims Courts.* Williamsburg: National Center for State Courts.

———, and Steven Weller (1978) *Small Claims Courts: A National Examination.* Williamsburg: National Center for State Courts.

Saltmarsh, Robert (1973) "Development of Empathic Interview Skills Through Programmed Instruction." *Journal of Counseling Psychology* 20: 375.

Sander, Frank E. A. (1976) "Varieties of Dispute Processing." *Federal Rules Decisions* 70: 111–134.

——— (1978) *American Bar Association Report on the National Conference on Minor Disputes Resolution, May 1977.* Washington, D.C.: American Bar Association Press.

———, and Frederick E. Snyder (1979) *Alternative Methods of Dispute Settlement—A Selected Bibliography* Washington D.C.: Division of Public Service Activities, American Bar Association.

Sarat, Austin (1976) "Alternatives in Dispute Processing: Litigation in Small Claims Court." *Law and Society Review* 10: 339–375.

——— (1978) "Understanding Trial Courts: A Critique of Social Science Approaches." *Judicature* 61: 318–326.

——— (1980) "Assessing Access to Justice: Citizen Participation and the American Legal Order." Paper prepared for the Social Science Research Council volume on Law and Society.

———, and Ralph Cavanagh (1980) "Thinking About Courts: Traditional Expectations and Contemporary Challenges on the Crisis of the Courts as a Social and Political Crisis." *Law and Society Review* 14: 371–420.

———, and Joel Grossman (1975) "Courts and Conflict Resolution: Problems in the Mobilization of Adjudication." *American Political Science Review* 69: 1200–1217.

Scheingold, Stuart (1973) *The Politics of Rights.* New Haven: Yale University Press.

Schlegal, Stuart A. (1970) *Tiruray Justice.* Berkeley: University of California Press.

Schön, Donald A. (1977) "Network Related Intervention." Unpublished paper, M.I.T.

Scull, Andrew T. (1977) *Decarceration, Community Treatment and the Deviant: A Radical View.* Englewood Cliffs, N.J.: Prentice-Hall.

Schwartz, Richard D. (1954) "Social Factors in the Development of Legal Control: A Case Study of Two Israeli Settlements." *Yale Law Journal* 63: 471–491.

Seeley, John R., R. Alexander Sim, and Elizabeth W. Looseley (1956). *Crestwood Heights: A Study of the Culture of Suburban Life.* New York: Basic Books.

Selznick, Philip (1980) "Jurisprudence and Social Policy: Aspirations and Perspectives." *California Law Review* 68: 206–220.

Shapiro, Martin (1979) "Access to the Legal System and the Modern Welfare State: An American Report." Paper presented at the Colloquium on Access to Justice After the Publication of the Florence Project series: Prospects for Future Action, Florence, Italy.

Sharp, Harry, and Morris Axelrod (1956) "Mutual Aid Among Relatives in an Urban Population," in Ronald Freedman et. al *Principles of Sociology: A Test with Readings*. New York: Holt, Rinehart and Winston.

Sheppard, David J., Janet A Roehl, and Royer F. Cook (1978) *Neighborhood Justice Centers Field Test: Implementation Report*. Reston, V.: Institute for Social Analysis.

——— (1979) *Neighborhood Justice Centers Field Test: Interim Evaluation Report*. Washington, D.C.: U.S. Government Printing Office.

Shonholtz, Raymond (1977) "Neighborhood Justice Centers: A Critique." Paper submitted to the U.S. Department of Justice.

——— (1978) Testimony before the U.S. House of Representatives Subcommittee on Courts, Civil Liberties and the Administration of Justice.

Siegal, Bernard J., and Alan R. Beals (1960) "Pervasive Factionalism." *American Anthropologist* 62: 394.

Silberman, Linda (1979) *Non-Attorney Justice in the United States: An Empirical Study*. New York: Institute of Judicial Administration.

Silbey, Susan S. (1979) *What the Lower Courts Do: The Work and Role of Courts of Limited Jurisdiction*. Mimeo, report prepared for the Federal Justice Research Program, U.S. Department of Justice.

Simmel, George (1955) *Conflict and the Web of Group Affiliation*. New York: Free Press.

Simmons, T. W. (1968) "Changing Residence in the City: A Review of Intraurban Mobility." *Geographical Review* 58: 622–651.

Simon, William H. (1980) "Home Psychologicus: Notes on a New Legal Formalism." *Stanford Law Review* 32: 487–559.

Singer, Linda R. (1979a) "The Growth of Non-Judicial Dispute Resolution: Speculations on the Effects on Justice for the Poor and on the Role of Legal Services." Mimeo. Washington, D.C.: Research Institute, Legal Services Corporation.

——— (1979b) "Non-Judicial Dispute Resolution Mechanisms: The Effects on Justice for the Poor." *Clearinghouse Review* (December 1979): 569–583.

Skinner, B. F. (1978) "Why Don't We Use the Behavioral Sciences." *Human Nature* 1: 86.

Smith, Christopher (1978) "Self-help and Social Networks in the Urban Community." *Ekistics* (March/April 1978).

Smith, David N. (1972) "Man and Law in Urban Africa: A Role for Customary Courts in the Urbanization Process." *American Journal of Comparative Law* 20: 223–246.

────── (1978) "A Warmer Way of Disputing: Mediation and Conciliation." *American Journal of Comparative Law* 26: 205–216 (Supp.
1978).

Smith, Gordon (1974) "Popular Participation in the Administration of
Justice in the Soviet Union—Comrades' Courts and the Brezhnev
Regime." *Indiana Law Journal* 49: 238–252.

Smith, Reginald Heber (1924) "Report of the Committee on Small
Claims Courts and Conciliation." *Legal Aid Review* 22: 1.

Snyder, Frederick E. (1978) "Crime and Community Mediation—The
Boston Experience: A Preliminary Report on the Dorchester Urban
Court Program." *Wisconsin Law Review* 1978(3): 737–795.

────── (1979) "Legal Implications of Mediation." *Perspective* 3 (Fall/
Winter 1979).

Solomon, Stephen (1979) "A Businesslike Way to Resolve Legal Disputes." *Fortune*, February 26, 1979, pp. 80–82.

Spence, Jack (1978) "Institutionalizing Neighborhood Courts: Two Chi-
lean Experiences." *Law and Society Review* 13: 139–182.

Srinivas, M. N. (1954) "A Caste Dispute Among Washermen of Mysore." *The Eastern Anthropologist* 7: 149.

Stanford Law Review (1952) "Small Claims Courts as Collection Agencies." *Stanford Law Review* 4: 237–243.

Stanley, Justin A. (1977) "The Resolution of Minor Disputes and the
Seventh Amendment." *Marquette Law Review* 60: 520–529.

Starr, June, (1978) "Mediation: Anthropological Perspectives." Paper
prepared for evaluation of Brooklyn Dispute Resolution Center.

──────, and Barbara Yngvesson (1975) "Scarcity and Disputing: Zeroing
in on Compromise Decision." *American Ethnologist* 2(3): 553–566.

Statsky, William P. (1974) "Community Courts: Decentralizing Juvenile
Jurisprudence." *Capital University Law Review* 3: 1.

Steele, Eric H. (1975) "'Fraud, Dispute and the Consumer: Responding to
Consumer Complaints." *University of Pennsylvania Law Review*
123: 1107–1186.

────── (1977) "Two Approaches to Contemporary Dispute Behavior
and Consumer Problems." *Law and Society Review* 11(4): 667–677.

Stirling, P. (1957) "Land, Marriage and the Law in Turkish Villages."
*International Social Science Bulletin* 9: 21.

Stolz, Preble (1968) "Insurance for Legal Services: A Preliminary Study
of Feasibility." *University of Chicago Law Review* 35: 417–476.

Street, Harry (1979) "Access to the Legal System and the Modern Welfare State." Paper Presented to Colloquium on Access to Justice,
Florence, Italy.

Stulberg, J. (1975) "A Civil Alternative to Criminal Prosecution."
*Albany Law Review* 39: 359–376.

Sussman, Marvin B. (1959) "The Isolated Nuclear Family: Fact or Fic-
tion." *Social Problems* 6: 333–340.

Swingle, P., ed. (1970) *The Structure of Conflict*. New York: Academic Press.

Sykes, Gresham M. (1969) "Cases, Courts and Congestion." in Laura Nader, ed., *Law in Culture and Society*. Chicago: Aldine.

Tamarkin, Civia, and Douglas Stanton (1979) "Courting Alternatives." *Ambassador* (March 1979) pp. 26–28.

The Small Claims Study Group (1972) *Little Injustices: Small Claims Courts and the American Consumer*. Washington: The Center for Auto Safety.

Thibaut, John, and Laurens Walker (1975) *Procedural Justice*. New York: Wiley.

Tittle, Charles, and Charles Logan (1973) "Sanctions and Deviance: Evidence and Remaining Questions." *Law and Society Review*: 7: 371–392.

Toch, Hans (1973) "Change Through Participation (and Vice Versa)," in John R. Snibbe and Homa M. Snibbe, eds., *The Urban Policeman in Transition*, Springfield, Ill.: Thomas.

Tomasic, Roman (1978a) *Lawyers and the Community*. Sydney: Allen & Unwin.

—— (1979b) *Drugs, Alcohol and Community Control*. Sydney: The Law Foundation of NSW.

—— (1980) "Mediation as an Alternative to Adjudication: Rhetoric and Reality in the Neighborhood Justice Movement." Paper presented at the 1980 Meetings of the Law and Society Association, and circulated as Working Paper 1980–2, Dispute Processing Research Program. Madison: University of Wisconsin, Law School [included in this volume].

——, and Ian Dobinson (1979) *The Failure of Imprisonment: An Australian Perspective*. Sydney: Allen & Unwin.

Tonnies, Ferdinand (1974) *Community and Association*. London: Routledge & Kegan Paul.

Townsend, Peter (1957) *The Family of Old People*. London: Routledge & Kegan Paul.

Truax, C. B., and Robert R. Carkhuff (1967) *Toward Effective Counseling and Psychotherapy*. Chicago: Aldine.

Trubek, Louise, and David Trubek (1979) "The Protection of Diffuse and Fragmented Interests: The 'Second Wave' in the Access to Justice Movement." Paper presented to Colloquium on Access to Justice, Florence, Italy.

Turk, Austin (1978) "Law as a Weapon in Social Conflict," in Charles Reasons and Robert Roth, eds., *The Sociology of Law—A Conflict Perspective*. Toronto: Butterworths.

Turner, Ralph H. (1970) *Family Interaction*. New York: Wiley.

U.S. Department of Justice (1977) "Neighborhood Justice Center Program." Mimeo. July 11, 1977. Office for Improvements in the Administration of Justice.

Unger, Roberto M. (1976) *Law in Modern Society*, New York: Free Press.

U.S. House of Representatives. Sub-committee on Courts, Civil Liberties and the Administration of Justice of the Committee on the Judiciary *Dispute Resolution Act* (June 10, 1978).

—— Sub-committee on Courts, Civil Liberties and the Administration of Justice of the Committee on the Judiciary. *Dispute Resolution Act* (s. 957) (Hearings, July 27; August 2, 1978).

—— *Joint Hearings Before the Sub-committee on Courts Civil Liberties, and the Administration of Justice of the Committee on the Judiciary and Sub-committee on Consumer Protection and Finance of the Committee on Interstate and Foreign Commerce, 96th Congress* June 6, 7, 14 and 18, 1979.

Utz, Pamela (1978) *Settling the Facts*, Lexington, Mass.: Lexington Books.

Vanderbilt, Arthur T. *The Challenge of Law Recofm*. Princeton, N.J.: Princeton University Press.

Van Velsen, J. (1969) "Procedural Informality, Reconciliation and False Comparisons," in Max Gluckman, ed., *Ideas and Procedures in African Customary Law*. London: Oxford University Press.

Vera Institute (1977) *Felony Arrests: Their Prosecution and Disposition in New York City's Courts*. New York: Vera Institute of Justice. Revised edition (1981) New York: Longman Inc.

Wahrhaftig, Paul (1973) "Disputes Resolved in the Communities." *Pretrial Justice Quarterly* 2: 1.

—— (1977) "Mediation in the Suburbs." *The Mooter* 1: 5.

—— (1978) "Citizen Dispute Resolution: A Blue Chip Investment in Community Growth." *Pretrial Services Annual Journal* 1978: 153–161.

—— (1979) "Prepared Testimony, Resolution of Minor Disputes." House Hearings, 1979, pp. 212–214.

—— (1981) "An Overview of Community-oriented Citizen Dispute Resolution programs in the United States." in Richard Abel 1982 ed. *Informal Justice*: The Politics of The American Experience New York: Academic Press.

——, and Michael J. Lowy (1974) "Mediation at the Police Station, A Dialogue on the Night Prosecutor Program: Columbus, Ohio." *Pretrial Justice Quarterly* 3: 37.

Wald, Patricia M., and Robert L. Wald (1968) "Law and Grievances of the Poor," in James M. Campbell, Joseph R. Sahib, and David P. Stang, eds., *Law and Order Reconsidered*. Washington, D.C.: National Commission on the Causes and Prevention of Violence.

Walsh, Elaine, and Sidney Splawn (1979) *The Neighborhood Mediation Pilot Project Annual Research Report*. Portland, Oreg.: Metropolitan Human Relations Committee.

Wanner, Craig (1974) "The Public Ordering of Private Relations, Part One: Initiating Civil Cases in Urban Trial Courts." *Law & Society Review* 8: 421–440.

Warren, Donald (1978) "The Neighborhood Factor in Problem Coping, Help Seeking and Social Support: Research Findings and Suggested Policy Implications." Paper presented at the 55th Annual Meeting of the American Orthopsychiatric Association, San Francisco, California, March 31, 1978.

———, and Rachelle Warren (1977) "The Helping Roles of Neighbors: Some Empirical Patterns." Draft NIMH Project "Helping Networks in the Urban Community."

Weber, Max (1967) *Max Weber on Law in Economy and Society* (Max Rheinstein, ed.). New York: Simon & Schuster.

——— (1968) "Ideal Types and Theory Construction," in May Brodbeck ed., *Readings in the Philosophy of the Social Sciences*. New York: Macmillan.

Weisbrod, Ann (1977) "Alternatives to Formal Judicial Process." *New Directions* 2(6): 180–182.

Weiss, Robert (1966) "Alternative Approaches in the Study of Complex Situations." *Human Organization* 25: 198–206.

Wellman, Barry (1978) "The Community Question—The Intimate Networks of East Yorkers." Mimeo April 1978.

Wheeldon, Prudence (1969) "The Operation of Voluntary Associations and Personal Networks in the Political Processes of an Inter-Ethnic Community," in J. Clyde Mitchell, ed., *Social Networks in Urban Situations*. Manchester: Manchester University Press.

Whitford, William L. (1968) "Law and the Consumer Transaction: A Case Study of the Automobile Warranty." *Wisconsin Law Review* 1968: 1006–1098.

Whyte, William F. (1955) *Street Corner Society*. 2nd ed. Chicago: University of Chicago Press.

Williams, Lynne (1980) Comment at session on Dispute Processing at 1980 Meetings of Law and Society Association, Madison, Wisc.

Wilt, G. Marie, James D. Bannon, and Ronald Breedlove (1977) *Domestic Violence and the Police: Studies in Detroit and Kansas City*. Washington, D.C.: Police Foundation.

Wimberley, Howard (1973) "Legal Evolution: One Further Step." *American Journal of Sociology* 79: 78–83.

Winch, Robert F. (1968) "Some Observations on Extended Familism in the United States," in Robert F. Winch and Louis Wolf Goodman, eds., *Selected Studies in Marriage and the Family*. 3rd ed. New York: Holt, Rinehart and Winston.

————, and Rae Lesser Blumberg (1968) "Societal Complexity and Familial Organization," in Robert F. Winch and Louis Wolf Goodman, eds., *Selected Studies in Marriage and the Family*. 3rd ed. New York: Holt, Rinehart and Winston.

Wirth, Louis (1938) "Urbanism as a Way of Life." *American Journal of Sociology* 44: 1–24.

Wiser, William H., and Charlotte V. Wiser (1969) *Behind Mud Walls*. Berkeley: University of California Press.

Wolf, Margery (1972) *Women and the Family in Rural Taiwan*. Stanford: Stanford University Press.

Wordsworth, William (1933) *The Prelude to Growth of a Poet's Mind 1805*. London: Oxford University Press.

Yaffe, J. (1972) *So Sue Me! The Story of a Community Court*. New York: Saturday Review Press.

Yale Law Journal (1970) "Legal Ethics and Professionalism." *The Yale Law Journal* 79: 1179–1197.

———— (1979) "Dispute Resolution." *The Yale Law Journal* 88: 905–909.

Yang, Martin C. (1945) *A Chinese Village: Taitou, Shantung Province*. New York Columbia University Press.

Yankelovich, Skelly and White, Inc. (1978) "Highlights of a National Survey of the General Public, Judges, Lawyers, and Community Leaders." in Fetter, Theodore ed. *State Courts: A Blueprint for the Future*, Williamsburg, Va.: National Center for State Courts.

Young, Michael, and Peter Willmott (1957) *Family and Kinship in East London* Glencoe: The Free Press.

Yngvesson, Barbara B. (1970) *Decision-Making and Dispute Settlement in a Swedish Fishing Village: An Ethnography of Law*. Unpublished Ph. D. dissertation, University of California, Berkeley.

———— (1976) "Responses to Grievance Behavior: Extended Cases in a Fishing Community." *American Ethnologist* 3: 353–374.

———— and P. Hennessey (1975) "Small Claims, Complex Disputes: A Review of the Small Claims Literature." *Law and Society Review* 9: 219–274.

Zander, Michael (1979) "Legal Services to the Poor: The First-Wave to the Access-to-Justice Movement." Paper presented to Colloquium on Access to Justice, Florence, Italy.

# Notes on Contributors

**Leonard G. Buckle**, Associate Professor of Urban Studies and Planning at MIT and Adjunct Research Associate at the John F. Kennedy School of Government at Harvard University, received his Ph. D from MIT. He is coauthor with Suzann Thomas-Buckle of *Standards Relating to Planning for Juvenile Justice Agencies* and *Bargaining for Justice* and has directed research projects in program evaluation, legal institutions, and informal networks. His current research concerns the role of negotiation in courts and their alternatives.

**William Clifford** has been the Director of the Australian Institute of Criminology for the past six years. Prior to that he was the Director of Crime Prevention Programmes for the United Nations, Senior United Nations Consultant for Social Affairs in the Congo, the first United Nations Interregional Adviser for Social Planning and the Senior United Nations Adviser to the United Nations Asia and Far East Institute for the Prevention of Crime and Treatment of Offenders in Fuchu, Tokyo, Japan. He is the author of criminological works on Africa, Asia, and the Middle East and has pioneered the subject of social and economic planning for the prevention of crime.

**Royer F. Cook** is the President of the Institute for Social Analysis in Reston, Virginia. He has previously held research management positions at the Army Research Institute for the Behavioral and Social Sciences and at the Institute for Research. His research interests include drug abuse prevention, criminal justice, and organizational behavior. He is currently studying the effectiveness of physical activities and other positive alternatives in preventing drug abuse among youth. Many of Dr. Cook's recent research projects and publications have focused on the areas of alternative dispute resolution mechanisms, juvenile offender programs, and evaluation methodology. He received his Ph.D. in psychology from Kansas State University in 1968.

**Richard Danzig** is currently a Principal Deputy Assistant to the United States Secretary of Defense (MRA & L). He was formerly a Professor of Law at Stanford Law School. His academic attainments include the following: B.A. 1965, Reed College; B. Phil, 1967, D. Phil, 1968, Oxford University; J.D. 1971, Yale Law School.

276

**Robert C. Davis** is Research Director of the New York Victim Services Agency. His fields of interest include victimology and criminal court decision making. He is currently conducting research on witness intimidation, the response of criminal courts to nonstranger violence cases, and crime victims' use of informal social networks for support.

**Malcolm M. Feeley** is Associate Professor of Political Science at the University of Wisconsin-Madison and the author of *The Impact of Supreme Court Decisions* (1973), *The Process is the Punishment: Handling Cases in a Lower Criminal Court* (1979), and with Austin Sarat, *The Policy Dilemma* (1980), as well as numerous articles on criminal justice administration and law and social sciences.

**William L. F. Felstiner** is Senior Social Scientist at the Institute for Civil Justice, Rand Corporation, Santa Monica, California. He was Director of the Program for Dispute Systems Research at the University of Southern California and has taught at the Yale and UCLA Law Schools. He has published many papers on dispute processing theory and alternatives to court process in the U.S. and Europe.

**Richard Hofrichter** is a legal sociologist in Washington, D.C.

**Daniel McGillis** is a Research Associate at Harvard Law School's Center for Criminal Justice, Director of the Center's Dispute Resolution Project, and Lecturer on Psychology and Social Relations at Harvard University. Dr. McGillis has published a number of papers on dispute settlement, including *Neighborhood Justice Centers: An Analysis of Potential Models*, and has worked closely with the U.S. Department of Justice and the U.S. Congress on dispute-processing mechanisms.

**Sally Engle Merry** is a legal anthropologist specializing in the role of law in urban societies. She is currently Assistant Professor of Anthropology at Wellesley College. She completed her Ph.D. in anthropology at Brandeis University, working on perceptions of danger and strategies of coping exercised by the residents of a multiethnic, inner-city, housing project of mediation in neighborhood dispute settlement processes, examining the effect of different community social structures, differential degrees of legal coercion, and different mediation processes on users' perceptions of legitimacy and justice. She has published an ethnography on crime in an urban neighborhood, *Urban Danger: Life in a Neighborhood of Strangers*, and several articles on cross-cultural views of mediation, court use in urban populations, and integrated housing.

**Janice A. Roehl** is a Senior Research Associate with the Institute of Social Analysis in Reston, Virginia. Among her research interests are alternative methods of conflict resolution, equity and perceptions of justice, and drug abuse prevention. Ms. Roehl is currently evaluating community-based crime prevention projects which concentrate on the social and economic causes of crime, and which include alternative dispute resolution services. She is currently completing her Ph.D in social psychology at George Washington University.

**Frank E. A. Sander** teaches Family Law and Dispute Settlement at Harvard Law School, from which he was graduated in 1952. He was a law clerk to Justice Felix Frankfurter at the United States Supreme Court in 1953–1954 and, following a period of practice, he began teaching at Harvard in 1959. He was asked to prepare the paper here included by the Chief Justice of the United States for delivery at the Pound Conference in 1976. He has also worked actively with the American Bar Association as a member of its special committee on minor disputes and has prepared a comprehensive bibliography on dispute settlement.

**Suzann R. Thomas-Buckle**, Associate Professor of Urban Studies and Planning at MIT and Adjunct Research Associate at the John F. Kennedy School of Government at Harvard University, received her Ph.D. from MIT. She served as a reporter on planning for the Joint I.J.A.–A.B.A. Juvenile Justice Standards Project and has directed research projects in juvenile justice, civil and criminal courts, and informal negotiation processes. She is coauthor with Leonard G. Buckle of *Bargaining for Justice*. Her current research interests are bargaining and negotiation and their relationship to social structure and organizational behavior.

**Roman Tomasic** is an Australian lawyer and sociologist currently teaching in the Department of Legal Studies, Kuring-Gai College of Advanced Education, Lindfield, Sydney, Australia. He has taught in the School of Law at the University of Wisconsin-Madison and been a Senior Research Officer with the Law Foundation of New South Wales. He obtained his PhD. in sociology from the University of New South Wales. He is the editor of *Understanding Lawyers: Perspectives on the Legal Profession in Australia* (1978) and *Legislation and Society in Australia* (1980) and the author of *Lawyers and the Community* (1978), *Lawyers and Their Work in New South Wales* (1978, with C. G. Bullard), and *The Failure of Imprisonment* (1979, with Ian Dobinson). Dr. Tomasic is currently writing a book on *The Sociology Of Law* with Dr. Pat O'Malley, to be published in 1982 by Allen & Unwin (Australia).

**Lynne A. Williams** has a Ph.D. in Social Psychology and a Master of Legal Studies degree from the University of Southern California. Her dissertation was on the mediation of interpersonal disputes. She is now a social services planner for the United Way in Los Angeles.

# Index